MONETA

MONETA

A History of Ancient Rome in Twelve Coins

GARETH HARNEY

|BH|

THE BODLEY HEAD
LONDON

1 3 5 7 9 10 8 6 4 2

The Bodley Head, an imprint of Vintage, is part of the Penguin Random House group of companies whose addresses can be found at global.penguinrandomhouse.com

Penguin Random House UK

First published by The Bodley Head in 2024

Copyright © Gareth Harney 2024

Gareth Harney has asserted his right to be identified as the author of this Work in accordance with the Copyright, Designs and Patents Act 1988

Map by Bill Donohoe

penguin.co.uk/vintage

Typeset in 12/14.75pt Bembo Book MT Pro by Jouve (UK), Milton Keynes
Printed and bound in Great Britain by Clays Ltd, Elcograf S.p.A.

The authorised representative in the EEA is Penguin Random House Ireland, Morrison Chambers, 32 Nassau Street, Dublin D02 YH68

A CIP catalogue record for this book is available from the British Library

HB ISBN 9781847927507
TPB ISBN 9781847927514

Penguin Random House is committed to a sustainable future for our business, our readers and our planet. This book is made from Forest Stewardship Council® certified paper.

To my father,
for placing ancient Rome in the palm of my hand.

Contents

Map		x
Introduction		1
Prologue	Moneta	9
Chapter I	Wolf	21
Chapter II	Nemesis	40
Chapter III	Dictator	61
Chapter IV	Ides	85
Chapter V	Pax	106
Chapter VI	Kingmakers	133
Chapter VII	Arena	162
Chapter VIII	Zenith	186
Chapter IX	Philosopher	214
Chapter X	Split	241
Chapter XI	Cross	266
Chapter XII	Collapse	289
Acknowledgements		313
List of illustrations		315
Recommended reading		321
Notes		323
Index		343

When wasteful war shall statues overturn,
And broils root out the work of masonry,
Nor Mars his sword, nor war's quick fire shall burn
The living record of your memory.

                        Shakespeare, Sonnet 55

Oceanus Atlanticus
Mare Germanicum
HIBERNIA
CALEDONIA
BRITANNIA
York
Colchester
London
Kalkriese
R. Rhine
GERMANIA INFERIOR
GERMANIA MAGNA
Trier
BELGICA
LUGDUNENSIS
Alesia (52 BC)
GERMANIA SUPERIOR
Carnuntum
Vienna
RAETIA
NORICUM
Aquincum
PANNONIA
Lyon
1
2
3
AQUITANIA
Milan
ITALIA
Aquileia
Turin
Nîmes
Arles
Ravenna
R. Rubicon
DALMATIA
TARRACONENSIS
Lake Trasimene (217 BC)
Split
LUSITANIA
Mérida
Tarragona
CORSICA ET SARDINIA
ROME
Ostia
Capua
Naples
Cannae (216 BC)
Pompeii
Saguntum
BAETICA
New Carthage
SICILIA
Syracuse
MAURETANIA TINGITANA
MAURETANIA CAESARIENSIS
Carthage
Zama (202 BC)
AFRICA PROCONSULARIS
Mare
GAETULIA
PHAZANIA
Leptis Magna
N
1. ALPES POENINAE
2. ALPES COTTIAE
3. ALPES MARITIMAE
Major battles
0
500 km
0
500 miles

The Roman Empire at the end of the reign of Trajan in AD 117

Introduction

'This is two thousand years old,' my father reminded me as he placed the small silver disc into the palm of my hand. It was still gleaming, cool to the touch, no bigger than a penny. My young mind could not possibly – and will always struggle to – comprehend such an expanse of time. This coin was older than both world wars, older than Shakespeare, had already existed for a millennium when Harold took an arrow in the eye at Hastings.

The details were worn but, peering closely, I could make out letters of an alphabet I understood; encircling the profile of a man whose determined stare seemed to reach far beyond the coin's edge, as if still planning his next move. Grasping the true antiquity of the shimmering metal might have been beyond me, but I was immediately curious about this man whose portrait was forever stamped into its surface. My father soon clarified: 'That's the Roman emperor, Trajan.' The leader, he went on to explain, who ruled over an empire so vast it stretched all the way from Scotland to Iraq, and this coin, known as a *denarius*, would buy my bread at each end of it.

I had to wonder, looking down at the stern face of an emperor of Rome, how he rose to become the most powerful man in the ancient world. Just as he lay in my hand, the fate of millions once lay in his. What might it have been like to meet him, and what would he make of our distant century – to know that children and their fathers were still gazing at his coins, speaking his name, and recounting his deeds after two millennia? The more I thought about the adventure that shining denarius must have taken through time, the more it seemed to tingle with electricity in my palm.

'Let's call that the first coin in your collection,' my father said.

A few decades and countless Roman coins later, it is safe to say that from that moment my imagination was captured. These were, after all, hand-held windows into a world inhabited by the most colourful

Silver denarius of the Roman emperor Trajan who ruled
AD 98–117, held by the author.

and entertaining characters, who wielded the power of gods while falling victim to the most human weaknesses. A world with no comforting distinctions between hero and villain, where triumph was balanced always by tragedy – and the best part was that this was no fanciful work of fiction. This rise and fall was a true-life epic, with many of its most dramatic scenes playing out before you in precious metal.

Perhaps more than any other artefact, coins offer us a tangible and immediate connection to our ancient past. Their invention in the seventh century BC represents a crucial spark in humanity's intellectual awakening: it has rightly been observed that wherever man began to think, money began to live.[1] They have been our close physical companions ever since, coveted and carried always about our bodies, designed to sit in our palms, to be passed between the hands of strangers and friends – a focus of human contact through much of recorded history. The relationship would soon become a sacred one: to this day we still throw them in pools of water and make a hopeful wish, place them in the foundations of new buildings, carry them as good luck charms, hide them in food, and give them as gifts.

First crafted as a convenient and mass-produced means of financial exchange, coins quickly turned into so much more, with the ancients treating the small discs of metal as a canvas on which to showcase the fundamental ideals of their culture. While the Greeks pushed the medium to its artistic limits, attaining levels of beauty and sophistication arguably never seen before or since, the Romans appreciated the practical power of coinage to disseminate their own civilisational brand. As cultural transmitters, coins promoted the very concept of *Romanitas* – what it meant to be Roman. Empire would be built as much by their silver and bronze, as it would by the iron of the legionary's blade.

Struck on an industrial scale under the might of Rome, coins truly became humanity's first mass media. Two thousand years before the printing press, they were efficiently spreading ideas, beliefs, news, and propaganda to the furthest reaches of the known world. Counting your change in the Roman market might also mean seeing the face of your new emperor for the first time – it seems beards are back in fashion again! – or learning of the latest military triumph over those trouser-wearing barbarians. You might even get your first glimpse of a new in-vogue god from the East – if Mars or Venus have yet to answer your prayers, why not try a sacrifice to them instead?

Ancient coins exist as stirring reminders of that intimate bond, though in my view their unique ability to place history at our fingertips is rarely harnessed to its full potential today. By their nature, coins are small and difficult to display effectively. While many museums around the world hold dazzling collections, contextualising them for the visiting public can present a seemingly impossible task; understandably, most institutions only exhibit the tiniest fraction of their ancient money.

Likewise, while the scientific study of coins and currency, known as numismatics, pre-dates other disciplines like archaeology and anthropology by centuries, it remains one of the most obscure academic fields. The literature is only for the brave, filled often with technical jargon that keeps at arm's length many who might threaten interest. Even among historians, numismatics is seen as an esoteric area of study. Coins are rightly valued by the archaeologist for the precise dating evidence they can provide for an ancient site – but they also risk being reduced to exactly that: just well-dated pieces of metal.

They need not be seen in such enigmatic terms; indeed, far from being exclusionary, coins can provide one of the most welcoming gateways into ancient history. Unlike other rare and untouchable artefacts, they survive in their millions, many in pristine condition; are conveniently held in the hand, and are still – for now at least – used much as they always were, instantly recognised by young and old. Coins were one of the few objects handled equally by people from every walk of ancient life, treasured by the slave and the senator alike. A universality that endures today as the ancient artefact most frequently unearthed by the general public; brought to light by farmers, construction workers, and metal detectorists far more than they are by archaeologists. Unless they were deliberately melted down, most ancient coins were accidentally lost or, in an age before banking, intentionally buried in hoards. People have therefore been finding them – in vast numbers and in the most surprising places – for centuries, and there remain untold amounts still to be discovered. So many survive that any history lover hoping to bring the classical world to life with a collection of its money can see it as a perfectly realistic goal. As such, they are the only handcrafted pieces of ancient art freely collected by enthusiasts of all backgrounds across the world.

Further adding to their accessibility is the fact that coins are an inherently visual art form: intrinsic stores of monetary value first and foremost, but also picture books of the past, specifically designed to cross cultural and linguistic barriers for appreciation by the widest audience possible. Their study provides a complete immersion in the enchanting myths and the harsh realities of the classical world, a visual manifest through the essential components of Western civilisation, diarising the evolution of art, language, architecture, war, government, and much more besides. It is no exaggeration to say that a dedicated ancient coin enthusiast might acquire in the pursuit of the hobby their own 'classical education'; before long they will be able to read a coin's Greek or Latin legends, identify its gods and goddesses, recount the myths it portrays, locate the cities where it was struck and, of course, recognise the faces of kings and emperors stamped on its surface as if they were old friends.

Yet as well as igniting the intellect, ancient coins also strike at the heart. Holding one in your hand, the mind inevitably imagines the countless others who have also looked down upon its designs, both in far-off millennia and in recent centuries. Maybe the coin once lay in the palm of a hardened legionary, a brutalised gladiator, an enterprising merchant; perhaps later, a British monarch or president of the United States – both surprisingly possible.[2] In the circle of a coin we find an uncanny portal connecting us not only to its makers, but to every one of its custodians, both past and future.

From the seed of that first denarius gifted by my father, my own collection of Roman coins grew steadily, alongside an inevitable fascination with the world that struck them into being. Researching their origin stories – often as intricate as the tiny designs stamped into their surface – took me to dusty libraries and grand museums; but most thrillingly of all, to the Eternal City where they were forged in fire and the still-standing monuments celebrated in their metal, as well as to ruinous towns where they had united people by a shared measure of exchange. Clambering over the broken fragments of once-magnificent structures, much like holding a coin, it is not so difficult to hear the voices of those people who surely looked around at their empire and thought it could never end. The remains of the classical world would take even the most enthusiastic traveller many lifetimes to fully discover; so far, I have been lucky enough to explore hundreds of Roman sites all over Europe, the Middle East, and North Africa, including in lesser visited countries like Libya and Albania. But returning always to the miniature realm of Rome's coins, to realise myself as part of the same history as immortal names like Julius

Caesar, Cleopatra, Caligula, Nero, Hadrian – to reach out and touch the face of the past.

This book sets out to celebrate the power and immediacy of coins as primary sources from the Roman world. Not faded and crumbled like painted frescoes, nor burned or corrupted in later centuries like fragile manuscripts; but durable, unchanging – 'a true reflection of their time'.[3] Striking into metal the faces of her rulers – earthly and divine – along with the deeds credited to them, Rome inadvertently left behind a near-unbroken personal record of her achievements. Coins told the story – at times they even *became* the story. As we will see, the shocking designs that some leaders dared to place on their money quickly had commentators reaching for their stylus pens, and political rivals reaching for their daggers.

The exploits of the ancient Romans are well-worn tales; embellished by historians, ornamented by Shakespearean tragedy, and reimagined by Hollywood epics. But the handcrafted coins they left behind invite us to see these stories newly minted, to experience the most climactic moments in Roman history, as if for the first time. Transported through the millennia by their imagery, we will witness, first hand, the mythical founding of the city; be thrown into the chaotic aftermath of Rome's most infamous assassination; jostle to our seat in the packed Colosseum; see unveiled the symbol of an invincible new God; and ultimately, watch with dread as a barbarian army masses outside the city walls.

Coins enchanted me by giving the intangible wonder of ancient history a physical form; granting it weight, vivid colour, and a human face. For the reader, this book hopes to do something of the same.

By no means will this be a guide to collecting coins, though if a reader is enthused to read more on the topic, or even search out their first Roman coin, then the book will have surely succeeded in its aims. Nor will this be an encyclopedic reference work on Roman coinage; the Republic and Empire of Rome struck coins across three continents for the better part of a thousand years. There will, no doubt, be many numismatic masterpieces that are painful to omit, but in this personally curated selection of coins from a variety of Roman denominational values – gold, silver, and bronze – I hope to give the reader the fullest possible experience of Roman money. The fact that this story could be rewritten a hundred times featuring different Roman coins with each telling, only serves as a testament to the art of their creators.

There will be no intimidating glossary of terms demanding study before we embark on this journey. In delving into the backgrounds of each coin, we will discover the mechanics of their creation and the anatomy of their design along the way. Their stories will be brought to life through rigorous historical research, but I will equally seek to embrace the excitement and flights of imagination that accompany the experience of holding these ancient time capsules in your hands.

Coins need little explanation to evoke a pang of recognition. They have been treasured friends on our human journey for over a hundred generations – and yet it seems increasingly likely that our very generation will be the one to break that long bond. As we prepare to bid farewell to physical money in our lives, and step into an intangible digital future, I believe it more vital than ever that we celebrate the role coins played in bringing humanity together.

Ancient Rome, meanwhile, shows no signs of losing its timeless appeal. Film and television productions continue to dig its rich history for inspiration, and seemingly every month there are new archaeological excavations, museum exhibitions, or scientific discoveries that make the Romans, once again, headline news.

Still, the Romans themselves are hard to grasp. At a distance they can seem to us strange, cruel, irrational – beings from another world. This book hopes to introduce you to them, face to face. We will pick up lovingly crafted coins made by their ancient hands and hold them in our own. Looking closely, we will read in the recognisable letters, sharp as the day they were struck, their names, their vain boasts, and their solemn vows. We will see what they believed and what they valued, their brightest hopes and their darkest fears – some of which we might still share. But their living portraits will be read most clearly of all. Familiar faces made immortal in precious metal, tenacious and vital, almost seeming to breathe; as if they might, at any moment, turn to us and begin to tell us of that world long gone.

Prologue
MONETA

'In a way the coin is our superior. The hardness of its metal secures for it "eternal" existence... A coin does not grow, it issues ready-made from the mint and should remain as it then is; it should never change.'

Elias Canetti, *Crowds and Power*

Silver denarius struck by the moneyer Titus Carisius, 46 BC.
Obverse: Head of Juno Moneta, 'Moneta' behind.
Reverse: Tools for striking coins: tongs, anvil die, punch die, and hammer.

Juno's Warning

The night was moonless, clear, perfect for the attack. From the summit of the citadel, the Roman defenders would never see them coming through the darkness, yet the silver glow of the starlight was just enough to illuminate a route for the Gauls up the rugged cliffs.

This siege had gone on long enough. Several months had passed since the Gallic tribe, led by their chieftain Brennus, had won an astonishing victory over the Romans a few miles from the city. So bewildered were the Gauls at their sudden success, they hesitated in marching upon Rome itself, suspecting an elaborate trap. The delay allowed many of the citizens to escape, and a steadfast contingent of warriors to fortify a position on the Capitoline Hill, Rome's most sacred summit and home of her gods. From their high stronghold, the remaining men watched helplessly as the barbarians rampaged through the familiar streets below, putting to the torch their revered temples and their beloved homes. A thousand terrors forced them to turn their eyes to the sea of calamities all around – the screams of those left behind, the roaring of flames, the crashing of falling masonry – as if 'fate had made them spectators to the nightmare of their country's ruin'.[1]

It seemed that before young Rome even had a chance to realise her potential, she had fallen.

The city was left a smouldering wreck, her last soldiers surrounded and massively outnumbered. Still, they were certain they would prevail. Romans, after all, embraced fearful odds. Not to mention that the Gauls lacked the discipline needed for protracted siege warfare. Rationing of supplies, guard details, watchwords: these things meant nothing to bearded barbarians. The attackers had also burned the city's grain supplies during their sacking and were now encamped in charred, malarial valleys strewn with the rotting dead. The Romans – hardened by disaster and defending ancestral soil – were confident that disease and hunger would break the invaders before long. They would soon be proved right.

The attack, though, when it came, took them by surprise. The Gauls had eventually identified the most vulnerable ascent to the citadel, if only by following the footprints of a Roman messenger who had passed freely though their lines. Tonight, navigating by starlight alone, they would scale the cliffs by the same route and put an end to this upstart republic.

It would prove a difficult scramble, especially when attempted in darkness and under arms. But with uncharacteristic self-control the Gauls ascended in silence, passing weapons between each other without a sound, and acting as footholds for their comrades as they hoisted themselves up the jagged rock face. The Roman sentries on duty heard nothing of the coming attack. Their guard dogs too, tuned to the slightest noise in the darkness, did not stir. As destiny would have it, a more unlikely animal was to play the role of Rome's saviour that night.

Cresting the summit of the hill, the Gauls emerged before a flock of geese left to wander the citadel. These were the sacred animals of Juno, chief goddess of the Roman state and protectress of the city. Despite the near starvation of the besieged soldiers, the birds had not been killed for food and were, indeed, kept well fed. That devotion was soon to be rewarded. Disturbed by the barbarians, the geese clapped their wings frantically and shook the night air with their honks, like trumpets rousing every soldier from his slumber.[2] First to the scene was the highly decorated and perfectly named officer Marcus Manlius, who charged the leading barbarian and with a crushing blow from the boss of his shield, sent him headlong back over the cliff. With more Romans arriving, other Gauls soon followed him into the void, tumbling down onto their fellows below. The defenders rained down javelins on the remaining barbarians clinging desperately to the rock face. As Juno's geese gabbled their approval, every one of the attackers was soon sent hurtling into the blackness.

Spurred by their successful defence, the Romans offered the weary barbarians a decisive battle and the chance to end the entire ordeal once and for all. Their victory was swift, bloody, and complete – the Gauls were annihilated. With her sacred geese, Juno had saved Rome from imminent destruction. The wife of Jupiter and queen of the gods had once again affirmed herself protectress of the city. Rebuilding commenced immediately. Rome, as she would do so often throughout her history, would return from disaster with more strength and resolve than ever before.

The Gallic sack of Rome in 390 BC would ever after haunt the Roman imagination. Having only thrown out its kings a little over a century before, the fledgling Republic had been brought to the brink and survived. Virtues that defined the Roman character – discipline, courage, endurance, piety – had been put to the test in the crucible of war and delivered a resounding victory over the enemy. For the next 800 years, no barbarian would breach the walls of the city.

A glorious new temple now rose on the site of the foiled Gallic attack.[3] It would honour Juno in her role as the goddess who warns Rome of imminent dangers. The Temple of Juno Moneta, 'the Warner' (from the Latin verb *monere*, meaning 'to warn'), would thereafter watch over the ever-growing city from its prominent outcrop on the Capitoline. Yet as well as guarding the Roman populace, Juno Moneta would also safeguard the wealth of the state. It was perhaps for this reason that the temple soon took on a second function: it became the mint of the Roman Republic. Here, Rome would strike her name not only into the coins that fuelled her economy, but into history itself. From the mint, a gleaming and seemingly endless river of lovingly crafted coins flowed by the million, ready to spread the dream of Rome far and wide. Coinage struck in this very building would travel to every corner of the world under Roman dominion and beyond – later to be unearthed as far afield as Iceland, India, and China.[4]

For centuries, those gathering in the Forum square – the epicentre of the Roman world – could, with a single glance, look from the coins in their palms up to the temple in which they were created. So connected were the two in the Roman mind that those precious discs of gold, silver, and bronze were simply called *moneta*, after the watchful goddess. In this way, the Temple of Juno Moneta continues to loom large over all our lives today. It is, of course, from her name that we derive the English word for that force which still makes our world go round: money.

Masterpieces in Miniature

Every single ancient coin was made by hand. When you hold one in your fingertips and marvel at its intricate design, it is vital to remember that each stage of its creation was completed by skilled craftsmen without any modern tools or machinery. Awed by the engineering perfection of a Roman aqueduct or the mind-boggling complexity of a Greek astronomical 'supercomputer', we may be forgiven for assuming the ancients must have devised a clever mechanised solution for something as simple as hammering coins.[5] In fact, the process was a manual one from beginning to end, remaining essentially unchanged until the sixteenth century's first experiments with machine-pressed 'milled' coinage.

Understanding the basics of how ancient coins were created helps to remind us that these cold discs of metal have a human story to tell – each one the product of human sweat, toil, and ingenuity. Essentially, ancient coins were made by placing a blank disc of metal called a *flan* between two engraved dies and striking them with a hammer. The lower die, set tightly into an anvil, would imprint the *obverse* or 'heads' side of the coin, while the hand-held upper die would imprint the *reverse* or 'tails' design. But this swing of the hammer was just the final step in an intricate process, demanding the skills of a diverse team of workers. Minting ancient coins was, in every respect, a collaborative endeavour.

The story of each coin can be traced as far back as the extraction of its metals from the earth. Of the many cruel fates that might await the enslaved across the ancient world, condemnation to the mines – *damnatio ad metalla* – was the most feared of all. Slaves in their thousands – an estimated 60,000 working at one Roman mine in Spain alone – were forced to hack endlessly at the rock in the near-total darkness of cramped, suffocating tunnels.[6] So horrific were conditions for those labouring in the mines, being sent to one was generally considered a prolonged death sentence. When not being mined directly, the precious metals required for coinage were plundered from conquered lands. The emperor Trajan is thought to have brought home from his conquest of Dacia (modern Romania) around 225 tons of gold and 450 tons of silver to fill the state treasury – enough to strike thirty-one million gold *aurei* and 160 million silver *denarii* coins.[7]

Questions of how much coinage to inject into the Roman economy were closely tied to state expenditure at the time, though little is known of the bureaucracy behind such decisions.[8] What is clear is that coinage has always helped, as one scholar put it, to 'facilitate exchange between people, the payment of taxes and external trade'; naturally, as the scale and population of Rome's dominion expanded, so would the demand for new coin from the mint.[9] Once a finance magistrate, consul, or emperor decided on the amount of coin needed, the allotted weight of precious metals was designated by officers in the Roman treasury situated in the Temple of Saturn at the base of the Capitoline. The bullion was then taken on a short journey to the summit and delivered to the mint, presumably under the tightest security. Going by the procedures at medieval mints, from which more evidence survives, we can assume that the metal passed through a network of officials and assayers who carefully tested its purity. Batches of blank circular flans of gold, silver or bronze were then pre-prepared by metal workers to exacting weight standards.[10]

No coin was complete until it was embossed with a carefully chosen design – the state's stamp of approval. Of all the skills involved in ancient coin production, perhaps none impresses more than the artistry of the die engraver. The detail and creativity of the designs stamped into the metal of ancient coins, often just millimetres across, continued to fascinate long after the ruin of the classical world. As the wonders of Rome faded from memory, the art of her coinage remained prevalent, inspiring many a great Renaissance mind.[11] The dies that punched both sides of a coin were cut entirely by hand. It is worth emphasising what this entailed: a craftsman engraving tiny images and lettering directly into the hard bell-bronze stamps, using only simple chiselling tools – and for good measure, cut in reverse so designs were read the correct way when imprinted. As no Roman die

The die-engraver's art: a startlingly lifelike portrait – just a few millimetres across – of Hadrian's heir, Aelius Caesar. Denarius struck in AD 137, from the author's collection.

engravers ever signed their creations, they remain to us anonymous masters.

All of this was completed without any eyeglasses or magnification. This feat seems even more miraculous today: many delightful details on coins from my own collection can only be revealed under the microscopic scrutiny of high-definition photography. While primitive lenses are known from the ancient world – and one anecdote reveals that the emperor Nero may have used a lens of sorts to better see the action at gladiator fights – these were rare curios.[12] It seems fair to assume that expert mint engravers would have suffered from significant short-sightedness by the end of their careers. Furthermore, the intense stresses placed on these hand-cut dies during the minting process meant they only survived a few thousand blows of the hammer – perhaps a single day's use – before they cracked or wore down to an unacceptable degree.[13] By that point, engravers needed to be ready with another set of dies without delay. Studies have shown that a single issue of Roman coinage would routinely require hundreds of engraved dies for each side of a coin.[14]

When it was time for the strike, the metal blanks were heated to soften them in readiness for the hammer blow. Visual or written descriptions of mint teams in action are all but non-existent in ancient sources, perhaps owing to the secrecy and security around the process; forgery was enough of a problem already, without giving counterfeiters an instruction manual too. But from the scant surviving evidence, we can surmise that a team of at least three men brought the minting process to its climax. A rare bronze token shows one man placing the flan on the anvil, another positioning the upper die over it, and another wielding the hammer, ready to strike.[15] Given the enormous output of the mint, it is likely that multiple teams like this were at work simultaneously, from dawn till dusk and possibly beyond; a later medieval chronicler states that the 'hammers of the moneyers are never still, day and night'.[16]

Before they bring the hammer down, we may ask, who were the craftsmen making these coins? Thousands must have worked in the mint during the many centuries it operated, yet not a single testimony from one of them has come down to us. Does that mean, then, that they were downtrodden slaves, not so far removed from those toiling in the mines? A fortuitously surviving inscription celebrates a selection of workers at the mint in the year AD 115.[17] It lists sixty-three names and whether they are *liberti* or *servi* – freedmen or slaves. Just over half are labelled as free men. In the great social dynamism of the era, many of the slaves would have hoped to earn their freedom through the quality of their work at the mint. Conditions were no doubt dangerous and unpleasant, but this was not a torturous workhouse. Skilled men worked together in small teams, with little distinction between the free and enslaved, to manufacture a precision-made product. While their voices have been sadly lost to time, they continue to speak to us through the countless artworks they left as a lasting legacy to the world.

The Hammer and the Anvil

With splendid irony, an intriguing glimpse of the tools used by our tireless mint workers is offered to us on a coin that they created.[18] The silver denarius was struck in 46 BC in the name of the moneyer, Titus Carisius. As moneyer, Titus was one of three junior magistrates at the outset of their careers who took charge of coin minting for a single year. In the highly competitive political world of the Roman Republic, a stint as moneyer was the perfect way to raise your profile, coming as it did with the privilege of placing your name on that year's coinage. It seems they were even given free rein over coin designs; while in the imperial age, the emperor surely had the final say – though how he reported his requests to the mint remains a mystery. A minor position it may have been, but Titus Carisius clearly took pride in his role as moneyer, choosing for the obverse of his coin the face of Juno Moneta herself. The patron goddess of the mint is shown with her hair tied back in a bun, wearing cross-shaped earrings and a necklace. Evidently, Titus also felt that the mint workers deserved a rare bit of recognition, presenting to us on the reverse the essential tools of coin production. We can see the tongs used to place the hot metal blanks in position, a pair of dies, and the all-important hammer. In a telling addition, the upper 'punch' die is shown garlanded with a laurel wreath, while another wreath artfully frames the whole design – triumphant symbols that emphasise coin production as a sacred craft and a driving force in Rome's unstoppable rise.

Though the mint in the capital would remain the most prominent, it would not be the only place to strike the coins of empire. As we will see, a general on a multi-year campaign far from Rome might need to create his own coinage with which to pay his soldiers. In these instances, a stripped-down travelling mint would operate while moving with the legions through enemy territory. Perhaps the most famous example would be that of Julius Caesar, who took a mobile military-mint with him on his epic conquests. In times of civil war, rival claimants to power might each strike their own coinage in the hope of legitimising their positions. And as Rome's sphere of influence expanded, other cities, especially in the East, would be granted the right to strike their own coins. This 'provincial' coinage in bronze and silver was designed to fulfil the needs of local economies and used locally recognised denominations. Without coins, the legions, ports, marketplaces – indeed, all the mechanisms of empire – would quickly grind to a halt.

Now we reach the final moment of creation: with a precise swing and deafening clang, the hammer meets the die exactly, and a coin is wrought into being. The explosive effort of the hammerer – the above-mentioned inscription reveals that these men were called *malliatores* – is often evocatively frozen on the face of a coin in the form of shockwaves called 'flow lines', radiating out through the metal. Many people, when they hold an ancient coin, ask why the design is not perfectly centred like our modern money – and sometimes so misaligned that part of the image or text has dropped off the edge. Having tried striking reproduction coins myself with similar tools, I can attest how difficult it is to keep the die perfectly placed over the blank as you bring down the hammer. With a little practice and a great deal of concentration, I just about managed one well-centred coin after many attempts. Now factor in the fatigue and the lightning pace of production needed to meet demand – some estimate one coin struck every three seconds – and it is no surprise that not every coin is perfect to modern eyes.[19]

In other instances, the reverberation of the impact caused the die to bounce and impress its design into the coin twice – known as a 'double strike'. An even more dramatic mishap sometimes occurred when a coin became lodged in the upper die. If this went unnoticed by the striking team, the obverse side of the trapped coin would be embossed into the next blank to be struck, instead of the reverse design of the die. This could result in error coins known as 'brockage', with mirror-image heads on both sides. Quality-control measures in place at the mint held each team accountable for their daily output, but inevitably some of these blundered coins slipped through. Indeed, many modern collectors enjoy seeking out such imperfect examples; all happy accidents reminding us that these coins were made by human hands that tired, that rushed, that made mistakes. Underlined by all this is a compelling truth: every single ancient coin is a unique work of ancient art. Even two coins struck seconds apart, by the same team with the same dies, will never be identical.

The coins produced by Rome, two millennia ago, must surely rank as the most widely surviving artefacts from all antiquity – still emerging from ploughed English fields and parched Israeli hillsides on an almost daily basis – yet surprisingly little is known about how exactly they were created.[20] Modern experimental archaeology and even cutting-edge atomic spectrometry is only beginning to reveal the secrets of the minting process. What we do know is that each coin was the result of a dynamic collaboration of metallurgists, assayers, smiths, artists, engravers, and labourers. Ancient coins were mass-produced, yet at the same time, artisanal. Labours of love crafted on an industrial scale.

A Forge of Ideas

A thousand noises compete in the cacophony. Flaming furnaces roar, quickened by blasting bellows. Molten metal spits out crackling sparks as it pours from glowing crucibles. Through clouds of hissing steam, overseers struggle to be heard as they call out commands to their teams. And always cutting through the din, the unending chimes of the striking hammers, like the peal of frantic bells ringing out over the heart of Rome.

Perched on the sacred hill of the gods, adjacent to the house of Jupiter himself, the temple-workshop of Moneta watches proudly over the city.[21] In the bustling streets below, close to a million people exchange her wares by day and night. Deals are made, bets are won and lost, exotic items from a boundless empire are bought and sold. Juno's coins connect those usually separated by gulfs, passed between the hands of the rich and the poor, the free and the enslaved – allowing them all to relate through a 'common measure'.[22] From the great metropolis paved roads emanate like arteries, carrying these coins to people in even the most distant province. A gleaming denarius fresh from the mint might go on to buy beer in Britannia or pepper in Syria.

The workshop of Moneta is many things simultaneously to the vast Roman world. An engine room, with hammering pistons that power the wheels of empire; and a newsroom, where the latest headlines are imprinted and rushed out to every corner of the Mediterranean. A cultural ground-zero bringing Roman gods, emperors, and fashions to the masses; yet equally, a Ministry of Truth, still controlling narratives and offering 'alternative facts' across the millennia.

Here Rome strikes gold, silver, and bronze coinage on an unprecedented scale, but the mint is also a workshop of ideas. Accompanying the heat of the forge is heated discussion of artistic composition, symbolism, and persuasion. On the enduring metal, Rome writes her unfolding biography; a visual journey from difficult childhood all the way to *caput mundi* – capital of the world. These will be tales of glory and sorrow, of heroism and betrayal; like the coins they are stamped into, there will always be opposing sides. In the end, as with most history, the genre will be tragedy. There will be a triumphant rise and cataclysmic fall – but even when the world that made them is long buried, the coins will still emerge, glinting in the dark earth, ready to tell their stories.

These are just a few of them.

Chapter I

WOLF

'Then Romulus, proud in the tawny hide of the she-wolf, his nurse, shall found the walls of Mars and call the people Romans after his own name. For these Romans I set no bounds in space or time; but have given empire without end.'

Virgil, The Aeneid

Silver *didrachm*, 269–266 BC, Rome mint. The first coin struck in Rome, under the name 'of the Romans'.
Obverse: Diademed head of young Hercules, with club and lion skin over shoulder.
Reverse: She-wolf suckling the infant twins, Romulus and Remus. 'ROMANO' in exergue.

Children of Mars

The flood had passed. Finally, the river had retreated to its tangled banks. From the dark undergrowth there, a pair of amber eyes scanned the waterline. Only when she was sure, did she emerge from the shadows into the open. Thirst often brought her down from the wild hills to drink here, most recently with the latest litter she had reared. Those pups had followed her so closely, grown so fast; until one day they needed her milk no longer, and bounded off into the woods. Now she was alone again. Planting her paws into the soft mud of the riverbank, she lowered her muzzle and lapped at the cool waters.

The scent reached her first, swept downstream on the brisk air. All at once her muscles tightened, her eyes narrowed, her pointed ears stood alert for every sound. A lone wolf quickly learned to sense danger everywhere. Then came the faint whimpering, almost lost as it mingled with the gush of the tumbling waters. She thought of running, but her curiosity – and her hunger – drew her towards the sound. Along the riverbank she stalked, closer and closer to the origin of that strange mewling. Pushing through the thick reeds at the water's edge, she bared her glistening teeth instinctively. And then she saw them.

They lay, writhing in river muck, next to the basket that had turned them out as the flood receded. Tiny arms and legs flailing, naked, utterly helpless before her. With every weak cry she padded nearer, until she stood over the two infants. Spittle dripped from her open mouth as she sniffed their shivering skin. Famished ribs showed through her fur. She was ravenous, deadly – yet still, a mother.

Curling her grey tail protectively around the pair, she began licking them down. Her slick tongue washed away the mud and warmed their blood. With their wails renewed and vigorous, she offered her teats, still distended and lactating from the recent rearing of her pups. She could hardly spare the energy, drained as she already was, but there on the banks of the Tiber, she suckled the twins with all the life-giving milk she could muster.[1] Milk imbued in equal measure with maternal gentleness and wolven ferocity. After the feed she carried each of the babies up to her shadowy cave, the Lupercal, where she would rear them as her own.

It was here, some time later, that the shepherd came upon them as he led his flock through the hills. He was struck dumb with astonishment at the sight before him: a wild wolf tenderly nursing motherless human twins that clung to her lovingly. Moved though he was at the almost supernatural scene, he drove the she-wolf away and took the boys up himself. The moment he held them, Faustulus sensed that they were no normal children, but surely of royal – perhaps even divine – heritage. And he had heard those rumours from the nearby city of Alba Longa; that the princess Rhea Silvia, daughter of the rightful king, Numitor, had given birth to twins after declaring that she had been raped by Mars, the god of war. Her uncle, Amulius, who had seized the throne, threw Rhea in prison and ordered that the illegitimate children be drowned. The servant tasked with the deed could not bring himself to see it through and instead sent the babies down the flooded river in a basket.

Whether the rumours of their parentage were true or not, the gods had clearly decided the miraculous twins should live. Besides, the life of a herdsman like Faustulus was tough, and sons would one day provide him welcome help. The boys needed names – and he would derive them from the Latin *ruma*, describing the teat at which they were found suckling.[2] In naming them, he could not have known he was also naming history's greatest city and empire. Back at his humble shepherd's hut, Faustulus presented to his wife their new adopted sons, Romulus and Remus.

Ab Urbe Condita

The story of Rome begins with an enigma: how did a hamlet of a few thatched huts on a hillside above a murky Italian marsh grow in just a few centuries to be the most powerful empire in the history of humanity? Even the Romans themselves struggled to answer this question, concocting a fascinating mythology to explain their staggering explosion out of Italy and seemingly predestined rise to greatness. In the prelude to his epic *History of Rome*, Livy declares that 'antiquity draws no hard line between the human and the supernatural'; boundaries that become especially blurred as historians, poets, and artists of every era turn their gaze back to the hidden origins of the Eternal City. Everywhere we encounter 'tales with more of the charm of poetry than of a sound historical record' and events which merely 'carry with them an appearance of truth'.[3] The narrative of the founding of Rome has always been a heady mix of primal myth, received tradition, and embellished reality, which even today's exciting archaeological discoveries struggle to separate from each other.

While they could not settle on a single definitive origin story for the Roman world, the accounts of most ancient writers converge in that sacred scene chanced upon by the shepherd in the woods: the wild wolf-mother suckling the feral human twins, Romulus and Remus. An image so evocative of the Roman character, it would remain an emblem of the city and its citizens across the upheavals of millennia. Any visitor to Rome — where there is no shortage of competition for religious icons — will be greeted by the wolf and twins at every turn, still nursing lovingly to this day. Yet before the strange diorama had been described by the earliest Roman historian in the third century BC, it had already been hammered into gleaming silver at the mint on the Capitoline Hill.[4] Rome had barely completed the conquest of the Italian peninsula, let alone the wider Mediterranean, but she had already struck a coin that presented her people with the defining image of her founding myth.

The origin stories that evolved in the Roman mind reveal much about their perceived place in the ancient world. Most accounts link the rise of their legendary city to the fall of another. Following the destruction of Troy — narrated for the ages in Homer's epic poems *The Iliad* and *The Odyssey* — the Trojan warrior Aeneas found himself exiled with a group of his followers, left to wander the Mediterranean in search of a new homeland. After many adventures and divine interventions that echo the journeys of the Homeric hero Odysseus, Aeneas eventually landed on the shores of Latium in Italy, where he chose to settle for good. The Trojans and Latins gradually merged into one people through intermarriage, and the descendants of Aeneas spread out to create cities of their own. His son Ascanius would go on to found the kingdom of Alba Longa, where generations later the princess Rhea Silvia would fall pregnant after apparently being raped by the god of war. These were claims of divine conception that even Roman historians would later question; Livy could not help but wonder if the sworn Vestal Virgin was 'merely hoping by the pretence to alleviate her guilt'.[5]

Down the River Tiber would go the twin sons of Mars, towards the teats of the she-wolf and the crook of the herdsman Faustulus. Incidentally, numerous other mythological and historical figures supposedly began their lives as the proverbial 'baby in the basket' cast down a river, such as Osiris, Sargon of Akkad, Moses, and Bacchus. The boys grew to be hardy shepherd lads, blissfully unaware of the royal blood in their veins. But signs of their noble lineage – or were they qualities imbued through the mother's milk of the wolf? – regularly showed themselves. The twins even became Robin Hood-like figures in the local community, attacking brigands and sharing the stolen goods among all the other shepherds. Eventually, they would push their altruistic escapades too far, with Remus being captured by a gang of ruffians and brought before the hateful king Amulius for judgment. Romulus rushed to rescue his brother, but not before his adoptive father Faustulus revealed to him the truth of their parentage: that they were the banished king Numitor's grandsons, exposed on the riverside by the evil brother who had stolen his throne. Romulus gathered a force of his fellow herdsmen and led a surprise attack on the king's palace, where he succeeded in rescuing his brother and killing Amulius. Returning to his kingdom, Numitor acknowledged the twins who had reclaimed his throne as his own kin, conferred on them royal titles, and together they led a jubilant parade through the streets.[6]

Buoyed by their successful revolution and new royal status, the brothers set out on a pilgrimage to find the mystic riverside where they had been rescued by the wolf; and there, do what any self-respecting young princes would do: found a city. Though just when their tale threatens a heroic end, we encounter the dangerous sibling rivalry that would plague Rome throughout her history. Whether it was actual brothers, or power-sharing consuls and co-emperors, many a fraternal bond over the next few centuries would crumble under the weight of personal jealousy and ambition, resulting in more than a few destructive civil wars that brought Rome to the brink of disaster.

A 'disgraceful quarrel' arose between Romulus and Remus concerning which brother should govern their new settlement.[7] Each stubbornly took to rival hills: Romulus settled on the Palatine and Remus on the Aventine, separated by the valley that would later become the site of Rome's great racetrack, the Circus Maximus. In what is surely one of history's most far-reaching neighbour disputes, the twins argued over where to place the boundary dividing their land. When Remus jumped the wall into his brother's territory, an enraged Romulus struck him down and killed him. 'So shall it be henceforth with all who leap over my walls!' he cried out over the body of his brother.[8] Fortifying his position on the Palatine Hill – leading to our modern word 'palace' and forever marking the hill as the home of the ruling class – Romulus proclaimed the name of his new city, known thereafter as Roma rather than Rema. Its people would chart all future events *ab urbe condita* – 'from the founding of the city'. That day of Rome's birth, by ancient tradition, was 21 April 753 BC.

A Public Thing

Romulus would be the first of seven kings to rule over Rome and her seven hills. We are told that this monarchy lasted for almost 250 years, yet the age of kings remains shrouded in the same fog of myth that cloaks the city's foundation. Almost no written records or inscriptions survive from Rome's infancy. Later Roman historians found themselves writing the biography of their all-powerful empire, without knowing the events of its youth that had given it its steel. A great city needed a great provenance, and as it often will, a colourful blend of fable and lore poured in to fill the void.

Modern archaeological discoveries have provided some tantalising insights into the city's earliest history, showing that at least a few facts may be concealed in the fiction. Romulus was said to have lived in a simple thatched hut on the Palatine that was carefully preserved, like a living museum, through the later Empire. In the mid-twentieth century, post holes of circular Iron Age dwellings were found cut into the tufa bedrock of the hill. Organic material helped date the settlement to between 900 and 700 BC; it would appear Rome did, in fact, begin as a small community on the heights of the Palatine, around the time of its traditional founding date.[9] Excavations of the Regia, the office of Rome's kings and later chief priests like Julius Caesar, uncovered a pottery sherd intriguingly inscribed 'Rex', meaning 'King'. The mysterious 'Black Stone' was also discovered nearby in the Roman Forum. Dating to around the sixth century BC, it carries the oldest known Latin inscription and seems to be a warning by the authority of 'the king' against desecrating sacred ground.[10] We cannot say if a king named Romulus truly founded the city, or to what extent the city was even 'founded' at all, but here we do have evidence of that first monarchy that, until recently, was merely the stuff of legend.

It may have been in these humble huts that Romulus and his mostly male followers soon found themselves struggling with a serious problem: a distinct lack of women in their new settlement. Unable to start families, they questioned the long-term future of their new Roman enterprise, which would 'now only last for one age of man'.[11] In desperation, Romulus resorted to drastic actions. The king arranged a lavish pastoral festival as an elaborate ruse and made sure to invite all tribes in the region. There would be games, spectacles, and of course, heavy drinking – the perfect opportunity to launch a strike against his rivals while their guard was down. Many tribes attended, curious to see the new city they had heard so much about; including the Sabines from the north, who happily brought along their wives and children. When all 'minds and eyes were intent upon the spectacles', Romulus gave his loyal followers the signal. In an instant, the Roman men set upon and kidnapped the young Sabine women, 'carrying off a great number of the virgins by force'.[12] The legend of the Abduction of the Sabines can be seen in the context of historical bride-kidnap or 'bridenapping' – a practice that has been

Soldiers of Romulus abducting Sabine women, shown on a denarius struck in 89 BC – from the author's collection.

prevalent in cultures all around the world and not only limited to the pages of ancient history.[13]

A Roman silver denarius, struck centuries later during the Republic, provides a startling visualisation of the legend in miniature, and perfectly exemplifies how coins were vital tools in crafting a collective sense of Roman heritage and identity. Two soldiers of Romulus can be seen, each carrying off a Sabine woman in his arms. The women strike out desperately against their abductors, their flailing arms and flowing robes adding movement and urgency to the scene. The two abductors are seen turning to each other, perhaps avoiding the defensive blows of the young women or maybe encouraging each other in their shocking collective act. That the moneyer responsible for the coin, Lucius Titurius Sabinus, traced his lineage back to the Sabine people might explain his numismatic tribute to the mass abduction, and it would not be his only memorial to his ancestral tribe. Another coin struck during his tenure as moneyer depicts the death of the Vestal Virgin Tarpeia, who defected to the rival Sabines hoping she might be rewarded with gold jewellery. Instead, she was crushed with shields and thrown from the cliff that would thereafter carry her name, the Tarpeian Rock.[14]

Such are the stories that Romans told themselves about their primordial past, celebrated for centuries to come in coins, art, and literature. Given the chance to invent their own grand mythos, they crafted unapologetic tales of refugees and outcasts, of kidnap, rape, abandonment, and murder. As surprising as these legends might seem to modern sensibilities, they can only be interpreted as the product of the ruthless Iron Age world in which they were forged, with Rome just one minor city-state jostling among many on the Italian peninsula. When life for most was short, threatened by violence, and dogged by hunger, something of the animal was surely needed to prevail. It may have been 'written in the book of fate that this great city should arise' but for Romans, there was no shame in their beginnings as the feral underdog of ancient Italy.[15]

Tales of a somewhat savage childhood also helped illustrate to contemporaries how far Rome had come since the age of kings. After centuries under the yoke of an increasingly tyrannical monarchy, Rome was ready to take a radically new direction. In 509 BC, the final king, Tarquin the Proud, was thrown out of the city by the great liberator, Lucius Junius Brutus. Instantly protective of their new-found freedoms, Brutus gathered the Roman populace together while the 'taste of liberty was still fresh upon their tongues' and made them swear a solemn oath that never again would a king – a *rex* – be allowed to rule in Rome.[16] With the monarchy overthrown, they would experiment with a revolutionary new form of government: one where power was held not in the hands of one man but shared among annually elected representatives; where Romans were no longer subjects, but citizens, guaranteed liberty under the authority of the law. The state and all its mechanisms would now be 'a public thing' – a *res publica*. In this new Republic, Brutus himself would become one of the first two *consuls* – a pair of leading magistrates elected for only a single year, each acting as a check on the other's power. These liberating systems of the Republic would quickly unleash the full force of Roman potential, resulting in what is surely one of the greatest explosions of human ambition in all of history. These children of Mars, suckled by the wolf, were ready to take on not just the rest of Italy, but the entire known world.

Heirs of the Owl

The young Roman Republic was a relative latecomer to the world of coinage. A hundred years before its foundation, the first coins had been struck in the kingdom of Lydia in western Anatolia (modern-day Turkey). Humans had been exchanging items through systems of barter for thousands of years — be it cattle, animal skins, or axe heads — but these transactions required negotiation and what economists call 'the double coincidence of wants'.[17] The concept of portable currency as a store of wealth evolved gradually, with bullion bars or measures of grain being exchanged at standardised values set by the community or state. Coins were the natural culmination of this journey towards the most efficient form of human exchange; highly portable, of set weight and worth, and guaranteed by the stamp of an authority. These early Lydian coins took the form of small lumps of the naturally occurring compound electrum, punched with the head of a roaring lion. Soon they were struck in glorious gold and silver and with increasingly complex designs.[18]

As an undeniable catalyst in trade and growth, the use of coins spread quickly through the Greek states that dominated the Mediterranean. This flourishing Hellenic world, with Athens at its heart, used coins as cultural messengers, transporting classical ideals to islands and colonies far and wide. The owl of Athena, symbol of the city of wisdom, now flew to distant shores, stamped on instantly iconic silver coins of Athens. Often called the 'dollar of the ancient world', these coins were so prevalent they were fondly known by the nickname 'Owls'.

Within a couple of centuries of their invention, coins struck by the Greeks achieved a quality of craftsmanship that would arguably never be surpassed. This perfection of the art is exemplified in the audacious coins minted at Agrigento and Syracuse, Greek colonies on the island of Sicily: miniature masterpieces to rival even the most famous classical sculpture. One of these large silver coins, known as a *tetradrachm*, bears a captivating portrait of the water nymph Arethusa, who turns to face the viewer as playful dolphins leap from the waves of her flowing hair. Described as 'easily the most beautiful coin of all time', its magnificence was also recognised by its maker; the coin's dies are proudly signed by the master engraver Kimon, who is known to have worked at the Syracuse mint in the late fifth century BC and included his signature on his finest creations, just as an artist might today.[19]

Romans meanwhile were still trading rough, unworked ingots of bronze. With the advent of the Republic these were refined into cast bronze currency bars embossed with simple designs, known as *aes signatum* or 'signed bronze'. The city's economic ambitions grew with her territory. Under the monarchy, Rome had gradually pushed her borders to become the largest city-state in Latium; now renewed as a Republic, the Romans would fully manifest as the progeny of the god of war and seek to dominate the entire Italian peninsula. The Etruscans to the north were an ancient civilisation that had greatly influenced Roman culture, language, and religion, yet their time had passed, and Rome gradually ate away at their lands in a series of bloody wars through the fifth century BC. Next came the tribes of the Samnites who occupied much of central Italy and the Bay of Naples, reduced in similarly gruelling and hard-fought campaigns through the fourth century. When a victory was achieved, Rome integrated each Italic tribe into her expanding orbit, enfranchising them as allies rather than ruling them as subjects. All the while her armies became more deadly, absorbing the most effective weaponry and tactics they encountered.

By 300 BC, Rome's advancing territory was pushing against the Greek colonies of southern Italy and the island of Sicily. The lasting power of this 'Greater Greece' can be felt even today when we visit sites like Paestum, Agrigento, and Segesta, where classical Greek temples still stand majestic on Italian soil. The Golden Age of Greece was nearing its end, but Rome seemed a vulgar, young upstart by comparison. When competing with such a titan – one whose empire was a byword for civilisation itself – there was no shame in using imitation as a shortcut to greatness. Rome would happily emulate Greek architecture, religion, battle tactics – and of course, her coins. The functional bronze currency bars issued by Rome appeared laughably primitive next to the showpieces struck by the Greeks. The time had come for Rome to announce herself on the world's stage with coins of shining silver that would rival all others.

The first silver coins minted in the name of Rome were struck around 280 BC, as her forces battled the Greek colonists led by the Hellenistic king Pyrrhus. These were probably minted in Neapolis (modern Naples) and used to pay allied troops on the frontlines. Appropriately, they show the portrait of Mars, divine father of the warlike nation, though the helmet he wears is of the Greek Corinthian type. After fierce fighting, the bloodied forces of Pyrrhus retreated from Italy in 275 BC and the final strongholds of Greek resistance were overcome. The wolf of Rome could now claim the whole of the Italian peninsula as her territory.

The Nurturing Beast

She would celebrate her fated ascendancy with this, the first ever silver coin struck at home, on Rome's Capitoline Hill. A coin that captures the spirit of Italy's new apex predator so perfectly, its design would remain emblematic of her to this day. The weighty silver piece might announce the arrival of a new superpower, but it is designed to fit seamlessly into the existing economic world of the third century BC. Struck from around seven grams of pure silver, the coin is a *didrachm*, meaning a double unit of *drachm* – a standard Greek denomination used across the Mediterranean. It also bears the youthful portrait of one of the most popular action heroes of the Greek pantheon, Heracles – or as the Romans would know him, Hercules. A demi-god born to a human mother but fathered by the mighty Jupiter, Hercules was renowned for his superhuman strength and thrilling Twelve Labours in which he battled a variety of mythic beasts. The pelt of one of them, the ferocious Nemean Lion, can be seen draped over his shoulder, along with the wooden club that was his weapon

The first silver coin struck in Rome, and the artistic introduction of the Lupa Romana she-wolf nursing Romulus and Remus.

of choice. The Romans quickly identified with the rough and tough folk-hero who won a place alongside the immortal gods, yet the portrait also evokes another superstar of the Greek world. Alexander the Great, the Macedonian conqueror who brought Greek culture as far east as India, had died only a few decades before this didrachm was struck. The famous coins that spread out in the wake of his conquests also showed Hercules wearing his lion skin. Fresh from their own takeover of Italy, the Romans presented themselves, with this coin, as potential new Alexanders – natural heirs to the classical world.

Yet turning the didrachm over in our hand, we see that it is not all mindless imitation. On the reverse we are greeted with a design that launches the brand of Rome – logo and all – with an advertising panache that would make any modern marketeer proud. The fearsome she-wolf dominates the frame with powerful musculature and flexing sinews; a ruffled mane makes her seem more lionly than wolflike. Intimidating as her physique appears, she turns her head to gently lick the two babies beneath that reach out for her lactating teats.[20] Below the scene, a single word announces to the viewer the name to remember: 'Romano', abbreviating the Latin *Romanorum* – the coin you hold is the product 'of the Romans'. The striking numismatic tableau shows how, even in their fiery adolescence, the Romans were keenly aware of their contradictory qualities. The she-wolf is both a frightful beast and a gentle mother. In the nourishment of twins with her lupine milk, the Romans saw the perfect reflection of their own duality: brutal yet maternal, wild yet civilised, warlike yet peace-loving.

The prevalence of the wolf in foundational myths and fairy tales from numerous cultures speaks of a primal connection between man and animal. A key figure in Norse mythology is the monstrous wolf Fenrir, son of Loki, who breaks out of all fetters and devours Odin at the doomsday of Ragnarök. Grey wolves of Japan – sadly extinct since the twentieth century – are embodied in various Shinto wolf gods that bring divine messages, inhabit lightning, or escort travellers across dangerous mountains. Wolves would also be of sacred importance to Native American peoples, with tribes sharing their hunting grounds with the revered animals in a symbiotic relationship; even modelling their own community structure on the cooperative wolf packs following an elder male leader.

The psychoanalysts Sigmund Freud and Carl Jung would later see the wolf as an elemental archetype, representing the struggle to suppress our wild and primitive instincts beneath modern civility and domestication, echoing ideas distilled in the ancient proverb '*Homo homini lupus est*' – 'Man is a wolf to his fellow man'.[21] The Brothers Grimm also made full use of the animal archetype in their collections of cautionary folk tales, several of which included a 'Big Bad Wolf' as a predatory antagonist with thinly veiled sexual undertones. Roman writers did not shrink from deconstructing their maternal icon either, candidly observing that the Latin *lupa*, meaning 'she-wolf', was also a word used to describe prostitutes. Brothels like those famously uncovered in Pompeii were called *lupanare*, or 'wolf dens'. Perhaps Romulus and Remus were nurtured, not by a mythic beast, but by a common prostitute.[22]

Roman revelling in these feral origins culminated in the ancient fertility festival of the Lupercalia. Each year on 15 February, a raucous crowd of young men assembled – naked except for animal skins – at the mouth of the Lupercal cave on the Palatine. There this 'brotherhood of the wolf' would sacrifice goats, smear themselves in their blood, and fashion whips from their hides. The Luperci then ran riotously through the streets of Rome, flogging young female spectators to bestow fertility, with many coming forward voluntarily to be lashed by the wolf men. The Lupercalia remained a key date in the Roman calendar for centuries; it was during the festival of 44 BC that, as well as being offered a kingly crown, Caesar was first warned by a soothsayer of his approaching demise. The unashamedly pagan ritual even seems to have been celebrated alongside Christian festivals in the later Empire, illustrating its fundamental importance to Roman identity.[23]

In the intimate nursing scene presented to us on this remarkable coin, we see real-time myth-making in progress. It would arguably be as close as Rome ever came to an artistic depiction of her Genesis, allowing the Republic to revere its own inception; simultaneously comparable to the Christian Nativity, a cradling Madonna and Child, or Michelangelo's *Creation of Adam*. An eagle swooping down on distant enemies like a bolt of lightning would become the feared symbol of Rome's military might, but it was the maternal image on this coin that would be her lasting badge of identity. In a largely illiterate world, its striking visual composition spoke quickly to those within and beyond Rome's borders. For those already under her sway, she would provide and protect, as this she-wolf nurtures her twins. And for all those yet to meet this lean and hungry Roman wolf – she was on her way.

Lupa Romana

At the heart of Rome's Capitoline Museum, on the very hill where our Roman coin was first struck, stands one of history's most iconic and influential statues. The Capitoline Wolf was part of a group of ancient bronzes donated to the city of Rome in 1471 by Pope Sixtus IV, leading to the foundation of the spectacular museum in which it still resides. Much like on our coin, this she-wolf stands sturdily on all four paws, with taut musculature and protruding ribs. A mane of curled fur also echoes the ancient beastly depiction, with little

The Capitoline Wolf, bronze statue of the she-wolf with Romulus and Remus. Capitoline Museums, Rome.

resemblance to an actual grey wolf. If she seems inattentive to the suckling infants reaching for her swollen teats, that is because the chubby twins – clearly executed in a different style – are known to be Renaissance additions. The wolf herself was long assumed to be an ancient Etruscan or early Roman work. Some even identified it with the bronze statue of the wolf and twins known to have stood on the Roman Capitol, dramatically struck by lightning in 65 BC.[24] The inauspicious event made quite an impact on the city, with the great orator Cicero describing how the 'martial beast, nurse of Roman dominion, suckling life-given dew' was 'stricken by lightning, toppling to the earth, bringing with her the children of the war god'.[25]

Recent scientific studies have dared to question the ancient origins of the iconic statue, however. Analysis revealed that the wolf was cast as a single piece in a manner akin to the bells and cannons of the Middle Ages, whereas ancient bronzes were typically constructed from multiple segments. Tantalising scorch marks on the back leg of the wolf are more likely lesions from errors in this casting process and not, as some imagined, damage from Cicero's lightning bolt. Organic material in the interior of the statue has recently been radiocarbon-dated to the eleventh or twelfth centuries.[26] However, references to a 'wolf' standing in the portico of the Pope's Lateran Palace go as far back as the tenth century.[27] Remnants of the clay core used in its moulding can be traced to the lands of Etruria, north of Rome, and metal for the statue is known to have been mined in Sardinia – all as would be expected from Etruscan production in the early fifth century BC.[28] Some also see in the highly stylised depiction of the wolf Etruscan visual motifs that would have been little known to sculptors of the Middle Ages: a composite creature given the body of a lion in an archaic fashion, with curly mane and crest of locks along its spine. A Greek historian in first-century Rome does indeed describe seeing at the mouth of the Lupercal cave a bronze statue of the she-wolf suckling the twins that was 'of ancient workmanship'.[29] The dating debate rumbles on, but the Capitoline Wolf's position as 'the ultimate image of Rome's tutelary beast' remains secure.[30]

Since being struck into our coin in the third century BC, the iconography of the Lupa Romana went on to represent city and empire in countless forms across the centuries. The motif would resurface regularly on later Roman coinage, especially when emperors such as Hadrian or Constantine celebrated the birthday of the city – perhaps even looking to cast themselves as new founders akin to Romulus himself. The wolf and twins would appear as late as the sixth century AD on the coins of Gothic kings ruling in the city, hoping to project a sense of continuity with the Roman state they had overrun. While the crude copper coins are wretched in comparison to our lustrous silver didrachm, their compositions of the nursing wolf, separated by 800 years, remain essentially identical.[31]

In every corner of the wide Roman Empire, citizens would incorporate the she-wolf into their dress and home decor as a patriotic symbol. An elegant silver brooch from Roman Iadera (modern Zadar, Croatia) shows the Lupa Romana suckling in her cave; dating to the second century AD, it was clearly worn by someone hoping to express pride in their membership of the Roman world. Two centuries later, the owner of a townhouse in what is today Aldborough, North Yorkshire, decided to install a mosaic floor showing the she-wolf with her twins. The finished product – affectionately nicknamed the

Roman silver brooch depicting the she-wolf suckling the twins Romulus and Remus, second century AD. Zadar Archaeological Museum, Croatia.

'Wonky wolf' of Leeds Museum where it is today displayed – is far from a technical masterpiece, but it survives as a testament to the lasting cultural legacy of Rome's foundational myth, even at the very edge of an empire nearing the end of its life.

In the nineteenth and twentieth centuries, the wolf became an unfortunate living symbol of the city, exploited by popes, kings, and Fascist dictators hoping to link themselves to the magnificence of ancient Rome. In 1872, a grey wolf was placed on display in a cramped cage next to Michelangelo's staircase to the Capitoline, in commemoration of Rome becoming the new capital of the Kingdom of Italy. Incredibly, captive wolves would remain caged in the heart of the city long after the Second World War and the formation of the modern Italian Republic; it was not until 1971 that the city's financial problems and changing attitudes to animal rights finally brought the pitiful display to an end.[32] The Fascist dictator Benito Mussolini had also embraced the imagery of the she-wolf as part of his quest to restore the glory of the Roman Empire. As well as making sure the wolf cage on the Capitol never stood empty, Mussolini named his Fascist youth organisation the 'Sons of the She-Wolf'. He would also send bronze copies of the Capitoline Wolf statue to numerous countries as diplomatic gifts from Fascist Italy, one of which still stood in Eden Park, Cincinnati, until it was stolen in 2022.

All around present-day Rome, La Lupa can be seen nursing her human children in the murals of churches, the decoration of palazzos, even on the city's litter bins. Football fans will instantly recognise the she-wolf from the jerseys of AS Roma, on which she decorates the club's famous crest. Once a surrogate mother for Rome's founding king, she has now become a proxy for the city itself; an eternal embodiment of 'Senatus Populusque Romanus' – 'The Senate and People of Rome'.

As the city's reach extended, the Roman wolf soon counted all the peoples of ancient Italy among her brood – and like that scene struck into pure silver, she would nurture and defend them as she had done her feral twins. By 264 BC the search for new hunting grounds could only bring her to the coastline, where she looked knowingly across the choppy waves to a dark horizon. From not-so-distant shores, another predator stared back. A superpower even more ancient, every bit as deadly, and commanding both land and sea. Their showdown was inevitable. Rome had successfully waged war on her Italian neighbours, but this was to be an all-consuming conflict that would test every principle of the young Republic.

The arena was readied for the battle to decide the future of the ancient world. The winner would rightly call themselves undisputed master of the Mediterranean. As for the loser – they would face an oblivion so profound, it might seem at times like they never even existed.

Chapter II
NEMESIS

'War is the father of all, and the king of all. Some he makes gods, others he makes men. Some he enslaves, others he sets free.'

Heraclitus

Rome's first silver denarius, struck from 211 BC.
Obverse: Helmeted head of the goddess Roma, with mark of value 'X' behind.
Reverse: The Dioscuri twins, Castor and Pollux, galloping right,
'ROMA' in exergue.

Blood Oath

The knife plunged, and in a moment, rich red blood spilled down the sides of the altar. With attendants holding the young lamb as its life drained away, the chief priest raised his arms to the sky and recited the necessary prayer. The general stepped forward. Placing his hand on the sacrificial animal, he called out to the king of the gods, Baal Hammon, to hear his solemn words. First a plea, to grant him victories in the coming wars. Then a vow, one of everlasting hatred towards the cursed enemy that had humiliated his homeland.

The gathered elders muttered their approval, while nearby, the general's three young sons watched the rites with fascination. With the offering made, Hamilcar relaxed and mingled among the city's nobles, all wishing him good fortune on his campaign. Tomorrow he would set out towards the Pillars of Hercules where the crossing to Iberia was shortest. There he would defeat the local tribes and build a new seafaring empire to make up for the one recently stolen by the treacherous Romans. With this added Mediterranean foothold, they could reclaim their islands of Sicily, Sardinia, and Corsica – even take the fight to the city of Rome itself.

The eldest of his boys could contain his enthusiasm no longer. Clasping his father's tunic, he pleaded to be allowed to join him on his conquest. A wave of warm laughter rippled around the assembly. If the fighting zeal of the nine-year-old was anything to go by, their city still had a bright future. Hamilcar ruffled his son's hair and shared in the delight of the crowd. Despite his youth, the boy could well prove a charm of fortune when they crossed the strait. He was named in honour of their god-king Baal, after all.[1]

Hamilcar's proud smile wavered then faded. He took the hand of his boy and led him towards the crimson altar. There the general guided the hand to rest on the neck of the animal where it was immersed in the warm blood that still seeped forth. Gravely, he asked his son: 'Do you vow, that if fate stops my sword from cleansing the dishonour of Rome and her unjust treaties from our lands, that you will bring a war to the Romans so widespread, all the people of Italy will rue the day of your birth?' His son – paler now – swore to his father that he would.[2]

Then with a voice as booming and resonant as the clash of shields, Hamilcar led his son in the recital of a public oath before the altar of Baal Hammon and the people of the city, the boy repeating each sentence exactly: 'When I come of age, I will chase the Romans with fire and sword, and re-enact upon them the fate of Troy. No god, no pact, not even the high Alps will deny me. I pledge my unending enmity towards the descendants of Aeneas. Hear these words, O great Baal Hammon – this is the oath of Hannibal, son of Hamilcar!'[3]

Father and son turned to meet the applause of the roused crowd. From the high citadel known as the Byrsa, they had a panoramic view over the vast metropolis that cascaded down to the sparkling waters of the Mediterranean. The capital of their empire was a modern marvel, with its impregnable circular harbour and towering six-storey buildings housing around half a million people. Carthage was not just the most magnificent city in North Africa, it might even claim to be the greatest city of the entire ancient world.

Like almost every aspect of his life, the blood oath made by a young Hannibal in 238 BC is relayed to us by the hostile voice of the enemies he would later terrorise. Ominous words imagined into his mouth by Roman historians desperate to make sense of the most destructive foe Rome would ever face. Hannibal would inflict such lasting trauma on the Roman psyche, it was vital for their pride that he be depicted as more ghoul than man, driven by irrational hatred and twisted oaths to barbaric gods. Though certain facts are undeniable. That boy would grow to be a charismatic leader able to unite disparate bands of men. In battle he would prove fiendishly inventive, entirely unpredictable, and utterly relentless in his pursuit of his enemy.[4] In short, he was Rome's worst nightmare. But the struggle against Hannibal was just one of three Punic Wars fought against his empire of Carthage. Together they formed the Great War of the ancient world – an existential struggle, apocalyptic in its scope – and it would drag on for almost 120 years. For it to end, an entire civilisation would need to be wiped from the face of the earth.

Rome would prevail in this, 'the most memorable of all wars ever waged', but only just.[5] Time and time again, she would suffer a knockout blow – losing multiple consuls, naval fleets, entire armies – only to haul herself back up and, inexplicably, return to fight with even greater resolve. The Punic Wars would be the proving ground of the young Roman Republic, revealing in it a wisdom beyond its years. When all hope seemed lost, Rome stubbornly refused to panic – in fact she was at her best. Perhaps the finest example of this fortitude came as the Carthaginian enemy massed at her very gates. While any normal state would be drafting terms of surrender, Rome calmly set about reforming her finances. In the midst of war, she would implement a whole new monetary system aimed at reviving her crippled economy. At its heart was a coin that would go on to become the staple of ancient commerce for the next 500 years. Its influence would last millennia. Every day, millions still refer to it without even realising. This was the coin that saved Rome. Its silver would be pure, yet at the same time imbued with the determination of a people who could lose many a battle, but somehow always seemed to win the war.

Uncharted Waters

By the time young Hannibal bloodied his hands at the sacrificial altar, Carthage and Rome had already fought 'the longest and most severely contested war in history'.[6] The First Punic War erupted in 264 BC, lasting almost twenty-five years and costing hundreds of thousands of lives. At its outset, the opponents were largely indifferent to each other; by its conclusion they were mortal enemies.

It was inevitable that the two worlds of Carthage and Rome would eventually collide. With Roman expansion into the toe of the Italian boot, she looked enviously across the narrow Messina Strait at the island of Sicily. The crossing was only two miles, but for landlubbing Romans that was barrier enough. Besides, these were dangerous waters. The mineral-rich islands of Sicily, Sardinia, and Corsica were out of bounds: proud jewels of the Carthaginian Empire. Every day, hundreds of merchant vessels of the North African superpower crisscrossed the lucrative trade routes of the western Mediterranean, unopposed, much of the wealth from their weighty cargoes of precious metals, olive oil, and grain flowing back to their glorious capital on the coast of what is today Tunisia.

While Rome was wary of wading into the shallows, Carthage was a city positively born of the sea. It began life in the ninth century BC as a trading outpost of mariners from the distant shores of Phoenicia, in modern Lebanon. The Phoenician civilisation (in Latin, *punicus* – hence 'The Punic Wars') was already a thousand years old when it began expanding to new coastlines. With it came rare spices, textiles, and the ancient world's only purple dye, known as 'Tyrian Purple', painstakingly extracted from the shells of murex sea snails.[7] But their intellectual cargo was even greater: secrets of seafaring, navigation, international trade, even the first alphabet. Carthage had also been striking impressive silver coins for two centuries before Rome had even considered the idea. Minted to Greek monetary standards that dominated at the time, this coinage allowed Carthage to pay its expanding armies more efficiently and to access the thriving sea trade of the Mediterranean. The first of these coins, a tetradrachm struck in Sicily around 400 BC, shows a superbly rendered date palm tree hanging heavy with fruit. The tree would become a numismatic logo of the Carthaginian culture, paying tribute to its ancestral home on the Lebanese coast where date palms grow in abundance to this day.

Carthaginians were famed mariners, and unsurprisingly their colony quickly flourished into a new empire of the waves, surpassing even their Phoenician homeland. This was a merchant sea power that preferred conquest by commerce to the sharp end of a sword – but if blood made business sense, Carthage was more than happy to oblige. Unlike Rome's conscripted armies, Carthage recruited mercenary soldiers from diverse lands, as and when she needed them. Their loyalty depended on their pay; but between them, a fleet of 350 battleships, and even 300 war elephants, Carthage could crush any rival. Rome knew the risks but would never sleep soundly with this giant on her doorstep. When a Sicilian colony appealed to Rome for help in freeing it from Carthaginian occupation, Rome had the pretext she needed. She crossed the strait, into an uncertain future.

Wars came and went for Carthage, as much a tool of trade as hard selling and negotiation. But for Rome, war was a sacred calling. Once declared by the children of Mars, it was an all-or-nothing commitment; a vocation soon made clear when Roman legions brutally sacked the Carthaginian stronghold of Agrigento and sold the entire population into slavery. Carthage might just have underestimated these scrappy Italian pretenders. Not to worry, the encircling sea was still a thoroughly African one. Rome had made the baffling decision to go to war with the world's ultimate naval superpower, without a navy of her own. If she wanted to survive, Rome would need to find her sea legs, fast.

The incident that followed perfectly showcases the audacity and resolve that defined the Roman character, helped always by a generous portion of what they called *Fortuna* – blind luck. When a Carthaginian warship ran aground on the Italian coast, Rome seized the vessel and with it, her opportunity. Dismantling the ship plank by plank, Roman engineers saw that each timber was helpfully marked with corresponding letters indicating its place in the construction. This was a flat-pack superweapon, and it had come with instructions. The fact that Rome had never built a warship before was no matter. Her carpenters set to work on a carbon-copy fleet with blistering speed. While their ships were being built, teams of would-be rowers sat on benches at the shoreline practising their drills.[8] In what is surely one of history's most impressive feats of enterprise, Rome built 120 state-of-the-art warships in just sixty days.[9]

Summoning up a navy was one thing, taking on the seasoned Carthaginians was another. Ancient maritime warfare was a ruthless test of seafaring skill: hundreds of warships battling for tactical position, each fronted with a lethal bronze ram designed to smash through the hulls of enemy ships and send them to the bottom of the Mediterranean. Since the game did not suit her strengths, Rome simply changed the rules. The ingenious addition of a drop-down boarding bridge to vessels, called the *corvus* or 'raven', meant that Roman soldiers could utilise their superior infantry skills even at sea – storming aboard enemy ships and dispatching their crews with trusty sword and spear. Rome had effectively turned naval battles into land battles.

Victories soon mounted. By the time the opponents met off Sicily's Cape Ecnomus in 256 BC for what may have been the largest naval battle ever fought, Rome was at home on the waves: thirty Carthaginian ships sent to the seabed and 40,000 of the enemy killed or captured. But these successes were hard won, and Rome was regularly reminded that any battle at sea had a third combatant – nature itself. When her fleet was caught in a freak storm near Tunisia's Cape Bon the following year, virtually every Roman vessel and a staggering 100,000 men were lost. Almost as soon as they had rebuilt the fleet, it was sunk again in another fierce tempest.[10] These were appalling losses for the young Republic. But somehow Rome was able to absorb each catastrophe, getting straight to work rebuilding ships and levying more men.

After many reversals of fortune, the two sides fought a decisive battle among the Aegates islands in 241 BC. Rome was the narrow victor, sinking fifty Carthaginian ships and losing thirty of her own. Today, their enormous bronze rams are still being lifted from the seabed at the site of the battle.[11] For Carthage it was one loss too many – war was no longer tenable. Hamilcar was ordered to negotiate a peace treaty with the Romans, a task that he rejected in disgust. Roman terms were harsher than expected, including a total relinquishing of Sicily and crushing reparations to be paid in silver over the next ten years. In a move that even ancient observers called 'contrary to all justice', Rome then altered the treaty, seizing Sardinia and Corsica too and demanding even more silver.[12] Once-mighty Carthage was powerless to object. She had lost an empire, but Rome had gained one: Sicily, Sardinia, and Corsica – the first overseas provinces of an expanding Roman world.

The next two decades could be labelled a peace, but they were more a pause for the two sides to gather their breath and simmer in bitter resentment before meeting again for the even bloodier rematch. Echoing the twentieth century's two cataclysmic world wars, the seeds of the second conflict had been sown in the perceived ignoble resolution of the first. A hard core of Carthaginians led by general Hamilcar would never accept the dishonour of the Roman treaty. They passed down a hatred of Rome to their sons as a dark inheritance. Oaths of enmity were sworn at bloody altars. Reckoning was in the air.

Scourge of Rome

The second contest between Carthage and Rome would be an entirely different beast to the first. For starters, Carthage was no longer a naval power. Instead she pushed west across North Africa, over today's Strait of Gibraltar and into the silver-rich lands of Spain. Hamilcar's quest to build new dominions there was a success, though he would die battling local forces before he saw the task completed. At the heart of this province would be the city of 'New Carthage' – its modern name, Cartagena, still echoing the resurgent empire. With Hamilcar's death, power eventually passed to the capable hands of his three sons: Mago, Hasdrubal, and the eldest, Hannibal.

By 221 BC, Hannibal was in sole command of the entire Carthaginian force while only in his mid-twenties. He was a chip off the old block, magnetically drawing together mercenary bands from varied lands behind a single cause: retribution against Rome. But this vengeance was not some vague notion – Hannibal had a plan of attack. A strategy so simple, and yet so audacious, the Romans would never see it coming. Hannibal's not-so-secret weapon stomped along with his army, shaking the earth with their approach. The mere sight of his forty African war elephants would make any sane opponent flee in terror. Stampeding into enemy lines, the destruction the animals wreaked was total and often indiscriminate; elephant riders were equipped with a mallet and chisel to drive into the animal's neck if they began trampling their own men. This was ancient 'shock and awe' – and Hannibal was finally ready to make Rome tremble.

The Republic had grown increasingly concerned about Carthaginian rearmament and expansion into Iberia, though it was distracted elsewhere. Delegations were sent to try and talk Hannibal down from whatever he was planning but it was no use. When his mercenary force struck at the Roman-allied town of Saguntum, in modern Valencia, a state of war existed once again between the old rivals. The Romans wondered what the Carthaginian maverick and his marauding elephants would do next; without a navy, however, they believed Hannibal would at least remain a distant annoyance. In the summer of 218 BC, Rome sent one consul north and another south to cover any eventuality, but at no frantic pace. Intelligence was vague, though each report added more ice to Roman blood. Hannibal was moving north with an ever-growing mercenary army; Hannibal had crossed the Ebro river, frontier of Carthaginian influence; Hannibal had skirted the natural barrier of the Pyrenees, near modern Perpignan. The unthinkable reality was slowly dawning on Rome, though it seemed too terrible to utter aloud. Hannibal intended on marching his elephant army across the Alps. He was coming to Italy.

A silver coin minted by Hannibal to pay his soldiers of fortune offers us a remarkable view of one of these elephants – perhaps even showing us the general himself on his personal mount named Surus, 'The Syrian'. This shekel, an ancient denomination from the East, was minted in Spain using high-quality silver from local mines now controlled by Hannibal. Historians often ask what species of elephant the Carthaginians deployed; this coin seemingly provides the answer, showing as it does an African elephant with large billowing ears and tall shoulders. This animal was a North African subspecies that could be captured close to Carthage, until it was hunted to extinction in the later Roman period. These were the four-legged tanks of the ancient world, and with them Hannibal thundered his way through the Rhône valley towards the Alps.

It was autumn when he reached the mountains. With temperatures dropping and snowstorms inbound, attempting a crossing now would surely be suicide. Hannibal's own generals warned him that there was no way through. He famously responded that he would 'either find a way or make one'.[13] With that, his army ascended into the cloud-capped peaks. The details of Hannibal's arduous crossing of the Alps are largely lost to time. Historians have long argued about the possible route by which the enormous force could have navigated

Silver shekel of Carthage, minted in Spain, 237–209 BC.

Europe's highest mountain range. Incredibly, a 2016 study of sediments in the Col de la Traversette pass on the France–Italy border discovered bacteria from the droppings of thousands of animals that could be radiocarbon-dated to approximately 218 BC – the exact year of Hannibal's expedition.[14] His army had to march in near single file, overcoming deadly terrain and deep snows, not to mention attacks from Alpine tribes along their route. It is unclear how many of Hannibal's elephants were able to endure the epic journey; some sources state that most survived, others that only the general's mount made it through alive. Yet a mere sixteen days after they had entered the Alps, the invasion force emerged miraculously from the mountains and rolled down into the plains of northern Italy near modern Turin.[15]

Rome was in shock but managed to hold her nerve, sending armies to eradicate the Carthaginians who were surely exhausted after their march. Hannibal trampled right over the first near today's city of Piacenza. He then ambushed the second on the shores of Lake Trasimene, slaughtering 15,000 Romans including the consul Flaminius. The name of the nearby village Sanguineto, translating to 'blood river', may still recall the horror. Huge pits, known as *ustrini*, found in the vicinity are thought to be industrial cremation ovens where Hannibal disposed of the rotting Roman dead – a rare example of an environmental clean-up operation from antiquity.

In the wake of these disasters, Rome opted for the new strategy of starving Hannibal out of Italy. His response was to make straight for the Roman supply depot at Cannae in Apulia and seize it for himself. It was there that Hannibal was cornered by the biggest Roman force yet, twice the size of his own and led by both of that year's consuls. It seemed that the game was finally up. The following engagement is still taught today at military academies as the textbook example of how to overcome a superior force. Hannibal intentionally weakened the centre of his line while placing his crack cavalry units at its edges. As the Roman legionaries pushed into the middle of his ranks, the Carthaginian flanks curved inwards creating a deadly crescent. Before they realised what was happening, the Romans were encircled.

What followed was sheer butchery: estimates have suggested that up to 600 legionaries were killed every minute, until nightfall forced an end to the bloodbath.[16] At the final count, Roman losses numbered more than twice those of the British on the first day of the Battle of the Somme: around 50,000 slain, including another consul and eighty men of senatorial rank.[17] When news of the disaster reached the city of Rome, it was met with a reaction so rare to her streets – sheer panic. Hannibal had fulfilled his bloody vow. This was a Roman apocalypse.

Gemini Rising

The question of why Hannibal did not immediately march on the exposed Roman capital in the wake of the massacre at Cannae is one that has intrigued military historians for centuries. Counting his victory as definitive, he likely assumed he would not need to; that the Romans would beg for mercy and he could punish them with a treaty every bit as harsh as the one suffered by his Carthaginian homeland. To help matters along, Hannibal offered the Roman Senate an opportunity to discuss their terms of surrender. They flat-out refused. Like his father, Hannibal was learning that when it came to war, the Romans operated from a different rule book. Reluctant to commit to what would be a gruelling siege of Rome, Hannibal stumbled into a cat-and-mouse game with remnants of the Roman army around the Italian countryside.

With a barbarian army ravaging Italy's agricultural land, famine was soon a real prospect. Debts were mounting. Soldiers were going without pay. Grinding wartime inflation led to a growing crisis of confidence in Roman currency. These were dark days for Rome – but as we have seen, that was when she often shone the brightest. In 211 BC, just as Hannibal prepared to besiege the city after all, Rome launched sweeping economic changes designed at reinvigorating her war effort. Massive wartime demand for bronze, desperately needed for the production of weapons and armour, had dramatically increased the value of the metal, motivating Rome to adopt a new silver standard in her money.[18] Out would go the old Greek denominations and a reliance on roughly made low-value coinage. It was time to launch an independent monetary system based around a new family of high-quality coins that were proudly Roman.

They would follow Roman weight standards, the base unit of which was the bronze *assarius*, or more simply, the *as*. A small silver coin worth five *asses* would therefore be called the *quinarius*. But the focal point of this new gallery of coins was the *denarius*. Taking its name from the Latin *deni* meaning 'containing ten', this coin was valued at ten asses – sometimes affectionately called the 'tenner' of the Roman world. Crucially, the denarius would be struck with 4.5 grams of the purest possible silver, unlike the recent wartime coinage that had been declining in weight and increasingly 'mixed with copper'.[19] By way of comparison, the 98 per cent silver of the first denarius (plural, *denarii*) far exceeds the 92.5 per cent standard of British 'sterling' silver coinage through the centuries, as well as the 90 per cent purity of America's iconic silver dollars.[20] With its unadulterated precious metal, the denarius was a coin designed to inspire confidence across the Mediterranean.

Portraits of Greek gods would not do for a coin that sought to break free of Greek monetary standards; the goddess Roma herself would be the face of the denarius and would remain so for the first century of its use. The personification of the city can be seen on the

Colossal statues of the Dioscuri twins, Castor and Pollux, unearthed in Rome in 1561 and re-erected in Piazza del Campidoglio on the Capitoline Hill in 1583.

obverse, wearing an ornate winged helmet topped with the fierce head of a mythical griffin (Plate section, 1). Rome was a city under siege when this first denarius was struck, and yet her patron goddess looks out fearlessly from the rebranded Roman money – a show of defiance, just like the coins themselves. Behind her portrait, an 'X' for 'ten' explains to the viewer the numerical value of this denomination. Placing a coin's face value on its surface is standard practice today, whether it is a British fifty pence or an American quarter dollar, but in the ancient world this was a novel idea, and here we see it used across a series of coins for the first time.

On the reverse, we meet not Romulus and Remus, but another set of twins beloved to the Roman mythos. Galloping across the coin are the brothers Castor and Pollux, known as the Dioscuri or 'Sons of Zeus'. Brandishing their spears, the astronomical twins of Gemini ride to the rescue of the city with their guiding stars shining out from above their helmets. In stark contrast to Romulus and Remus, the Dioscuri twins shared an inseparable bond. When Castor alone was offered a place among the gods of Mount Olympus, he voluntarily sacrificed half his immortality to remain with his brother. They were transformed into the two central stars of the Gemini constellation but were forced to spend half their time as gods on the heights of Olympus, and the other half as mortals in the depths of Hades – a delightful explanation for why we can view the constellation of Gemini only in winter and spring each year. The Dioscuri have also long been associated with the atmospheric phenomenon known as St Elmo's Fire, which causes dazzling discharges of electrical plasma around the tall masts of ships. When this colourful display occurred in ancient times, it was deemed to be the divine presence of Castor and Pollux watching over a vessel. The twins of Gemini were therefore seen as protectors of those on dangerous voyages, their attributes later associated with the ever-wandering apostles Peter and Paul in the New Testament.

As the backbone of a dependable and easily understood monetary system, the denarius signalled a Roman resurgence in the struggle against Hannibal. In the very same year it was implemented, the Romans successfully besieged the city of Capua which had defected to Hannibal after the disaster at Cannae. When the starvation could no longer be endured, Capua threw open its gates to the Romans. The magistrates of the fallen city were publicly beheaded; a clear message to any others who dared to consider defecting to the enemy. With his mercenary army of Numidian cavalry, Spanish infantry, slingers from the Balearic islands, and other contracted warriors, Hannibal might have assumed that allegiances to Rome across Italy would be equally opportunistic. While some cities like Capua did defect, others such as Naples turned him away. No doubt he was surprised by the loyalty shown to Rome among its young coalition of allies.

Also in that critical year of 211 BC, a momentous appointment was made in Rome. When the Senate asked for volunteers to lead a daring attack on the enemy's Spanish base of operations at New Carthage, they were met by stony silence. Surely this was a suicide mission. Just one man eventually came forward. Despite the fact he was only twenty-five years old – technically too young for the command – Publius Cornelius Scipio was promptly granted sweeping proconsular powers and sent on his way to Spain. He soon showed his brilliance. Hannibal's brothers, Hasdrubal and Mago, were unprepared for the arrival of this energetic young general who made straight for their capital. Scipio led a multi-pronged assault on the walls of Cartagena, while secretly sending a force across a tidal lagoon that went unwatched to the rear. When the surprise attackers scaled the walls with ladders and got inside the city, panic erupted. They opened the main gate for their Roman comrades and so began one of the bloodiest slaughters documented from the ancient world. The historian Polybius memorably describes how the Romans killed 'all they encountered, sparing none'. In the furious release of violence after a difficult siege, it was customary to see 'not only the corpses of human beings, but dogs cut in half, and the dismembered limbs of other animals'. And as Cartagena fell, 'such scenes were very many'.[21]

Not long after, a mysterious object was hurled over the barricades into Hannibal's camp. On closer inspection it was revealed to be the head of his brother Hasdrubal, fallen in battle to the Romans. The general was devastated. Things soon went from bad to worse. After smashing the remaining Carthaginian resistance in Spain, Scipio brought the fight directly to their North African homeland. A desperate Carthage ordered Hannibal back to Africa immediately. He had been ravaging Italy for fifteen years. Near the remote town of Zama in central Tunisia, Scipio and Hannibal lined up their forces for a decisive clash in 202 BC. Hannibal had never lost a battle and was confident of victory, his home advantage, superior numbers, and massive force of eighty war elephants adding to his certainty. But after decades of facing down the unstoppable beasts, the Romans had built a defensive strategy. When the elephants charged, the Romans channelled them into narrow corridors between their ranks. A mass of spears then overcame each unfortunate animal. The rest of the elephants fled in panic, stampeding over the Carthaginians as they escaped. One by one, Hannibal's lines buckled to the Roman counter-attack. When Scipio managed to outflank the Carthaginians with cavalry and strike them from behind, it was all over. Fighting on home soil, the Carthaginians lost up to 20,000 dead and a similar number captured. Scipio would thereafter be given the name 'Africanus' in honour of his extraordinary victory.

Hannibal had finally been beaten, and he lived to taste the shame of defeat. In the following years, he fled in exile to the cities of the East. There, the ageing general who had once brought the Roman Republic to its knees, eked out a living as a freelance military adviser to foreign kings. A poignant anecdote survives that reveals the character of the grizzled general who, while still a proud Carthaginian, could not help but respect the Roman genius who had ultimately bested him. Many years after the Battle of Zama, Scipio was part of a Roman delegation visiting the rich city of Ephesus, where he met none other than his old nemesis. Despite the earth-shattering consequences of their earlier conflict, the two generals conversed amiably. Scipio could not resist asking Hannibal, who did he think were history's greatest generals. Hannibal placed Alexander at number one, for conquering most of the known world before the age of thirty. For his number two, he selected King Pyrrhus, who had fought the Romans so bravely in the Pyrrhic War. Pressed for his number three, Hannibal chose himself.

Scipio laughed and asked, 'Where would you rank yourself if you had beaten me?'

Hannibal thought for a moment before responding, 'If I had beaten you, I would rank myself before Alexander, before Pyrrhus – in fact, before all other generals.'[22]

An Empire Erased

Each time the old man struggled to his feet the other senators all knew what to expect. Whatever the issues of the day, Cato managed to bring every speech back to that same tired topic. Dire warnings that their sworn enemy was once again rearming, doom-laden predictions that their rebuilt fleet could set sail for Italy at any moment.

Today though, Cato had something special, quite literally, up his sleeve. From a fold in his toga, he revealed some ripe, juicy figs, spilling them theatrically onto the Senate floor. Where had such fresh and bounteous fruits come from, he asked the senators. He quickly answered his own question: Carthage, just three days' sail away. Rome's nemesis, who had twice been overcome at terrible cost, was clearly in fine health once again. Cato finished with that same trademark line he used to round off every speech he delivered to the Senate: *'Carthago delenda est'* – 'Carthage must be destroyed!'[23]

The old hawk had been a teenager when Hannibal marched on Italy, and a soldier in his thirties when Hannibal was defeated at Zama. Now Cato was in his eighties, one of the few who remembered first-hand the terror rained upon Rome by the African invader. Indemnities after the second war had been even more punishing than after the first; for Carthage there could be no overseas territories, no war elephants, and only a measly ten warships. But like Rome, Carthage displayed an almost supernatural ability to rise from even the deepest grave. She had paid off her war debts decades earlier than expected. Her economy was flourishing. She was indeed rebuilding her fleet. The spectre of Carthage was haunting Rome once again.

The fresh figs achieved the desired result: in 149 BC, a massive Roman force set sail for North Africa to solve the Carthaginian question once and for all. For three gruelling years the Romans blockaded the enemy capital and attempted to breach its defences. When they eventually broke in through the harbour, their pent-up wrath was unleashed. Cato would finally have his wish. After a week of house-to-house extermination, the streets of Carthage had become rivers of blood. Special squadrons were tasked with clearing the dead and dying from the roadways and dumping them in mass graves.[24] With hundreds of thousands of Carthaginians slaughtered, the remaining 50,000 were sold off into slavery. Then the demolition of the city commenced. Even the Roman commander, adopted grandson of the Scipio who had fought Hannibal, is said to have been moved to tears at the sight of the famed metropolis being razed to the ground. The younger Scipio gazed out over the destruction and 'wept openly, realising that all cities and nations must, like men, meet their doom'. Even as he reflected on his triumph, he was 'filled with a dreadful foreboding, that one day the same doom might be pronounced on his own nation'.[25]

Scipio the Younger was ordered to obliterate Carthage and he followed his instructions to the letter. The idea that the Romans ploughed salt into the land, ensuring nothing could ever grow there again, is a nineteenth-century literary invention, though it may well hold an element of truth. On the Byrsa citadel, the most sacred quarter of the city where young Hannibal had once made his bloody oath, Scipio proclaimed an oath of his own: that no one would ever again build on the accursed site.

With the physical annihilation of Carthage complete, the eradication of its history and identity became the new battleground. Carthaginian libraries were put to the torch, all works of Punic literature turned to ash. After three devastating Punic Wars, even the word 'Punic' could now only be uttered in disgust. The entire story of a distinctive and ancient civilisation was to be curated by the very enemy that erased it from existence. In this historical drama, Carthage would be cast as Rome's villainous foil. Where Rome was noble, just, and civilised, her antagonist across the sea was barbaric, treacherous, and perverted.

One of the most emotive accusations directed at the fallen empire – and one which endures to the present day – is that they practised not just human sacrifice, but child sacrifice. Numerous ancient commentators describe elaborate rites where, in times of crisis, first-born sons were placed in the hands of a bronze statue of the god Baal Hammon, which then dropped the crying infant into a flaming pit.[26] Many visitors to modern Tunis will have explored the Tophet, a Carthaginian cemetery where 20,000 urns containing the burnt remains of young babies were unearthed. Upon its discovery in 1921, the site was quickly interpreted as sinister confirmation that Carthage incinerated its own children. Well-meaning critics saw this view as an extension of ancient biases; surely the Tophet was merely a child graveyard, and a tragic reminder of the ancient world's shocking rate of infant mortality. However, even those scholars most wary of Roman propaganda are now coming around to the idea that it may not all be ancient smears.[27] In 2014, Oxford University announced, after a meta-study of the latest evidence, that Carthage did in fact sacrifice its own young in periods of unrest.[28] That the question is still intensely debated after two millennia only demonstrates the extent to which the Romans were successful in erasing the voices of the Carthaginian people from the history books.

Aside from the mysterious Tophet and a few uncovered sandstone walls – still a burnt orange from the inferno that consumed the city – almost nothing of mighty Carthage remains. Theirs is a mostly vanished empire. In its place sits a modern, sprawling capital. The medina, mosques, parks, and palaces of Tunis now look out over the glittering waves of the Mediterranean. Waters that, with the end of the Punic Wars and the eradication of their greatest rival, Romans now rightfully called *mare nostrum* – 'our sea'.

Coin of Ages

Rome had entered her first war with Carthage as a land-bound nonentity; by the culmination of her third, she was the dominant power of the Mediterranean. The very same year Rome sacked Carthage, her armies laid waste another famous city of the classical world. With the destruction of Corinth, mainland Greece was also brought under Roman dominion. The Republic seemed invincible. This sudden ascendancy is perhaps nowhere better symbolised than in the silver denarius launched at Rome's lowest ebb, now circulating on every shore of her wide empire. In the markets of Spain, North Africa, and Greece, traders looked at the coins in their palms and saw that same warrior goddess: Roma.

The denarius would become the coin of choice for everyday transactions across the ancient world, though its buying power would naturally evolve in the five centuries of its use. Where gold coins were used mainly by the elites for sizeable purchases such as property, it was the silver gleam of the denarius that was familiar to the average Roman – particularly welcome in the payment of their salaries. In his parable of the workers in the vineyard, Jesus describes the denarius as the 'daily wage' of a labourer – an oversimplified characterisation, but one that provides a fair sense of the coin's value.²⁹ At around the same time in the first century, a professional Roman legionary soldier was paid 225 denarii a year, later increased to 300. A denarius for a day of skilled work was therefore a reasonable rate. In general, one coin might buy a working Roman their daily bread for the week, and a few cups of wine for good measure.

The iconic designs and Latin letters of the denarius would soon prove so influential that even those outside Rome's borders would try to imitate them. Decades before the Roman invasion of Britain, native British kings of southern England struck their own coins emulating features of the Roman denarii they came across through their close trading links to the continent. Celtic rulers like Cunobelin, Eppillus, and Verica proudly copied Roman designs on their coinage and even gave their name and titles in Latin, notably styling themselves 'Rex'. This spread of Roman coins beyond the limits of their control can be seen as a first wave of Romanisation, acquainting foreign peoples with Roman language and culture in preparation for a future absorption into the Empire.

So intrinsic was the denarius to booming Mediterranean trade, its name eventually became synonymous with coinage itself. When Arab caliphs issued the first Islamic coinage in the seventh century AD – complete with Quranic inscriptions – they simply called it the *dinar*, after the Roman denarius. In the following century, the Carolingian dynasty resurrected the denomination even more explicitly. After unifying much of Europe into a new Holy Roman Empire, Charlemagne became the first emperor to rule in the West since the fall of Rome three centuries before. His *novus denarius* or 'new denarius' – more generally called the denier – was almost indistinguishable from its ancient counterpart. It was struck in high-quality silver, used Latin legends, and even showed the ruler dressed as a Roman emperor.

King Offa, one of the most powerful kings in early Anglo-Saxon England and a contemporary of Charlemagne, was in turn inspired by the Carolingian silver denier. He ordered the minting of his own coin in the same style and weight to promote trade with the continental power. On his new 'penny' (from the Old English *penning*, and the same origin as the German *pfennig*) he too was shown in profile much like a Roman emperor, encircled by Latin legends. The silver penny proved such a success, it would be the only coin minted in England for the next 500 years.

In the King James Bible of 1604, the word 'denarius' (more specifically, the Greek *dēnárion*) was simply translated as 'penny' – both being silver coins of roughly equal size, stamped with a ruler's portrait. When Jesus is questioned by the Pharisees if it is 'lawful to give tribute to Caesar', he therefore asks that one of them bring him a 'penny' that he may see. After inspecting the portrait and titles of the Roman emperor on the coin, Jesus famously responds that one should 'Render unto Caesar the things that are Caesar's, and unto God the things that are God's'.[30] The story will be a familiar one to coin collectors, as well as Christians, around the world. Since the adult life and eventual execution of Jesus fell under the reign of the second Roman emperor, Tiberius (AD 14–37), the silver denarius of Tiberius has come to be known as the 'Tribute Penny'. Many a collector has since secretly suspected their own Tribute Penny may be the very one that was held by Jesus. The somewhat confusing abbreviation of pennies and pence to the letter 'd' in pre-decimal currency was another echo of its links to the ancient Roman coin, with 'd' of course being short for 'denarius'.

Twenty-two centuries after it was first struck in the Roman Republic's darkest hour, the denarius remains embedded in the cultural and linguistic memory of both East and West. Every day, millions of Spanish speakers around the world will refer to *dinero* when they talk of money, just as the Portuguese will discuss *dinheiro*, and Italians *denaro*. Several monetary currencies took their name directly from the denarius, including the Macedonian *denar* and Catalan *diner*. And of course, in bustling souks across North Africa and the Middle East – but perhaps especially in the markets of modern Tunis, watched over by the spirit of the city's most famous son, Hannibal – the dinars still change hands.

Chapter III

DICTATOR

'Our master Caesar is in the tent
Where the maps are spread,
His eyes fixed upon nothing,
A hand under his head.
Like a long-legged fly upon the stream
His mind moves upon silence.'

W. B. Yeats, 'Long-Legged Fly'

Lifetime portrait denarius of Julius Caesar, February–March 44 BC.
Obverse: Laureate head of Caesar, CAESAR DICT PERPETVO –
'Dictator for Life'.
Reverse: Venus standing, holding winged Victory and a sceptre with star.

The Pirates' Ransom

The young man seemed, at first, quite the prize. A Roman aristocrat, heir of a noble house, kidnapped on his way to study oratory in Rhodes. What vast weight of silver might a wealthy family pay for his return? While the pirates debated the size of the ransom demand, their twenty-five-year-old captive sat on the deck, thoroughly bored by the whole proceeding. Eventually, one of the dagger-wielding outlaws stomped over to him and delivered their decision. The price of his freedom? Twenty talents – over 600 kg – of silver. He was met with unrestrained laughter. Clearly, the fools had no idea who they had abducted. Their Roman hostage demanded they ask fifty talents for his release and no less. The pirates were bewildered. Prisoners normally tried to negotiate ransoms down, not up. But as they would quickly learn, this was no normal prisoner. He expected a ransom worthy of his name: Gaius Julius Caesar.

Pirates like these had infested the seas by 75 BC. Operating out of bases in Cilicia on the coast of Anatolia, they plundered vessels with increasing impunity and had even begun to attack the ports of Italy. Here, Rome was a victim of her own recent success. Mighty powers such as the Macedonian and Seleucid empires, that once helped police the waves, had collapsed under the force of the expanding Roman Republic. Freebooters flourished in their wake, threatening to destabilise trade networks across the entire Mediterranean. Rome launched a few half-hearted campaigns to eradicate the plague of piracy, but each time the pests merely scattered, only to return to their nests once the threat had gone.

Cilician pirates were known to be the 'most murderous of men', but this Roman captive stubbornly refused to be intimidated.[1] Having sent out his agents to gather the necessary funds for his ransom, Julius Caesar was determined to make the most of the time with his captors. He insisted on joining in their games and exercises. Soon he was dictating their daily routines. Before long, the pirates found themselves being bossed around by their own prisoner. Caesar treated the heavies tasked with watching him as his own personal bodyguard. Since his education had been disrupted, Caesar took to writing poems and speeches which he forced the pirates to listen to. Any that failed to appreciate his rhetorical talent he dismissed as 'illiterate barbarians' to their faces. At night, when Caesar wanted to sleep, he had his attendant call out for the pirates to be quiet.[2]

Far from drawing their anger, the captors were delighted by the boldness of their Roman hostage. Even when Caesar promised to return after his release and have them all crucified, the pirates laughed heartily. They were almost disappointed when, after thirty-eight days, the hefty payment of silver finally arrived. There was something irresistible about this Roman youth and they would miss the entertainment he provided. Reluctantly, they said goodbye to their prisoner. The pirates had honoured their word – and Caesar would honour his.

Immediately, he made for the nearby metropolis of Miletus, one of the wealthiest Greek cities on the coast of Anatolia. In his midtwenties and holding no political office of any kind, Caesar used his personal magnetism to quickly assemble his own fleet of ships. He found the pirates where he had left them, returning before they had even lifted anchor.[3] Their booty he seized for himself, including his fifty talents of silver. Back on dry land, wooden crosses were soon assembled. On the orders of the enigmatic young man whose company they had enjoyed for over a month, iron nails were driven through the pirates' arms and feet. To tortured cries, the crosses were hoisted upright and fixed into the ground. Crucifixion was an agonising, drawn-out death, sometimes taking days. But Caesar had heard the pirates' pleas – and he would always be famed for his mercy. One by one, he cut their throats, to quicken the end.

Twilight Republic

Caesar's pirate adventure is a ripping yarn, recounted by multiple ancient authors and, in all likelihood, embellished in the telling by the man himself, but it also perfectly distils the essential character of the most famous name in all Roman history. We are presented, almost fully formed, the arrogant aristocrat, certain he is destined for greatness; the charismatic scoundrel whose lethal charm cut like the blade of his dagger; and the brilliant general, born to lead and whom men loved to follow. Even in an age of giants – Pompey, Cicero, Antony and Cleopatra – Caesar would tower above all, bestriding the world like a colossus. As Shakespeare noted, all most could do was peep about in his shadow to find dishonourable graves; and many graves would be needed in the bloody twilight days of the Roman Republic.[4]

Gaius Julius Caesar was born in 100 BC, not on the lofty heights of the Palatine Hill, but in the depths of Rome's overcrowded Subura. So infamous was this district of the city, attitudes towards it live on in the modern Italian word *suburra*, still used to describe places of disrepute. The high-rise apartment buildings of the notorious neighbourhood had risen around the family's townhouse over the decades, a clear sign of the capital's explosive growth. Rome housed over half a million people at Caesar's birth – already the largest city in the ancient world – and like the towers surrounding them, Caesar's branch of the Julian clan were also reaching new heights: all four of Caesar's uncles had held the consulship, and his father had governed the rich province of Asia. Young Julius was as blue-blooded as they came, but growing up among the Subura's urban poor surely helped him develop that common touch, later so beloved by the Roman people.

The Roman Republic was by now over 400 years old. Its creaking constitution struggled to cope with the rate of its recent expansion. In less than two centuries, Rome had gone from minor Italian city-state to master of the Mediterranean world. With its greatest rival Carthage wiped off the map, the Republic had claimed in quick succession lucrative lands in North Africa, Iberia, Greece, and western Anatolia. Observers noted that the constant threat of Carthage had once kept Rome disciplined and virtuous – now freed from the fear of her nemesis, she had fallen into idleness and greed. The balance of power between the Roman Senate, magistrates, and the people they governed was always a delicate one. With the temptations offered by rich new provinces and subjects to exploit, it teetered more than ever. Increasingly, the hand of the Republic was guided not by its founding principles, but by ambitious provincial governors who amassed money, influence, and military might for themselves.

Doing their bidding were the feared Roman legions, who fell like lightning on any who dared to question the Republic's dominance. In radical reforms around the time of Caesar's birth, the Roman army was made a permanent and professional standing force. Rome had always relied on the levy of citizen soldiers – the honest farmer who downed tools when the call came and proudly did his duty for the Republic. But with such vast territories to protect, the sword of Rome would now be held by hardened, full-time legionaries. Once they fought to defend the sacred soil of their family farm, now they were motivated by the weight of their purse and, increasingly, intense personal loyalty to the commander who held their lives in his hands.

The world of Caesar's youth was one of near-constant political violence. Time-honoured democratic systems of the Republic were everywhere trampled by strong men who saw the sword as a valid alternative to the ballot box. Wildly ambitious statesmen commanding loyal legions as their own personal armies – it was a flammable combination, and a teenage Julius Caesar would only barely survive the eruption that followed. Caesar's uncle, Gaius Marius, had become locked in a tug-of-war battle for power with another ruthless general, Lucius Cornelius Sulla. Each time one left the city on campaign, the other seized power and attacked his rival's supporters. This bitter feud culminated in 88 BC, with an event as inevitable as it was unthinkable.

Blood of the Gods

Sulla's march on Rome was unprecedented. Since the age of kings, commanders returning from war were strictly forbidden from entering the capital with their troops, except for the single day of a triumphal procession. To do so would represent an outrageous violation of ancient law, tradition, and the hallowed delineation between Roman military and civic identity. Sulla had no time for such taboos.

The moment he led his legions across the city's sacred boundary under arms, the Republic changed forever.

The appalling act would have made a great impact on young Caesar who likely watched events unfold with both fear and boyish fascination. His family were spared in the wave of executions that followed, but worse was still to come. When Sulla left for the East to campaign against a rebellious king, the Marian faction took hold in Rome yet again. There would be no mercy a second time. Caesar was eighteen years old when Sulla marched on the city once more and began a nightmarish reign of terror. As he addressed the fearful Senate, a ghastly chorus of screams drifted across the city – the sound of 7,000 captured enemy soldiers being executed on his orders.[5] Sulla then implemented the grim programme of 'proscription' – any Roman who found their name posted on his wanted list was now an outlaw, their property confiscated, a bounty offered for their head. Before long, the heads of hundreds of proscribed, arbitrarily deemed 'enemies of the state', rotted on spikes in the Forum.

Caesar was now the head of his family after the recent death of his father, and closely tied to Sulla's enemies. As well as being related to Marius, he had just married the noble Cornelia, daughter of another of Sulla's hated rivals. Surely, his name would be added to the list of condemned at any moment. Caesar called in favours, sent out bribes, and twisted the arm of anyone who might have the tyrant's ear. In a rare show of leniency, Sulla eventually agreed to let Caesar live, so long as he divorced his wife, Cornelia. A small demand in return for his life. Incredibly, Caesar refused. It is hard to imagine how anyone could survive such bold defiance against a bloodthirsty tyrant, yet somehow Caesar did. Perhaps Sulla saw something of himself in the fearless young aristocrat. Counselled that he was 'just a mere boy', Sulla allowed Caesar to keep his head, against his better judgement – but with the prescient parting words that 'in that boy, I see many a Marius'.[6]

Not content with marching on his own city and slaughtering his opposition, Sulla dug deep into the constitution of the Republic, blowing the dust off an ancient title that had not been used since the Punic Wars. Unlike the two consuls who ruled annually and watched each other's actions closely, the *dictator* ruled alone – appointed to steer the Republic through an emergency that threatened its very survival. His powers were unlimited – and when the crisis had passed, he was expected to voluntarily lay them down. To the surprise of many, Sulla did just that. After a year in total control of the Republic, he resigned his office, disbanded his legions, and disappeared into retirement. Caesar was dumbfounded that a man could surrender the absolute power he had shed so much blood to achieve. He had watched a Roman general march devoted legions on his own city, destroy his opponents, declare himself a dictator, and live to die a natural death. He may have also been inspired by the pithy epitaph later engraved on Sulla's tomb: 'No better friend, no worse enemy.'[7] Now Caesar embarked on his own political career: that slow ascent up the *cursus honorum* or 'ladder of offices'. Each job leading reliably to the next, with a select few gaining the ultimate prize of a consulship. Its hierarchies were strict, and its rules were clear. But if Sulla had taught Caesar anything, it was that rules were made to be broken.

To begin with, Caesar's rise followed the trajectory of the career politician. After he raised a fleet to capture and execute the Cilician pirates, there was the obligatory stint of military service as an officer in the East. Then two years as *quaestor* – a type of financial inspector – in Spain. His next job as *curule aedile* in Rome was far more up his alley, giving him responsibility over public games and festivals. Caesar spent lavishly, offering the people banquets, theatre performances, and hundreds of gladiator bouts. Before long the adoring public were actively seeking out any new office and honour that they could bestow on him – popular appeal he would soon cash in.[8] When the prestigious post of 'Pontifex Maximus' became available in 63 BC, Caesar saw a chance to leap a few rungs of the career ladder. The Pontifex was the chief priest of the Roman state, the man who linked the people to the gods – indeed, the word translates to 'bridge builder'. Not unlike the modern Pope who still holds the same job title, the Pontifex Maximus was expected to be an elder statesman who had proved his piety over a long career. Caesar, on the other hand, was a swaggering showman condemned by crusty senators for wearing his toga loose and his belt slung low.[9] There were far more suitable candidates, but with the winner chosen by popular vote, Caesar knew he had a fighting chance. He turned up the charm and dished out enormous bribes he could not afford to all those who wielded any influence. Leaving his home in the Subura on the day of the election, he kissed his mother goodbye and told her he would 'either return as Pontifex, or not at all'.

Caesar had another weapon that he was more than happy to use when the political game required. Through his illustrious bloodline, Caesar claimed a descent from the Roman kings and ultimately, the gods themselves. His Julian clan traced their lineage back to the Trojan hero Aeneas, and therefore also to his divine mother, Venus. Caesar made sure to remind the people that his stock not only had 'the sanctity of kings, whose power is supreme among mortal men', but 'the reverence of the gods, who hold sway over kings'.[10] Venus, goddess of love, desire, and war, would forever be Caesar's patron deity. On his later coinage, her alluring visage would feature regularly, reinforcing to viewers that in Caesar's veins ran the blood of the gods. The divine beauty is shown wearing a regal diadem and accompanied by an adoring winged Cupid. In his final years, Caesar would even build a glorious temple in the heart of Rome dedicated to Venus Genetrix, his 'ancestral mother', where the goddess – and perhaps by extension, he – could be worshipped.

Caesar would embrace his mother again. In a shock victory, he was elected as spokesperson for the gods while still only in his thirties. The title was for life, granted its holder sweeping powers, and even came with a house in the Roman Forum. A consulship followed soon after. Though meant to rule in unison, Caesar overshadowed his consular colleague to such an extent that Romans joked it was the consulship of 'Julius and Caesar'. His ascendancy seemed unstoppable – but the extravagant spending and shameless bribery that helped his rise had left him with crippling debts. Many noticed that provincial governors often returned from their provinces far richer men than when they had set out, able to settle their debts and still have plenty left over. How exactly, it was best not to ask. If only Caesar could secure the right province to govern. Perhaps even make war and win prestige, along with the booty that accompanied it. He would soon

Portrait of the goddess Venus on a silver denarius of Julius Caesar, 45 BC — from the author's collection.

get his chance. Roman Gaul was not the richest of lands but Caesar knew it had potential. Beyond its northern frontier, the barbarians of independent Gaul – roughly equating to modern France – were restless, stirring, whole tribes were on the move. In 58 BC, Caesar set out for his new province at the head of four legions. Certain that whatever awaited him in Gaul, he was bound for glory.

The Scarlet Cloak

'All Gaul is divided into three parts.' With this simple line, Caesar begins his own account of his Gallic War – an eight-year conflict that would forever change the course of European history and leave millions dead or enslaved. The war is unique in that we can follow its events from beginning to end in the surviving reports of Caesar himself. His first-hand dispatches from the front, written in the regal third person, were probably published annually in Rome, unfolding for fascinated audiences like a serialised drama. Even Caesar's opponents would compliment his clear and clinical Latin prose, as no-nonsense as the man himself. While Caesar undoubtedly writes with one eye on his public image, his commentaries cannot be dismissed as mere propaganda; they were read by senior officers who had witnessed the events, not to mention scrutinised by Caesar's many political enemies. Indeed, archaeological excavations in modern France have corroborated many of Caesar's descriptions of battle sites and the enormous scale of Roman defences. Today the broad narrative of his commentaries is deemed to be largely accurate.[11]

This bloody war of conquest began as a localised migrant crisis at Rome's border. Before Caesar could even reach his new posting, word arrived that the Helvetii tribe, from the region of modern Switzerland, were migrating to new lands. Fully committed to their exodus, the tribe had even burned their homes before setting out on their march. When they requested permission to cross his province on their way to western Gaul, Caesar stubbornly refused. The moment their enormous wagon train entered Roman territory anyway, Caesar had all the reason he needed to attack. The tribe were no match for his legions: of the 370,000 men, women, and children who had gathered at Rome's border, Caesar boasts that just 110,000 survivors returned to their native land. A subsequent incursion into Gaul by Germanic tribes drew Caesar further north, deeper into hostile territory. Exacerbated by the presence of the Roman legions, the whole of Gaul soon erupted into open war.

Battling and besieging one Gallic tribe after another, Caesar eventually determined that his only option was to pacify the entirety of Gaul and form a new Roman province. The fighting was brutal even by the standards of the ancient world. Overcoming a rebellious Gallic town, Caesar matter-of-factly explains how he ordered the hands cut off every man of fighting age who had taken up arms against him. Though he reminds us that, since he let them live, his famed reputation for leniency was still intact.[12]

Caesar's eye was always alert to any audacious escapade that might generate publicity for him during his years away from Rome. In 55 BC he led the first of two expeditions to the mysterious island of Britannia, claiming British kings had been assisting the Gauls in their revolt. He scuffled with British tribes and gave them a quick taste of Roman strength before returning to Gaul. A public relations coup more than any serious invasion, news of Caesar's crossing of the sea to lands unknown would have amazed the Roman public much like an ancient equivalent of the moon landings. Indeed, paralleling that modern venture, conspiracy-minded commentators claimed that Caesar had fabricated the fantastical story, since as everyone well knew, Britain did not exist and never had existed.[13]

Though Gaul had been more a selection of quarrelsome tribes than any unified nation in the modern sense, it now found a cause to unite behind: hatred of the Romans. A charismatic chieftain emerged to rally the various tribes against their common enemy. Vercingetorix led a huge alliance of Gallic warriors with renewed purpose. At one battle he even forced Caesar into a rare retreat. Taking on individual tribes was one thing; now Caesar faced a coalition numbering in the hundreds of thousands, led by a born leader of men not so different from himself.

The fate of Gaul would be decided at Alesia. As Caesar pursued Vercingetorix to the hilltop settlement, the Gallic leader would not have been overly concerned. He held the high ground with massively superior numbers and supplies for a month. The Gauls must have watched in disbelief then, as the Roman legions set to work. With lightning speed, they built an eleven-mile ring of fortifications, including twenty-three forts, completely encircling the hill of Alesia. Before the Roman trap closed around him, Vercingetorix managed to send out a desperate plea to all remaining Gauls to come to his aid. He just needed to wait for the relief force to arrive and crush Caesar and his legions. The united peoples of Gaul answered the call. A staggering quarter of a million warriors descended on Alesia. As they approached, victory for Vercingetorix must have seemed certain – the triumph of a new Gallic nation.[14]

Once again, Caesar called upon the boundless energy of his legionaries. Now they built another fortification facing outwards from Alesia, this time completing a circuit of almost thirteen miles. These siegeworks were no mere wooden palisades, but turreted battlements defended by deep moats and high ramparts, all bristling with lethal traps for good measure: iron spikes, caltrops, and camouflaged pits filled with wooden stakes. Numerous French hilltops have claimed to be the fabled site of Alesia over the years, but recent research has confirmed suspicions that the climactic battle took place around today's Alise-Sainte-Reine in eastern France. Aside from the obvious similarity of the village's name to 'Alesia', remarkable 3-D laser imaging of the area has revealed the unmistakable lines of Caesar's fortifications striking across the landscape, matching the dimensions he describes in his account.[15] Here Caesar and his men – outnumbered five to one – prepared to fight to the last man in a war that was now total. Unable to feed the thousands besieged in Alesia, Vercingetorix sent the women and children out of the town towards the Roman lines below, hoping they would be allowed through to safety. His hopes were misplaced. Caesar ordered that none be allowed to pass. Trapped in no man's land, the women and children slowly starved to death, in full view of their husbands and fathers in the fort above.[16]

With the arrival of hordes of Gallic reinforcements, Caesar now fought two ferocious battles simultaneously. The sheer weight of enemy numbers seemed impossible for the legionaries to withstand. Gauls penned inside the Roman defences called to their countrymen on the outside, strengthening their will to fight. Caesar kept close watch on the unfolding battle, directing reinforcements to any weak points in the Roman lines. But everywhere Gallic warriors were scaling the walls. His men were being overwhelmed.

They knew him by the colour of his general's cloak. Even in the confused carnage of battle, that flash of scarlet proclaimed his arrival. A great shout went up from the Romans manning the barricades as Caesar rode into the fray. Charging along the defences, he shouted out to his men that every battle they had ever fought led them to this day, to this very hour. The legions were lifted by the presence of their general. They renewed the hail of their spears and thrusts of their swords. A thundering Roman cavalry charge followed, spreading panic among the Gauls. All those that turned to flee were cut down easily. The battle descended into a slaughter. Vercingetorix watched the massacre of his comrades, and any hope was abandoned.

Caesar's demands were clear: all enemy leaders, especially Vercingetorix, handed over alive. At a Gallic council, Vercingetorix took responsibility for the defeat, stating poignantly that he had

Dictator

made war against Rome 'not in his own interests but for the liberty of all'. Now, whether it meant for him life or death, he would 'yield to fortune'. The following day, Caesar sat proudly on a podium in front of the Roman fortifications, awaiting his defeated enemy.[17]

'Noble Savage'

The face of the proud Gallic leader who rode up to Caesar that day, threw his weapons to the ground and offered his surrender, may be revealed to us on an astonishing Roman coin minted in the aftermath of the war for Gaul. The denarius carries the carefully engraved portrait of a Gallic chieftain with a long, pointed beard. He wears a beaded necklace and is shown with an oval Celtic shield. His hair is drawn back into wavy spikes in a style that matches ancient descriptions of Celtic warriors who were known to use an Iron Age 'hair gel' to craft their fierce appearance. One observer describes how Gauls 'wash their hair with a lime solution' to artificially whiten it and then 'pull it back from the forehead to the top of the head' much as we see here.[18] Recent analysis of uncannily preserved 'bog bodies' of Celtic warriors from the same era has even identified that their hair is styled with a gel made of plant oil and pine resin originating from France or Spain.[19]

After almost a decade of hard fighting in Gaul, Caesar had learned to respect his enemy and regularly references their 'great bravery' in his commentaries – an esteem personified in this dignified portrait of the defeated.[20] The unprecedented character-study of an adversary might be seen as an ancient precursor to the 'noble savage' prevalent in the art and literature of the Enlightenment, an archetype meant to convey the innate goodness of man even when existing outside the bounds of civilisation. This Romantic primitivism would become most evident in Western depictions of Native American culture from the sixteenth century onwards. Here it could be argued that the humane portrait of the barbaric freedom-fighter Vercingetorix is echoed in the famous 'Indian Head' gold pieces struck by the United States in the early twentieth century. The coins show a nameless

The face of Vercingetorix? A noble portrait of a Gallic
captive on a denarius of Julius Caesar, 48 BC.

Native American chief wearing a magnificent traditional feather headdress – the first Native American to be shown on American coinage – with the simple legend above, 'Liberty'.

Whether the face of the anonymous Gaul is truly intended to represent Vercingetorix, we cannot say for certain, though it was undoubtedly interpreted as such by many Roman viewers. The portrait is executed with a naturalism that suggests a living model. Caesar would later shock the people of Rome by becoming the first leader to place his portrait on coins during his own lifetime; if this is indeed the face of Vercingetorix, then somewhat poetically, Caesar's Gallic nemesis was commemorated on Roman coins years before Caesar himself.

His uniting of the Gallic tribes against the Roman invader would later make Vercingetorix a potent symbol of French nationalism. Looking to inspire the French people in the lead-up to the Franco-Prussian War, Napoleon III would commission an enormous bronze statue of Vercingetorix to stand on the hilltop at Alise-Sainte-Reine where he staged his final defence against Caesar. Erected in 1865, the statue of the Gallic chieftain continues to watch over the battlefield, a lasting embodiment of French Liberty,

Equality, and Fraternity. As the inscription on its base proclaims: 'Gaul united, forming a single nation, animated by a common spirit, can defy the Universe.'

Caesar might have helped create a future national hero in Vercingetorix, but for now the rebel was a prisoner in chains, to be displayed in Caesar's inevitable triumphal parade. Yet such celebrations would have to wait. Caesar had suppressed the entirety of Gaul, but back in Rome the Senate was by no means hailing him a conquering hero. Instead, he found himself accused of vast overreach in his authority, subject to prosecution the moment he gave up his command and the immunity it granted. The senators most anxious about Caesar's military strength had united behind his old colleague Pompey the Great – ruthless defender of the Republic and probably the only living general who could rival Caesar's brilliance. The bond between the two men had originally been cemented by Pompey's marriage to Caesar's daughter, Julia, but since her death in childbirth a few years earlier, their political partnership had wavered. Caesar offered to lay down all arms if Pompey did the same; and for a moment compromise seemed possible. When talks suddenly broke down and Caesar's envoy, Mark Antony, was chased out of Rome, Caesar felt he was left with only two choices: either give up his legions and return to be tried like a common criminal or . . . The other option was equally unthinkable. But he had seen it done before.

Caesar's political and military authority to command – known as *imperium* – was only valid within the borders of his assigned province, the southern limit of which was marked by an insignificant stream. In January 49 BC, Caesar paused on its banks. Behind him massed the devoted soldiers of his Thirteenth Legion who had distinguished themselves for their commander in countless Gallic battles. To cross the small stream and enter Italy with his men would be a declaration of war. Caesar and his troops would, in an instant, become enemies of Rome. The men of the legion waited patiently as their general deliberated with himself in silence, weighing the implications of such a fearful step. What evils crossing this river might unleash upon mankind – and what fame the story of it might leave to the ages.[21]

That misty morning, the flowing waters of the Rubicon looked especially dark.

Veni, Vidi, Vici

Caesar was a born gambler. His gambit on the pirates' ransom, his voyage to the terra incognita of Britain, his double wall at Alesia – all made clear his belief that Fortune favoured the bold. Abandoning any further calculations, he shook the reins of his horse and pressed forward into the shallow water of the Rubicon, again entrusting his fate, and the fate of the whole Roman world, to chance. As he hastened across the river he was heard to proclaim: '*Alea iacta est*' – 'The die is cast', likening his decision to a throw of the gambler's dice. His legion dutifully followed him, and with that, Rome was again at war with herself.

Despite holding the capital and commanding superior numbers, Pompey abandoned Rome to Caesar and made a tactical retreat across the Adriatic. A military prodigy in his younger years, Pompey had not seen any action in over a decade, and he also knew his untested troops would be no match for Caesar's battle-hardened legions. Caesar swept into Rome and took the city without bloodshed. Pompey and the Senate had fled in such a rush, they had left the state treasury intact in the Temple of Saturn. Caesar happily seized its bullion to pay the loyal troops who had followed him across the Rubicon. Throughout his Gallic campaign, he had largely been paying his men with plunder – after the Battle of Alesia, every one of his soldiers was given a Gallic captive to sell as a slave.[22] Now he struck for them one of the largest Roman coin issues in history, an estimated 22.5 million denarii, and a coin beloved by collectors to this day.[23]

Caesar was evidently not quite ready to break the taboo of placing his living face on a coin. Instead, he is represented on this iconic denarius by a marauding elephant, trampling under its feet what has variously been identified as a serpent, a dragon, or more likely, a Gallic war trumpet known as a *carnyx*.[24] As evident on the coins struck by Hannibal, the elephant had long been a symbol of military

The 'elephant denarius' of Julius Caesar, showing an elephant trampling a serpent (?), and the emblems of the Pontifex Maximus, mint moving with Caesar, 49–48 BC.

might, and here Caesar may well be equating himself with the Punic conqueror. As the elephant of Caesar treads on the beastly carnyx, the viewer is reminded of Caesar's victory over the unified tribes of Gaul and more generally, the triumph of good over evil. Beneath the design, the simple mononym 'CAESAR' proclaims the name that was on the lips of millions. Distinguished Roman men usually had three names, the *tria nomina*, but as a superstar of the ancient world, Caesar needed to present only one. 'Caesar' would thereafter be more a brand than a name – an imperial title bestowed on his successors, and one reincarnated in the names of the German 'Kaiser', Ottoman 'Qaiser', and Russian 'Tsar'.

Where the obverse casts Caesar as the unstoppable military leader, the reverse reminds us that he is also Rome's spiritual guide, giving us a glimpse of the priestly tools of the Pontifex Maximus. We see a ladle, ceremonial sprinkler, sacrificial axe, and the pointed hat of a priest – sacred instruments that affirm Caesar as earthly spokesperson for the Roman gods, perhaps even close to the divine himself.

Caesar was now able to pay his men handsomely and he did just that, doubling the annual pay of the Roman legionary to the generous rate of 225 denarii, where it would remain for well over a century.[25]

Consolidating his power in the following years, Caesar took his legions on a victory lap around the Mediterranean world. In August 48 BC, he caught up with Pompey at Pharsalus in Greece where, despite being outnumbered as usual, he won a convincing victory. Pompey sought refuge in Egypt, only to be assassinated there on the orders of the ruling Ptolemaic dynasty. When they sycophantically presented Caesar with the head of his rival, he was appalled and wept openly, denied the chance to show his famous clemency to an old friend. While in Egypt, Caesar became embroiled in a dynastic struggle between the boy-king Ptolemy XIII and his twenty-one-year-old sister Cleopatra. The fifty-two-year-old Caesar was quickly beguiled by the tenacious Egyptian queen. Not only did he help Cleopatra win the throne from her brother, but he soon fathered a child with her – a son boldly named Caesarion or 'little Caesar'.

By the time Caesar returned to Rome in 46 BC, bringing with him his exotic young queen and infant son, there was a backlog of victories to celebrate. A single triumphal parade would have been spectacular enough – Caesar held an unprecedented four in a row, marking conquests in Gaul, Pontus, Africa, and Egypt. Notably, he chose not to celebrate a triumph for his defeat of Pompey, accepting there was not much glory in the taking of Roman lives. Among the seemingly endless procession of foreign treasure and captives rolling by, a large banner caught the eyes of the cheering crowds. It was emblazoned with three simple words that perfectly summed up Caesar's unparalleled achievements and unmatched ego: '*Veni, Vidi, Vici*' – 'I came, I saw, I conquered'.

Adoring spectators clamoured to see the general himself as he trundled by on his chariot. Caesar wore a dazzling purple toga embroidered with gold, and his face was painted red in the guise of Jupiter, king of the gods. A slave stood behind him, holding a laurel crown of victory above his head. That slave had another critical role. Over the thunderous applause, he called out an important reminder repeatedly into Caesar's ear: '*Memento mori, memento mori*' – 'Remember you are mortal'. The magnificent parade eventually culminated in front of the Temple of Jupiter, where sacrifices were made and notable captives executed, all in honour of the thunder god. One dishevelled prisoner was brought forward with particular anticipation. He was pale and emaciated after six years in an underground jail. But somewhere behind his tangled hair and beard, there was still a defiant spark, a glimmer of the man who had united Gaul against Rome – and whom Caesar had even immortalised on one of his own coins. To round off the day's spectacles, Vercingetorix was slowly strangled, to the delight of all.

Behold the Man

The shopkeeper stared in disbelief at the silver coin in his hand. A gleaming denarius, fresh from the Roman mint. He picked it up between his thumb and forefinger to inspect it more closely. Even without the letters proclaiming his name and title, the portrait was unmistakable. The high cheekbones, wrinkled neck, and piercing gaze. The face of the dictator, Julius Caesar.

Roman coinage had always followed strict traditions. It celebrated sacred gods and legendary heroes. At most, an aspiring politician might place on their coins the portrait of a famous and long-dead ancestor. Never the living. Granted, in the decadent lands of the East, Hellenistic monarchs had been placing their faces on coins for centuries. There, people expected coins to carry the head of their king. But this was Rome, and Rome was no city of kings.

Caesar's lifetime portrait appearing on Roman coins in January 44 BC was a shock to be sure, though it continued a long list of outrageous honours recently granted him by a grovelling Senate.[26] The right to continue wearing his triumphal purple and gold toga, his own statue beside that of the resident god inside temples, and a suspiciously throne-like golden chair from which he now refused to rise when greeting senators.[27] Worst of all, the title of 'dictator' had returned to haunt the Roman people. Dictatorships were previously granted for six-month periods in times of crisis. At the culmination of his quadruple triumph, the Senate proclaimed Caesar dictator for the next ten years. Even the tyrant Sulla had never accepted such an obscene honour. In fact, Caesar was recently heard to comment that in laying down his dictatorship, Sulla showed he did not know his political ABCs.[28]

Caesar's portrait denarii usher in the 'Age of Men' on Roman coins. They allow us the only verified contemporary view of the face that stared down deadly pirates, bloody tyrants, and rebellious Gauls: Julius Caesar the man – still mortal, for now. As with many legendary figures of the Republic, sculptural likenesses of Caesar are difficult to identify with certainty. Statues rarely provide a name for their subject and often differ greatly from one another in style and execution. Coins are the key, presenting uncannily lifelike faces of power, helpfully encircled with names and titles. Caesar's coins show the dictator in his mid-fifties, with hollowed cheeks and pronounced creases on his neck. His hair is drawn forward towards a high forehead, though his famed receding hairline is conveniently covered by a laurel crown, exactly matching descriptions from Suetonius. The scurrilous imperial biographer claimed Caesar's 'baldness troubled him greatly' and that 'of all the honours voted him by the Senate, there was none he made use of more gladly than the privilege of wearing a laurel wreath at all times'.[29]

Sculptural portraits widely accepted as Caesar are surprisingly rare for such a giant of history. Most are idealised likenesses crafted in the decades after his death, with wrinkles smoothed and hairline strengthened. However, one possible lifetime portrait of the dictator was dredged up from the Rhône river near Arles in 2007 (Plate section, 2). The impressive marble sculpture depicts a middle-aged man with the 'warts and all' artistic naturalism prevalent in the first century BC. Caesar had been intensely active in the region of its discovery in southern France; in 46 BC he refounded Arles as a Roman colony where he settled retired veterans. While the rush to identify the face lifted from the river as that of Julius Caesar was rightly criticised, it certainly portrays a powerful figure of the late Republic.[30] The receding hair combed forward, furrowed brow, and distinctive neck creases are all present and correct – along with an aura of cold command that speaks of a leader men would gladly follow into battle.

The political situation in early 44 BC was fast-moving and unpredictable. As ever, coins were the most convenient way to quickly relay

The true face of Julius Caesar, on a lifetime denarius shockingly declaring him 'Dictator for Life'.

information to the masses on the latest developments. So it was that in the first weeks of February, Romans noticed a disturbing update to the denarii of Caesar pouring out from the Roman mint. Instead of being labelled merely 'dictator', an ominous new title encircled Caesar's bust. His coins now proclaimed him 'Dictator Perpetuo' – 'Dictator in Perpetuity'. Put plainly, Caesar was now dictator for life.

Romans of all ranks were dumbstruck. This was surely a coin and a title too far. Even Caesar's closest allies who had fought alongside him in the Gallic Wars now struggled to defend their old commander against the charge of tyranny. Some argued that Caesar's enemies were intentionally heaping on him absurd honours that would drive even the mildest citizens to outrage.[31] And there were further disturbing rumours: that at the upcoming celebrations of the Lupercalia, Caesar's right-hand man Mark Antony planned to present him with a kingly crown. Senators huddled in corners and conversed in whispers, some held the coin and gestured to it emphatically. The denarius showed the dictator as he lived and breathed. Ironic then, that it would prove to be the coin that killed him.

Eternal Dictator

For many, Julius Caesar is synonymous with ancient Rome itself. He represents the arrogant, even cartoonish, personification of the ultimate empire. Yet Caesar was never an emperor. Like many towering figures of history, he continues to confound – challenging each generation to reconsider his legacy. A complex man living in remarkable times, the real Caesar can perhaps be best seen in his contradictions: a ruthless warlord who was renowned for his clemency, an autocrat who was adored by the common people. After his death he would even be worshipped as a god – but the human face on our denarius reminds us that, as the slave behind him had reminded him during his triumphs, Caesar was a mortal man. To those closest to him, he was a son, a husband, a father. To Cleopatra he was a lover, to Mark Antony a trusted friend. As a general he was beloved by his troops and despised by his foes.

Few would question Caesar's military brilliance – especially the many enemies he overcame – but his tactical genius also helped him outmanoeuvre his rivals in the cut-throat world of Republican politics. Unlike many of his contemporaries, Caesar was able to dominate both the field of battle and the marble floor of the Senate. As a rising politician, he pioneered a new brand of populism that bypassed age-old mechanisms of the Republic by appealing directly to the people. Caesar was no working-class hero, but he was adored by the Roman populace, walking among them and listening to their concerns. As Shakespeare would later write: 'When that the poor have cried, Caesar hath wept. Ambition should be made of sterner stuff.'[32] After his triumphal celebrations, Caesar gave every citizen a gift of 400 *sestertii*, equivalent to 100 denarii, and paid the rents of Roman tenants for a year.[33] Cynical ploys, maybe – but the people would also feature heavily in Caesar's will and testament, in which he left them vast sums of money and his private gardens to be used as public parkland.

Alongside his military prowess and political savvy, Caesar was also an intellectual, respected by the great minds of his age. He authored a multi-volume linguistic treatise entitled *On Analogy* exploring the theory underlying Latin grammar and eloquence, and the elegant prose of his *Gallic War* is still admired by students of Latin around the world. Between battles he even found time to focus his intellect on the confused calendar year which had drifted hopelessly out of sync with the seasons. Caesar worked closely with astronomers and mathematicians to solve the problem. His 'Julian Calendar' took effect on 1 January 45 BC and gave our year its twelve months and 365 days. The month of his birth would thereafter be named in his honour – July.

Caesar was also passionate about architecture and engineering. He commissioned a new Senate house and forum complex in the heart of Rome. Planning was also under way for improved harbours and roads to serve Italy, as well as ambitious proposals further afield; he hoped to revolutionise Mediterranean travel by cutting a navigable canal through the Isthmus of Corinth, an engineering feat not achieved until 1893. In his calendar reforms and civic projects, we perhaps see Caesar at his most godlike – literally reshaping time and space to his liking around the people of Rome.

His seismic wars of conquest helped form the Europe we see today. The entire region of Gaul was forever transformed by his campaigns, with its ancient Celtic culture replaced by Roman language, laws, and the relative comforts of urban living. Caesar's intrepid voyages across the Channel introduced a whole new realm to the classical world: Britannia. Those who pass a point of no return may still be said to have 'crossed the Rubicon', an idiom that evokes Caesar's greatest gamble.

No surprise then that Caesar has been a continuing source of inspiration for leaders across time. Napoleon Bonaparte devoured books on Caesar, and both he and his nephew Napoleon III wrote their own lengthy biographies of the Roman general. The Fascist dictator Mussolini would take 'invincible lessons' from Caesar, whom he described as 'an unsurpassed genius in war and politics'.[34] Winston Churchill held similar views. When asked who he thought was the greatest leader in history, he stated definitively: 'Julius Caesar, because he was the most magnanimous of all the conquerors.'[35]

In the nineteenth century, the term 'Caesarism' would be coined to describe an authoritarian ruler whose absolute power is seemingly legitimised by popular appeal. Napoleon, as a so-called 'people's emperor', was initially singled out as the concept's clearest exemplar, yet Caesarism remains a common charge against world leaders in the twenty-first century – directed at those who preserve only the outward forms of democracy, validating radical changes to their constitutions by putting them to the public vote. Although he once ruled the city as eternal dictator, to this day a full-length ancient statue of Caesar stands in the council chamber of Rome's city hall, presiding over meetings of the democratically elected local government.

Caesar was the first Roman leader to fully exploit the persuasive power of coinage. Realising that an icon needed iconic coins, Caesar's were a masterclass of propaganda and self-promotion, helpfully punctuating each step on his path to absolute power. Our silver portrait of Caesar offers the perfect opportunity to reflect on his life and legacy, giving us the face of a man who would help bring down the Republic that created him. With almost unbearable dramatic irony, it declares him 'Dictator for Life'. The title proved to be accurate, though for all his godlike power, Caesar could not foresee how little of that earthly life remained.

Chapter IV

IDES

'The tyrant may be gone, but the tyranny remains.'

Cicero

Brutus 'Ides of March' denarius, military mint travelling with
Brutus and Cassius, 42 BC.
Obverse: Head of the assassin, Marcus Junius Brutus,
BRVT IMP L PLAET CEST.
Reverse: Pileus cap of liberty flanked by two pugio daggers,
EID MAR. 'Eidibus Martiis' – 'On the Ides of March'.

Hero of the Republic

Dawn was yet to show itself through the windows of the townhouse, and the flames of oil lamps still danced in every room. By their meagre glow, the two slaves unfurled the garment. Before them their master stood motionless; with his sharp features illuminated only by flickering fire, he could have been mistaken for a temple statue. The first slave heaped the white wool over his master's left shoulder until it cascaded down as far as the mosaic floor, while the second swept the other end of the fabric around his back and reappeared on his right side. The slave waited a moment before whispering any prompt.

'Your arm, master.'

Brutus blinked and raised his arm at the reminder, allowing the slaves to draw the woollen expanse across his chest and wrap him fully in its deep folds. Like sculptors, they then set to work perfecting the intricate creases and layers of the garment, loosening it here, adding tension there, until every inch of its complex drapery flowed as intended.

The toga was the formal wear of every male Roman citizen. So fundamental was the garment to national identity that the poets Virgil and Martial would both classify Romans as simply the 'toga-wearing race'. A weighty cloth of white wool up to five metres in length, it signified not only the proud citizenship of its wearer, but announced him everywhere as a political being with a stake in the success of the Republic. Indeed, it marked him as a true man. Its pleats did not, however, make all men equal. Where most wore the plain white *toga virilis* or 'toga of manhood', senior magistrates like Brutus had the privilege of wearing the *toga praetexta* or 'bordered toga', edged with a broad crimson stripe that clearly distinguished its wearer amid the crowds of the Roman Forum. Over time, the brilliance of the toga's white wool also became a proxy for a man's character and nobility. Citizens of lower rank were easily identified by the duller hues of their garments, while the wealthiest ensured their togas were expertly laundered to the most pure and unblemished snowy white. Candidates for office were even known to rub chalk into the fabric, hoping to make it shine ever brighter in the eyes of prospective voters.

Key to the formal associations of the toga was the fact that every man needed assistance to properly enrobe themselves in its unwieldy fabric. For many this help came in the form of wives and children, but for those who could afford them, wardrobe slaves ensured the garment achieved an immaculate appearance. And finally it seemed the slaves of Brutus were satisfied with their master's attire. While his left arm carried the weight of the toga and held its carefully curated folds in place, his right arm remained free for the shaking of hands, the wide gestures of oration ... and another task that would be required of Brutus that day.

The voice of a woman rang out from the shadows, dismissing the slaves. Only when their scurried footsteps had faded away did Porcia emerge from the deep darkness between the oil lamps. She stepped slowly towards her husband, carrying the weapon in her open hands like a sacrificial offering. The dagger lay there before him, glinting in its gilded scabbard.

Brutus gripped it by its hilt and slowly unsheathed the blade. Turning it in his hand, he reminded himself of the weapon's weight, and inspected the leaf-shaped iron blade which widened slightly in the middle before tapering gradually to the deadliest of points. The dagger was military issue – more formidable, and more difficult to conceal, than the compact blades usually preferred by assassins. The choice was intentional. It was, after all, to be wielded in glorious defence of the Republic, not for some cowardly murder done in the dark. A worthy weapon for the deed, he concluded as he slid it back into its sheath.

Gently parting the thick folds of his toga, Porcia helped her husband in hitching the dagger onto the belt of his tunic, before restoring the garment just as it was.[1] She stepped back and scanned the tumbling drapery, confirming the blade was invisible underneath its layers, and answered a question her husband had not asked.

'A hero of the Republic,' Porcia announced proudly, 'ready to take on the gods themselves.'

Brutus met her gaze and saw the trembling firelight reflected there. 'I only ask that the gods make me worthy of so noble a wife.' Since Brutus had entrusted her with his all-consuming secret, Porcia had been the only woman in the entire Republic who knew of the events planned for this day – and true to her word, she had not told a soul.

Dawn was aglow now, bringing with it all the tumult and the traffic of an awakening city. After embracing his wife one last time at the door of their home, Brutus strode out into the already bustling street, closely followed by his attendants – off to see to the business of the day. Porcia watched her husband go for the longest time, following the progress of his pristine white and crimson toga through the early morning crowds, until finally she could see him no longer.

Public calendars across the city reminded all Romans that this was the fifteenth day of the month of Mars – the Ides of March. The Ides marked the date of the full moon halfway through each lunar month, and were a traditional deadline for Romans to settle their outstanding debts.

Many debts were to be settled on that spring morning in 44 BC.

Call of the Ancestors

The Romans worshipped a colourful and seemingly endless pantheon of gods. Whether you were heading off to war, starting a new business, or trying to keep the sewer system running smoothly, there was a god or goddess expecting an offering.[2] Roma watched over her city, but every home was guarded by its own household deities. A flame would be kept burning in the shrines of these protective spirits, where offerings of food and drink might be placed by those hoping for a long and prosperous future for their family. In the atrium of any self-respecting aristocratic home, the lamplight from the shrine would also illuminate a selection of ghostly faces nearby: the masks of the ancestors. Mounted on the walls, these wax death masks served as a constant reminder of the great deeds achieved under their family name. The more faces looked out from the walls, the more prestige a family had earned – and needed to maintain. The spirits of the ancestors were as omnipresent as the gods, their uncanny eyes always watching, always judging.[3]

Elite patrician families of the Roman Republic enjoyed the trappings of incredible wealth — villas for every mood, slaves for every possible chore — but their lives were also lived under the crushing weight of expectation. There were only so many political offices to be won with each election cycle, and every man dreamed of crowning his career by winning the Republic's top job, the consulship. Existence meant competition. A dog-eat-dog race where the stakes were impossibly high. Try for position and fail, and your once-respected family could be left in the wilderness, the ancient prestige of their name lost in an instant. Of course, most political careers end in failure, but in the rowdy and unpredictable world of the late Republic, they also routinely ended in death. Candidates employed mobs of heavies to cudgel their rivals. Loyalists fought running battles on the streets. The very real risk of manure being spattered over your white toga was the least of your concerns.[4]

As uninviting as it all sounds, this quest for prestige was what defined the life of a Roman patrician. Their wives and daughters equally so. Though women could not hold political office directly, their manoeuvrings, persuasions, and marriages always sought to advance the cause of those who could. The rise of Julius Caesar completely stalled the time-worn mechanisms of this world. Where the best and brightest of Rome once vied to outdo each other with spectacular achievement in the name of the Republic, now they were expected to keep their heads down and swear allegiance to one man.

This half-life did not suit Marcus Junius Brutus, watched over as he was by a selection of glowering death masks more numerous than most. Being able to trace your aristocratic lineage all the way back to a legendary figure from the old Republic could be a leg up to any political career, but most could only dream of a family tree as illustrious as Brutus and his Junii clan. The bust of one ancestor surely occupied the most prominent position in their Roman townhouse: Lucius Junius Brutus, the liberator of Rome. Half a millennium earlier, this legendary figure had cast out the last king and founded the Roman Republic, no less. As if this was not enough, Lucius had made

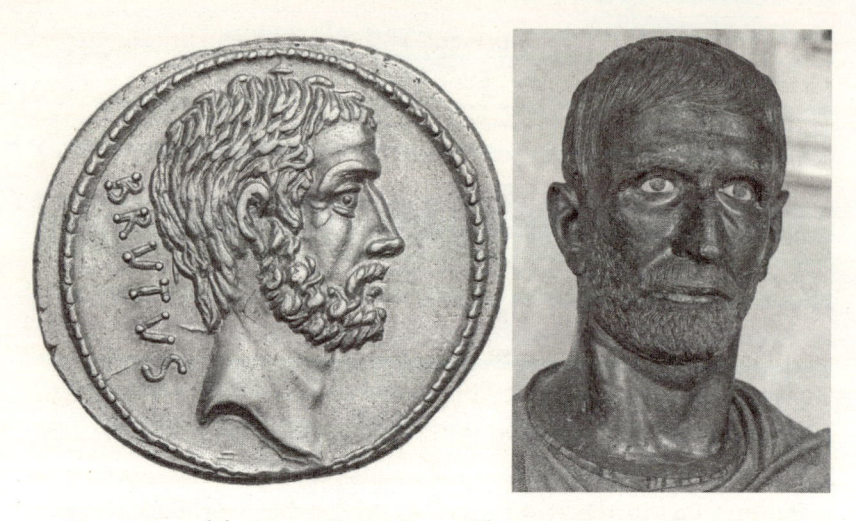

Denarius struck by Marcus Junius Brutus (the assassin) as moneyer in 54 BC, showing his ancestor, Lucius Junius Brutus; compared with the Capitoline Brutus in Rome's Capitoline Museum.

the populace join him in swearing a communal oath, that no monarch would ever again be allowed to rule in Rome. An oath that would have echoed in the conscience of his descendant all these years later.

The power that this revolutionary inheritance held over Brutus is made clear in coins he struck a decade before the dictatorship of Caesar. He began his journey up the political career ladder in 54 BC, with an obligatory year as moneyer overseeing the Roman mint. It was a junior position, but it gave young up-and-comers like Brutus the chance to stamp their names on coins and on the consciousness of the voting public. The early designs chosen by Brutus are revealing: on one denarius he presents us with the face of Libertas, goddess of freedom; on another we see, sure enough, a portrait of his heroic ancestor, Lucius Junius Brutus. The ancient liberator is shown with a thick beard and resolute gaze. A famous bronze bust in Rome's Capitoline Museum has come to be known as the 'Capitoline Brutus' thanks solely to the subject's striking resemblance to the helpfully named face on this coin.

The similarities in the bearded portraits are undeniable, and while the bronze cannot be identified as the elder Brutus with certainty, he clearly represents a noble hero of the old Republic. Just as ancient sources speak of a bronze statue of the she-wolf standing on the Capitol, they also describe a statue of the Liberator, Lucius Junius Brutus, raised there alongside depictions of the Roman kings, with sword drawn ready to defend his new Republic.[5]

Years before he picked up a dagger in the defence of liberty, the coins of Brutus show he was already defining himself by the radical republicanism of his ancestor. Kingly ambitions were to be answered by the sword, and by February 44 BC, Rome was at the mercy of one man – a king in all but name.

Not that Marcus Junius Brutus was suffering under Caesar's domination in Rome. He had recently completed a governorship of Gaul and now held the respected position of *urban praetor*, overseeing the city's courts. He had even been promised a consulship in three years – positions all gifted him by Caesar.[6] These were venerable offices established by his ancestor, to be competed for by Rome's best men, now doled out meaninglessly by a dictator to his most obedient followers.

Some said Brutus was lucky to have any position at all, being as he was a notable beneficiary of Caesar's famous clemency. Just a few years ago he had taken a principled stand against the warlord who crossed the Rubicon with his troops and marched on his own city. Brutus not only opposed his old friend, but he sided instead with Pompey the Great, even though his own father had been put to death by Pompey – no doubt, this was a time of difficult compromises. Caesar, however, not only forgave Brutus and other nobles who opposed him, he embraced them closely. Some chose death over such a humiliating pardon. Perhaps now more than ever, Brutus envied their bravery.[7]

As a popular scion of the liberty-loving Junii, all eyes now looked to Brutus. Seemingly every day, a new outrage to the traditions of the Republic brought cries that Brutus had forgotten his ancestry. Caesar may have just publicly refused a royal crown offered him three times by his loyalist Mark Antony but such theatrics were fooling nobody. Straight after this spectacle, Caesar had given himself the unprecedented title of 'Dictator for Life' – the sickening phrase stamped proudly on his coins fresh from the mint. Now a targeted campaign tried to goad Brutus into action. Each night, graffiti appeared around the city urging that Brutus act swiftly to save the Republic. Messages like 'Brutus, where are you?' sprang up on monuments and street corners faster than they could be scrubbed off. 'Are you asleep, Brutus?' was daubed on a statue of Caesar shamelessly erected alongside those of the Roman kings. One message stung more than others, evoking as it did the ever-expectant face of his ancestor, Lucius the Liberator. Scrawled for all to see in the public square, it proclaimed: 'You are no descendant of Brutus.'[8]

Fatal Days

The Romans saw omens in all things. Clouds of starlings whirling in the dusk sky revealed the future – and mesmerise residents with their displays to this day. The guts of sacrificed animals offered grave warnings. Cryptic dreams were clues to the gods' intentions. By late February 44 BC, the streets of Rome, darkened by the eclipsing shadow of the dictator, were rife with ill omens. After Caesar bodged the sacrifice of a bull at the festival of Lupercalia in mid-February, the fortune teller Spurinna announced that his life – and by extension the Roman state – would be in mortal danger for one lunar month, up to and including the Ides of March. This portent of a thirty-day period of danger, the *dies fatales* or 'fatal days', was not just an astrological forecast but had basis in Roman law, denoting the length of time given to pay fines or make an appeal in court. Caesar had little time for such superstitions.

He was far more preoccupied with final preparations for his most ambitious conquest yet, assembling a massive force of sixteen legions for a reckoning with Rome's troublesome neighbour in the East – Parthia. If he pulled it off, he would return to Italy as master of the world, a living god surpassing even Alexander himself. Rumours of an ancient prophecy stating that Parthia could only ever be conquered by a king did not put the minds of his opponents at ease. If

Caesar was to be crowned 'Rex', it would likely be on the eve of this great expedition.[9]

As the dangerous days passed, news of increasingly disturbing omens swirled in the city streets. One concerned the horses that Caesar dedicated to the Rubicon, set free to wander at the spot of his famous crossing of the river. The animals were now said to be catatonic, refusing all nourishment and weeping constantly.[10] An owl was seen to swoop down and perch in the crowded Roman Forum, hooting and shrieking – an omen of death, most agreed.[11] The citizen who seemed least perturbed was Caesar himself. On the contrary, he had dismissed his bodyguards and walked freely among the people as he surveyed his various building projects around the city.

With Caesar planning to leave for his Parthian campaign on the 18th, the Senate called a special session for the 15th – the Ides of March. Senators were used to holding their meetings in various makeshift spaces around the city since the previous curia burned down eight years ago. Caesar was, predictably, in the process of building its replacement to his own design. The meeting of the Roman Senate on the Ides of March would therefore take place in the curia of Pompey's grand theatre complex. If Caesar was indeed to be crowned king, what better venue for the ceremony than the hall of his old rival?

The night before the meeting, Caesar dined with some of his most loyal generals: Mark Antony, Lepidus, and Decimus, a cousin of Brutus who remained faithful to Caesar throughout the civil war when many others had not. A few friends had made their excuses and could not attend – Cassius, Casca, Cimber, and most notably Brutus himself. But Caesar was not concerned; he was absorbed with other matters. As was usual for the restless leader, even at the banquet table he continued to read and dictate documents to multiple secretaries at once.[12] Conversation among the generals inevitably turned to the coming Parthian campaign and soon enough, to the best sort of death. Asked what type of death he would choose given the chance, Caesar was concise in his response: 'A sudden and unexpected one.'[13]

'The Ides of March are come . . .'

No single day from antiquity can be reconstructed as forensically as 15 March 44 BC. By sheer good fortune, blow-by-blow accounts from several literary giants like Cicero, Plutarch, and Suetonius all survive, each adding their own colour to events. Examining and comparing each one carefully, it is possible for historical detectives to piece together the unfolding narrative of this most fateful of days.

It had been a restless night for Caesar and his wife Calpurnia, both left unsettled by vivid dreams. Caesar had dreamed he was flying above the clouds and clasped the hand of Jupiter. Surely a sign he would one day be welcomed into the pantheon of gods. Calpurnia could not help but offer a more pessimistic interpretation, especially after her own nightmare in which their home crumbled around them and she was left holding her husband's bloodied corpse in her arms. Caesar had never seen his wife so distressed by such superstitions. Bowing to her pleas, the dictator announced reluctantly that the day's senate meeting would be postponed.[14]

At the Theatre of Pompey, senators had been assembling since dawn. When a messenger finally arrived to announce that owing to ill-health, Caesar would not be attending, they saw it for what it was: yet another snub to the esteemed Senate. The dictator had recently caused outrage by not standing to greet them; now he did not even honour them with his presence at all. An anxious Brutus and Cassius urged Decimus to rush to Caesar's house and persuade him to come. To a chorus of disgruntled mutterings, Caesar's gold and ivory chair – or was it a throne? – was carried out of the curia by slaves, seeming to confirm his non-attendance. Still, Brutus and Cassius assured the assembly that Caesar would be there.

Decimus arrived breathless at the dictator's door in the Roman Forum. A trusted voice who had served Caesar loyally for over ten years, Decimus asked if he really intended on disappointing all the gathered noblemen who were expecting him. Caesar explained the portents, but Decimus would not hear it: 'Will you Caesar really be swayed by the dreams of women and the omens of fools?' Calpurnia protested of course, but the words of a concerned wife were ultimately waved away. What, in the end, had the mighty Caesar to fear? With smiles and reassurance, Decimus led Caesar from his home.

Back at the Theatre of Pompey, word now spread that Caesar was, in fact, on his way. An old senator sidled over to Brutus and Cassius, waiting anxiously in the portico, and whispered: 'I join you in prayer for the enterprise you both have in mind.' Inside the hall, containers awaited holding the scrolls for today's meeting, carried into the curia by slaves earlier that morning; some noticed they were heavier than usual but, being slaves, they said nothing.

As soon as Caesar arrived, he was accosted by men with the usual petitions. In the scrum, one tried to pass him a scroll with what he claimed was an urgent message but was quickly shoved back. A short religious ceremony was needed to inaugurate the meeting of the Senate, and it would be led by none other than Spurinna, the soothsayer who had presided over Caesar's failed sacrifice exactly one month earlier. The dictator could not help but comment wryly to Spurinna that 'the Ides of March are come'. For all the portents of doom, he had survived the month of dangerous days so ominously foretold to him.

'They are come', Spurinna agreed, 'but not gone.'

Scoffing at the warning, Caesar turned and ascended the marble steps into the hall. Inside, senators pressed tightly around him, all vying to get his attention for their own individual causes. Glances and nods were quickly exchanged between several of the crowding men. As one loudly petitioned the dictator about pardoning an exiled brother, glinting objects were revealed from the folds in togas and pulled from scroll boxes. Caesar casually dismissed the appeals, until his toga was forcefully yanked from his shoulders.

'This is violence!' he called out angrily. Suddenly from behind, Casca lunged at Caesar, stabbing him in the neck with a dagger. Then the flash of blades from all around: almost every senator seemed to suddenly brandish a weapon. Caesar hemmed in on all sides, driven back and forth like a wild animal entangled with his attackers. Cassius slashed at his face. Others at his back. But the sight of his beloved Brutus thrusting a blade was his final despair. By chance, Caesar fell under a statue of Pompey, as if his old rival was presiding over the vengeance. Looking up at his assassins, his allies, friends, with daggers drawn – Brutus, Cassius, Decimus – Caesar summoned his last ounce of energy to draw his bloodied toga over his face, veiling himself.

He sank and died at the base of Pompey's statue. Mortal after all.

Blood-spattered senators burst out of the theatre complex, unleashing panic and terror in the surrounding streets. Caesar's staunch ally Mark Antony, who had been held up at the door by one of the conspirators, now saw what they had done to his dearest friend – and he did not linger. As a pool of crimson spread out on the white marble floor around their victim, the assassins breathlessly debated what they should do next. One suggested they complete the deed by dragging Caesar's corpse to the Tiber and confiscating his property like a criminal. It was Brutus who reminded them all how closely their subsequent actions would be scrutinised; this was meant to be a cleansing of the Republic, not a bloody revolution.

The assassins wrapped their togas around their left arms to act as shields against the mob and marched out of the curia in a group. With daggers raised high they cried out that they had 'killed a king!' and 'slain a tyrant!' Caesar's body was now left alone in the silent hall. He had been stabbed twenty-three times, with perhaps only one wound, to his chest, being fatal. Up to sixty conspirators, his most trusted friends among them, took part in his assassination.[15]

The Liberators

Before the sun had even set on the Ides of March, the battle for control of the day's narrative was under way. The daggers of Brutus and his men had cut down a dictator, but they had also cleaved the Roman populace in two. Where many called them 'conspirators', they cast themselves as the *liberatores* – defenders of the Republic, who had freed Rome from the grip of a tyrant. They assumed that once Caesar's boot was lifted from the city's neck, applauding citizens would congratulate them on their courageous deed. They were sorely mistaken. Despite being as blue-blooded as any patrician, Caesar really had been a man of the people: he had mingled with them in the Forum, noted their concerns, shared in a bawdy joke – treating them much as he did his soldiers. He had not invented populism, but he had perfected it. Noble Brutus and the rest were all honourable men, but they were darlings of the establishment. In killing Caesar, they forced upon all Romans an ultimatum which would only be met with resentment.

The Liberators soon realised that any dreams of being hailed as heroes may have been naive. Caesar's loyal legions, full of zeal for their coming campaign, were encamped just outside the city; when the news arrived of their beloved commander's murder, their fury was barely contained. Mark Antony was also presiding consul in Rome at the time. If the Liberators were truly defenders of the Republic, the ancient office made Caesar's most loyal supporter untouchable. While the assassins dithered, Antony seized the initiative, along with the state treasury. He fortified his residence as a new base of operations and sent orders for Caesar's furious troops to march on the city. Dusk settled on the Ides with the city in a tense stand-off – Caesar's killers holding out on the Capitoline while a sea of the dictator's loyalists churned below.

For all his reputation as a brawler and a drunkard, Antony now appeared positively statesmanlike. The assassins may have been perched on Rome's most sacred hill but it was Antony who held the moral high ground. He stated he would not let 'private grudges' dictate his actions – yet in the next breath reminded Romans that a heinous crime had been committed and 'many oaths to Caesar broken'.[16] The tyrannicides, eager to appear reasonable, agreed to a decree that all Caesar's recent appointments would stand and that he would even be granted divine honours. In short, Caesar was to be made a god.

Just how far the abilities of Caesar's right-hand man had been underestimated became abundantly clear a few days later, when Antony stepped onto the podium to address an emotional crowd at the dictator's funeral. His speech, so masterfully imagined by Shakespeare, included a full reading of the oaths sworn by the assassins to protect Caesar. He also read part of the dictator's will that announced a generous gift of coin – 300 sestertii or seventy-five denarii – for every Roman citizen. Even in death, Caesar clearly loved the people of Rome. Among the heirs to his estate, Caesar had listed several of his assassins, infuriating the crowd even more. Finally, Antony revealed that Caesar would now be known as 'Divus Julius' – the 'divine Julius'. He had joined the pantheon of gods after all. As for Brutus, he was now a god-killer as well as an oath-breaker.[17]

Antony's oration whipped the mob into such a frenzy, they seized the body of Caesar and cremated him right there in the Forum. Spectators fuelled the blaze with anything they could get their hands on: dry branches, chairs from the surrounding courts, even their own clothes – turning the pyre into an inferno. Some snatched flaming brands and announced they would use them to burn down the houses of Brutus and Cassius.

In the event, the Liberators survived in Rome for a few weeks, but their situation was becoming increasingly untenable. Matters were not helped by the arrival of a new Caesar: the dictator's young grand-nephew, Octavian, named as heir in his will. He had been a non-entity before the Ides but since taking on the name of Caesar – and becoming the 'son of a god' in the bargain – he had undergone quite a transformation. Between Octavian, Antony, and Caesar's angry soldiers, Rome seemed less welcoming by the day.

As Pompey had done five years earlier, Brutus concluded that the best course of action was a tactical retreat to the rich provinces of the East. In the old kingdom of Macedonia and the spectacular cities of Asia, his ancient name would still be respected. There he could amass his own legions and even have a guilty taste of that awesome power Caesar had enjoyed. With his mighty armies he could march on Rome and re-establish the Republic. Perhaps finally make his ancestor, Lucius, proud. But armies required soldiers, and soldiers needed paying. Brutus would need to start striking coins.

Cap and Dagger

Things worked differently in the East. As soon as a Roman crossed the Adriatic Sea, the rulebook of the Republic, with its strict codes and traditions, often seemed to get misplaced. Macedonia, Asia, Bithynia – these were vast and ancient lands where Roman rule was young. The word 'king' need not be whispered here; the people were used to crowns. A tapestry of kingdoms had been left behind in the wake of Alexander's conquests, gradually absorbed into the expanding Republic. Where Rome did not rule directly, she allowed tame client-kings to do the job for her, though the magistrates sent to govern these Eastern provinces had a habit of fleecing them for all they were worth. Brutus himself had been embroiled in such a scandal just a few years before, when during a posting in Cyprus he had been caught lending money at four times the going interest rate – the stink of the extortion uncovered by none other than the Republic's greatest legal mind, Cicero himself.[18] Now Brutus was back, and on the make again.

With their newfound tyrant-killing fame, Brutus and Cassius criss-crossed the province of Asia amassing money and men. They had been delighted by updates from Rome describing how the heirs of Caesar were busy squabbling among themselves. With Antony and the young Octavian locked in a power struggle, the Senate had looked to the Liberators to unite the Republican cause. Fortune finally seemed to be smiling on the assassins. Then, one day in late 43 BC, news arrived of an unthinkable event in politics: two rivals had agreed to put aside their differences. At a secret summit, Antony and Octavian had shaken hands and formed a new alliance. Their combined forces were massive, and they were coming after the assassins. As an added insult, they had rammed through new legislation that retroactively outlawed the killing of any dictator. Brutus and Cassius were now criminals.[19]

The Liberators needed to mount a defence. How could they quickly remind their armies of the nobility of their aims? How could they explain their actions to people across the Roman world, reigniting in them the Republican fire? Brutus knew of only one way. He had already deployed the unique power of coins to help make his name during his stint as moneyer; on those silver denarii he had celebrated the cause of liberty and the bearded face of his revolutionary namesake who loomed so large over his upbringing. Now it was time to step out of his shadow. Being far away from the workshops of the Roman mint on the Capitoline Hill, the coins of Brutus would be struck by a travelling mint moving with his forces through Asia Minor and northern Greece. They would follow standard Roman denominations closely – with a denarius comprising four grams of pure silver – sending the message that these were the official coins of the true Republic.

The dictator's violent death was in answer to many wrongs, but one of his acts that had most shocked the sensibilities of Rome was daring to place his portrait on a coin in his own lifetime. Why, just two years later, the leading face of the assassins would choose to do the very same is a question that has intrigued historians for centuries. Had so much changed in that short time? Evidently it had. In the turmoil of the dying Republic, people united less behind ideas and more around strongmen and their cults of personality. Values, principles, even the gods, could only get you so far; besides, these were men who increasingly seemed to hold the power of gods. It was also a question of intended audience: here in the East, mortal men had been vainly striking their faces on coins for centuries. If Brutus was to truly unite these provinces behind him, they would expect to look on the man they were to follow into the fray.

A thrilling aspect of many coins from this era is that they often give us our only verified look at the face of a legend. Museum galleries are filled with broken busts hopefully identified as some titan of history; but coins, quite literally, put a face to the name. So it was with Caesar, so it is here also with his assassin.

In Shakespeare's timeless play, Caesar warns of the dangers posed by men with a 'lean and hungry look' – he could almost be describing the face of Brutus that we see here stamped in silver.[20] He was clearly once a handsome man; now in his forties and with the weight of the Roman world on his shoulders, he appears drawn. The die engraver has even included a growth of beard, a small but revealing detail. Beards carried several symbolic associations, evoking portraits of the wise philosophers of Greece and the stern elder statesmen of the old Republic. In this sense, Brutus may have been trying to further resemble his legendary bearded ancestor. But the growth of facial

The face of the tyrannicide, Marcus Junius Brutus.

hair also carried with it a performative element: in a tradition that persists today, beards were grown by those in mourning after a tragic loss. Those accused of a crime might also ensure they were unshaven in court, hoping to elicit pity by their wretchedness. We might discern a combination of these motives in the Brutus we meet here: both mourning the loss of his beloved Republic and, for good measure, being wrongfully accused of her murder.

As riveting as it is to meditate on the face of Caesar's killer, it is the reverse of Brutus' coin that made it so instantly recognisable that even ancient authors took time to describe its design. Well over two centuries after it was struck, the historian Cassius Dio remembered its motifs vividly; no doubt the infamous coin could still be viewed in state archives and the collections of contemporary coin enthusiasts. Dio wrote that Brutus not only stamped on the coin 'his own likeness' but also 'a cap and two daggers, indicating that he and Cassius had liberated the fatherland'.[21] We are indeed presented with a pair of military-style *pugio* daggers, evidently the type wielded by the assassins on the Ides of March. The daggers are even differentiated by the designs of their hilts, possibly representing the distinctive blades of Brutus and Cassius themselves. That the coin was minted, first and foremost, to pay the armies of the assassins, would have also

The daggers of the assassins shown with a cap of liberty.

influenced its notorious design. The denarius speaks a visual language easily understood by military men; of course, every soldier who held it would have also had a pugio dagger – the standard Roman legionary sidearm – slung at their hip (Plate section, 3). With these two blades, Brutus and Cassius had slain a tyrant but that was only the beginning of the great battle for liberty. Clearly, it was now down to each and every one of their troops to use their own blades in finishing the fight.[22]

If the daggers provide the weapon, the object they flank provides the motive. Between them sits a *pileus* cap, a felt hat ceremonially placed on the heads of those being freed from slavery; an abiding symbol of Libertas carried by the goddess of freedom herself on her coin depictions. The assassination was therefore to be perceived as a ritual act, placing this cap of freedom on the head of an enslaved Republic. The cap and daggers explain the actions of the assassins in the most clear and elemental terms; the only way to achieve one was by the other. Beneath this enigmatic still-life, Brutus could have clarified his message or inspired the viewer with a slogan of freedom. Instead, the coin's inscription simply proclaims the fateful day and assumes viewers will draw the necessary conclusions: 'Eidibus Martiis' – 'On the Ides of March'. As with various 'Revolution Days' still marked by nations around the world, the Ides had apparently become, to Brutus at least, a byword for liberty won by the violent overthrow of tyranny.

Like the greatest artistic masterpieces, the coin has drawn different interpretations from audiences since the day it was struck in 42 BC. Viewers are still trying to decide whether the Mona Lisa is smiling or not, after all. Does the 'cap and dagger' denarius represent the desperate justifications of traitors with their backs against the wall? Or is the coin a memorial to the never-ending battle for freedom across time? Perhaps those daggers are a warning to tyrants in every era, what awaits them when they seek to stifle the human spirit. Whether the coin is, in the end, a solemn commemoration of the day's events, or an exuberant celebration of them, is not clearly defined. Brutus leaves it all to us to decide.

In a final irony, Brutus was not done with the dagger he shows us here. He would soon need to use it one last time.

Sic Semper Tyrannis

At the graphic culmination of Dante's *Inferno* (1320), the poet descends into the Ninth Circle of Hell – the realm of Treachery – where he finally meets the Devil himself. Dante's Satan is a giant three-faced demon, trapped forever in a frozen lake. The monster is unable to speak as his mouths are otherwise occupied, endlessly devouring the three most terrible traitors in history: Judas, Brutus, and Cassius.[23]

A couple of centuries later, Shakespeare concludes his play *Julius Caesar* (1599) with a moving description of Brutus as 'the noblest Roman of them all', the only conspirator motivated not by 'envy of great Caesar' but by the 'common good'.[24] Dante and Shakespeare, writing at either end of the Renaissance, disagree so profoundly on what Brutus represents, any attempt to reach a consensus today might seem an impossible task. For some he will always be the arch-traitor, next only to Judas Iscariot as the ultimate embodiment of betrayal. For others he personifies the unending struggle for freedom and democracy throughout the ages. To say that, since his last stand on the plains of northern Greece in October 42 BC, Brutus has remained a controversial figure, is perhaps an understatement.

When the forces of the Liberators met those of Antony and Octavian at Philippi, the result was one of the bloodiest single battles in all of history. Pitting Roman against Roman, estimates suggest up to 200,000 troops fought to decide the future of the ancient world. Cassius fell first but Brutus carried on a spirited defence. In the end, he too was surrounded. Brutus resolved to die like a Roman of old, running himself through with the same pugio dagger he had used against Caesar on the Ides of March.[25] Even the enemies of Brutus were split on how he should be remembered; while Antony ordered his body wrapped in his finest purple cloak, Octavian demanded his head be cut off and sent to Rome to be thrown at the foot of Caesar's statue. In the end, the wishes of Antony prevailed and, following a respectful cremation, the ashes of Brutus were carried back to his devastated mother in Rome.[26]

Nineteen hundred years later, Ford's Theatre in Washington, DC was packed for the evening's performance. The audience had been enjoying a popular comedy, until the final act when their laughter was halted by the crack of a pistol shot. In the presidential box, Abraham Lincoln slumped forward in a cloud of gun smoke. His assassin dropped his small Deringer pistol and instead drew a dagger before leaping to the stage – being an actor, this was where John Wilkes Booth felt most at home. Before the shocked crowd he raised the dagger theatrically above his head and cried out in Latin: '*Sic semper tyrannis!*' – 'Thus always to tyrants!'

Though no ancient sources directly attribute it, the phrase was long associated with Brutus, imagined into his mouth as he stood over the body of the dictator. The dramatics of Caesar's killing were at the forefront of Booth's mind, having staged a version of Shakespeare's *Julius Caesar* with his thespian family just a few months earlier. Indeed, his own father, the famous English stage actor Junius Brutus Booth, was even named after the tyrannicide. Like Caesar, Lincoln had been troubled in the days before his assassination by premonitions of his own demise, dreaming of attending his own funeral wake at the White House.[27] Lincoln's death had likewise been brought about by a large band of 'conspirators' led by a figurehead convinced he was carrying out a patriotic service on behalf of his nation. Booth's Latin rallying cry was also closely entwined with American independence, becoming in 1776 – and remaining today – the state motto of Virginia. Since then, the slogan, and by extension the identity of Brutus himself, has been co-opted by radicals and revolutionaries in many forms – invoked by protesters, rebels, even by terrorist bombers in the hope of galvanising people behind their cause.[28]

Owning a 'cap and dagger' coin of Brutus is a dream for many coin collectors today but only the wealthiest aspire to make the dream a reality. While not excessively rare – around a hundred examples are currently known to survive – the sheer historical magnitude of the coin means it usually achieves a six-figure sum at auction.[29] The story of the Ides of March evidently enthrals more than ever, but it should always be treated as a cautionary tale. For all the self-congratulating imagery we see on this denarius, it could be argued that those two daggers of Brutus and Cassius brought about the death of the Republic more effectively than Caesar himself. Killing the dictator turned him into a god and his name into a hereditary title. The power vacuum left behind would soon be filled by ruthless men who respected the values of the Republic less than Caesar ever did. It would lead to fifteen further years of cataclysmic civil war, at the end of which the last man standing would be crowned the first Roman emperor.

The Republic, which had lasted 482 years and made Rome the capital of the world, would thereafter be just a memory – a half-remembered dream, recalled only in the minds of honourable men.

Chapter V
PAX

'There was peace after all this, no doubt, but it was a peace stained with blood.'

Tacitus

Denarius of Octavian/Augustus showing the goddess Pax (Peace), *c.*29 BC.
Obverse: Bare head of Octavian, soon to be renamed Augustus.
Reverse: Pax holding olive branch and cornucopia, CAESAR DIVI F.
'Divi Filius' – 'Son of a God'.

The Julian Star

The messenger's breathless arrival proclaimed urgent news from Rome – so much for a peaceful afternoon of study. The letter was dated to the Ides, its ink already ten days dry. Bad news may travel fast, but in the ancient world even the gravest reports were limited to the speed of a galloping horse or a ship's billowing sail.[1] Word of bloody deeds radiated from Italy like a shockwave across the Mediterranean and with this letter it shook the sleepy Illyrian shores of Apollonia (in modern Albania). Here all eyes turned to its recipient: a bright but sickly young aristocrat completing his education in the city. The first eighteen years in the life of Gaius Octavius had been largely unremarkable, apart from the obvious fact that the titan Julius Caesar was his great-uncle. Or rather, had been. As the hastily penned words of his panicked mother revealed, the mighty Caesar was no more, cut down by the daggers of countless assassins.[2]

Not one for rash action, Octavius carefully weighed the advice of his inner circle. Most trusted among the voices were those of his two closest friends accompanying him in Apollonia, the rugged Agrippa and the refined Maecenas. Some counselled caution: after all, what could an untested teenager like Octavius hope to achieve by throwing himself into the snake pit that was Rome? Others, like Agrippa, urged that he take up his great-uncle's legions and strike at once against the assassins. Octavius chose the middle way, already embodying the approach of what would become his favourite motto, '*Festina lente*' – 'Make haste, slowly'.[3]

Crossing the choppy Adriatic in a small boat, Octavius landed quietly at a town on Italy's boot heel. There he learned from locals the full scale of the treachery in Rome. Some had even been in the Forum to witness Caesar's fiery funeral; and from them Octavius heard for the first time the contents of Caesar's will, read aloud by Mark Antony with so much stagecraft it had incited a riot. They revealed that it was Octavius, not Antony, whom Caesar had named as heir to his titles and fortune. In that instant, the course of his young life, and that of the entire ancient world, was forever changed.[4]

As Caesar's newly adopted son, he stood to inherit the dictator's wealth, network of allegiances, and most crucially, the loyalty of his troops. Yet Octavius saw that perhaps his most potent inheritance was a name. When he cautiously entered Rome that spring, he did so as Gaius Julius Caesar Octavianus. The assassins surely despaired – they had barely wiped the blood from their daggers and already there was a new Caesar in town.

The power players in Rome underestimated the adopted Caesar – or 'Octavian' as he became known to history – from the very start. The statesman Cicero remarked in his letters that despite his 'impressive natural qualities', it should be easy to 'keep him in line'. Continuing with trademark smugness, 'the boy is convinced – and I may have done some of the convincing – that he is the one who will save us'.[5] The strongman Mark Antony was similarly contemptuous of the teenager, dismissing him as a mere 'boy who owes everything to a name'.[6] As executor of Caesar's will, Antony held the pursestrings on the sizeable inheritance due to Octavian – and he was understandably in no hurry to pay up. Octavian instead borrowed the huge sums needed to pay Caesar's indignant troops, and in doing so, not only secured the loyalty of the legions but cast himself as the noble heir fighting to defend Caesar's legacy against corrupt forces. As ardent 'Caesarians' rallied to the dictator's fresh-faced namesake, Antony saw that this 'boy' might have just outmanoeuvred him.

Like his great-uncle, Octavian knew an opportunity when he saw one. When, in late July, a blazing comet appeared in the sky over Rome, he could hardly have believed his luck. Never mind that comets were usually seen as evil omens that struck the ancients with dread; this fiery spectacle had appeared during Caesar's birth month as games were being held in his memory: clearly it was the soul of the divine Caesar taking his rightful place among the immortal gods. The Sidus Iulium or 'Julian Star' is said to have shone for a whole week, burning so brightly it was visible even by day. While some historians have dismissed the appearance of Caesar's comet as fantastical propaganda, many such cometary outbursts have been studied in the last century, most recently Comet Hale-Bopp which made its closest approach to Earth in 1997, and Comet Holmes which underwent history's largest recorded outburst in October 2007. In recent years, a comet matching the Julian Star (today known by the snappy designation C/-43 K1) has even been identified in the detailed astronomical records kept by Han China, where at magnitude -4 it shone as brightly as Venus in that very summer of 44 BC.

Octavian quickly co-opted the auspicious omen, encouraging its celebration in literature, art, and coinage. After all, if the gods had welcomed Caesar with such a dazzling display, surely they also favoured his son and heir. The great poet Virgil, writing soon after, would portray Caesar's comet as herald of a new age of fertility and prosperity, 'by which the fields ripen with wheat, and the grape deepens its colour on the sunny hills'. Ovid would also vividly describe Caesar's ancestral goddess Venus carrying his soul to the heavens until 'she felt it glow and take fire, and loosed it from her breast' where it 'climbed higher than the moon, drawing behind it a fiery tail'.[7]

A Julian Star was soon added to a statue of Caesar raised in the Forum at the place of his funeral pyre.[8] In subsequent decades, a Temple of the Deified Julius Caesar would be built on this spot, its pediment adorned with an enormous gilded representation of the star – so prominent, it was labelled by Pliny as the only temple in the world where people apparently worship a comet.

The heavenly symbol was eventually venerated across the Roman world on a coin, struck by an all-powerful Octavian in his later incarnation as ruler of an empire. The denarius shows the flaming Julian Star, blazing with eight shining rays. Its simple inscription, brilliantly emphasised by the explosive composition, leaves no doubt as to the meaning of the comet – 'Divus Julius'. That Caesar had become a 'god' was impossible to question in the face of such a celestial sign, here recreated for every single Roman to see.

For all the talk of Caesar's soul, the shining star was just as much a manifestation of the young Octavian, the new Caesar, the guiding light destined to save the Republic. Some speculated that Octavian secretly believed the omen was meant for himself all along. With

The Sidus Iulium (Julian Star) shown on a denarius of Octavian/Augustus, 19 BC.

every elevation of Caesar's memory, he of course elevated himself. As Shakespeare would later observe: 'When beggars die there are no comets seen. The heavens themselves blaze forth the death of princes.'[9] With his adopted father sitting safely among the gods, the question was: what did that make Octavian? The answer came in his newly proclaimed title, 'Divi Filius', sure to be of help as he consolidated his position in Rome and planned bloody vengeance against Caesar's assassins. He was barely twenty years old, but his rivals were now up against the 'son of a god'.

Last of the Pharaohs

The peace between them was grudging, but it allowed Antony and Octavian to combine their forces and crush the assassins on the Greek plain of Philippi. Antony took the lead as commander, not least because Octavian was bedridden with illness on the day of the battle. Throughout his life, Octavian would struggle with a weak constitution and bouts of illness after exertion; some have suggested that, like Caesar, he may have suffered from the 'falling sickness' which today we understand as epileptic seizures, or possibly even depressive episodes brought on by stress.

With both Brutus and Cassius run through with their own blades, the debts of the Ides were mostly repaid. Their goal achieved, Antony and Octavian again looked uneasily to each other. A proposal was made in the hope of strengthening their fragile alliance and avoiding another civil war. Just as Caesar had offered Pompey his daughter's hand in marriage to bolster their partnership, so Octavian would offer Antony his sister, Octavia. The fact that she was currently pregnant with her previous husband's child was no obstacle. It would not be the only time that Octavian would dictate the lives of women in the Julian house, deploying them like chess pieces in the game of Roman politics.

Their coalition secured for now, the Roman world was free to carve up as Antony and Octavian chose. Antony would be master of the East, enjoying the decadent delights of rich cities like Ephesus, while also dusting off Caesar's plans for a glorious invasion of Parthia. Octavian would meanwhile remain in Rome to manage the less glamorous provinces of the West. As Antony chased military glory, Octavian learned the essentials of governing an empire: resettling veterans, rebuilding cities, and putting down rebellions. In the event, Antony's campaign descended into debacle, as have so many incursions into those vast and unforgiving lands, before and since. With his supply train overstretched and his legions struck by disease, he was forced into an embarrassing retreat. Octavian's reluctance to send money and reinforcements had not helped matters. Instead, Antony had been financed by the considerable wealth of an old flame in Alexandria. Defeat would soon send him wholeheartedly back to her arms.

In 35 BC, Octavian's sister returned to Rome, humiliated. Her marriage to Antony had been a political arrangement, but she had proved a loyal and devoted wife to the wayward general. In return, he had abandoned her to take up with the Egyptian queen Cleopatra in Alexandria. A virtuous Roman matron, cast out in favour of a suspicious foreign queen – the people of Rome were appalled. Even more so after Octavian took to the speaker's platform in the Forum to denounce Antony publicly. Clearly, he had been 'drugged' and was 'no longer master of himself'.[10] Naturally, he failed to mention that this was the second Roman general to 'go native' in Egypt and fall for Cleopatra; embarrassingly, Octavian's divine adoptive father had also been ensnared by her charms.

The climax of Octavian's propaganda assault came when he demanded a public reading of Antony's will, deposited in the sacred temple of the Vestal Virgins. Even those who despised Antony saw this for the sacrilegious act that it was, questioning if 'a man should be called to account while alive for what he wished to have done after his death'.[11] Undeterred, Octavian assembled the Senate and reeled off the document's private instructions, each more outrageous than the last: the children Antony had fathered with the queen were to be named heirs; and wherever he died, Antony wished for his body to be buried in Egypt with Cleopatra. Proof, Octavian claimed, that he had been 'bewitched by the accursed woman', taken on 'barbaric customs', and no longer honoured 'his father's gods'.[12] Octavian's ultimate demand was clear yet cunning: henceforth 'let no one count him a Roman, but rather an Egyptian'. Antony was promptly declared an enemy of the state – but if he was no Roman, then the coming conflict was no civil war. Octavian was also careful to declare war solely against Cleopatra, and not her spellbound lover. This would be a battle fought with propaganda as much as clashing swords, and Octavian was winning it before it had even begun.

The allure of Cleopatra, Queen of the Nile, has lost none of its lustre over millennia. For many, her name instantly conjures golden images of Egyptian extravagance, hedonistic pleasures, and in all likelihood, the timeless beauty of Elizabeth Taylor. Her reputation veers from that of seductive femme fatale whose charms entranced multiple Roman leaders, all the way to feminist heroine who, for decades, held her own against the most powerful men in the ancient world. So concerted was the Roman propaganda effort against the queen and her ancient realm, it still shapes perceptions of Cleopatra today: the exotic temptress and very embodiment of Egyptian decadence. Satirical depictions of Antony and Cleopatra's debauched escapades amid fantastical Nilotic landscapes soon became an entire artistic subgenre. A marble relief in the British Museum shows caricatures of the couple enjoying erotic pleasures on their Nile barge, while the helmsman steers the boat round the river's hippopotami. On Octavian's instigation, Egypt was depicted as an absurd, degenerate wonderland, under the sway of a sorceress queen who bewitched any Roman commander who strayed into her lair.

As intended, the human face of Cleopatra was soon lost in the onslaught. Though she was born in Egypt, the queen actually traced her origins to Macedonian Greece – the last of her Ptolemaic dynasty that ruled in the wake of Alexander's conquests. During her youth in Alexandria she was tutored by the Greek philosopher Philostratus, and she displayed her formidable intellect by becoming the only member of her family to also learn the Egyptian tongue. The Ptolemies maintained the 'purity' of their bloodline through intermarriage and Cleopatra followed the tradition with marriages to both of her younger brothers. Modern pop-culture depictions of Cleopatra would likely meet Octavian's approval, focusing less as they do on the shrewd political player, well versed in mathematics, history, and astronomy, and instead relegating her to an ancient beauty icon.

We can judge for ourselves Cleopatra's beauty on coin portraits of her and Antony, struck as the renegade regents in the East prepared for a final clash with Octavian. Silver tetradrachms showing the couple were minted in Antioch for circulation in the eastern Mediterranean, yet surprisingly their faces also appear on Roman denarii more associated with Antony's estranged homeland. Portraits of the lovers take up both sides of the denarius equally, demonstrating an egalitarianism in their relationship that would be quite alien to the Roman viewer, and surely confirming in their mind allegations that Antony had been enslaved and emasculated by his Egyptian mistress.[13]

Antony is portrayed as the rugged Roman commander with a strong jaw and striking aquiline features. We may expect his rough-hewn profile to be contrasted on the other side of the coin by the delicate aspect of his beloved queen; yet, as we see, Cleopatra is presented as no classical beauty. Coin portraits of living women on Roman coinage were still a rarity and female faces usually came with

Tragic lovers: the faces of Mark Antony and Cleopatra,
on a denarius struck in 34 BC.

the soft, graceful lines and otherworldly expression of a goddess. Cleopatra, however, is shown with a vigorous stare every bit the equal of her partner.

Though Cleopatra met Caesar and his general Antony when she was just twenty-one, this coin shows an older queen now in her late thirties. Just as the couple shared in all things, the die engraver has gifted Cleopatra with the same hooked nose, protruding chin, and low forehead as her husband. While this trend of echoing features of a male ruler in the face of his consort would be a continuing one in Roman art, it does seem from wider sources that Cleopatra's undeniable appeal stemmed less from her looks and more from her personal charisma and intelligence. Plutarch states that while her physical beauty was not immediately striking, the 'peculiar force of character in her every word and action made the charm of her presence irresistible'.[14] Such self-confidence from a female ruler primed many in the Roman establishment for instant dislike. In his letters, Cicero, who had met Cleopatra when she accompanied Caesar to Rome in 46 BC, made it clear that he despised 'the insolent Queen'. This denarius would certainly not have helped matters, with its legend proclaiming her 'Regina Regum', 'Queen of Kings' – proof for the Roman on the street that the ambitious queen had unmanned one of their finest leaders and now presented herself as the senior partner.

The fate of the tragic lovers and that of the classical world would be decided at sea. In September 31 BC, Antony and Cleopatra were finally cornered by the forces of Octavian and his steadfast general Agrippa at the Greek promontory of Actium. Antony lined up his forces at the mouth of the gulf with Cleopatra's vessels nestled behind. As battle commenced, their lumbering warships were soon swamped by Octavian's smaller, more agile galleys. Yet the most painful blow for Antony came not in the enemy onslaught, but in the sight that followed. Commotion in the rear, sails being unfurled. To his disbelief, Cleopatra's vessels ploughed through the ongoing battle and disappeared on the open sea. His lover had abandoned him. An inconsolable Antony took off after Cleopatra, and, left without its commander, his fleet at Actium was quickly destroyed.

Octavian pursued the couple relentlessly, eventually besieging them back in the Egyptian capital of Alexandria. In a tragic denouement that needed little embellishment by Shakespeare, Antony fell on his sword after hearing a false report that Cleopatra had already done the same. Learning she was still alive and hiding in their pre-prepared tomb monument, he clung to life long enough to be borne to her. There, after one last drink of wine, he died in his lover's arms. Octavian would make every effort to bring Cleopatra back to Rome alive, imagining the glorious spectacle she might make paraded in gold chains at his inevitable triumph. The queen – wily to the end – would deny him the pleasure. Arranging for a deadly asp to be smuggled into the place of her captivity, she held the snake to her skin and accepted its lethal venom. Her dying wish was to be buried with her greatest love, Antony, which Octavian grudgingly allowed. In the end, he could not help but admire her spirit.

With Cleopatra died the line of pharaohs that had ruled Egypt for over 3,000 years. Finally, there was no one left to fight; after two decades of near-continuous civil war, Octavian stood alone as the sole ruler of the Roman world. His divine father had once been in the same lofty position – but before long, assassins had been unsheathing their daggers. Octavian would ensure he did not meet the same fate. He would need to become more than a man, but he knew better than to declare himself a god. Avenging Caesar and eradicating all rivals had also left his hands stained with noble Roman blood. Only with a new name and form could he rightly be revered as the sacred saviour of the Republic. Nothing less than a reincarnation was needed.

Revered One

The senators could hardly believe what they were hearing. Octavian had entered the hall that day in January 27 BC as uncontested master of the world, sure to be voted all manner of excessive honours. Now he stood before them calmly explaining how, having delivered the Republic from evil, he was handing it safely back to the Senate and people of Rome. In his bombshell speech, a version of which is preserved in full by a later Roman historian, Octavian lamented that destiny had called on him at such a young age to save his homeland. Now, having avenged Caesar and freed his country from the grip of his murderers, let no one claim he did it to win absolute power: 'I shall lead you no longer,' Octavian announced. 'I resign my offices completely and restore to you everything you committed to me. Receive back your liberty, and your Republic.'[15]

Octavian's feigned retirement was a masterclass in political manipulation. Even as he spoke, some senators cried out begging he reconsider. Others remained silently suspicious of his words, but all marvelled equally – either at his generosity, or his cunning. As he relinquished control of 'the army, the laws, and the provinces', a compromise was proposed. The Senate urged him to, at least, accept the honour of a new name, a sacred title worthy of the Republic's saviour. The initial suggestion was 'Romulus', casting him as a second founder of Rome, but its regal associations were far too blatant. Another distinctive epithet was soon settled on that evoked all the necessary qualities. Like the hallowed art of augury that foretold the future in the flight of birds, and the augural priests who communed with the heavens, he would be 'Augustus'. Loosely translating as 'Revered One', the venerable Augustus would be sacrosanct and inviolable. More than a man, but by no means a monarch.

Having showcased his virtue by voluntarily renouncing his power, Augustus could now in good conscience have it gifted back to him by a fawning Senate. He refused to govern all provinces but reluctantly agreed to take responsibility for those that were the most precarious: lands like Gaul, Spain, and the newly acquired jewel of Egypt. Some observed the convenient fact that these provinces were the most heavily garrisoned by loyal legions, but Augustus insisted that he merely wanted the Senate to enjoy the most peaceful portions of the Empire. Further adamant that his position not be seen as any perpetual dictatorship, the unparalleled power – or imperium – of Augustus would only be granted in ten-year periods. That it would then be promptly renewed for another decade was beside the point – all that mattered was that the appearance of representative government had been retained. Where Caesar had trampled over the constitution as 'Dictator for Life', Augustus subtly blended his sovereignty into the workings of the state in a manner tolerable to proud senators.

Along with his new name came the title *princeps* designating him the 'first among equals'. While he technically held no more official power than the next man, he paradoxically remained 'above all in authority'. Augustus needed no tarnished title like 'rex' or 'dictator' for his will to be done; the moral and spiritual obligation of his great deeds would be enough. He would be untouchable, but just in case anyone thought of recreating the Ides of March, his newly formalised bodyguard would allow him to 'live in security and suffer no harm'. His handpicked Praetorian Guard would be fiercely loyal to him alone – helped no doubt by his revealing first decree which awarded them double the pay of a normal legionary.

In the creation of Augustus, Rome revelled in a comforting lie. Her people were exhausted. The past century's destructive cycle of civil war had left their families and farms destroyed. If the paternal hand of Augustus offered a return to order, then so be it. As long as consuls still swore oaths of office each new year, and the Senate still met for its boisterous assemblies, all could convince themselves Augustus had saved the Republic rather than dissolved it.

A spectacular Roman cameo, today held in Vienna's Kunsthistorisches Museum, most likely commemorates these honours bestowed on Augustus in January 27 BC (Plate section, 4). Cut by a master engraver exploiting the natural colours of the layered onyx, the cameo shows a majestic eagle spreading its wings. As the messenger of Jupiter, the eagle would hereafter represent the might of the Imperium Romanum – what we today recognise as the Roman 'Empire'.

In one talon, the eagle grasps a palm branch as a symbol of victory, while in the other it holds an oak wreath. This *corona civica* or 'civic crown' was another honour awarded Augustus, granted only to a Roman who had saved the lives of his fellow citizens. This crown of oak leaves would hang above the entrance of the house of Augustus on the Palatine, a permanent reminder that he had rescued not just one citizen, but the entire Roman world.[16]

The evolution of Augustus' coin portraiture perfectly illustrates his journey from boyish obscurity to heroic, ageless demigod. On a denarius from my collection, struck soon after his defeat of Antony and Cleopatra at Actium, Octavian is shown in his early thirties on the cusp of absolute power (Plate section, 5). His hair, which we are told was 'inclined to golden', lies ruffled and un-styled with little sign of vanity. The 'Roman nose' also described by Suetonius, with its small hump on the bridge, is present and correct.[17] A slender neck with pronounced Adam's apple and delicate chin remind us of his fragile constitution, no match for the physical toughness of enemies like Antony. Even so, his 'clear and bright eyes held a kind of divine power', and while the coin gives one of the last glimpses of Octavian the man, there is something in the wide-eyed stare that hints at his coming elevation to a higher plane of existence.

The human face of Octavian on coins would be gently classicised in his reincarnation as Augustus, a stronger jawline and fuller features adding a touch of the hero to the individual seen on the earlier denarius. Embarking on his lengthy reign as Rome's first emperor, the stability of his leadership would be reflected in the stolid permanence of his public image. Throughout his extraordinary forty years as ruler, the portrait of Augustus would stay virtually unchanged. Even as he neared the end of his life at the impressive age of seventy-five, the Augustan profile stamped into his coins remained all but indistinguishable from the young man on this denarius. This timeless visage of the emperor essentially presents his accession as an 'end of history' event. Having ushered in a tranquil golden age, Augustus would be frozen forever at the moment of his greatest triumph.

The immutable image of Augustus would soon be omnipresent across the Roman world, not just on coinage, but in the busts and statues that seemingly watched over the citizens of every city. Today, over 250 sculptural portraits of Augustus survive in museums around the globe, more than any other figure from the ancient world.[18] The strict uniformity of his likeness across all media suggests that portraits were meticulously copied from a state-approved original. The agreed-upon features of the emperor's public face are indeed so systematic, experts have carefully mapped the exact placement of each lock of hair. Even a newcomer to ancient art will soon be familiar with his curled sideburns and distinctive forked fringe swept to the right of his forehead – details already present in the portrait on this coin. While we know little about their process, it seems logical to assume that die engravers in the Roman mint worked from an authorised imperial portrait bust placed in their workshop, at least until they had committed every detail of the emperor's profile to memory.

The denarius not only presents us with the ubiquitous face of the Revered One; turning over the coin we are shown the somewhat surprising manifesto of his coming reign. Celebrated on the reverse is a goddess who was probably unfamiliar to many ancient viewers – it was the first time she had been venerated on Roman coinage.[19] As they beheld her, Romans may have spared a wistful thought for their ancient Republic that – despite the onslaught of propaganda celebrating its salvation – most now recognised was lost. It had once promised them liberty, but few could remember it delivering anything but chaos and destruction. Granted, they now lived under an 'Empire', but at least it was an empire at peace.

The Altar of Peace

'Peace is the best thing that man may know; peace alone is better than a thousand triumphs.' The simple affirmation of a first-century Roman poet echoes the fundamental shift in worldview that came with the age of Augustus.[20] Since the founding of the city, conquest had been seen as a noble end in itself: a vital outlet for the ambitions of great men, unifying the people against barbarian outsiders. As the sons and daughters of Mars, Romans had, since the birth of their city, defined themselves by their martial prowess and ability to overcome any foe. No surprise then that the helmeted god of war had been a mainstay on Roman coinage throughout the Republic's rise. But as worthy opponents became fewer in number, the insatiable need for military glory could only turn Rome's commanders against each other. A century of internal chaos and bloodshed had been the result. War would always be Rome's vocation – it had won her an empire and would help her defend it – but it would now be in service of a higher goal.

The reverse of the denarius gives us our first declaration of peace throughout the Roman world. With all enemies subdued, the goddess Pax reigns supreme. As we might expect, she quite literally extends to us an olive branch, signifying an end to all hostilities. For centuries, the resilient and seemingly immortal olive tree had been associated with the prosperity of peaceful times. Greek foundation myths tell of Athena planting the world's first olive tree on the Acropolis and being granted possession of the city in thanks for her bountiful gift to the world. As emblem of cooperation and accord, an olive sprig also accompanied the owl of Athens on the city's iconic tetradrachms struck from the sixth century BC onwards.

In her other arm, Pax holds a cornucopia or 'horn of plenty', overflowing with the fruits of peace. If war-weary Romans needed any persuading as to the benefits of peacetime living, it came here in the promise of its associated abundance and prosperity. With Rome's infighting over, citizens and soldiers could return to the land and the pastoral existence celebrated by poets like Hesiod and Virgil. On their fertile farms, unmolested by hungry legions, they would enjoy many a plentiful harvest. The symbol of the cornucopia would later be used to advertise the great abundance awaiting settlers in the New World, and to this day it remains a common decoration on the American Thanksgiving dinner table.

Romans understood the harsh reality that peace was by no means

The goddess Pax offering her olive branch for the first time on Roman coinage.

the default state of nature in the ancient world. As the Greek philosopher Plato had concluded centuries earlier, 'peace' was merely the name for the short armistice in the 'perpetual war between nations'.[21] Our enlightened revulsion at the very thought of invading the territory of our neighbours would appear quite strange to most ancient cultures, whose borders were constantly contested and to whom melting snows signalled the 'campaigning season' just as much as they did the coming of spring. If the last century had taught Rome anything, it was that peace was hard won and only maintained with force. As Augustus himself observed, his was a 'peace secured by victories'.[22] The vast lands of his unified Empire stretched from dank Germanic forests all the way to the Saharan sands of modern Sudan, and close to thirty professional legions would be kept busy defending its borders. This would be an internal peace, ensured by barbarian blood spilled at the fringes of the world.

Oxymoronic notions of a bloody peace are perhaps best explained in the root of the word 'pax' itself, deriving from the verb *pacisci*, used to describe the forming of a pact or treaty upon acceptance of an enemy's surrender. In this sense, the concept of pax may be better translated in another linguistic descendant, 'pacification'. Pax was therefore less an idyllic life free from war, and more the reward of a war fought well – the total submission of the enemy to Roman superiority.[23]

The goddess Pax now took a prominent position in the Roman pantheon, completing a new triumvirate with the deities Mars and Victory. All three would feature heavily in Augustan art and coinage, a trinity that revealed the essential reckoning behind the emperor's rule: war inevitably led to victory, which in turn secured peace. Just as this denarius represents a 'Mission Accomplished' moment for Rome's new sole ruler, at around the same time it was minted, a heavily symbolic public event also announced to the Roman people that their wars were done. The Temple of Janus was a small but important Roman temple that stood at the northern edge of the Forum. By ancient tradition, its doors were kept shut in times of peace and open in times of war. Romans were therefore used to seeing the gates left open – and inside, the statue of Janus, god of transitions and new beginnings. In fact, Livy records that in seven centuries since the reign of King Numa, the gates were only briefly closed a single time, in the aftermath of the First Punic War. Now with great ceremony, Augustus was granted permission by the Senate to close the doors of the shrine, pronouncing peace 'throughout the whole domain of the Roman people on land and sea'.[24]

The veneration of Pax culminated in 9 BC, with the consecration of a monumental altar dedicated to the goddess. The Ara Pacis Augustae or 'Altar of Augustan Peace' was constructed, with intentional irony, on the Field of Mars – the large plain in the north of the city where Rome's citizen-soldiers once mustered before setting out to war. The Ara Pacis has today been fully reconstructed from surviving marble fragments, guided in part by its depiction on bronze coins struck by the successors of Augustus. An enormous sacrificial podium surrounded on all sides by a lavishly decorated marble screen, the Ara Pacis is a tour de force of Augustan art. Its intricate friezes – originally vibrantly painted – celebrate the fertility and abundance of a world at peace, with spiralling plants, blossoming flowers, and weighty garlands of fruits.

Mythological scenes of the founding of Rome dominate the front and back of the altar, along with a panel depicting a seated goddess usually identified as Pax Augusta (Augustan Peace), giving the altar its name. The veiled goddess holds two cherubic infants, one of whom picks out an apple from the many fruits collected in her lap. Animals graze around her and nearby a swan takes flight, scenes of pastoral harmony showing the connectivity in the Roman mind between the affairs of men and the health of the natural world. A grand procession of figures make their way along the upper registers on the sides of the altar, possibly depicting the inauguration of the monument itself. Among the dense crowd we see men, women, and children of the Julian house; notably, the trusted general Agrippa with his illustrious wife, Julia, daughter of Augustus, with their own infant son tugging on his father's toga. Augustus, of course, leads the sacred procession, ready to offer thanks to Pax in the form of warm animal blood. Despite his unageing image, he would not live forever, and on the altar we see the crucial formation of his future dynasty.

Today, the reconstructed Ara Pacis stands in a strikingly modern museum on the banks of the Tiber, a few blocks from its original location. The incongruous building has been the subject of some criticism since its opening in 2006. Inside, the monument's ancient reliefs are illuminated by shafts of sunlight streaming through towering walls of glass. The self-proclaimed Augustan Peace that they celebrate also found itself subject to scrutiny before long. Pax reigned over land and sea, yet disturbing news reached Rome of catastrophic battles on northern frontiers. The Republic had apparently been restored, yet democratic elections had quietly been phased out of Roman politics. The Ara Pacis was where Romans offered thanks to Pax for the delights of their golden age – but on that altar of peace, much would need to be sacrificed.

A Dynasty of Ashes

Through those same windows that now cast sunlight on the Altar of Peace, visitors are given a panoramic view of an imposing brick cylinder dominating the neighbouring piazza. Many may be forgiven for not realising the neglected structure is all that survives of the once-spectacular Mausoleum of Augustus, final resting place of Rome's first and longest-reigning emperor. Augustus began construction on the monumental tomb for himself and his family at the very outset of his reign. He would surely have been surprised to learn, given his sickliness in youth, that his own ashes would not be interred there for forty years – by which time the tomb would already be well populated with the urns of other family members. The gods seemed to smile on the long-lived emperor, just as they cut down any hopeful heir who might dare claim Rome as a birthright.

For all its apparent stability, the reign of Augustus was plagued by anxieties around the true nature of his powers, and to what extent they might be passed on to an eventual successor. After all, the great deeds of Augustus were his alone, not as easily bequeathed to a son as a name or fortune. An obvious fact complicated matters further: there was no son of Augustus awaiting any grand inheritance. His marriage to Livia – indomitable matriarch of the imperial family – would last for more than half a century. A union that would have been perfect if it had produced any children.

Augustus, in his younger incarnation as Octavian, was instantly taken with Livia when they first met in 39 BC. That he already had a heavily pregnant wife did little to curb his desires. On the very day his wife gave birth to their daughter, Julia, he announced he was divorcing her to pursue the new match. Livia was also married and pregnant at the time, but after some strongarm persuasion by Octavian, her husband agreed to a divorce. Octavian and Livia quickly married, and three months later she gave birth to her second son. While complications from a subsequent miscarriage seem to have rendered Livia incapable of giving Augustus the son 'he earnestly desired', it is testament to their bond that, with no chance of children, they remained at each other's side until death.

Without sons to call his own, Augustus would need to cast a wider net in the Julian bloodline in search of an heir. The first candidate to emerge was his sister's teenage son, Marcellus. Popular and capable, he seemed a natural successor to his uncle, and was hastily married to Augustus' daughter, Julia, to strengthen his position even further.

The gods would laugh at such best-laid plans, however. Following a short illness, the gold urn containing the ashes of Marcellus was the first to be carried with solemn ceremony into the imperial tomb.

Widowed at just sixteen, Julia was quickly married off again – this time to her father's lieutenant, Agrippa, who was in his forties. The match proved to be a fruitful one for the imperial house, producing five children in under a decade. Augustus was especially delighted with his two grandsons, Gaius and Lucius, in whose blood mingled the divine ancestry of Caesar and the steel of his most trusted general. The emperor placed all his dynastic hopes in the boys, officially adopting them as sons, and hailing them 'Principes Iuventutis' or 'Leaders of the Next Generation'. To publicly identify them as joint heirs, the brothers were granted silver shields and spears, as well as being depicted with these symbolic gifts on coins duly circulated far and wide. The future of the dynasty seemed secure, but as the contemporary historian Livy reflected: 'When Fortune is at her most giving, she is least to be trusted.'[25] Both of the beloved heirs would subsequently be 'snatched away by fate' within eighteen months of each other in the first years of the first century; Gaius succumbing to an infected wound, and Lucius dying of an unspecified illness. With each death, another mournful procession wended its way to the mausoleum, where, by shimmering lamplight, Augustus dedicated with prayers the ashes of another hopeful prince.

The urns of the brothers were placed alongside that of their father, Agrippa, who had died of illness in 12 BC. Widowed yet again, Julia had barely been given time to mourn her husband before being redeployed once more in her father's quest for an heir. The next betrothal dictated to her was to Livia's eldest son. Tiberius had already gained a reputation as a capable military commander, but he was also known to be dour and morose; traits only exacerbated when Augustus forced him to divorce a wife he truly loved so that the new marriage could take place. When Tiberius burst into tears at the sight of his ex-wife on the Roman street, Augustus gave strict orders that he never be allowed to see her again.

If the emperor hoped this union would provide him another supply of heirs, he was sorely mistaken. Hopelessly mismatched,

Julia and Tiberius were soon living separate lives. Worse still, rumour circulated that Julia – no doubt tired of her role as her father's dynastic pawn – had become a serial adulterer. Augustus despaired. Hoping to elevate Roman morality and increase population, he had passed legislation incentivising marriage and threatening strict punishments for adultery; laws now made a mockery of by his own daughter. The identity of her most prominent lover was the final straw: Lullus Antonius, son of the emperor's old nemesis, Mark Antony. The choice almost seemed designed to wound her moralising father. Lullus was promptly charged with treason and compelled to commit suicide. As for Julia, being the emperor's only child would spare her none of his rage.

The narrow, windswept island of Ventotene lies thirty miles from the coast of Italy. Even at its widest point, just 800 metres separate its jagged cliffs. Along the sheer rock faces echo the cries of migrating birds and the crash of the sea breaking far below. Julia would become well accustomed to the sights and sounds of the wild island on her permitted walks. There was little else to enjoy in this perfect prison, where her every move was watched by vigilant guards enforcing her father's instructions to the letter. Julia was allowed no visitors, certainly no male company – Augustus even ordered that she never again enjoy the taste of wine. After three marriages in service of her father's dynasty, Julia would live out her days in solitary exile. Even her eventual death by slow starvation could not free her from her father's control. There had been one more command: never would her ashes join those of her family in the imperial tomb.

The banishment of his daughter cast a shadow over the final years of Augustus' reign. The people marched in protest against her treatment, and against the morality laws that saw Augustus try to control their private lives in the same way he micromanaged the affairs of his close family. Amid the popular strife, the persistent problem of succession remained unsolved. As Livia never failed to remind her husband, only one serious candidate remained: her son, Tiberius. He was not of Julian blood, but rather a Claudian – one of Rome's most ancient families – but with his adoption he now became Augustus' son and heir.

Knowing that his unique position and titles had little reason to be gifted to any successor, Augustus carefully orchestrated a gradual handover. Tiberius was first given the power of tribune, an important tool in the emperor's arsenal, granting him inviolability while in office and the right to veto any legislation put forward by the Senate. He was presented to the legions and, even more crucially, to the Praetorian Guard as the man who would soon be paying their generous double salaries. Finally, in AD 13, Tiberius was given equal imperium over the Empire, effectively making him co-ruler. It was a shrewd manoeuvre, ensuring that when Augustus died there would be no dangerous interregnum – just seamless continuation.

On his deathbed the very next year, Augustus asked his assembled family and friends: 'Have I played my part in the comedy of life well? If so, applaud me as I leave the stage.' The theatrical analogy was apt. Augustus had played the role of benign ruler to perfection and the Republic he left behind had long been a fiction. As Tacitus noted, thanks to Augustus' long life 'most alive had been born after his victory at Actium. Few were left who could even remember the Republic.' The magistrates carried the old titles, the provinces were tranquil, but when Augustus breathed his last, a month before his seventy-sixth birthday, he truly left behind 'an altered world'.[26]

The transition of power to his stepson Tiberius ultimately proved to be peaceful, though its implications were seismic. Here was confirmation, if any was needed, not only that Rome was an empire, but that 'the Empire' was now an heirloom to be passed down in the blood of a single family. A stern and miserly leader, Tiberius would make little effort to endear himself to the Senate or people, but as long as he kept the backing of his powerful Praetorian Guard, he knew his position was secure.

Like Caesar before him, Augustus was declared a god after his death, though he would not ascend the heavens as a fiery comet. Forty years after his grand mausoleum was built, the ashes of 'Divus Augustus' were laid to rest at its heart. Other god-emperors would join him there in death over the decades. The irony of it all was not lost on the famous satirist Martial, who remarked wryly on 'the tomb nearby, teaching us that the gods themselves can die'.[27]

Pax Romana

While the mortality rate of those in the imperial household would remain perilously high, the reign of Augustus ushered in two centuries of unprecedented stability and economic prosperity across the Mediterranean world. At the height of the 'Pax Romana' or 'Roman Peace', close to one hundred million people were united by language, law, and a single monetary currency within an area spanning over two million square miles. More than 50,000 miles of paved roads connected the Empire's diverse lands, allowing for unparalleled movement of people, ideas, and previously unknown commodities.[28] A wealthy Roman Briton might enjoy fine wine imported from Italy and olive oil from North Africa, poured from glossy red pottery made in southern Gaul, all the while wearing vibrant silks that travelled the silk roads from China.

No surprise then that the Pax Romana initiated on this Augustan denarius has long fascinated academics and politicians seeking to replicate the formula for such widespread human flourishing. Particularly between the conflagrations of the twentieth century – easily the most murderous century in human history – the alchemical secrets of the Roman peace seemed all the more aspirational. Writing in the wake of the Second World War, Churchill stated that in his 'precarious age, where all is in flux and nothing is accepted', it was impossible not to respect that period 'when widespread peace in the entire known world was maintained from generation to generation'.[29] Subsequent ascendant empires claimed their own incarnations of the great peace – from the Pax Britannica to the Pax Americana. Augustus had declared peace in his time – but while many agreed that it was the coming of a new golden age, others sensed the 'delights of peace had become a siren song, seducing the Roman people' and leading them blindly into tyranny.[30] Roman thinkers would question the reality of the Pax Romana just as commentators do today. How peaceful was it really? Were its blessings to be enjoyed by the many or the few? And ultimately, was it worth the weight of an empire's boot heel?

Pax may have been celebrated on Roman coins and altars, but the era was by no means without military action or even defeats. The Empire in fact suffered one of its greatest military disasters in the final years of Augustus' reign. In AD 9, the general Publius Quinctilius Varus led three whole legions into Germany's vast Teutoburg Forest. They would never emerge again. Betrayed by their German guide, Arminius, the legions were surrounded by warrior tribes and annihilated. Hardly any soldiers survived the ambush, but those who did talked of hellish slaughter in the dense forest, and their general, Varus, falling on his sword when he saw all was lost. Any Romans unlucky enough to be taken alive were variously burnt in wicker cages, nailed to trees, or sacrificed on bloody altars. A final few were sold into slavery; incredibly, some of these survivors were liberated by a Roman raid into German territory forty years later.[31]

Augustus, then in his seventies, was almost undone by the catastrophe. For several months he did not cut his hair or beard, and at any reminder of the massacre he is said to have struck his head against the palace walls, crying out: 'Quinctilius Varus, give me back my legions!' The numerical designations of those lost legions – seventeen, eighteen, and nineteen – were never used again by the Roman army. For two decades, the emperor had focused his military efforts on the Germanic frontier, hoping to quell the unruly tribes and eventually turn Germania into a Roman province. If not for the Teutoburg disaster, Germany might one day have been fully Romanised like Gaul or Hispania, dramatically altering the cultural dynamic of modern Europe. Instead, the Rhine would effectively come to mark the northerly limits of Roman ambition. No straight roads were unfurled across the landscapes of Northern Europe and no classical cities arose. Where legions once dared to march, the raven-call echoed over piles of rusting Roman weapons, animals picked through clattering bones, and smiling skulls decorated the trees. It was peaceful, in its own way.

Elsewhere, the olive branch of Pax was only extended selectively to those who submitted to Roman power. Conquest continued apace with the lands of Britannia, Judea, Dacia (modern Romania), Armenia, and Arabia all added to the Empire in the following two centuries, sometimes by diplomacy and coercion, but more often by force. Rebellion against Roman occupation would on occasion lay waste whole cities, perhaps most famously in the great revolt led by the British queen Boudica in AD 60. As part of their efforts to subjugate Boudica's defiant Iceni tribe, Roman soldiers decided to publicly flog the queen and rape her daughters. Londinium (London), Camulodunum (Colchester), and Verulamium (St Albans), and their 80,000 inhabitants were soon incinerated in the flames of Boudica's vengeance. The cities burned with such ferocity that anyone excavating in them today will soon encounter a scorch-layer filled with charred tiles and blackened pottery, named by archaeologists the 'Boudican Destruction Horizon'.

Probably the most powerful contemporary critique of Roman imperial dominance comes from the subversive pen of one of its own historians. In imagining the rousing speech given by the Caledonian chieftain Calgacus prior to battle, Tacitus uses the voice of the enemy to rail against the oppression of his own 'rapacious Romans', who in their 'lust for dominion' have 'exhausted the land by their universal plunder'. The speech is widely remembered for one devastating metaphor: 'To robbery, slaughter, plunder, they give the lying name of empire; they make a desert and call it peace.'[32] The proverbial peaceful desert evoked by the rebel Calgacus endures in challenging our perceptions around the price of peace – when the battle is done, can the smouldering wasteland left behind truly be called 'Pax'? And what of the entire ancient cultures – Carthaginian, Gallic, Druidic – that were lost to the advance of Roman civilisation?

For all the desolation imagined by Calgacus, it was rare for Rome to adopt a scorched-earth policy in her expansion. Provinces were expected to be stable and profitable, with the price of their conquest measured against the possibility for future returns; a cost-benefit calculation largely responsible for keeping Ireland, Scotland, and sub-Saharan Africa outside the limits of the Empire. Once law and order were implemented, Roman investment in provincial infrastructure was monumental in scale – still embodied today in the Pont du Gard Roman aqueduct bridge that soars fifty metres over France's Gardon river and once helped carry 200,000 cubic metres of water a day to the city of Nemausus (modern Nîmes); or the Via Egnatia Roman road which stretched for 700 miles from the Albanian coast all the way to Byzantium (modern Istanbul).

The universal benefits of this 'long festival of peace', as Edward Gibbon would describe it, were 'warmly felt and honestly confessed by provincials as well as Romans'.[33] Once within imperial borders, the multiplication of human living standards – and, by extension, human population – was real. Still, the Pax Romana remains best described as a relative peace. At intervals it brought its own oppression and bloody revolts, but when viewed in opposition to earlier civil wars, the chaos of the later Empire, and the state of constant tribal warfare that existed for many outside its bounds, the full colours of Pax are revealed. As the final centuries of Roman rule would demonstrate, entire peoples wanted in on the imperial project more than they ever wanted out.

Long after her debut on this denarius, Pax would continue to offer her olive branch and overflowing cornucopia on the coins of almost every emperor, even those bloodthirsty rulers who had no business celebrating the goddess. As part of his efforts to project continuity with the reign of Augustus, his successor Tiberius' coinage would also be dominated by Pax. Just as the second emperor lacked the personality of his predecessor, so too did his rather unimaginative coinage; throughout his twenty-two-year reign, his silver and gold coins would be based around a single design, the aforementioned 'Tribute Penny' famously referred to by Jesus in the New Testament. The reverse of the coin proclaims the continuation of the Augustan Peace, showing the enthroned goddess Pax holding a sceptre and olive branch – though the goddess also looks suspiciously like Tiberius' ageing mother, the empress Livia. As much as the coin celebrates the prevailing Pax Romana, it appears to equally give personal thanks to the eternal matriarch of the imperial house who seems to have secured Tiberius his place on the throne.

With curious irony, the Pax Romana celebrated on the Tribute Penny had been inaugurated by an emperor calling himself the 'son of a god'. He promised 'peace on earth', was reincarnated, and the 'good news' of his coming was proclaimed across the world.[34] If we follow the accounts of the New Testament, it was also during Augustus' reign that a baby was born to a carpenter's wife in the Roman province of Judea. That child, named Jesus, would grow up to be

The reverse of the famed 'Tribute Penny' denarius, showing the enthroned figure of Pax/Livia holding a sceptre and olive branch, AD 14–37.

described with the same phrases. Handed this denarius in the Temple of Jerusalem, Jesus would have inspected the glum portrait of Tiberius and the image of Pax enthroned; peace that must have seemed a distant promise when soon after, by order of the Roman governor, nails were struck through his limbs, and he was hoisted high on a cross outside the walls of Jerusalem.

The execution of the dissident Judean made little immediate impact across the Roman world in the early first century. But in the following decades, a growing number of disillusioned Romans were drawn to his teachings. Before long, magistrates throughout the Empire wondered what to do with these seditious believers in their one God, rejecting the peace promised by Rome and hoping instead for an eternal peace in a life yet to come. On roughly carved gravestones, they expressed their wish to 'rest in peace' (*requiescat in pace*) alongside images of an olive branch, held not by a Roman goddess, but by a dove symbolising a Holy Spirit.

Emperors of the Pax Romana may have kept barbarians at bay, but they could not keep out these subversive ideas – ideas that, with some irony, spread easily on the straight roads and calm waters of the Roman peace.

Chapter VI

KINGMAKERS

'. . . but who will watch the watchmen?'

Juvenal

Gold *aureus* of Claudius commemorating the Praetorian Guard proclaiming him emperor in AD 41.
Obverse: Laureate head of Claudius, TI CLAVD CAESAR AVG P M TR P IIII.
Reverse: The praetorian fortress with guard inside, across the battlements IMPER RECEPT – 'The Reception of the Emperor'.

Behind the Curtain

The starlings soared and tumbled in the evening sky above Rome. Bathed in dying light, the palace on the hill seemed almost at peace, as if the day might be done with its bloodshed. But inside, screams echoed through the flickering hallways. Bodies sat crumpled against red-smeared frescoes. Others, somehow clinging to life, dragged themselves across glistening mosaics to nowhere. Around them, statues of their fallen emperor and his family lay in jagged pieces, toppled and smashed by the rampaging guards. Surviving slaves clung to the shadows, and in their hiding places held their breath as praetorians charged by, the robes and armour of some still spattered with the blood of the emperor they had sworn to protect. Having slaughtered the tyrant, they scoured the palace for any who might share his cursed blood.

In a lofty room of the palace, a praetorian named Gratus searched the gloom with his *gladius* sword drawn. The breeze of the January dusk entered from an open balcony and shivered the drapery around the room, but otherwise, all seemed still. Just as he turned to leave and continue the hunt, he paused. One curtain covering an alcove seemed to quake beyond the incitement of the wind. Gratus stepped closer and focused his eyes through the failing light. Only then did he notice the sandalled feet protruding below the quivering fabric. And presently, from beneath the covering, a pained whimper that could no longer be stifled. Gratus gripped the ivory hilt of his sword tightly – and in one swift movement, he whipped back the curtain.

With a shriek, the uncovered figure collapsed out of the shadows. Clawing at the praetorian's purple cloak, he begged to be spared. He swore, stuttering between sobs, that he knew nothing of the day's bloody events. Gratus lifted the trembling chin of the man to better comprehend him. His silver hair shone in the twilight, as did the spittle running from the corner of his mouth. This was the mad emperor's uncle. Brother of the beloved Germanicus. The harmless old fool of the family: Claudius.

The praetorian's thoughts were quick and calculating. After the day's massacre, here was the last remaining heir to the Julio-Claudian house helpless before him. One swift strike of his gladius would liberate Rome from the clutches of that ruinous bloodline for good. After decades of tyranny, the Republic could be restored. And yet, without an emperor to protect, what would become of the Praetorian Guard – and their handsome salary?

'No more of saving yourself, my lord,' said Gratus, hoisting the shaking man to his feet and fixing his dishevelled toga. 'Time to elevate your thoughts. The gods have entrusted you with an empire this day.'

Bewildered and weak-kneed, Claudius almost had to be carried to the doorway. 'W-Where are you taking me?' he pleaded.

'To the throne of your ancestors, my lord.'

A thunderous chant could soon be heard emanating from the palace, drifting out across the tense city: 'Imperator! Imperator! Imperator!'

The Praetorian Guard had found their new emperor.[1]

Sting of the Scorpion

The troops who would assassinate one emperor and choose the next on that fateful day in January AD 41 were part of a notorious military unit that had been growing in strength and influence for almost seventy years. Created as a loyal and disciplined imperial bodyguard, the institution would evolve into an uncontrollable force, more lethal to Roman rulers than the assassins it was meant to guard against. Before long, their name would become a byword for palace intrigue, greed, and betrayal. Making and unmaking emperors at will, the Praetorian Guard would rise to become the true power brokers of the Roman Empire.

No doubt haunted by the daggers of the Ides, the very first act of the emperor Augustus upon his accession in 27 BC had been to formalise his own elite security force. His Praetorian Guard would thereafter be the sworn protectors of the emperor and his family, though their origins actually stretched back centuries. During the

Republic, praetorians were the best and bravest men chosen to guard generals against assassins, especially while campaigning in enemy territory. This prestigious escort took their name from the commander's headquarters or *praetorium*, placed at the heart of any Roman fort. As part of his enormous issue of 'legionary denarii' minted to pay his troops prior to the Battle of Actium in 31 BC, Mark Antony made sure to remember this specialist unit. A rare variant within the coin series pays tribute not to the usual numbered legion, but to his 'Cohortium Praetoriarum' – his 'Cohort of Praetorians' – the first reference to the Guard on Roman coinage. After his momentous victory, Augustus merged the remainder of Antony's praetorian forces with his own to form the unified imperial guard.

Membership of his Praetorian Guard was open only to the most trusted, homegrown Italian soldiers and came with numerous privileges. Their term of enlistment would be sixteen years, as opposed to the twenty years demanded of a legionary. They would be based in and around Rome, serving in close proximity to the emperor, rather than risking their lives on the frontiers. As an immediately obvious sign of their status, Augustus decreed that his praetorians would be paid double the legionary's salary of 225 denarii a year, as we have seen. At the end of his career, a guard could also expect a grant of fertile land and a retirement payment or *praemium* of 20,000 sestertii/5,000 denarii – almost ten years' salary.[2] Not to mention the bonuses he might receive during his service: Augustus bequeathed each guard 250 denarii in his last will, setting a trend for generous gifts or *donatives* to the praetorians in reward for their loyalty.[3] These cash gifts would escalate to absurd amounts in subsequent centuries, with each emperor implicitly expected to outdo the generosity of his predecessor.

The praetorians were the only troops permitted to bear arms within the *pomerium* – the sacred boundary line demarcating the city limits of Rome. Though founded as a personal security escort to the imperial family, the convenience of having nine armed cohorts close at hand – around 4,500 well-trained and well-equipped men – soon saw emperors deploying the Guard for all manner of tasks in the capital.[4] Romans became accustomed to seeing praetorians act not just as bodyguards, but as riot police at public events, firefighters, civil engineers, executioners, and even participants in arena shows. Less visibly, members of the Guard were also employed in covert action as what we might today describe as spies or secret police, working to uncover plots against the emperor.

In a dual command structure that mirrored the power-sharing consuls of the Roman Senate, the Guard was usually led by a pair of prefects both answering directly to the emperor. This shrewd system meant prefects competed with each other to please the emperor and, with each commander keeping a careful eye on his colleague, checked the ambitions of any one prefect who might have designs on seizing the throne for himself. As another hierarchical failsafe, prefects were selected from the equestrian order rather than the senatorial elite. While *equites* or 'knights' were a prosperous business and landowning class, coming from outside the patrician bloodlines of Rome's ruling families, it was, in theory, unthinkable that any prefect would have the prestige and connections to make a play for direct political power.

It was during the twenty-two-year reign of Tiberius that the Praetorian Guard would truly emerge as an influential political force in its own right, equally ensuring and threatening the emperor's grip on the throne. Upon the announcement of the death of Augustus, the first act of Tiberius was to issue the praetorians with that day's watchword, a symbolic act that displayed the transferral of their allegiance to a new *imperator*. Safely surrounded by soldiers of the Guard – what Suetonius calls 'the actual power of sovereignty' – Tiberius could begin the charade of refusing the imperial titles offered him. As the Senate pleaded with him to accept the accumulated powers of Augustus, Tiberius affected such great reluctance that one senator eventually lost patience and demanded that he 'take it or leave it!'[5] But once the feigned equivocation was over, it is notable that the first oath of allegiance Tiberius accepted was from his praetorian prefect; only then did he concern himself with the pledges of consuls and senators.[6]

The growing interdependence between the emperor and his bodyguard may be reflected in the presentation of the praetorians during Tiberius' reign. While surprisingly little is known about the exact appearance of the Guard's uniform and regalia, a small number of surviving depictions suggest that they took a symbol closely connected to Tiberius as their new emblem. A marble relief from Puteoli shows members of the Praetorian Guard holding distinctive oval shields – rather than the rectangular shields of the typical legionary – decorated with the insignia of a scorpion. Just as it does today, the poisonous arachnid with its stinging tail signified the astrological sign of Scorpio, which also happened to be the zodiac sign of Tiberius, born on 23 November. A bronze sestertius coin showing the praetorian cohorts being addressed by a subsequent emperor depicts their armour in such minute detail that a tiny scorpion can be seen on a guard's shield.[7] The surviving grave memorial in Rome of a praetorian named Marcus Pompeius Asper also shows a scorpion placed prominently on the Guard's elaborate military standards.[8]

The privileged position of the Praetorian Guard soon drew the resentment of the average Roman legionary. This bitterness was made abundantly clear in AD 14 when, upon hearing of the death of Augustus, a large-scale revolt broke out among the legions stationed near the Danube. When troops along the Rhine followed suit, the whole northern frontier garrison of the Empire was soon in open rebellion. Many of the leading instigators would have previously served under Tiberius and most likely resented the demand that they switch their allegiance to the surly new emperor. The tentative transferral of power from one emperor to another was also the perfect opportunity for the disgruntled soldiery to renegotiate their pay and conditions. Tacitus tells us that one of the key legionary demands was to be 'paid a denarius a day', especially since 'the Praetorian Guard received two denarii a day, despite being restored to hearth and home after just sixteen years' service'.[9] Interestingly, this report reveals that by the reign of Tiberius, praetorians were being paid around 750 denarii a year – three times that of the standard legionary – a generous ratio that would also be mirrored in their donatives and discharge payments. Though as Tacitus reminds us, no one could argue their lavish salary was due to 'risking more danger' than frontline troops, who endured brutal daily discipline, meagre rations, and the constant threat of attack from an enemy 'visible from their very tents'.[10]

Tiberius dispatched two rising stars of the imperial family to put down the revolts. His only son, Drusus, found the Danube legions downtrodden and ashamed of their actions – prompt execution of the rebellion's ringleaders quickly restored order to the ranks. Appeasing the angry troops on the German lines would prove much more difficult, even for a prince as beloved as Germanicus. Dashing, charismatic, adored by citizens and soldiers alike, the young Germanicus was everything Tiberius was not – and with an illustrious bloodline that perfectly united the Julian and Claudian branches of the imperial house. On his father's side he was nephew of Tiberius and grandson of Livia, while his mother was none other than the daughter of Mark Antony and Augustus' sister, Octavia. Further marking him as the golden boy of the imperial family, Germanicus was already enjoying a fruitful marriage to Agrippina, daughter of the great general Agrippa and Augustus' only child, Julia. Tiberius had his own natural son in Drusus, but it seemed to many that Germanicus was the fated heir to the Empire.

His popularity with the troops caused its own problems when Germanicus arrived at the rebellious camp with wife and children in tow. Legionaries came forward to kiss his hands, and at the same time 'pushed his fingers into their lips so he could feel their toothless gums'. Worn out soldiers – some claiming to have fought thirty campaigns – begged Germanicus for relief from their grinding service and, most troublingly, assured the prince that if he wanted to seize the throne from his miserly uncle, they would help him do it. When Germanicus emphatically refused the offer, placing a sword against his chest and stating he would commit suicide if they persisted in their pleas, the troops became dangerously irate.[11]

Germanicus promised the soldiers he would double the gift bequeathed to them by Augustus and that he would discharge all who had completed their term of service. But their anger would not be quelled. Swords were drawn. The hopeful young family were hemmed in. Only when Germanicus begged for safe passage for his pregnant wife and infant son did the legionaries regain their senses. Seeing the noble granddaughter of the Divine Augustus selflessly protect her small child from their threatening violence filled the troops with shame. But the pitiful crying of her little boy was what truly ended the rebellion. The son of Germanicus and Agrippina had been born in their very camp and the surprisingly sentimental legionaries had embraced the adorable toddler as their mascot. They had played with him, even made for him a miniature soldier's uniform. Their affectionate nickname for the sweet child playing soldier had followed naturally – they called him 'Little Boots', or in Latin, Caligula.[12]

Another individual had been sent from Rome on behalf of the emperor to monitor the situation on the fragile frontier. The prefect of the Praetorian Guard, Lucius Aelius Sejanus, observed the progress of the young princes very closely. Back in Rome, he reported everything he saw to Tiberius – especially how the troops had clamoured for Germanicus as their emperor instead. Tiberius was always a reluctant ruler; soon he would be paranoid and isolated too. If he wished to take a step back from the toils of leadership, his always-obedient prefect Sejanus would gladly step forward to fill the void. Under his command, the praetorians would be made indispensable to the emperor, moving ever closer to the throne, and closer to power.

The Damnation of Memory

The endless traffic of modern Rome trundles by under the forbidding walls of the fortress. All along the avenue, bleak brick ramparts, pockmarked and speckled with wildflowers, tower over oblivious pedestrians running their errands. On the long side of its massive rectangular plan, the fortification strikes down the thoroughfare for almost half a kilometre. This busy intersection, now a short walk from the bustle of Termini station, once marked the very edge of the ancient city. Here, as they did two millennia ago, the walls of the Castra Praetoria maintain their watch over the comings and goings from Rome. This region of today's city, Castro Pretorio, takes its name from the gloomy fortress (*castrum* meaning 'fort/camp' and giving us our modern word 'castle'), but few who walk in its shadow give any thought to what once lay behind its high walls.

Tiberius authorised the building of a Roman base for the Praetorian Guard in AD 21, doubtless on the advice of his trusted prefect, Sejanus. So complete was the emperor's confidence in Sejanus that the prefect had been given sole command of the praetorians, breaking the model of two-man leadership established by Augustus. Before construction of their forty-acre fortress, praetorians had been loosely garrisoned around the city, making their cohorts hard to manage and slow to muster in a crisis.[13] In establishing a permanent and centralised camp for them in Rome, Tiberius had hoped to reinforce strict military discipline to their ranks and keep them close at hand to respond quickly to security emergencies in the capital.[14] In reality, he had gifted Sejanus and the Guard a strongly fortified power-base from where they could increasingly dictate events in the city as a unified and intimidating force. For centuries, the first sight greeting anyone arriving at the capital from the east were the toothed battlements of the praetorian fortress.

The concentration of his military power in the Castra Praetoria represented a key step in the patient and calculated rise of Sejanus. Only a couple of years earlier, one of his main competitors had been helpfully removed from the dynastic equation. The sudden death of Germanicus in AD 19 provoked an unprecedented outpouring of grief across the Empire.[15] The beloved heir-designate died under extremely suspicious circumstances in Antioch, Syria, at the height of a feud with the province's governor. While mysterious deaths in the ancient world were often attributed to poisoning, Roman historians are particularly united in their assertions that Germanicus was the victim of foul play. Suetonius recounts ominously that 'when Germanicus was cremated, his heart was found whole among the ashes; for when steeped in poison it cannot be destroyed by fire'. Tacitus goes as far as to describe letters sent from Tiberius with instructions to the poisoner and observes how the emperor merely 'assumed an air of sadness' in the aftermath of the tragedy.[16] That the accused provincial governor conveniently took his own life before a trial could be held, only added to suspicions that the envious emperor was somehow behind the death of his popular nephew.[17]

The very year that Sejanus moved his guardsmen into their new fortress, another competitor for the emperor's affections succumbed to sudden illness. As the only son of Tiberius, Drusus had naturally emerged as leading heir to the throne. Unsurprisingly, a bitter feud with his father's ambitious prefect followed. Drusus had even punched Sejanus in the face during one of their heated arguments. Soon after, the heir lay dead. Poison, once again, the suspected cause. Rumour was rife that not only had Sejanus eliminated the emperor's son, but the deed was done with the help of Drusus' own wife, whom the prefect had seduced.[18] However damning the circumstantial evidence, Tiberius seems to have paid it little heed. Moving to resolve any succession crisis, the emperor sent for the two teenage sons of Germanicus, with a third brother, Gaius 'Little Boots' Caligula, still too young. Before the assembled Senate, Tiberius adopted the boys with solemn ceremony, placing all his hopes in the 'great-grandchildren of Augustus, descendants of a most noble ancestry'. Sejanus stood, stony-faced, at his side.[19]

Not only did Tiberius maintain confidence in his prefect after his son's death, but in his grief entrusted Sejanus with more responsibility than ever, even labelling him 'partner in my labours'.[20] A contemporary historian describes Sejanus 'sharing the burdens of the imperial office'; increasingly, senators and petitioners approached him with their causes, rather than the emperor himself.[21] With his prefect's encouragement, by AD 25 the emperor had effectively retired to a palatial hideaway on the rugged island of Capri. Sejanus was left the leading man in Rome. Gilded statues of the regent duly sprang up all around the city, his birthday was publicly celebrated, and sacrifices were made to his health. For many, Sejanus actually 'seemed to be the emperor and Tiberius a kind of offshore monarch', who had abandoned his offices for a secluded life of debauchery and indulgence.[22] With almost unlimited power at his disposal, Sejanus set about clearing his pathway to the throne with little concern for subtlety.

In quick succession, both sons of Germanicus and their popular mother, Agrippina, were arrested on nebulous treason charges and put to death. Few remained who could stand in Sejanus' path to supreme power. A physically disabled brother of Germanicus – the limping, drooling, family-embarrassment named Claudius – was of little concern. Caligula, last living son of Germanicus, was a mere teenager, out of reach after being summoned to the emperor's island retreat. That the praetorian prefect would soon be named heir to the throne seemed certain, especially when, in AD 31, he was granted the ultimate political prize of a consulship, taking office alongside his colleague, the emperor himself.

The fall of Sejanus, when it came, was swift, bloody, and total. Even when Tiberius finally acknowledged the heinous machinations of his trusted confidant, it was only through 'craft and deceit' that he could overthrow him, illustrating the extent to which his position had been supplanted.[23] A surprise meeting of the Senate was called on 18 October 31, during which, it was rumoured, a letter from Tiberius would be read out bestowing tribunician powers on his praetorian prefect – effectively designating him successor. That morning, a hopeful Sejanus was escorted to the assembly by a subordinate named Macro, no doubt buoyed by the prospect of achieving his ultimate goal. Backslapping senators greeted Sejanus heartily on his arrival, some already congratulating him on his imminent honours. Anticipation filled the hall as the emperor's letter was read aloud.

Smiles soon faded from the assembled faces. Rather than praise Sejanus, the rambling letter began to reel off criticisms of the prefect. Confused mutterings filtered through the packed Senate. Gradually the emperor's slights grew into all-out condemnations. As the reality of the situation dawned on the assembly, senators shuffled away from Sejanus, some rising and scuttling out of the hall altogether. The long-winded missive had meanwhile allowed Macro to take his leave and rush to the Castra Praetoria. At the fortress he assumed the position promised him by Tiberius in secret correspondence; as new prefect of the Guard, Macro readied the troops for the inevitable chaos about to ensue. Back in the curia, the scathing letter finally culminated in a demand that the treasonous Sejanus be arrested. The assembly erupted. Senators who had earlier lavished their praises now hurled vicious attacks. A bewildered Sejanus was led out into the Forum to the waiting crowds, and a grim fate.

The anarchy that followed gives, as Cassius Dio soberly puts it, 'enough proof of human frailty to prevent anyone from ever again becoming puffed up with pride'. The man whom senators had welcomed that morning as a supreme being was now dragged through the streets in chains, beaten and mocked all the way. Having risen that day expecting to be hailed heir to the Empire, Sejanus was summarily garrotted and his body thrown to the crowds to be abused. After three days, when the mob's fury had run its course, what was left of his corpse was dragged on a hook to the Tiber and cast into the dark waters.[24] The violence unleashed in such revolutionary moments of Roman history often extended to the innocent wider family of the condemned; the young son and daughter of Sejanus were also dragged, terrified, to their deaths. Since Roman law dictated that no virgin could suffer capital punishment, the executioner raped the girl while the rope was around her neck, before strangling the children and hurling their bodies to the crowd like their father. Witnessing the horror, the children's mother, Apicata, promptly committed suicide.[25]

The traitor and his family were dead, but that was only the beginning of the purge. Sejanus would become the first individual to suffer an Empire-wide *damnatio memoriae*: the condemnation of his very memory. With the decree issued by the Senate, it was beholden upon Romans to ensure that every statue of Sejanus was torn down and that every mention of his cursed name was obliterated. While complete removal from the historical record was near-impossible – indeed, efforts to deface statues and excise inscriptions remain as evidence in themselves – the damnation of Sejanus appears to have been particularly thorough. Of the countless likenesses we are told were raised in honour of the regent, not a single one can be positively identified today.

A remarkable piece of numismatic evidence reveals the effort even those far from Rome put into erasing the name Sejanus from history. In the months preceding the bloodbath, the town of Bilbilis in northeast Spain had decided to mint a coin honouring that year's co-consuls. The copper *as* (a quarter of a sestertius and a sixteenth of a denarius) bears the portrait of the emperor Tiberius on the obverse as expected,

Two examples of a provincial coin minted in the Spanish town of Bilbilis in AD 31. The first shows the name of Sejanus, L AELIO SEIANO, intact (lower right), while on the second the name has been carefully chiselled away.

while naming on its reverse the consular colleagues of AD 31: Tiberius Caesar, holding the office for the fifth time, and his partner, Lucius Aelius Sejanus.

Of roughly thirty specimens of the provincial coin catalogued today, the name of Sejanus has been completely obliterated from almost half. Struck to advertise the town's allegiance to Rome, the local coin issue would have instantly become a source of embarrassment when news arrived of the prefect's downfall and damnation. In contrast to conspicuous public statues and inscriptions, the small and transient nature of coinage usually precluded it from such systematic iconoclasm. The coin therefore presents intriguing questions around the practical measures employed to erase the name from circulating money; it may be that a recall of the coins was announced by local officials – a decree evidently not followed by all. Alternatively, individuals may have been compelled to enact the damnatio independently wherever they came across an untouched example. The uniformity by which the name has been precisely chiselled or filed away, crucially leaving the emperor's name and portrait untouched, seems to suggest the eradication was completed in an official capacity.

However it was implemented, magistrates surely accepted that erasing the name of Sejanus from every single example was unfeasible. In this sense, the coin also represents the ritualistic nature of damnatio memoriae; just as the town showcased its obedience to the Roman state in minting the coins, futile attempts at amending them afterwards merely served as a continuation of the performative display of loyalty.

Attacks on the memory of the damned would continue at intervals throughout Roman history, and eventually be echoed in the political purges of modern totalitarian regimes. As part of its quest to control information and shape narratives of both the future and the past, Stalinist Russia employed large groups of photo re-touchers to erase disgraced figures from documentary photographs. Nazi Germany similarly went to great lengths to expunge all references to the fallen SA officer Ernst Röhm from German history, unsuccessfully attempting to destroy every copy of a propaganda film in which he appeared. Ancient concepts of damnation remain relevant in today's information age. When popular reputations can seemingly crumble into ruins overnight, a digital damnation has the potential to delete 'unpersons' from the public consciousness with a completeness undreamed of by Roman emperors.

The inexorable rise and spectacular fall of Sejanus, just as he reached the pinnacle of his powers, presents us with a timeless tale of ambition, hubris, and betrayal. In 1603, the famed playwright Ben Jonson would adapt the downfall of the praetorian prefect into a tragedy for the Jacobean stage. *Sejanus, his Fall* was performed at London's Globe Theatre by the King's Men acting company, with a certain William Shakespeare taking on the role of the Roman emperor, Tiberius. The very next year, Shakespeare would premiere his own tragedy *Othello*, featuring an uncannily Sejanus-like character in the two-faced officer Iago, who presents 'shows of service' to his lord, while boasting 'I am not what I am.'

That the praetorian prefect Sejanus continued to serve as such a warning from history ultimately attests to the futility of his damnation; for all Rome's efforts to chisel his name from every monument and every coin, he would never be fully erased from memory.

Divine Madness

When Tiberius eventually succumbed to ill health in AD 37, it was the praetorian prefect Macro who ensured power passed seamlessly to Gaius Caligula (Plate section, 6). Having befriended the prefect during his captivity on the island of Capri, Caligula was assured that he had the Guard's backing when the time came. Tacitus goes as far as to claim that time was accelerated by Macro when – impatient at the ailing emperor's refusal to breathe his last – he smothered Tiberius with a pillow. True or not, it is revealing in itself that the praetorian prefect was now the one expected to lead the transfer of imperial power, sending pronouncements to Rome and the provinces, and ensuring the Guard swore allegiance to the new leader. Caligula would subsequently be the first ruler to publicly advertise his indebtedness to the Praetorian Guard upon his accession. Not only did he ensure that each soldier received the 1,000 sestertii/250 denarii bequeathed by Tiberius, he added his own generous bonus on top and even ordered the striking of a special series of bronze coins with which the reward could be paid. A finely executed bronze sestertius shows Caligula's 'Adlocutio Cohortium' – 'Addressing of the Cohorts' – and depicts the new emperor addressing armed praetorians from a high platform, no doubt praising them for their support.

Despite modern efforts to re-evaluate the reigns of various notorious emperors, the unanimously scathing sources describing the unbridled cruelty and insanity of Caligula have made his reputation hard to rehabilitate. Yet any exploration of his short reign should be prefaced by highlighting the trauma of his youth. Born and raised in military camps, he watched helplessly as his family was systematically destroyed through his childhood. One by one, he lost his father, mother, and both elder brothers, before being taken as an effective hostage by the man ultimately responsible for their deaths. Summoned to the paranoid emperor's forbidding clifftop palace, Caligula surely expected to follow his family to the afterlife. In the event he survived under an ever-present sword of Damocles by projecting total, silent obedience. Even when goaded by Tiberius about the ruin of his family, Caligula maintained such unfeeling deference it was said 'there was never a better slave, or a worse master'. At the age of just twenty-four, the orphan still known by his detested nickname 'Little Boots' would be handed, in a single day, powers that his predecessors had amassed over decades.

Revealingly, once Tiberius was safely dead, Caligula commemorated his family members on coins more than any other emperor. Among these were silver and gold coins with portraits of his murdered parents; and an exquisite bronze sestertius showing a procession held in honour of his mother, its bold inscription dedicating it 'Memoriae Agrippinae' – 'To the Memory of Agrippina'. It is perhaps no surprise that Caligula would become obsessively attached to his three sisters who survived the purges of Sejanus. A sestertius struck at the outset of his reign shows his cherished female siblings – Agrippina the Younger, Drusilla, and Julia – as Roman goddesses holding cornucopias. The adoring coin very likely contributed to salacious rumours that Caligula routinely committed incest with all three of his sisters. Whatever the nature of their family relationship, the madness of Caligula's reign would soon see two of his beloved sisters become embroiled in plots to assassinate their brother.

As the only surviving son of Germanicus, Caligula had come to the throne with 'the highest hopes of the Roman people' – and initially the young man more than lived up to expectations.[26] He completed public works left unfinished by his tight-fisted predecessor, released those jailed on spurious treason charges, and staged generous public banquets. Six months into his reign, however, Caligula was struck down with a mysterious illness from which it seemed he might not recover. He pulled through – but the emperor who emerged was dramatically changed.[27] Some modern analysts have questioned if his sudden transformation might have been caused by a psychotic break triggered by the overwhelming pressures of power foisted on the young ruler. Others have theorised that Caligula suffered from a brain injury, acute lead poisoning, or, like other notable Julio-Claudians, the 'falling sickness' we today know as epilepsy. Indeed, many of the emperor's afflictions described in sources – sudden falls, severe insomnia, depression, delusions, and paranoia – match

Sestertius struck under Caligula honouring his three sisters as goddesses: Agrippina the Younger (as Securitas), Drusilla (as Concordia), and Julia (as Fortuna), AD 37.

symptoms of what modern medicine defines as epileptic psychosis.[28] Though the diagnosis remains uncertain, in the wake of his sickness Caligula seems to have abandoned all pretences of fair rule and embarked on a new 'career as a monster'.[29]

Shocking stories of Caligula's sadism abound in the ancient sources. Watching the drawn-out torture of the condemned became one of his favourite pastimes. Demanding that death come gradually by numerous little wounds, his instructions to the executioner became notorious: 'Strike him in such a way that he can feel himself dying.' Even as he sat for lunch, Caligula often requested that capital torture or a decapitation be carried out for entertainment while he ate. Once, when confusion over names led to the wrong man being executed, Caligula merely said that the dead man probably deserved it too. With the fierce Praetorian Guard at his side, Caligula had little concern for his wider popularity; he was heard to say of Rome's elites: 'Let them hate me, so long as they fear me.'[30]

For all its horrors, Caligula's rule also showed a definite flair for anti-establishment mischief, the emperor never missing an opportunity to ridicule the senatorial class. At a gladiator auction, Caligula noticed the senator Aponius was falling asleep and instructed the auctioneer to pay special attention to the senator and his nodding head. When bidding was done, the dozing senator had unwittingly bought thirteen gladiators.[31] Some senior senators were made to run behind the emperor's chariot in their heavy togas, while others were forced to wait on him with napkins as he dined. His contempt for the once-hallowed body of the Senate probably explains the famous anecdote that he planned to elevate his favourite horse, Incitatus, to the order and make him consul; if true, surely another glimpse of Caligula's caustic sense of humour.[32]

Perhaps the final straw came in Caligula's insistence that he be revered as a living god. He set up a temple for his own worship, with its own priests and cult statue of himself in gold, shown in the guise of Jupiter. Despite his childlike fear of thunder and lightning, he wished to be called 'Jupiter' in official documents and even began building a new house on the sacred Capitol where he intended to live alongside the king of the gods.

While Caligula's extravagance and generosity seem to have helped maintain his popularity with the common people, such outrages quickly alienated Rome's ruling class. Fatally, this breach would soon extend to the praetorians. He might have had Macro to thank for his smooth accession to the throne, but a year into his reign Caligula stripped the prefect of his powers and compelled him to suicide, perhaps wary of creating another Sejanus. Reverting to the two-prefect model of Augustus, he otherwise made little effort to keep the Guard on side. He greatly enjoyed humiliating senior praetorians, such as the tribune Cassius Chaerea, whose duties included asking the emperor for the new watchword each day. Caligula never failed to use the ritual to ridicule the praetorian's high-pitched voice, issuing sexually suggestive watchwords like 'Venus' and 'Priapus' in a mockingly effeminate impersonation of the soldier.

If goading your own lethal bodyguard seems like a peculiar brand of suicide, this is exactly what has been proposed about Caligula's inevitable demise by thinkers, ancient and modern. The historian Josephus, writing later in the first century, concludes that in teaching his closest allies to regard him as an intolerable enemy, Caligula had 'become a conspirator against himself'.[33] Similarly, in the preface to his play *Caligula* (1938), philosopher and dramatist Albert Camus theorises that the emperor's self-destruction was deliberate – the logical final goal of a concerted nihilist. In driving his praetorians to kill him, he argues that Caligula's fall is less the story of an assassination, and more 'the story of a superior suicide'.[34]

The end for 'Little Boots', and the bloody apogee of the Praetorian Guard, came on 24 January 41. Caligula was slow to rise that morning, queasy after a heavy banquet the night before. Persuaded to take an invigorating walk on the Palatine, he came across the lively preparations for spectacles being held that afternoon. As any sovereign might do today, Caligula stopped to meet some young stage performers rehearsing their routines. He encouraged the theatre troupe and said he would have eagerly attended their performance later if not for the cold. At that point, his praetorian tribunes cleared away the crowds and asked the emperor for the day's watchword. Caligula thought for a moment and replied with the watchword 'Jupiter'. From behind him, the tribune Chaerea yelled out, 'So be it!' Drawing his gladius in an instant, he struck Caligula as he turned his head, splitting his jawbone. Caligula fell and lay twitching on the ground – but still managed to splutter defiantly through the choking blood: 'I am still alive.'

The frantic order went round the guards: 'Strike him again!' Eventually Caligula succumbed to thirty further wounds including deliberate sword thrusts to his genitals. His litter bearers had tried unsuccessfully to defend him using their litter poles as spears; and when soldiers of his ultra-loyal German horseguard appeared, they were too late to be of any help – but in the confusion killed several of the assassins and a few innocent bystanders into the bargain.[35]

As if driven to a frenzy by the spilling of their emperor's blood, Chaerea then led his praetorian assassins in storming the imperial palace where the massacre would continue for many hours.[36] In one of the rooms, a guardsman named Lupus came across the emperor's wife, Caesonia, bravely shielding her baby daughter. Caligula had doted on the infant Drusilla – his only child – even naming her after his favourite sister. The praetorian ran Caesonia through with his sword, before lifting the baby by her legs and dashing her brains out against a wall.[37]

Elsewhere in the palace, another praetorian stalked the shadows. Pulling back a quivering curtain, he unveiled Caligula's last male relative, and an unmissable opportunity.

Making an Emperor

The troops hoisted him high. Even after the day's violence, Romans lined the streets to see the passing spectacle; cheering praetorians taking turns to carry the litter, upon which their captive rolled and tumbled without dignity. In the torchlight, only some recognised the bewildered man swept along above the soldiers' heads. Claudius was brother of the great Germanicus, though for most of his fifty years he had been kept from public view on account of his physical disabilities. He had survived the bloodshed of Sejanus and Caligula by posing absolutely no threat to anyone, and onlookers were saddened to see Claudius now the picture of terror – cruelly paraded by the Guard before his inevitable execution. At the edge of the city, the jagged ramparts of the Castra Praetoria eventually loomed into view. Claudius trembled as he was carried through the ominous gateway of the praetorian fortress, and into the belly of the beast.

The Senate convened at daybreak. With Caligula dead, a return to liberty – to the Republic – seemed possible. But before any plans could be put into action, the problem of the praetorians and their hostage remained. A small embassy of senators was selected to travel the two kilometres to the Castra Praetoria and talk the Guard down. Arriving at the fortress, they not only found Claudius alive and well, but surrounded by hundreds of heavily armed praetorians already treating him as their new leader. When the senators demanded that Claudius attend their meeting, he gestured to the sentries all about him and, with the faintest hint of a smile, advised that unfortunately he was 'being detained by force'. The ambassadors soon found themselves being ushered out of the fort by intimidating soldiers, but before leaving they called out to Claudius that he of all people should hate the burden of tyranny, that all in the rebellious camp must submit to the law.

Hours of bickering and indecision followed back at the Senate house. For all the idealistic speeches praising the return of liberty, they knew that power ultimately lay with the faction commanding the most military strength. The urban cohorts – a kind of paramilitary city police – had tentatively allied with the Senate and occupied the Forum, but they would be no match for the praetorians. Pressure on the dithering senators mounted when an angry mob pushed through the military cordon and surrounded the building. They cried out that to avoid civil war, Rome needed an emperor – and the brother of Germanicus was as good a choice as any. The chant of the crowd outside drowned out the debate: 'Claudius, Claudius!'[38]

When word reached the praetorian base that the Senate had fallen into complete disarray, all within realised the time had come. The jubilant troops carried Claudius to a raised podium at the centre of the fortress, behind which the standards of the cohorts were proudly displayed in a sacred shrine. With a deafening clamour, the sea of massed praetorians raised their weapons and acclaimed Claudius their new 'Augustus'. Less than twenty-four hours before, he had been a stuttering family reject, busying himself with his studies in backrooms of the palace. Now, whether he wanted the title or not, Claudius was Roman emperor.

After delivering their oath of allegiance, the cohorts waited expectantly to hear how generously the new emperor would reward their loyalty. Claudius thought quickly before addressing them, composed himself, steadied his quivering knees, and dabbed away the spittle that sometimes foamed at his mouth. To the soldiers who had not only spared his life but made him the most powerful man in the world, he promised the enormous sum of 15,000 sestertii/3,750 denarii per man – the equivalent of five years' salary. The resulting cheer of the troops shook the high walls of the fortress.[39]

Paying each guard such a large sum in silver denarii would clearly be impractical, so the donative would be awarded to the praetorians mostly using the gold *aureus* – translating simply as 'golden', from the Latin *aurum* meaning 'gold' – the highest-value coin in the Roman monetary system. A single aureus was equivalent to twenty-five silver denarii, allowing the emperor's gift to be issued in the much more manageable quantity of 150 gold coins for every man.

The Roman mint quickly got to work striking the hundreds of thousands of coins needed to pay the donative. Consequently, many of these coins survive today – spellbinding time capsules connecting us to an individual praetorian gifted the gold in return for his loyalty almost 2,000 years ago. The messaging in the coin's carefully crafted design further adds to its fascination, custom-made for its intended audience and starkly revealing where power truly resided as Claudius took the throne. On the obverse we see a portrait of the new emperor, shown with the 'majesty and dignity of appearance' that he exuded despite his stammering and shaking. It is thought that Claudius probably suffered from cerebral palsy or infantile paralysis as a result of polio – physical infirmities that he more than compensated for with his keen intellect and voracious scholarly studies.

On the reverse we are presented with a remarkable recreation of the location any praetorian holding the aureus would know intimately. Creatively rendered within the coin's tiny canvas, we see the crenellated battlements of the Castra Praetoria, with two arched gateways granting entry. Inside the defensive wall, a praetorian soldier holding a spear stands sentry before the temple-like shrine of the standards. The oversized soldier most likely represents the entirety of the Guard and, more specifically, may personify the 'Fides Praetorianum' or 'Loyalty of the Praetorians' to the new emperor – if not the old – during those critical days in January 41.

The inscription across the face of the coin (as opposed to a coin's 'legend' which curves around its edge) speaks directly to the new power-dynamic established by the Guard's elevation of Claudius. Imaginatively emblazoned across the battlements of the fortress is an abbreviated description of the scene: 'Imperator Receptus' – the 'Reception of the Emperor'. When fully considered, the implications of the commemoration are seismic, openly acknowledging realities that would have previously been unthinkable. The fact that the Guard is shown ready to 'receive' the emperor at the Castra Praetoria presents the fortress as nothing less than the true seat of imperial power in Rome, a fortified satellite-palace at the edge of the city, exerting its gravitational influence over all events in the capital. In welcoming the emperor under their battlements, the praetorians are cast as gracious hosts, and Claudius as their guest, permitted to stay on the throne as long as they are appeased.

This donative issue is made even more extraordinary by the fact that this gold aureus is actually one of a pair of coins, intended to complement one another in their messaging (Plate section, 7). Together the companion coins offer viewers a choice of lenses through which they can interpret the same momentous event. Where the first shows the Praetorian Guard greeting Claudius, its sister coin mirrors it with a depiction of Claudius instead greeting the Guard. Also mirrored are the accompanying written dedications; this time we have the legend 'Praetoriani Recepti' – the 'Reception of the Praetorians'. A toga-clad Claudius is shown shaking hands with a praetorian *signifer* or 'standard bearer' who wears an animal-skin over his helmet. As it does today, the handshake symbolises friendship, harmony, and mutual trust between the two parties – a visual motif that would become a popular one on Roman money any time alliances were forged.

While it may be tempting to see this second coin as redressing the balance of power back towards the emperor, the revealing composition of the figures in the scene betrays the truth. The scale of figures often served to communicate their hierarchy in ancient art; here, Claudius and the guard are presented as the exact same height – equal in size within the frame and by extension, equal in status. The coin inadvertently presents to us a new balance of imperial power: the emperor as the toga-wearing public face, and the praetorians as the armed enforcers – mutually dependent and each granting the other legitimacy.

The unprecedented donative coins tell a dual narrative of Claudius' elevation, almost prefiguring postmodern ideas of subjective truth in their parallel depiction of events. The alternating scenes may even reflect the precision with which coins targeted their intended audience; it is possible that the coins showing the emperor received like a subordinate in the praetorian camp were specifically intended to pay the Guard, deliberately feeding their egos; whereas the coins showing Claudius receiving the praetorians may have paid the donative of other military units, reminding all that the emperor had the Guard's backing while allowing Claudius at least a modicum of agency in his own rise. Afterwards, the valuable aurei would have circulated mainly among the wealthy Roman elite, affirming to the great and the good that, however he came to power, Claudius had the full support of the military's most feared unit.

They may vary in their viewpoint, but the coins make one thing clear: Claudius would be forever indebted to the Praetorian Guard – both figuratively and literally. Every year, Claudius would mark the anniversary of his elevation to the throne with an additional gift of 100 sestertii – or a single gold aureus – to each guardsman.[40] Even with his massive donative, Claudius evidently realised that praetorian loyalty was not purchased for life, but needed annual renewal. Through the numbered titles of Claudius on the obverse, which tallied how many times a ruler had held annual offices such as the tribuneship, we can see that this coin series was still being struck six years into his reign, no doubt being used to pay these anniversary gifts.

Backed by the swords of his praetorians, Claudius would go on to surprise the Empire with his successful thirteen-year reign. The bookish, physically infirm ruler even proved himself quite the military conqueror, launching the full-scale invasion of Britannia two years into his tenure. The mysterious realm at the edge of the world, last visited by Caesar a century earlier, was soon criss-crossed by straight Roman roads connecting newly founded cities like Camulodunum (Colchester), Eboracum (York), and of course, Londinium (London). There would be initial resistance to Roman rule, but ultimately the province would go on to be a prosperous and productive part of the Roman Empire for 400 years. Claudius visited the island soon after the initial invasion, bringing with him his trusted praetorian cohorts and, for added impact, the first recorded elephants to set foot in Britain.

His close relationship with the military unit that made him would continue throughout his reign. When a disturbing plot against the emperor was uncovered in AD 48, the place he sought refuge is most telling: Claudius made a 'cowardly flight' straight to the praetorian camp, where his emperorship was born and evidently where he felt most safe in a crisis.[41] As well as his anniversary bonuses, Claudius is said to have staged gladiatorial displays inside the Castra Praetoria for the entertainment of the Guard.[42] He even made them active participants in shows wherever possible. When an unlucky orca became stuck in the great harbour of Rome at Ostia, Claudius decided to turn the event into an impromptu spectacle for the people. Travelling to Ostia with his praetorians, the emperor and his men took to boats and staged a hunt of the trapped killer whale, showering lances down upon the creature. But the hunt was not totally one-sided. Pliny the Elder, who claims he was there watching the action, says the orca put up such a fight and splashed so much water that it sank a boatload of praetorians that ventured too close.[43] The surreal incident may have given Claudius the idea for his subsequent renovation of Rome's port. Soon after, he ordered that a huge vessel be sunk in the harbour to provide strong foundations for a massive new breakwater and lighthouse.[44]

Suetonius dismisses Claudius as the first emperor to buy the loyalty of the troops, referring indirectly to our infamous gold aureus. Yet soldiers' allegiance had long depended on the weight of their purses. Besides, as most sources make clear, Claudius had little choice. Either he paid, or he died. In this way, his gift to the praetorians was less a bribe, and more his ransom payment. The real first was that the throne was now the Guard's to grant. They had killed one emperor and made another; and this coin, honouring them as Rome's kingmakers, was the price of power.

The Empty Palace

The Praetorian Guard are the ultimate embodiment of the dilemma plaguing powerful rulers across the millennia. Those who sit on the throne will have no shortage of enemies wishing them harm, yet protection against these foes means granting intimate access to an armed and deadly force on whose loyalty everything depends. Long before emperors ruled in Rome, these dangers had been illustrated in one of history's most far-reaching assassinations. On 21 October 336 BC, as King Philip II of Macedon held a celebration in the theatre for his daughter's marriage, he was suddenly stabbed to death by one of his own bodyguards. His twenty-year-old son Alexander immediately ascended the throne, soon embarking on his epic campaign of conquest that would see Greek culture spread as far east as India, and give Alexander his famous title, 'the Great'.

Like the Medjay guards who protected Egypt's pharaohs, or the 10,000 Immortals who formed the bodyguard of Persian kings, world leaders continue to rely on the protection of elite security forces that often achieve their own fame or notoriety. Adolf Hitler would form his SS 'Personal Protection Squadron' in 1925, originally consisting of fewer than a hundred men. By the end of the Second World War the SS would have numerous branches, hundreds of thousands of members, and be regarded as the primary organisation behind the war crimes of the Holocaust. Libya's Colonel Gaddafi would memorably place his trust in an all-female 'Amazonian Guard' who accompanied the dictator everywhere and swore oaths of chastity as part of their service. The Swiss Guard, instantly recognised by their exuberant Renaissance-style uniforms, have protected the Pope and the sites of Vatican City since the sixteenth century. Perhaps the most well-known contemporary bodyguards are those of the US Secret Service, charged with protecting the President of the United States and renowned for their meticulously planned operations.

Ensuring the loyalty of such elite guards – who are by definition highly trained, ambitious, and constantly close to power – has always been a delicate balance, and one that Rome would never fully master. Unable to rely solely on fanatical adherence to a political or religious ideology, Roman emperors were forced to purchase the loyalty of the Guard through material rewards exemplified by our gold aureus; a transactional relationship that over time would only encourage greed and treachery. Inviting armed praetorians so completely into the Roman capital, into the Senate, even into the private rooms of the palace allowed them to exert the implicit threat of violence over every aspect of Roman political life. Even more fatally, as Gibbon observed, the praetorians were taught 'to view the vices of their masters with familiar contempt, and to lay aside that reverential awe, which distance only, and mystery, can preserve towards an imaginary power'.[45] As the folk tale warns, they saw that the emperor had no clothes. Imperial authority once granted by august institutions and revered ancient titles was now theirs to give and take away as they saw fit.

After placing Claudius on the throne, the Guard would continue to play a key role in the rise and fall of emperors for almost 300 years. Numerous rulers would find themselves at the business end of praetorian blades, some just months after paying huge donatives to secure their loyalty. The nadir of the Guard would come in AD 193 when, after murdering the emperor Pertinax, the unit auctioned off the Empire to the highest bidder. The pitiful sale, held at the walls of their fortress, saw them take competing monetary offers for their support from naive senators and eventually opening the gates to the winner, Didius Julianus. After purchasing the throne with an obscenely large gift to the Guard, he would be killed by them just nine weeks later. Praetorians continued to sully the succession process and effectively hold the Empire hostage until 312, when they would finally be disbanded by the emperor Constantine – and only when he had slighted the high walls of their Roman fortress was Constantine certain that he had ended the Guard's supremacy.

Tellingly, it was direct to these walls that the teenage Nero had been rushed upon the death of his great-uncle, Claudius. The first priority for any new emperor going forward would be to make straight for the Castra Praetoria to address the soldiers and give the necessary promises. We can only imagine how intimidating this was for Nero, Rome's youngest emperor yet, ascending the throne at the tender age of sixteen. Like Caligula, he came to power on a wave of goodwill and hopeful expectation. In an inaugural speech, written by his famous tutor Seneca, Nero promised that his would be a just rule, 'not motivated by hatred or vengeance'. Promises that – also like those of Caligula – would soon ring hollow.

The first watchword he ever gave to his praetorians was '*Optima*

Mater' – 'the best of mothers' – but Nero soon tired of his domineering mother, Agrippina the Younger (one of the sisters featured on Caligula's sestertius), who acted more like his co-ruler than his parent. This resentment culminated in Nero's most infamous crime: the calculated murder of his mother in AD 59. Freed from her interference, the flamboyant youth could embark upon a decade of excess and indulgence – indeed Nero's masterful coin portraits record his dramatic weight gain in these years with surprising honesty.

Nero was far more passionate about music and the arts than the mundanities of administering an empire. He became the first ruler to take to the stage, giving lengthy musical performances that audiences were forbidden to leave. As a committed aesthete, Nero also sought to beautify his surroundings at any expense. His taste for luxury was shamelessly demonstrated in the building of his *Domus Aurea* or 'Golden House'. After the catastrophic Great Fire of Rome conveniently cleared vast areas of city real estate in 64, Nero decided to seize the land for a sprawling urban pleasure-palace covering around 200 acres of central Rome. Construction of his decadent palace scandalised the age, with Suetonius calling it 'ruinously prodigal'. At its heart lay a huge artificial lake upon which Nero held floating feasts, and nearby a hundred-foot gilded bronze colossus of the emperor which dominated the Roman skyline. With the completion of his Golden House, Nero claimed he could 'finally begin to live like a human being'.[46]

But no sooner had his palace been completed than Nero's reign and with it the bloodline of Augustus came to a dramatic end. As provincial governors began to revolt against his tyrannical rule, Nero hoped he might weather the storm; the death knell came when the Praetorian Guard publicly declared for one of his rivals. Nero realised the game was up and escaped the city in disguise before the Guard could dispose of him as they had done Caligula. Holed up in a suburban villa, Nero lamented 'what an artist dies in me', before ordering his loyal freedman to drive a dagger into his throat.

After his suicide, Nero's newly completed palace would be stripped of all its valuables and filled with earth to act as foundations for new buildings. And from the ruins of the Empire's founding family, a new dynasty would also arise. In reclaiming the heart of the city for the people, the site of Nero's private lake was chosen for the construction of a spectacular monument to be enjoyed by all – the largest of its kind ever built in the Roman world. It would be the ultimate embodiment of the strength, the reach, and the brutality of the Empire. A building so iconic that, for many, it would become the prevailing symbol of Rome itself.

Chapter VII
ARENA

'Nothing is so damaging to good character as idling away time at the games, where vices have a way of creeping in disguised as entertainment. I personally return from the shows more greedy, more ambitious, more luxurious, indeed, even more cruel and inhuman.'

Seneca

Posthumous sestertius of Titus commemorating the inauguration of the Colosseum, AD 81.
Obverse: The Flavian Amphitheatre (Colosseum), with Meta Sudans fountain to left, and Baths of Titus to right.
Reverse: Titus seated left on *curule* chair holding olive branch and surrounded by arms.

Let the Games Begin

Trumpet blasts herald the start of the parade. An orchestra of musicians playing flutes, horns, lyres, cymbals, drums, even a water-powered pipe organ, strike up a jubilant tune as the grand procession emerges onto the sand. Their notes transcend even the thunderous cheers of the crowd, swirling around the steep stands of the new arena. The organiser of the coming spectacles leads the pageant, accompanied by the young sons of Rome's most noble families. Following are troupes of mime artists, twirling dancers, and leaping acrobats – all dressed in elaborate costumes and garlanded in the brightest flowers. The parade is an explosion of colour.[1]

Huge cheers greet the appearance of the beast hunters who will entertain the masses during the morning, and pulled alongside, some of the tamer exotic animals that will be displayed from every corner of the Empire. One wrangler struggles with the chain leading his fierce-looking lion as it recoils in fear at the overwhelming sights and sounds. But the most deafening clamour is reserved for the undisputed stars of the arena, marching proudly onto the sand that will soon absorb their blood. The gladiators, many of whom will not survive these inaugural games, wave to the adoring spectators as the sunlight flashes off their gleaming ceremonial armour. The warriors are surrounded by an entourage of attendants that carry their polished metal helmets and placards announcing the name and career statistics of each fighter to the crowds.[2]

All who tread the sand of the new amphitheatre feel, for a moment, like a god, but last to enter the arena are the gods themselves: ivory statues of Jupiter, Juno, Mars, Venus, all the deities of the pantheon, carried high on men's shoulders around the full circuit of the sands. Priests of their cult escort them, swinging incense burners that billow pungent smoke. At the culmination of the procession, the gods will be placed on a sacred ringside platform from where they can watch the action as the most honoured spectators – every drop of spilled blood ultimately dedicated to them.[3]

In the imperial box, the emperor stands to address the Roman people, visible to all in his dazzling gold and purple robes. The crowds instantly hush to hear his echoing words. Titus welcomes all to the inauguration of this, the greatest amphitheatre in the Empire, built with the spoils of Rome's triumph in the Jewish War. As the first son ever to succeed his natural father to the imperial throne, Titus expresses his sadness that his father, Vespasian, did not live to see this grand monument to his Flavian dynasty completed; to see Rome finally restored to herself and to her people. Yet this celebration, an unprecedented one hundred consecutive days of games, filled with never-before-seen wonders, will be his gift to the populace.

There will also be endless bounties drawn from Rome's vast dominion. Titus gestures skyward and to the astonishment of the spectators, a shower of gifts begins to rain down on them from the heights of the amphitheatre — sweetcakes, pastries, and ripe produce conjured from the most distant lands: dates from Arabia, figs from Anatolia, plums from Damascus. But these tasty fruits of empire are the least of the presents on offer.[4] Some are lucky enough to catch small wooden balls inscribed with the designation of even greater prizes, to be exchanged after the show for jewellery, horses, perhaps even a slave.[5]

Also being dispensed through the crowd is a shining souvenir created especially for the historic occasion: a lustrous bronze sestertius coin, fresh from the Roman mint. Delighted recipients, young and old, marvel at the intricate design on the weighty medallic coin, recreating the amphitheatre surrounding them in precise detail — its endless arcades of arches framing statues of Roman heroes, its miraculous retractable awning stretching out over the stands, shielding spectators from the hot sun. Even the people themselves are shown — up to 80,000 of them now packed into this temple of entertainment. The Flavian Amphitheatre was built for them, its oval arena an eye through which Romans of every class can witness the spectacle of the world. Where once stood a palace to the folly of a single man, now stands a palace of the people — and their rapturous applause answers the last announcement of the emperor: 'Let the games begin!'

Reclaiming Rome

The suicide of Nero in AD 68 presented the Roman state with a conundrum. The imperial throne had long been a grand inheritance, bequeathed in the bloodline of a single family, yet decades of murderous paranoia, combined with a distinct lack of sons, had whittled down the branches of the Julio-Claudian tree until not a single male heir remained. With no descendants of Caesar left to hoist onto praetorian shoulders, Rome could only ask herself one question: could a new dynasty arise to claim the Empire?

The answer would only be revealed after a chaotic civil war, the likes of which Rome had not seen since the dying days of the Republic. A succession of ambitious provincial governors would claim the throne with the help of their troops, only to be murdered by them after mere months in power. When the popular general Vespasian was hailed as emperor by his legions in July 69, he became the fourth man to go by the title that year. The commander had been busy crushing a massive Jewish revolt in the province of Judea when destiny called. Leaving his capable son Titus to complete the siege of Jerusalem, Vespasian swept back into Rome to be affirmed as emperor by an obedient Senate. The new dynasty of the Flavians had arrived. Imperial power was evidently no longer reserved for those who shared the blood of Caesar and Augustus; it had become a transferable asset.

Vespasian had, at least, some ties to the old regime: Claudius had entrusted the hardened general with pacifying the south-west of Britannia during his conquest of the island. On his return from Britain he was rewarded with a consulship, serving alongside Claudius himself. An impressive rise for the son of a middle-class tax collector. Vespasian later accompanied Nero on a cultural tour of Greece, though apparently he lost the artiste-emperor's favour after falling asleep in one of his interminable lyre recitals.[6] Now the military man with a country accent and earthy sense of humour was master of Rome – his reign bolstered in its first year by welcome news from the East. His son Titus had breached the walls of Jerusalem in AD 70, massacred the rebellious Jewish population, and burned down their sacred Second Temple for good measure. But not before looting its many treasures, most notably the temple menorah – a solid gold seven-branched candelabrum – which would be proudly displayed with all the other spoils at the joint triumph of Titus and Vespasian the following year.

A man of humble origins and simple tastes, Vespasian quickly set about demolishing Nero's sprawling golden palace with the intention of reclaiming the heart of the city for the people. Some wings were flattened, others were simply buried and built over. Many centuries later, the artists Michelangelo and Raphael would rappel down into these accidentally preserved corridors and meticulously sketch the fantastical ancient frescoes by candlelight. Their studies of the vibrantly painted interiors sent shockwaves through Renaissance Europe, with Raphael even recreating the 'grotesque' decoration of Nero's palace in his subsequent redesign of the Vatican.[7]

The imposing bronze Colossus of Nero was allowed to remain standing, though its features were altered and a radiate crown added to rebrand it as a depiction of the sun god, Sol. As for the enormous artificial lake where Nero enjoyed pleasure-boating in the centre of Rome, Vespasian ordered it drained and conferred with his architects at the edge of the huge basin, pointing and gesturing as if planning one of his military campaigns. He now had the space – and with the spoils from Jerusalem, the funding – for a popular monument bigger than anything Rome had ever attempted. A building that would stand testament to his obscure family name for all eternity.

Rome may have borrowed the concept of the semi-circular theatre from the Greeks, but the *amphitheatre* was a profoundly Roman invention. As its name suggests – with the prefix 'amphi' simply meaning 'double/both' – the amphitheatre effectively combined two theatres to create an exhibition space in which the action is viewable from all sides. To further maximise the visibility and energy of displays, Roman architects stretched the resulting circle into an ellipse – a dynamic shape that both encouraged movement and prolonged contests by ensuring there were no corners for fighters to become trapped in. This emphasis on the viewing experience of the spectators highlights an emerging difference between the Greek and Roman mind; where Greeks were expected to be active participants in physical competition and to maintain fitness in readiness for military duty, Romans of the first century had become passive observers, increasingly distanced from the realities of combat thanks to professional armies which saw to the Empire's defence.[8]

Romans had been thrilled by chariot races in the Circus Maximus for centuries, but a permanent stone amphitheatre had been a long-awaited addition to the city. Hunting and gladiatorial displays were previously held in temporary wooden arenas, quickly constructed in the Forum square whenever a politician needed to boost their popularity. Uniting the masses in close proximity and inflaming their passions with spectacles of blood could be a risky gamble for city magistrates, potentially inciting violence and unrest. Everyone had heard about the events in Pompeii, after all. The provincial town in the shadow of Mount Vesuvius had enjoyed its own stone amphitheatre for over a century. That was until a gladiatorial show in AD 59 during which fighting broke out between the Pompeiian home crowd and visiting fans from a rival town. The brawling spilled out of the arena, becoming an all-out riot that left many dead. As a stern punishment, Nero banned gladiator displays in the town for ten years. Still, some Pompeiians evidently took pride in their showing that day; one resident commissioned a large wall fresco for his home depicting the amphitheatre riot. Just as the fresco is preserved today thanks to the eruption of Vesuvius, so too is the battleground of Pompeii's arena – the oldest surviving Roman amphitheatre in the world.

Owing to the amount of land required, as well as the noise, waste, and general raucous atmosphere they generated, amphitheatres were usually placed at the very edge of a city. Not so the grand arena we today call the Colosseum. It would be built in the political and religious heart of the capital. All the Empire's roads led to Rome, and once inside the city, all roads would lead to the new Flavian Amphitheatre.

In every sense, the sand of its arena would be the centre of the Roman world.

The Emperor's Gift

The ruin rises in the midst of the city, triumphant yet forlorn, as if abandoned by the Empire that once surrounded it. While it continues to capture the imagination of millions of visitors every year, the Colosseum stands a beaten and broken survivor, testament equally to 'Rome's grandeur and Rome's decay'.[9] We might assume that in its prime, this architectural wonder at the epicentre of Roman culture was depicted by countless artists in fresco, marble, and mosaic. If it was, no such tributes survive. Only one artefact can allow us a historically priceless glimpse at the majesty of the monument when newly constructed.

This bronze sestertius was struck to commemorate the lavish inauguration of the Flavian Amphitheatre in AD 80, and stamped into its golden-brown metal we see the Colosseum in all its ancient splendour (Plate section, 8).[10] Building work on the arena had taken around eight years to complete, demanding the mobilisation of vast amounts of resources and labour. Just as the project was funded by spoils taken in the sack of Jerusalem, the construction workforce would have also included thousands of Jewish slaves brought back from the war. Before the 'mass of the far-seen amphitheatre' could begin to rise over Rome, a complex network of drains was installed to carry excess water from the marshy valley to the Tiber river.[11] With the hydraulic system prepared, 250,000 cubic metres of concrete were packed into the excavated bed of Nero's lake to create a massive oval foundation thirteen metres deep. The superstructure of the amphitheatre would then take shape, built using an estimated 100,000 cubic metres of the finest travertine limestone transported from quarries twenty miles away. Individual blocks weighing upwards of four tons were hoisted high into position using human-powered treadwheel cranes, before being fixed in place with over 300 tons of iron clamps.[12]

The sestertius shows the completed fifty-metre-high outer walls of the amphitheatre, a section of which still stands today thanks to a lucky underpinning of hard volcanic bedrock that dampened vibrations of destructive earthquakes over the millennia. As we can see in its depiction of the facade, the Colosseum was designed as nothing less than a celebration of that architectural feature that helped Rome engineer an empire – the arch. Held in place by their central keystone, arches both minimised the weight of a structure and distributed that weight evenly through walls below. Roman engineers masterfully exploited the potential of arches in their construction of soaring bridges and aqueducts that still seem to defy gravity as they leap across entire valleys.

Three stacked tiers of arcades wrapped around the facade of the Colosseum, each comprising eighty arches. While these stand empty today, the sestertius reveals that the second and third tier arcades originally framed 160 statues, almost certainly depicting mythological heroes and famous Roman generals. Also visible on the coin is the grand entranceway reserved for the emperor, topped by a statue of a four-horse triumphal chariot. Other ground-floor entrances were reserved for senators, patricians, and performers, leaving seventy-six gateways for the general public. A Roman numeral engraved above each gate corresponded to a ticket issued to those attending the games, directing spectators on the most efficient route to their assigned seat. Entrances numbered XXIII (twenty-three) to LIIII (fifty-four) still survive today, offering a handy lesson in ancient Roman numerals as you stroll the circuit of the ruins.[13]

Despite being dedicated to entertainment, the building also sought to provide visitors with an education in architectural history. The three tiers of arcades correspond to the three orders of classical architecture: plain Doric columns on the ground level, elegant Ionic columns on the second level, and ornate Corinthian columns on the third. In its incorporation of all three canonical orders, the Colosseum almost presents itself as a glorious architectural culmination, showcasing the pinnacle of what classical architecture can achieve. At its highest level, our sestertius reveals that the Colosseum was adorned with large shields, most likely made in gilded bronze, that would have shone like jewels in a crown under the Roman sun.

Vespasian would die of illness in AD 79 just as his ambitious amphitheatre was being completed. Even on his deathbed he displayed his signature down-to-earth humour, exclaiming: 'Dear me! I think I am becoming a god.'[14] Titus, conqueror of Jerusalem, therefore became the first son to inherit the throne from his father in over a century of imperial rule. He would also be depicted on the reverse of the inauguration sestertius – in place of the usual deity – sitting atop piles of captured weapons and armour, offering the obligatory olive branch of peace.

The coin already captivates in its vivid contemporary snapshot of Rome's most recognisable building, yet recent research into the context of its creation has only added to its significance. Study has suggested that the sestertius was not merely minted for general circulation but was perhaps struck as a souvenir, gifted to crowds attending the Colosseum's opening games. A number of unusual features hint at the coin being produced for such a special purpose. Notably, it lacks a key attribute of almost all imperial coins: the bust of the emperor. In place of an obverse portrait of Titus, we have the rendering of the Colosseum, presenting the building as the true honouree of the issue. The arena is also shown in an aerial view that offers a revolutionary three-dimensional perspective of the structure, as opposed to the two-dimensional renderings usually seen on coins. The larger flan of the bronze sestertius has provided an expansive canvas for the ambitious design, which reveals the Colosseum to be part of a wider complex of new Flavian monuments. Beside the amphitheatre we see the pointed Meta Sudans – a twenty-metre monumental fountain that took its name from the *metae* turning posts of the circus racetrack. With *sudans* meaning 'perspiring', water is thought to have flowed gently down the cone of this 'sweating post' rather than jetting out. The core of the fountain would stand next to the Colosseum until 1936, when it was demolished on the orders of Mussolini. Also visible on the coin is the columned portico of the new Baths of Titus, hastily erected next to the Colosseum on top of Nero's Golden House. Together, the image represents the first time a public entertainment complex was celebrated on a Roman coin, which usually reserved their honours for triumphal or religious monuments.

While careful thought has clearly gone into its design and engraving, the sestertius is also extremely rare. Study of the handful of known dies used to strike the issue suggests a production of well under 100,000 examples, a small number if intended for use as currency across the Empire. Intriguingly, the Colosseum's seating capacity was between 50,000 and 80,000. All of these elements, as well as the general medallic quality of the coins, point to them being souvenir pieces given as public largess, either gifted to every attendee at the opening games or distributed at intervals throughout the hundred-day inaugural celebration.[15]

Most spectators probably spent their money medallion, but with the sestertius being a relatively low-value coin (a quarter of a denarius), some may have kept them for their sentimental and artistic worth. Incidentally, while each attendee might have been gifted a single sestertius, the construction of the Colosseum itself has been estimated to have cost something on the order of one hundred million sestertii – roughly equating to between £1 billion and £2 billion today, matching the cost of most modern stadiums.[16]

Entering the amphitheatre embossed on the coin, we will see that it was a place of engineering marvels and theatrical wonders, where Romans of every class came to feel at their most alive – yet for untold numbers of humans, and for entire species of animals, the Colosseum would deliver nothing but torture and death.

Populus Romanus

Recipients of the coin saw in its design more than just a celebration of the building around them. For the first time ever, they saw themselves. Appropriately enough for a monument of the people, their heads are picked out in microscopic detail by the engraver, filling the stands of the amphitheatre. An inspired self-referential touch and one that makes this, incredibly, the only Roman coin ever to depict the assembled *populus Romanus* – the common people of Rome.

In the steep incline of those Colosseum stands, we see the full sweep of Roman society. The hierarchy was clear. At the front podium, closest to the bloody action, were the seats reserved for the senators, the Vestal Virgins – chaste priestesses who tended the sacred hearth of the goddess Vesta – and of course, the emperor himself.

Behind them sat men of Rome's wealthy patrician families, and higher still, equestrian men of the upper middle class. The second and third tiers of seating were occupied by the men of the plebian class – ordinary working citizens – in descending order of wealth and status. In the very heights of the amphitheatre, kept furthest from the arena sands, sat foreigners, slaves, and women. Aside from these groups sitting in the gods on rickety wooden benches, Romans of every rank perched on seats of fine Carrara marble from enormous quarries in Tuscany that provided the gleaming white stone for many of Rome's most famous structures – as well as Michelangelo's *David* – and are still in operation today.

A range of state-of-the-art engineering sensations ensured the comfort of spectators as they enjoyed the carnage in the arena. Most conspicuous among these was the astonishing *velarium* – a giant awning extending miraculously above the crowds to protect them from the blazing Roman sun. The velarium was operated by a detachment of sailors from the Roman naval base at Misenum, expertly manipulating the complex rigging of the awning much like the cloth sails of their vessels – indeed, its name derives from the Latin *velum* meaning 'sail'. Also visible on the sestertius are the 240 poles rising from the top of the structure supporting the weight of the twenty-four-ton sunshade, their empty sockets still to be seen encircling the rim of the Colosseum today. With its giant sails, adjusted throughout the day following the passage of the sun, the Colosseum effectively became the first ever stadium to benefit from a retractable roof.

The velarium not only cast a cooling shadow on the crowd but its sails are also thought to have encouraged a ventilation updraft, promoting air circulation and a refreshing breeze in the arena. Yet despite the sailors' best efforts, the awning could not shield every audience member and the heat of a Roman summer surely remained blistering for many. Luckily, on the hottest days the crowds might also enjoy *sparsiones* or 'sprinklings', refreshing water-mist blown from manually operated force pumps. Pleasing aromas of balsam or saffron added to the water might even help conceal the smell of your more fragrant neighbours in the stands.

The luxurious surroundings and expansive facilities of the

Colosseum would have made a welcome escape for Rome's urban population, most of whom worked laborious jobs and lived in cramped, teetering apartment buildings without toilets or plumbing. In vaulted corridors decorated with dazzling painted stucco and fresco, one hundred drinking fountains delivered a constant flow of refreshing water to thirsty spectators, piped into the building from the Claudian aqueduct.[17] Large communal toilets, similarly washed by the flow of the aqueduct, also served the needs of audiences. Recent exploration of the Colosseum's drainage system has even uncovered remains of the various snacks enjoyed by spectators during their day at the games. Remnants of olives, figs, grapes, cherries, peaches, plums, walnuts, hazelnuts, and blackberries have all been discovered, along with bones of chickens and pigs that some suggest may have been cooked by spectators on portable braziers during breaks in the performances.[18]

The refined decor, the comforts afforded audiences, and the jubilant atmosphere in the stands all provided a stark contrast to the brutal spectacles playing out in the oval of the arena. The Latin *arena* simply translates as 'sand', describing the sand spread across the wooden floor of the Colosseum to soak up the blood of countless men and animals. A high podium enclosing the arena kept the killing at a safe distance, with ivory rollers and gold netting suspended from elephant tusks further protecting the front-row elites from leaping beasts.[19] Mornings at the games were reserved for thrilling animal hunts known as *venationes*, featuring exotic creatures from across the Empire, when every eye was locked on the trapdoors opening in the sand, waiting to see what marvellous beast might emerge, as if by magic, into the theatre of death.

The Killing Floor

Such was the popularity of the Colosseum's elaborately staged wild-animal hunts, the building came to be known by some as simply the 'hunting theatre'. Slaughter took place on an industrial scale. We are told that during the inaugural games, a staggering 9,000 animals were

A bronze *quadrans* showing an anatomically correct African rhinoceros, and a denarius of Titus showing an African elephant.

slain for the entertainment of the crowds.[20] A few of these fantastical creatures captured the imagination of the populace to such an extent that they were even immortalised on coinage after the games. In his poetic celebration of the spectacles, Martial pays tribute to an African rhinoceros whose ferocity made its own keepers tremble. The rhino was pitted against a bull and later a bear, tossing them in the air like ragdolls. The 'double-horned' beast was eventually vanquished by the famed hunter Carpophorus, who managed to pierce the animal's tough hide with his precisely aimed spears.[21] The rhinoceros would thereafter be memorialised on small bronze coins with an anatomically accurate depiction showing its two horns and stocky armoured body.

An African elephant also achieved similar fame in the inaugural games when it emerged onto the sand and apparently knelt in reverence to the emperor Titus.[22] Martial reports that the animal's gesture was done without instruction, but the intelligence and training potential of elephants had long been appreciated by the Romans. Julius Caesar had paraded forty of them through the streets of the city during his Gallic triumph. Claudius had even established an elephant farm near Ostia, where the animals could be bred on Italian soil, rather than being imported with great difficulty from Africa.[23]

While their awesome destructive power sadly made elephants an inevitable addition to the games, their uncanny intellect gave even the Romans pause on occasion. Plutarch tells a heart-breaking anecdote of a group of elephants that were being trained to perform complex routines in the arena. One of the animals struggling to learn the tricks was repeatedly berated and punished by the trainers. Plutarch claims: 'That night, the elephant could be seen all alone in the moonlight, practising what he had been taught.'[24] Cicero was similarly struck by the gentle nobility of the animals. After watching a display of elephants in 55 BC, he wrote that while the crowd were astonished, they gained no pleasure from the show at all: 'No, indeed, a great sense of pity arose for the animals, and a feeling that they are somehow deeply connected to mankind.'[25]

This affinity would not stop the animals being hunted in such vast numbers that the North African elephant, a subspecies that once roamed the Atlas Mountains, would eventually be driven to extinction in the Roman era. Indeed, the Roman obsession with *venationes* already threatened the survival of multiple animal species before the Colosseum was even constructed, as evidenced in another of Cicero's letters. During his time as governor of Cilicia (in southern Asia Minor), Cicero was bombarded by requests from the Roman *aedile* in charge of organising games, urging him to supply panthers from his province for display in the capital. After an increasingly desperate exchange, Cicero is forced to concede that 'the animals are in remarkably short supply' and that 'fearing for their safety, the panthers have decided to depart from my province'.[26] Excessive hunting in ancient times would similarly drive out the hippopotamus from Egypt's Nile region and contribute to the extinction of North Africa's majestic Barbary lion.

Supplying exotic animals for hunts staged not only in the Colosseum but in more than 200 amphitheatres across the Roman Empire would remain a lucrative business for centuries. Sicily's sprawling Villa Romana del Casale, a fourth-century Roman estate housing the largest selection of in-situ mosaics in the world, is thought to have belonged to a wealthy individual involved in the capture and trade of wild animals. All around the palatial residence, mosaics celebrate the dramatic live capture of beasts of every description: a leopard is surrounded by hunters as it feeds, a rhino bound by ropes is hauled from its savanna; one scene even depicts hunters in India snatching tiger cubs while their mother is distracted by a mirror. Unfortunate creatures are then shown being dragged up ramps onto transport ships – ostriches, gazelle, elephants with chained feet – destined for display and death in amphitheatres all over the Empire.

Animals that came to the Colosseum after journeying sometimes hundreds of miles by land and sea eventually found themselves caged in the amphitheatre's *hypogeum*. Literally meaning 'underground', this complex labyrinth of passages and cells concealed under the arena floor operated as the Colosseum's backstage area. The hellish conditions in this subterranean world can barely be imagined. Animal handlers and performers rushing through cramped tunnels. The constant roar of frightened beasts adding to the deafening clamour of the crowds above. Stifling air filled with the stench of blood, sweat, and excrement – and all in near-darkness lit only by feeble lamplight. As their time approached, an ingenious system of man-powered elevators raised animals up from the depths to the killing floor above. Props and scenery could also be hoisted to the surface, creating elaborate backdrops for the battles. At the precise moment the action demanded, one of thirty-six trapdoors would fall open and the animal would emerge, starved and terrified, onto the arena sand (Plate section, 9).

After the morning *venatio*, ravenous animals were also put to use in the midday intermission. The gruesome execution of convicted criminals provided light entertainment to audiences as they enjoyed their lunchtime refreshments, with many prisoners suffering *damnatio ad bestias* – condemnation to the beasts. Runaway slaves, thieves, murderers, and members of the dissident sect known as Christians might be thrown defenceless to lions or tied to stakes to be slowly eaten alive by bears. Such grisly executions provided not only welcome distraction during the interval, but also served as a regular reminder to audiences of the fate that awaited all enemies of the established Roman order.

Discerning viewers, however, soon tired of seeing criminals being mindlessly torn to pieces. By the time of the Colosseum's inauguration in the late first century, indulged crowds demanded constant novelty and spectacle. Executions therefore became increasingly theatrical recreations of classical myths and famous historical battles. The promise of the new Colosseum to the people of Rome was clear: 'Whatever legend sings, the arena offers you.' This was where myth came to life. A notorious temple robber strung up to have his innards slowly devoured by animals, just like that thief of fire, Prometheus. Or another criminal fitted with wings and hoisted up to the top of the amphitheatre to re-enact the doomed flight of Icarus. After being dropped from a great height, the broken body of the condemned was ripped apart by wild boars.[27]

To watching Romans, these were wondrous sights, but they served as mere prologue for the show that was to come. As the carcasses were dragged from the blood-stained sand, anticipation built for the contests that would be fought in the heat of the afternoon. Spectators rushed back to their seats as the trumpets sounded. To thundering applause that somehow exceeded all that came before, the fighters marched out into the natural spotlight blazing through the gap in the velarium. These were the most adored and the most despised warriors of the Roman world.

'Those who are about to die . . .'

The curve of the Colosseum perfectly describes the Roman contradiction: an elegant architectural masterclass, built to celebrate death and cruelty; where people of apparent cultural sophistication and modernity gathered to applaud the torture of humans and animals. As the arena continues to challenge modern sensibilities around blood sports as entertainment, so too we remain fascinated by the enigmatic persona most associated with its walls. The gladiator stands a paradoxical figure. Their fighting prowess inspired the soldier, their stoic bravery impressed the philosopher, and their virile displays made them the object of sexual fantasy. Yet all acknowledged them to be *infames* – the most contemptible of slaves with no legal or social standing, segregated from society even in death. Unlike the animals of the arena, no gladiator would ever grace a Roman coin.

Gladiatorial contests known as *munera* began in the third century BC as part of the funeral rites of elite Romans, with a few fighters drawing blood in honour of the dead. These displays quickly grew in scale, evidently speaking uniquely to the martial character of the Romans. In 183 BC, a deceased nobleman was honoured by three whole days of games in the Roman Forum, during which 120 gladiators fought. The political capital to be gained from staging such spectacular events could not go unnoticed. By the late Republic, political heavyweights like Caesar and Pompey vied to outdo each other with ever more lavish contests, 'no longer held in honour of the dead but in honour of the living'.[28]

Most gladiators were either prisoners of war or criminals sentenced to death, though down-on-their-luck Roman citizens were known to sacrifice their freedom and take to the sand seeking money and fame. Gladiators lived in a fortified training school called a *ludus*, where they honed their fighting skills under the watchful eye of their *lanista*. Overseeing his own troupe of gladiators, the lanista bought and sold men much like a sports manager today, while holding absolute power of life and death over all in his school or *familia*. Upon entering their ludus, gladiators made their sacred oath – the *sacramentum gladiatorium* – before their new master: 'I will endure to be burned, to be bound, to be beaten, and to be killed by the sword.' As the wording suggests, conditions were harsh, discipline severe, and prospects bleak in gladiatorial *ludi* across the Roman world.[29]

The remains of the Empire's greatest training school, the Ludus Magnus, can still be seen next to the Colosseum today. Clearly visible is the practice ring where up to 3,000 fans could watch the gladiators sparring in the run-up to the games, as well as the cramped cells where the men were locked up after a hard day's training. As home to potentially hundreds of elite fighters, security in the ludus was robust. Rome would never forget the lessons learned in 73 BC, when a band of gladiators led by a Thracian named Spartacus broke out of their training school in Capua and quickly formed a 120,000-strong rebel army that almost brought the Republic to its knees.

With spectacles approaching, the lanista would rent out his gladiators to the organiser of the games known as the *editor*. The more popular his fighters, the more money he could demand, and he would expect to be fully compensated for lost earnings if an editor insisted on fatalities in his show. Gladiator contests are usually depicted in popular culture as no-holds-barred battles to the death, preceded by that fatalistic greeting to the emperor: 'Those who are about to die salute you!' The phrase is indeed reported as being addressed to Claudius by convicted criminals preparing to fight a mock naval battle, though we do not know if a similar salute was ever used in the Colosseum.[30] Contests were intended as thrilling displays of weapon mastery, and many of these were very likely exhibition bouts, with blood drawn for dramatic effect. Gladiators were certainly prepared to die, and did in large numbers, but when they met their end depended on more revealing factors than simply their fighting skill.

Gladiators represented sizeable investments to their lanista. Not only did he pay to feed, house, equip, and train his fighters, he would also pay for the best medical care available to treat their inevitable injuries. The ancient world's most famous doctor, Galen, began his career as a gladiator physician treating fighters in the city of Pergamum. A successful gladiator could bring great prestige and even greater profits to his school, making him a valuable commodity. Modern comparison to a prize-winning racehorse – with its associated care, training, risks, and rewards – may go some way to convey the dynamic between the star gladiator and his master. His death was therefore an expensive business.

With so much at stake, ensuring the fairness of contests was vital – and this was guaranteed by a crucial figure sadly absent from film and television recreations. The referee, known as the *summa rudis or* 'highest authority', closely supervised the action just like in combat sports today (Plate section, 10). Dressed in a white tunic and wielding a wooden rod with which he could strike or separate fighters, the referee established a level of fair play we may not often associate with the Roman arena. He could pause a fight to replace broken equipment, allow a fighter to fix their twisted helmet, or warn men about illegal moves. While no gladiator rulebook survives from the ancient world, the fact that referees – sometimes teams of referees – presided over contests, suggests there were clear regulations to follow. A number of ancient mosaics show the summa rudis getting dangerously close to the swinging blades and tussling to separate fighters. Unsurprisingly, the decision making of the referee came under much scrutiny. One gladiator named Diodorus even used the epitaph on his gravestone to blame a 'treacherous' referee for getting him killed.[31]

The referee would be especially important in overseeing the culmination of a fight. If an injured or outclassed gladiator wished to submit to his opponent, he could extend his index and middle fingers to the emperor or editor presiding over the games. With this appeal for mercy, known as *missio*, the life of the defeated gladiator hung in the balance. The cries of the crowd – '*Mitte!*' ('Let him go!') or '*Iugula!*' ('Kill him!') – surely influenced judgements, but factors such as the age, fame, and future earning potential of fighters no doubt also came into consideration. An ageing fighter on a losing streak might have raised his fingers optimistically, despite knowing that retirement-by-sword was his likely fate. The infamous 'thumbs down' of the emperor still signals his verdict in most cinematic depictions, inspired by the dramatic 1872 painting *Pollice Verso* by Jean-Léon Gérôme. The title, meaning 'with a turn of the thumb', is taken from descriptions in a small number of ancient sources where spectators demand death with an ambiguous thumb gesture. Whether the thumb was pointed down, sideways, or jabbed like a stabbing sword we cannot know.[32]

Death – when that was the verdict – was delivered execution-style and received with a stoic acceptance that impressed Rome's greatest minds. Cicero marvelled at the bravery shown by these 'dregs of mankind', asking movingly: 'What gladiator, of even average reputation, ever gave a sigh, ever turned pale? Ever disgraced himself when about to die? When defeated, ever drew in his neck to avoid the stroke of death?'[33] A stone relief in Durrës, Albania, shows a gladiator kneeling as his opponent plunges a sword between his shoulder blades. Analysis of a skull from the gladiator graveyard in Ephesus, discovered in 1993, revealed a similar scenario. The man's head had been impaled from above by the three prongs of a trident in a downward strike delivered as he knelt before his opponent.

Yet the chances that a competent gladiator might survive for years or even decades during the Republic and early Empire were

1. Rome's first denarius, with its portrait of the goddess Roma, shown in the hand of the author.

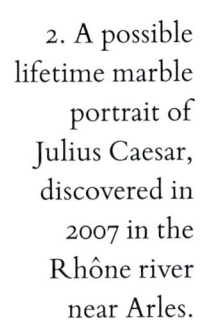

2. A possible lifetime marble portrait of Julius Caesar, discovered in 2007 in the Rhône river near Arles.

3. A Roman soldier's *pugio* dagger of the same type used by Brutus and his fellow assassins. Denmark National Museum.

4. Roman eagle onyx cameo, thought to have been commissioned in 27 BC to celebrate Octavian receiving the title 'Augustus'. Vienna KHM.

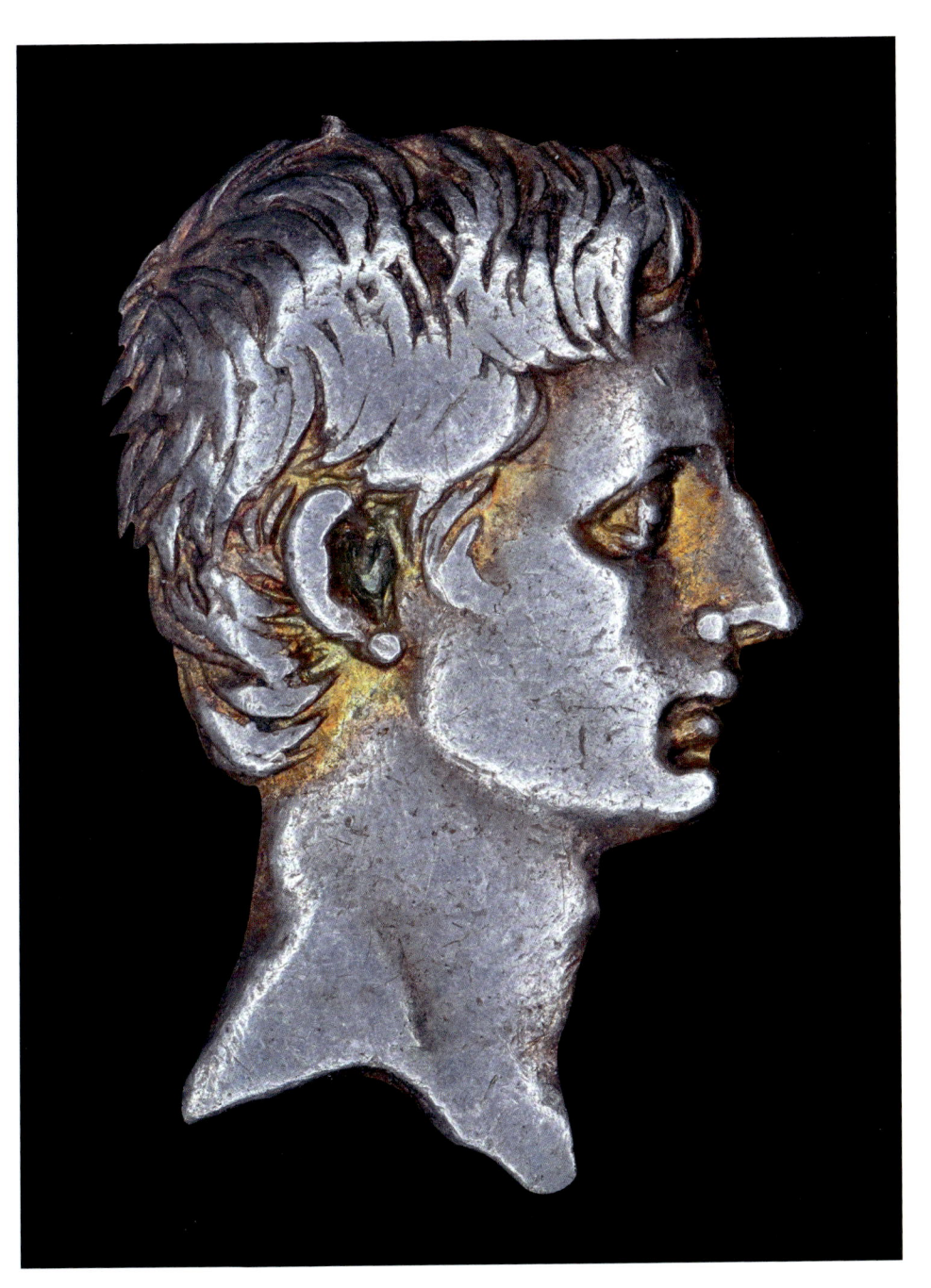

5. Detail of the portrait of Octavian/Augustus, on a denarius from the author's collection.

6. Marble portrait of the emperor Caligula, AD 37–41. Ny Carlsberg Glyptotek, Copenhagen.

7. Two gold aurei minted to pay Claudius' donative to the Praetorian Guard. The first shows the 'Reception of the Emperor' in the Castra Praetoria; the second shows the 'Reception of the Praetorians' as Claudius greets a personification of the Guard.

8. Sestertius showing the Roman Colosseum (Amphitheatrum Flavium) as it appeared upon its completion in AD 80.

9. A hunter (*venator*) fighting a lioness, fragment of the long fresco that decorated the balustrade of the amphitheatre in the Roman city of Emerita Augusta (modern Mérida, Spain), first century AD.

10. Gladiatorial combat overseen by a referee (*summa rudis*), second-century mosaic from the Roman Villa Nennig, Germany.

11. Gold aureus showing Trajan's Column at the time of its inauguration, topped with a statue of the victorious emperor holding the orb of the world in his hand.

12. Some of the 2,650 aurei in the Trier Gold Hoard, concealed under a cellar floor when the city was besieged in AD 167.

13. The *Portrait of the Four Tetrarchs*, carved in imperial porphyry around AD 300. The sculpture group was brought to Venice after the sack of Constantinople in 1204 and fixed into the wall of St Mark's Basilica.

14. The peristyle courtyard at the monumental heart of Diocletian's retirement palace in Split, Croatia, completed in AD 305.

15. A spectacular parhelion observed in Rhône-Alpes, France in 2015, largely matching descriptions of the vision witnessed by Constantine before the battle of the Milvian Bridge.

surprisingly favourable. Data collated from one hundred known matches in the first century showed that nineteen of the 200 fighters died, providing 9/1 odds of surviving a single bout, and 4/1 for those who pleaded missio.[34] On his gravestone in Thessaloniki, the gladiator Leukaspis made sure to display the thirteen victory wreaths he won in his many career matches. The epitaph of a Syrian gladiator named Flamma ('Flame') gives an overview of another exceptional career. Flamma lived to the age of thirty after fighting a remarkable thirty-four matches, of which he won twenty-one, drew nine, and was granted missio in four.[35] Estimating that Flamma entered the arena at age seventeen, he would have fought on average every four months, actually more often than most gladiators whose records survive. For every popular veteran like Flamma who could rely on the affections of the crowd, we must sadly assume there were many novices killed at the beginning of their careers and buried in unmarked graves. As desensitised audiences demanded increasingly bloodthirsty displays, the death rates of gladiators rose sharply. A magistrate who funded games in AD 249 boasts that in eleven matches between first-class fighters, eleven gladiators died. That every match ended in death for the defeated may imply that combat now took place under an ugly policy of *sine missione* – 'no mercy shown'.[36]

Faced with such grim prospects some fighters chose to go out on their own terms, again inspiring the respect of Rome's greatest Stoic philosophers. Seneca tells the story of a German gladiator who asked to visit the latrines before the games – the only thing he was allowed to do in private away from guards. In the latrine he quickly seized the sponge-stick 'kept there for the vilest uses', and rammed it down his throat, blocking up his windpipe and choking himself to death. Seneca, one of the Empire's richest and most influential figures, reflects: 'What a brave man he must have been. Cut off from every resource, he still found a way to furnish himself with death – knowing well that the foulest death is preferable to the fairest slavery.'[37]

Their lethal fighting skill and constant closeness to death made gladiators the superstar athletes of the Roman world – fame exemplified perfectly in the souvenirs available to buy at stalls surrounding the amphitheatre. There you could purchase your child a terracotta figurine of their favourite fighter, or perhaps a brightly glazed oil lamp for your home in the shape of a gladiator's helmet. Maybe even a vial of precious gladiator blood, known to be a 'draught of life' curing ailments like epilepsy.[38] But only the wealthiest could afford a bottle of *strigimentum* – the grimy mixture of olive oil, sweat, and dirt scraped from the bodies of famous gladiators and sold to the public at huge prices. Vendors cried out that these 'scrapings' from Rome's most virile warriors were a medical wonder drug, curing inflammation, stimulating blood flow, and relieving all manner of aches and pains.[39]

Echoes of the Colosseum

The poet climbs higher and higher through the cavernous ruin. Guided only by the faint rays of moon and stars, he clambers up collapsed stairways and delves into dark tunnels hidden by falls of hanging ivy. Finally, he emerges at the summit, atop grey walls garlanded by wildflowers. He pauses there to gaze out on the vast skeleton of the amphitheatre. Arches upon arches, through which moonbeams shine like natural torches, illuminating the vacant stands where the cries of Roman millions once meant life or death to their playthings below. Far down there in the void of the arena – in that 'magic circle' where heroes once trod – Byron is certain of a figure in the shadow. A fallen gladiator, leaning on his hand. Defeated, the man has conquered agony and consents to death. With the strike of the final blow, the arena swims around him and he is gone. Byron cannot help but join the inhuman shout of the invisible crowd. Rounding the shattered oval, the echo of his lone voice returns to him through the empty galleries.

His moonlit exploration of the ruined Colosseum in 1817 would have a profound impact on Lord Byron, being immortalised in the final part of his epic narrative poem *Childe Harold*, published the following year. Over the centuries, countless other poets and painters would find inspiration in the mystical arena rising in the heart of a depopulated Rome – Canaletto, Piranesi, and Turner all made numerous studies of its overgrown arcades. Incidentally, ongoing botanical surveys of the diverse plant life growing in the ruins of the Colosseum have so far recorded a total of 684 different species, with some of its rare flowers being found nowhere else in Europe.[40] A poignant explanation for the presence of these non-native plants has been suggested: that the seeds of many were brought to Rome in the fur and droppings of the exotic animals that died in the arena two millennia ago.

After its completion was celebrated on our sestertius, the Colosseum would remain in active use by the Romans for almost 500 years. Marking his victories over the Dacians in AD 107, the emperor Trajan outdid the inaugural games of Titus by hosting 123 consecutive days of spectacles in which 11,000 animals were killed and 10,000 gladiators fought. Soon after, the emperor Hadrian used twenty-four elephants to haul the bronze Colossus from Nero's palace to a new position beside the amphitheatre. Surprisingly, the towering Colossus may have survived the ravages of the fall of Rome to remain standing in the Middle Ages, being evocatively described in the eighth-century poetry of the Venerable Bede.[41] With the original name of the Flavian Amphitheatre gradually lost in the mists of time, the adjacent statue would contribute to the arena's new nickname – it would become the 'place of the Colossus' or as we know it today, the Colosseum.

The rise of Christianity had seen the moral character of the games increasingly called into question, though misgivings had always been present. Cicero acknowledged that gladiator combat may be 'cruel and inhuman' yet he felt that in watching the guilty fight 'we receive by our eyes and ears no better training to harden us against pain and death'.[42] Seneca, on the other hand, warned his friends in no uncertain terms not to attend the games. He had dropped in one lunchtime expecting 'sport, wit, and some relaxation' but was greeted instead by 'plain butchery'.[43] Early Christian writers like Tertullian and Augustine railed against the vices encouraged by the pagan spectacles, and after repeated attempts to restrict them, gladiatorial contests were finally banned in 438. Use of the ageing Colosseum for animal hunts – no doubt far smaller in scale than those of earlier centuries – would continue for a time. An inscription dating to 484 commemorates the restoration of the arena after an earthquake, with the last recorded hunts taking place there in 523.

As the Roman capital crumbled around it, the Colosseum became home to medieval housing, a chapel, a cemetery, even being repurposed as the fortified castle of a noble Italian family. Repeated earthquakes did great harm to the neglected structure, particularly one devastating tremor in 1349 which destroyed the entire south side of the amphitheatre. Romans happily carted away the resulting mountain of marble and travertine for use in the many Renaissance palaces and churches being built around the city. In 1452 a single building contractor working under Pope Nicolas V removed 2,522 cartloads of marble from the Colosseum for use in building the New St Peter's Basilica. Later, during construction of the Farnese Palace, Pope Paul III granted his nephew Alessandro Farnese permission to take as much stone from the Colosseum as he could in a twelve-hour period. Alessandro subsequently hired 4,000 labourers to work furiously for a single day, stripping the ruins of as much precious stone as possible. Thankfully, what remained of the building was protected by the popes from the seventeenth century onwards, claiming it to be a sacred site where Christian martyrs had died but also wishing to use its grand arches as the backdrop to their processional parades through the city.

Though abused and neglected, the revolutionary architecture of the Colosseum continues to inspire. Its efficient design incorporating a large number of entrances and exits, allowing the entire building to be emptied in as little as ten minutes, has influenced stadium architecture around the world. Just as the Colosseum stands as a reminder of the transience of even the greatest empire, so too it forces us to confront uncomfortable truths about human nature and the continuing appeal of blood sports throughout history. To this day, Roman amphitheatres in southern France play host to traditional bullfights. These spectacles held in their ancient venue make the millennia melt away – though Camargue bullfighting merely involves trying to snatch a ribbon from the bull's horns and thankfully the animal prances off the sand at the end of the show. Blood is certainly drawn, however, in the ferocious Florentine sport of *calcio storico*, which sees teams of men fight bareknuckle in an open-air arena of sand, not so far removed from the contests of old. Similarly, the spirit of the gladiator lives on in today's boxers, MMA fighters, and superstar wrestlers, all billion-dollar sporting industries watched by hundreds of millions of fans worldwide.

The Colosseum struck onto this medallic bronze coin – Rome's arena of death – endures as the eternal symbol of the Eternal City. Just as Byron's voice echoed through its wild ruins, so too he chose to echo in his poem the lasting sentiments of an ancient verse: that as long as the Colosseum stands, so Rome shall stand. If the Colosseum falls, then Rome shall fall. And when Rome falls – so falls the world.

Chapter VIII

ZENITH

'It is a rare delight of the present time that we can think what we wish, and say what we think.'

Tacitus, *c.* AD 100

Aureus of Trajan showing Trajan's Column which still stands in Rome, telling the story of his Dacian Wars, AD 113.
Obverse: Laureate, draped bust of Trajan.
Reverse: Trajan's Column surmounted by statue of the emperor, eagles on base, SPQR OPTIMO PRINCIPI.

Story in Stone

The morning mist hangs low over the wide Danube. All along the south bank of the gliding river, guard towers rise above spiked palisades. The frontier is on high alert. Sentries keep constant watch on the opposing shore, with signal flares ready to be lit at the first sign of enemy activity. At the waterline, the last careful preparations are under way. Mountains of essential supplies are loaded into barges – barrels of wine, tightly bound sacks of grain; everything the legions might need for the coming offensive. With the angle of the climbing sun nearing the critical hour, the river fog melts away to reveal the full scale of the Roman construction. The massive wooden pontoon bridge undergoes final checks. Built atop a line of anchored boats, the floating walkway stretches the better part of a mile to the barbarian shore. The crossing is firm, all is ready.

Soon a deep rumble descends on the river, like an unending peal of thunder rolling down from the Carpathians. Bright blasts of horns and trumpets cut through the clamour as the marching column emerges onto the bridge. Mounted cavalry, auxiliaries from around the Empire, and thousands of hardy Roman legionaries all advance in perfect step, their freshly polished weapons and armour gleaming in the sun. The formation bristles with colourful standards hoisted proudly above the troops. Most revered among them is the *aquila* – the golden eagle grasping a thunderbolt – sacred emblem of each legion.

At the head of the column, the emperor himself marches on foot with his officers and attendants.[1] Trajan was already a conquering general before he ascended the throne. Beloved by the troops, respected by senators, wildly popular with the people – he now sets out to become one of the greatest conquerors Rome has ever seen. Perhaps even a rival to Alexander himself. With his scarlet cloak thrown across his shoulder, Trajan's determined eyes are fixed on the far shore, and the realm of the rebel king beyond.

From the depths of his flowing river, the bearded god of the

Danube rises. The giant figure can only watch in awe as the seemingly endless column of soldiers stomps across the bridge they have quickly unfurled over his waters. With grudging respect, the river god beckons the Roman emperor and his troops by, even steadies the bobbing pontoon to smooth their crossing. The broad span of the Danube had long been a natural barrier separating the civilised and barbarian worlds. Now with Trajan's unstoppable advance, the old deity and his unbridgeable waters must yield to the might of Rome.

At the northern end of the bridge, countless hobnail boots tread onto enemy soil. The mountain kingdom of Dacia had become one of the Empire's most troublesome neighbours in recent decades. Led by their shrewd king Decebalus, Dacian warriors had raided Roman territory, humiliated a Roman army and even set their own peace terms. Lesser emperors had accepted the shameful arrangement, but not Trajan. Now this realm of dense forests and deep gold mines will finally be brought to heel. Decebalus can either kneel before Trajan, or have his head paraded in a Roman triumph.

The energetic emperor mounts a high tribunal to inspect and encourage his troops as they march by. With multiple Roman legions in convoy, each comprising over 5,000 men, the invasion column stretches out for miles. On distant clifftops rising above the gloomy forests, figures can be seen silhouetted and motionless. The long-haired Dacian warriors grip their curved swords, and watch gravely as the unending Roman tide floods their land.

So begins the astounding visual narrative of the Dacian Wars, as carved into the spiralling marble relief of Trajan's Column in Rome. Like an ancient cinema epic, the story of the emperor's conquest unfolds for the viewer in a continuous sculpted scroll of interconnected scenes with a cast of thousands. The unprecedented war diary seamlessly blends documentary retelling, myth, and propaganda. The gods will occasionally intervene on the side of Rome, and no Roman fatalities will be directly shown at any point; yet this winding frieze tells a real story of two earth-shattering conflicts fought between AD 101 and 106. Here for the first time, the average Roman could follow their lethal army in action on distant frontiers and

The opening of Trajan's Column: armoured Roman legionaries cross a pontoon bridge over the Danube, watched by a divine personification of the river.

experience brutal combat against barbarian foes – all playing out in glorious colour, for the reliefs were once brightly painted.

With Trajan's stunning victory over the rich kingdom of Dacia, hundreds of tons of gold and silver would pour back into Rome. The emperor used the spoils to reshape the monumental heart of the city, commissioning a vast forum complex that included markets, libraries, and a grand basilica. Crowning the spectacular civic space would be his triumphant Column, exquisitely carved with its twisting tale of how the wars were won. At its pinnacle, a gilded statue of the conquering emperor looked out over his mighty works. Romans were invited to join him there at the top of the world. Entering the Column through a door at its base, they could climb the spiral staircase that ascends inside the marble pillar. Emerging onto a balcony at the summit, they would surely gasp in awe at the sprawling vista that greeted them. A forum plaza larger than all before, built of vibrantly coloured marbles from across the Empire; and beyond, a thriving, cosmopolitan city of over a million people.

Just as the marble spiral of Trajan's Column raised the viewer to lofty heights, so the Column itself would come to represent the apex of Roman imperial power. Trajan would push the borders of the Empire to their maximum extent, and his successful reign would see a remarkable flourishing of the arts, architecture, education, and living standards at every level in society. As a symbol of Rome at her zenith, the image of Trajan's Column would be struck into coins of gold, silver, and bronze for circulation across the wide Roman world, from northern Britain to the Persian Gulf. Indeed, these coins would soon be used to proclaim Trajan's new title of 'Optimus Princeps' – the greatest of all emperors. When Trajan eventually died of illness after a tireless reign of almost twenty years, the Column would become his mausoleum, his ashes interred in its base – the only emperor ever buried within Rome's sacred boundary.

The majestic complex that once surrounded it has long been swept away, but Trajan's Column still stands true at the heart of the modern city, in proud defiance of every earthquake and pillaging invader across the millennia. Above the traffic and tourists, its thrilling narrative continues to play out on a winding ribbon of marble, depicting the brutal birth of a new nation. The story of Rome as *caput mundi* – capital of the world – and the Roman Empire at the height of its power.

The War Machine

Trajan came to the throne a man on a mission. For too long Rome had been on the defensive, harried at her frontiers, low on morale. In AD 85, a barbarian army led by a charismatic Dacian chieftain had swarmed across the frozen Danube from their mountainous homeland roughly equivalent to the modern country of Romania. The Dacians burned Roman towns and annihilated the Roman legions sent to stop them. Incredibly, the emperor Domitian – the second son of Vespasian to rule the Empire – decided to come to terms with the invader. Not only was the Dacian chief allowed to lead his people as a client king, but Rome also supplied him with engineers to help fortify his strongholds, and an annual tribute of eight million sestertii for good measure.[2] The damage to Roman prestige seemed irreparable. Having thoroughly embarrassed his giant neighbouring empire, the victorious Dacian king assumed the honorary name Decebalus, meaning 'the strength of ten men'.

When Domitian was assassinated in 96, an elderly and childless senator named Nerva was selected as a steady pair of hands to right the ship. A career politician with no military achievements to his name, Nerva proved unpopular with the army. Pressure quickly mounted for him to nominate a vigorous successor who could give Rome back her confidence. His choice of heir was perhaps Nerva's greatest deed, setting the precedent for much of the next century. During this prosperous era, emperors would be selected not by their birth but by their worth, with each ruler adopting the man he felt was best equipped to lead the Empire forward after him.

As governor on the turbulent Germanic frontier, Marcus Ulpius Traianus lived and breathed the military life. His offensives against the barbarians north of the Rhine had already won him the impressive title of 'Germanicus'. When letters reached Trajan in Cologne notifying him firstly of his imperial adoption, and soon after of his accession to the throne, Rome had her first true soldier-emperor. Born in Hispania, near present-day Seville, he also became the first ruler to originate from outside Italy. As one contemporary observed, the Spaniard was 'a general of the old school, who had earned his title on fields heaped high with slaughter'.[3] Conquerors like Caesar and Alexander were his heroes, and like them, the new emperor believed the best defence was an unrelenting offence. In 101, Trajan crossed the Danube with a gigantic force, determined to humble the Dacian king.

The unravelling frieze of Trajan's Column provides the most complete visual record of the feared Roman army at war. While the emperor has the starring role in the epic, appearing fifty-eight times in its carved reliefs, the ubiquitous figure of the untiring Roman legionary is never far away. Marching into the Dacian wilds, legionaries are shown living up to their nickname of 'mules' by carrying all the equipment needed while on campaign in enemy territory. In packs borne over the shoulder we see a satchel of rations, cloak, cooking pot, and mess tin. Minimising reliance on a sluggish baggage train increased the speed and manoeuvrability of the legion and made each soldier a highly mobile engine of technical warfare. As well as doing battle, legionaries are shown chopping down forests, laying roads, and building one fortified camp after another.

All while wearing their iconic segmented plate armour. Made from overlapping iron strips, this intricate *lorica segmentata* was lighter than chainmail and allowed the wearer freedom of movement while still protecting against enemy weapons.[4] Each legionary carried the long *pilum* javelin, hurled in unison at the advancing enemy to break their charge before closing in. Freed right hands then instantly drew the famed *gladius* short sword. Leading with their large rectangular *scutum* shield, soldiers knocked the enemy off balance and struck in a lightning flash of bared blade. Legionaries were taught not to slash but to thrust their gladius from behind cover with ruthless efficiency, their opponent feeling the point before even seeing the sword. As one military expert noted, 'a stab from their gladius, penetrating but two inches deep, is generally fatal'.[5] It has been estimated that until the invention of the firearm, the Roman gladius sword took more human life than any other hand-held weapon.[6]

These legions of citizen-soldiers formed the heavy infantry of the army, though much of the initial skirmishing was done by Trajan's equally large force of auxiliary soldiers drawn from the diverse lands of the Empire. Agile cavalry units made up of Batavians, Gauls, and Thracians struck at the enemy flanks, riding down and spearing any who fled in panic; slingers from the Balearic isles launched their stone bullets with deadly speed and accuracy; while archers from Syria lobbed a hail of arrows. Only after completing twenty-five years' service to Rome would each auxiliary soldier earn his ultimate reward: a bronze diploma granting full Roman citizenship to him and his children. Altogether, Trajan had amassed the greatest expeditionary force ever deployed by Rome; around 100,000 men shaking the earth as they marched into war.

At the head of this massive army, Trajan cautiously advanced north towards the forbidding Iron Gates. This deep river gorge cut through the Carpathian mountains, opening into the rolling forests of the Dacian heartlands, today the mystical landscape of Transylvania. After forcing the pass, Trajan could strike directly at Dacia's royal capital, the mountain stronghold of Sarmizegetusa. Reliefs on the column reveal that in initial engagements with the enemy, the emperor held back his legionaries and allowed auxiliary regiments to showcase their fighting prowess. The foreign soldiers were clearly eager to impress. They are shown hacking off Dacian heads and rushing to present the grim trophies to Trajan. One auxiliary even fights on while a severed head hangs by its hair from his clenched teeth.

Trajan's forces progressed methodically through enemy territory, clearing thick forests, fording rivers, and burning villages as they went. However, the column also emphasises Trajan's clemency in war, accepting the surrender of overawed Dacian warriors and offering passage to women, children, and the elderly out of the combat zone. As the Romans closed in on his capital, a decisive clash with Decebalus neared. The full commitment of the Roman army, legionary and auxiliary alike, was deployed in the bloody battle. While the dreaded gladius sliced through enemy lines, the Dacians had their own weapon to fill the invaders with fear. Their curved *falx* was the legionary's nightmare. With a wild downward swing, the scythe-like blade could reach over the Roman shield and puncture the helmet of the soldier behind. Adaptable as ever, the Romans quickly engineered a design solution to protect themselves against the vicious falx; a reinforcing crossbar added to the crown of legionary helmets is clearly visible in the Column reliefs, illustrating the exacting detail achieved by the sculptors.

Still, casualties began to mount. The ferocity of Dacian resistance is acknowledged on the Column with a humanising tableau showing Roman legionaries receiving treatment at a dressing station as the battle rages. In a scene that could have come straight from a modern war film, medics unroll bandages over the wounds of injured comrades. When the bandages ran out, we are told that Trajan even cut his own cloak into strips to be used as dressings for his bleeding men.

In addition to their sophisticated weapons, armour, and tactics, the battle also called for the use of Rome's cutting-edge war machines. Legionary gunners are seen taking aim with *ballista* bolt-throwers which could fire a dart as far as 500 metres. The historian Josephus, who had been on the receiving end of this revolutionary mechanised artillery decades earlier in the Jewish War, describes his horror at once seeing a single ballista bolt impale a whole row of his men. He recalls the psychological trauma caused by the unending 'terrifying shriek of incoming Roman missiles' and the 'constant thud of dead bodies as they fell one after another from the ramparts'.[7] Teams of legionaries are even shown firing the weapons on the move from horse-drawn carriages, essentially making them the world's first mobile field artillery.

Faced with such an onslaught, Decebalus soon accepted that the Romans could not be resisted. The pragmatic king knew that if the enemy ram touched the wall of his stronghold, it would be the end of him, his capital city, and the golden treasures hidden within. Brought before the emperor, Decebalus fell to his knees and swore his future obedience to Rome. Trajan accepted. He had achieved his immediate goals of forcing back the Dacian threat, humbling the barbarian king, and securing a punishing new treaty. Roman prestige was restored, for now.

Today it is hard to discern if either side truly sought an end to the conflict, or just a temporary respite, before regrouping for the deciding contest. The subsequent actions of both parties certainly hint at mutual bad faith behind the ceasefire. Back in Rome, Trajan had barely finished celebrating his victory when news arrived that Decebalus had launched another raid and taken a Roman commander hostage. Yet this attack may have been in response to the colossal construction he saw quickly taking shape over the Danube: a permanent bridge on massive stone piers, carrying a Roman highway directly into his lands – the longest bridge ever constructed in the ancient world. Despite the fresh treaty, Trajan had commissioned this crossing over the Danube so 'that there might be no obstacle to his going against the barbarians beyond it'.[8] It would be completed in time for the emperor's arrival. Trajan was returning to Dacia, and this time there would be no mercy.

Dacia Capta

Demanding a mighty bridge that would subdue the Danubian river god once and for all, Trajan turned to his chief military architect. Apollodorus of Damascus was a brilliant engineer from Roman Syria who had caught the emperor's attention with his innovative designs for war machines and siege engines. Surviving extracts from his treatise on military engineering propose, in true Da Vinci fashion, a range of fantastical battle hardware, from mechanised siege ladders and battering rams all the way to armoured assault rafts and fire hoses made of animal intestines.[9] Now tasked with designing a permanent bridge spanning one of Europe's greatest rivers on a volatile military frontier, Apollodorus had the chance to show the emperor his true genius.

The bridge would be constructed in just two years and stretch an incredible 1,135 metres across the broad river; to provide some sense of scale, the world's tallest skyscraper, Dubai's Burj Khalifa, laid alongside would not meet its length. For the next thousand years Trajan's Danube Bridge remained the longest arch bridge ever constructed. The crossing rested on twenty piers built using bricks, mortar, and that Roman wonder-ingredient: *pozzolana* cement. Mixed with quicklime and volcanic ash from the Bay of Naples, Roman cement not only hardened underwater but recent analysis has shown it actually became stronger over time, self-healing any cracks before they spread.[10] Apollodorus also minimised water resistance against the piers with their sophisticated diamond-shaped cutwater design. Enormous wooden arches leapt thirty-eight metres between each pillar, supporting the roadway above. If any proof were needed as to the resilience of the construction, Trajan and Apollodorus might be proud to know that the bridge supports were still a hazard to Danube shipping well into the twentieth century.

The completed Danube Bridge is shown in all its glory on Trajan's Column, stretching out behind the emperor as he leads solemn sacrifices at the opening of the second campaign. The bridge would also become the first of many architectural wonders designed by Apollodorus to be celebrated on Roman coins. A stylised representation of the bridge appears on bronze sestertii struck soon after the war, shown with triumphal arches at each end and a boat sailing by underneath. For most in the Empire, this coin would be the only way they could see one of the ancient world's greatest engineering marvels. As well as serving a practical purpose in allowing Trajan to renew his invasion, the bridge was also an instrument of psychological warfare: Dacians must have watched with dread as its arches bounded ever closer to their shore. The sacred waters that had long acted as a natural barrier, keeping invaders from their native land, were now rendered meaningless by Rome. Taking shock and awe to new levels, Trajan marched his armies across his Danube Bridge to end the reign of Decebalus once and for all.

Now more knowledgeable of the enemy terrain, Trajan split his invasion force into two columns and converged on the royal capital in a lethal pincer movement. Dacian warriors mounted a spirited defence of their hilltop towns, hurling down rocks and arrows on the attackers, but the Roman advance was relentless. Some fought to the bitter end, other clans fell to their knees before the emperor, begging his clemency. With the Dacian cause becoming increasingly hopeless, the reliefs of the Column show natives setting alight their own villages rather than have them captured by the approaching army. Behind the high walls of Sarmizegetusa, desperate men gather around a large cauldron from which a chieftain distributes cups of liquid. The poison quickly does its work, and the men fall dead one by one. In a heart-rending scene that almost anticipates the sorrow of a Renaissance Pietà, an elder Dacian weeps into his cloak as he cradles the lifeless body of a young man, probably his son.

The Roman army once again at his walls, Decebalus can be seen holding a final council with his followers. They urge him to accept that all is lost and escape while he can. With a small cavalry contingent, the king abandons his royal city and gallops into the deep forest. Trajan, learning of the breakout, sends his best cavalry detachment after his nemesis. In a frenetic final act worthy of a modern blockbuster, a heart-pounding chase ensues as the Roman riders close in on the rebel king. The cavalrymen gallop furiously through the trees wielding their spears, each competing for the honour of saying he captured the king and ended the war. Finally, an exhausted Decebalus is cornered in a wooded clearing. The thundering hooves of Roman horses pummel the earth all around him. In a moment between heartbeats, he envisions himself in chains, paraded through the streets of a decadent city, tortured to death before jeering crowds. A charging Roman cavalryman, now just feet away, reaches out his hand towards the kneeling king. Decebalus turns his thoughts to the boundless and free hills of his precious homeland – and drags a dagger across his own throat.

The Roman propaganda machine might have preferred an alternative ending to its war story – the king captured alive, or at least executed on Trajan's orders – but the climactic scenes at the heights of the Column concede that Decebalus went out on his own terms: a worthy foe until the very last.[11] Another glimpse at this decisive moment was granted by an extraordinary archaeological discovery in 1965. Near the ruins of Philippi in northern Greece, a farmer ploughing his field struck an enormous stone covered with Latin letters. Expert examination revealed it to be the gravestone of a highly decorated Roman cavalryman named Tiberius Claudius Maximus who served in the Dacian Wars. The memorial of Maximus was an astonishing nine feet tall and inscribed with the most detailed career summary of any Roman soldier known – and for good reason. In his epitaph, Maximus boasts that he was the very reconnaissance scout who 'captured Decebalus' and 'brought his head back' to Trajan, receiving an instant promotion for his deed.[12] While no artistic match for the scene shown on the Column, a relief panel on his gravestone also depicts Maximus bearing down on Decebalus, who lies on his back raising his curved sickle. Maximus claims to have 'captured' the king, though if Decebalus was still alive he was surely mortally wounded. His severed head was promptly displayed to Trajan's cheering soldiers before being sent to Rome.[13]

Another gift would soon be making its way back to the Roman capital: the vast royal treasure of the Dacian king. We are told that, hoping to keep his riches out of Roman hands, Decebalus had a river near his palace diverted, burying his wealth in the riverbed before bringing the waters back on course.[14] The tactic was employed

Denarius of Trajan showing an improvised victory trophy in the form of a tree stump decorated with captured Dacian armour and weaponry.

numerous times in the ancient world, notably by the later Gothic king Alaric who is said to have buried the treasures of Rome in a riverbed after sacking the city. Such tales may contribute to, or be inspired by, mythic associations between rivers and the discovery of precious metals. Wherever it was concealed, the location of the royal treasure was divulged by a Dacian prisoner and a mountainous hoard of gold and silver was soon on its way to flood the Roman state coffers.

Returning to Rome as perhaps the greatest warrior-leader since Caesar himself – rulers like Augustus and Claudius had largely entrusted generals with conquering on their behalf – Trajan wasted no time in making Victory the order of the day across his celebratory coinage. The winged goddess is shown crowning the emperor with a laurel wreath, and inscribing shields with the pronouncement of 'Victoria Dacica' – 'Victory in Dacia'. Also depicted are battlefield trophies in the form of a tree stump decorated with captured armour and weaponry. One such denarius from my collection shows in tremendous detail highly decorated Dacian shields, behind which are mounted spears and the curved blades of the Dacian falx. Also fixed to the trophy is a pair of crossed greaves (shin guards), and topping the makeshift monument, a distinctive pointed cap worn by Dacian

Colossal rock carving of the Dacian king Decebalus, overlooking the Danube river near Orşova, Romania.

nobles as seen on Trajan's Column. Perhaps most poignantly, another widely issued denarius depicts a Dacian captive seated on a pile of his countrymen's weapons, weeping for the loss of his homeland. Underneath, the coin declares proudly to the viewer: 'Dacia Capta' – 'Dacia Captured'. The free kingdom of Decebalus was now the newest province of Rome. Colonists, merchants, and miners poured across Trajan's Bridge into the newly opened lands, and its old capital was soon rebuilt to a rigid Roman plan.

Two thousand years later, the inhabitants of the region now hold both antagonists of the conflict, Decebalus and Trajan, in high esteem. The rebel king who fought to the death defending the liberty of his homeland; and the conquering emperor who brought classical culture and the Latin language to their nation. Tourists cruising down the Danube today look up in astonishment at a colossal portrait recently carved into the grey cliffs of the Iron Gates. The face of the freedom-fighter Decebalus is the largest rock sculpture in Europe, three times the height of the presidential portraits on Mount Rushmore. For eternity, he will gaze out from the limestone barrier guarding the land he tried to defend. Yet the king is named in the Latin letters of his enemy, 'Decebalus Rex' – and the home he died for is now known as Romania: the land 'of the Romans'.

The Upward Spiral

To the victor went the spoils, and the riches that Trajan brought back from Dacia were truly astounding. Surpassing even the Temple treasures seized in the sack of Jerusalem, the royal treasure of Decebalus would alter the economic and physical landscape of Rome. Even conservative interpretations of the amounts described in sources estimate that over 225 tons of gold and 450 tons of silver flowed into the state treasury – enough bullion to strike thirty-one million aurei and 160 million denarii.[15] In addition, there was the revenue that came with Roman exploitation of Dacia's mineral wealth. Through mining of gold, silver, copper, and lead, as well as the sought-after commodity of salt, the new province would go on to contribute hundreds of millions of denarii annually to the treasury of the Empire.[16]

Recent isotope analysis of Trajan's coinage has confirmed that during the period of the Dacian Wars, a brand-new source of precious metal began to supply the Roman mint. While the origin of the metal cannot yet be scientifically determined, it is reasonable to assume that Trajan wasted no time in striking coins with his bounty of Dacian gold and silver.[17] This influx of precious metals would be used to finance one of the most ambitious building programmes

Rome had ever witnessed. Soon the name of Trajan would adorn so many structures it was said to be as prevalent as 'wall ivy' growing around the city — and many of these marvellous monuments celebrating the defeat of Dacia would be immortalised on Roman coins struck with bullion from the conquered land.[18]

With the ancient market square of the Roman Forum increasingly crowded with monuments, ambitious rulers had begun adding their own public plazas to the heart of Rome — statements of their own prestige as much as they were gifts to the Roman people. Before long, Caesar, Augustus, Vespasian, and Nerva had all secured their posterity with magnificent marble squares dedicated in their name. Now Trajan sought to outdo them all. Calling once again on the architectural genius of his master builder Apollodorus, plans were drawn up for a civic complex of unprecedented scale and grandeur.

The Forum of Trajan, inaugurated in AD 112, would be the glorious culmination of the sequence of imperial fora, paying homage to the design of the adjoining squares while consciously seeking to surpass them in every way. Little of the spectacular public space remains to be seen today but we can tour the complex using the vistas presented on coinage, which as it so often does, provides our only view of the long-lost structures. Entering from the south we pass through an imposing monumental gateway. Coins show it surmounted by a statue of Trajan riding in a six-horse chariot and decorated with circular medallion busts depicting past emperors and empresses. The 110-metre-long Forum square stretches out before us paved with 3,000 slabs of shimmering Carrara marble, now identifiable only by their rectangular imprints in the ground.

Around the plaza rises a forest of columns cut from the Empire's rarest and most beautiful stones: dazzling yellow marble from North Africa, purple-veined 'peacock' marble from Anatolia, steel-grey granite from the deserts of Egypt. Close to a hundred statues of bearded Dacian noblemen look down on us from the attic surrounding the square, like Atlases seemingly holding up the massive structures. Indeed, the entire complex was in many ways a single triumphal monument celebrating Trajan's Dacian conquest.

Coins also reveal the colossal equestrian statue of Trajan dominating the centre of the plaza, its pedestal decorated with reliefs of captured enemy weapons. The gilded emperor on horseback directs our eye to the far end of the square, where coins show the ornate facade of the Basilica Ulpia towering over the complex. The forty-metre-high basilica was the largest in Rome, dedicated to public use as law courts, a place of business, or for Romans to simply stroll and socialise. This archetypal Roman basilica with a colonnaded central nave, side aisles, and apses would become the model of the early Christian basilica; where a presiding judge sat in the Roman apse, a bishop would later preside over the Christian Mass.

However massive the basilica, from our spot on the plaza another wonder can be glimpsed rising beyond it: an enormous gilded statue of Trajan, holding a sceptre in one hand and the orb of the world in the other. A spiralling marble pillar elevates the emperor perfectly, creating the illusion of him standing atop the roof of the basilica, surveying his works. Thankfully we need not rely solely on the ancient coins depicting this monument to imagine its glory. Rome may have fallen around it, but Trajan's Column refused to be toppled.

Coinage of all three metals celebrates the inauguration of the Column, presenting it much as it appears today – the pinnacle of Trajan's Forum, both in terms of physical space and in the completeness of its triumphal message (Plate section, 11). On all four sides of its base, relief carvings show dense piles of captured Dacian arms: oval shields, scale armour, curved falxes, and the mysterious *draco* – a fearsome military standard that emitted a terrifying howl when ridden into the wind. Coins faithfully depict the Roman imperial eagles, symbols of Jupiter and military strength, grasping each corner of the Column plinth with garlands of oak leaves strung between their sharp beaks. Though badly damaged, the birds of prey are still perched there today.

The Column is composed of twenty-nine blocks of the white Carrara marble beloved by emperors, each floated down the Tiber from the distant quarries in Tuscany. Stone workers expertly cut a section of spiral stair inside each drum before they were lifted into place. With each block weighing around thirty-two tons and the capital block estimated at an incredible fifty-three tons, Apollodorus would have needed to call on all his engineering genius to raise the drums into position. It is thought that a huge lifting tower was specially constructed for the job, incorporating a sophisticated system of pulleys and human-powered capstans. Inside the lifting scaffold, the marble drums were hoisted to terrific heights and carefully secured on top of one another.[19] Only then did sculptors begin chiselling the famous spiral frieze into the marble. Though some have questioned whether the carvings were completed in Trajan's lifetime or added later, well-preserved coin depictions clearly show the spiralling band encircling the Column, confirming that the narrative reliefs were part of its original design.

From its base to the feet of its crowning statue, the Column rises thirty-eight metres into Rome's blue sky – its shaft measuring exactly one hundred Roman feet. There was, we are told, an important reason it soared to this precise height. The flat expanse of the Forum was once occupied by the steep southern slope of Rome's Quirinal Hill, and Apollodorus was given the unenviable task of excavating away the entire saddle of the hill to create the space needed for the construction. Trajan and his architect literally had to move mountains in their realisation of the ambitious project, overpowering nature itself as they had previously done with their Danube Bridge.

The iconic Latin inscription above the pedestal doorway declares Trajan's lengthy titles and reveals that the Column is intended to 'show the height of the mountain and area of ground cleared for these mighty works'. After climbing the spiral staircase lit by forty small windows in the marble shaft, a Roman visitor would emerge onto the balcony where the scale of this engineering feat was best appreciated.[20] The sweeping view would have been one of the most spectacular in the city, looking over the gilded roof of the Basilica Ulpia, down the length of the Forum square and the line of imperial fora beyond, all the way to the distant arcades of the Colosseum. Notably, the elegant Latin letters of the Column's dedicatory inscription have achieved a lasting fame all of their own. Charcoal rubbings of the beautiful Roman letterforms taken by calligraphers would be used to create the 'Trajan' typeface in 1989. The font family is instantly recognisable for its ubiquitous use on movie posters in recent decades, the default choice for any graphic designer hoping to imbue a creative project with a sense of gravitas.

While the inscription clearly establishes the Column's primary function as a high belvedere providing a panoramic view over the complex, today the rising spiral of the Column's narrative frieze is easily its most recognised feature. Like an ancient reel of celluloid film, the visual retelling of Dacia's conquest wraps around the Column twenty-three times on its way to the summit and incorporates 2,662 individual human figures in its scenes. Unravelled, it would stretch for 200 metres – over twice the length of the equally famous Bayeux tapestry.[21]

Admired from viewing balconies by a cosmopolitan audience with varying levels of literacy, the Column achieves the broadest possible appeal through its purely visual storytelling. Interpretations of the frieze as a form of proto-cinema may come all too easily, yet many of its presentational choices are undoubtedly cinematic in the modern sense. Dramatic fade-ins and fade-outs open and close the action on the tapering frieze; an omniscient point of view alternates between Roman and Dacian perspectives; scenes are composed to maximise both their clarity and visual dynamism; the narrative even features an 'intermission', with a large figure of Victory separating the events of the two conflicts. The war epic could further be described as a literary adaptation, functioning as an illustrated version of Trajan's own written account of his wars, the *Dacica*, now sadly lost. Educated Romans may have enjoyed reading the work in Greek and Latin libraries that once flanked the Column, before strolling the high terraces outside and seeing the conquest come to life in full colour.

The Column's presentation of Rome at war is often dismissed as imperialist propaganda, though its imagery, while certainly a narrative written by the victor, does not seek to diminish or dehumanise the Dacian foe as we might expect. Like the imposing statues that surrounded the Forum square, Dacians are continually shown to be broad and noble. Evoking the complex humanity of Homeric heroes, they are seen undertaking individual acts of immense courage and sacrifice, as well as weeping for lost comrades. Trajan, of course, sought to benefit by presenting the conquered peoples not as contemptible figures, but as worthy foes who could only be vanquished by Roman military genius. As such, the experience of viewing the Column for a modern Romanian may be a complex one of intermingled national pride and melancholy reflection. With ruthless irony, our greatest insight into the lost culture of ancient Dacia is the Roman monument celebrating its very destruction.

Coins like the gold aureus showing Trajan's Column pay tribute both to the emperor's triumphant monument and the triumphs themselves. Quickly transported to the furthest edges of the Empire, even the newly conquered province of Dacia itself, each coin became a portable victory monument all of its own. As the most efficient tools of advertising and publicity in the ancient world, they also disseminated to millions the honorific title bestowed on Trajan by the Senate. Who could doubt they lived in a golden age, when every coin legend reminded them that they were led not just by an emperor, but by the greatest emperor of them all?

Optimus Princeps

Even before Trajan had sent them the head of Decebalus, the Senate had seen fit to grant him the lofty title of 'Optimus Princeps'. Whether he could justly be ranked the 'best of emperors' remained to be seen, yet the label would quickly encircle the victorious designs on his coins. The nickname would become Trajan's numismatic trademark, appearing in full or abbreviated form on all his subsequent coinage. Matching – maybe even exceeding – the brand recognition achieved by today's most famous celebrities and corporations, soon tens of millions of people across the Empire all knew Trajan as the 'best' ruler.

Numismatic portraits of Trajan faithfully capture the vigorous military man of simple habits described in sources. Contemporaries were pleased to see that his hair was becoming grey, a welcome sign of distinction and experience, especially after the reigns of youthful despots like Caligula and Nero. The historian Cassius Dio notes that Trajan, being in his early forties, came to the throne at the perfect

A stunningly realised coin portrait of Trajan from the author's collection.

age, 'when his mental powers were at their highest, so that he had neither the recklessness of youth nor the sluggishness of old age'. We see his short cropped hair swept forward in the plainest of styles, contrasting the effete curls of rulers before and after. While beards were becoming fashionable among younger senatorial men – many scenes on the Column show Trajan surrounded by bearded officers and attendants – the conservative soldier-emperor always remained clean-shaven.

As Optimus Princeps, Trajan ruled over an empire that stretched 5,000 kilometres across the entire Mediterranean and into the Middle East, unifying by language, currency, and custom the lands of around fifty modern nations. Just as his coins celebrated the beautification of urban Rome – his Forum, Basilica, Column, and restoration of the Circus Maximus – they equally honoured the functional wonders of infrastructure that the emperor and his architect built to improve quality of life for all across the Empire. A new Roman road constructed at the emperor's own expense, the Via Traiana, struck east across the boot heel of Italy and shortened the journey to the Adriatic coast by a whole day. The divine personification of the new road is shown on coins reclining and holding a wagon wheel – just one of a vast network of roads that now facilitated free and speedy movement throughout the Roman world. Placed end to end, the roads of Trajan's empire would have circled the entire globe twice.

A new aqueduct would also be constructed to bring additional clean water to the ever-growing capital. Using only the force of gravity, the precisely surveyed channel of the Aqua Traiana delivered an endless flow of fresh water from a lake twenty-five miles north of Rome. Bronze sestertii show the spirit of the man-made river resting under an ornately decorated arch with water cascading beneath, possibly depicting a real fountain built in the city. It has been estimated that by the third century AD, Rome's eleven aqueducts supplied the city with up to 300 gallons of water per person every day, many times the amount provided in most modern cities and more than twice the average daily water consumption in the USA.[22]

With over a million inhabitants, Rome's import economy had become insatiable. Most crucially, the city imported from Egypt and North Africa all the grain needed to feed its populace – an estimated 350,000 tons unloaded from grain ships each year. On top of this was the equally colossal tonnage of other staples shipped from around the Empire, such as wine, olive oil, and fish sauce – not to mention specialist imports like luxury goods, slaves, and wild animals.[23] Rome was the market of the world, but with the old port of Ostia increasingly unfit for purpose, Trajan and Apollodorus oversaw the construction of a modern port and canal system to supply the city. The new hexagonal harbour of Portus covered an area of almost one hundred acres and could accommodate hundreds of cargo ships simultaneously. One observer noted that 'the arrivals and departures by sea never cease. It is a wonder, not just that the harbour has sufficient space for so many vessels, but that the sea has enough.'[24] An ambitious sestertius celebrating the 'Portum Traiani' shows some of these vessels at anchor in the hexagon lined with porticoes and warehouses. As a result of extreme silting in later centuries, the harbour now lies stranded three kilometres inland next to the busy runways of Rome's Fiumicino airport. It remains one of the few Roman constructions clearly visible from space.

As well as striving to improve the infrastructure of the Empire, Trajan implemented benevolent government policies that sought to ease financial burdens and improve living standards for poorer citizens. He expanded Rome's grain dole to thousands more residents, cancelled many outstanding debts, and gave generous gifts of money to the people on special occasions. His forward-thinking *Alimenta* scheme even provided a welfare allowance to the children of impoverished Italian families. Coins proclaiming the charitable programme show a toga-clad Trajan offering aid to a small boy and girl, who both reach up to the emperor needily with outstretched hands. He spent lavishly on public entertainment, celebrating his Dacian victories with a record-breaking 123 consecutive days of games in the arena. The satirist Juvenal would dismiss these gifts of 'bread and circuses' as cynical ploys designed to distract the masses, though in his consistent humanitarian efforts to improve the health and well-being of all Romans, we can discern in Trajan a genuine concern for his subjects.

Commentators were left wondering whether the emperor was more excellent in the art of war or the art of peace. One contemporary observed that in his 'deep political wisdom', Trajan realised that 'a government succeeds by what it does in trivial matters no less than in grave ones'.[25] This clinical – at times even obsessive – attention paid to the administration of every corner of his empire is nowhere better evidenced than in the extraordinary surviving correspondence between Trajan and Pliny the Younger. Appointed governor of the mismanaged province of Bithynia and Pontus on the Black Sea coast in AD 111, Pliny would write to Trajan sixty-one times in two years, asking the emperor for specific guidance on forty occasions. Meanwhile, Trajan's dominion encompassed more than fifty provinces, each with their own governors, letters, and concerns.[26]

The letters between Pliny and Trajan provide a unique record of the day-to-day challenges of administering the Roman Empire at its height. Personalities of governor and emperor shine through – Pliny: meticulous, dedicated, always deferential; Trajan: patient, decisive, and intensely paternal. Pliny seeks the emperor's guidance on the most precise cases involving the fate of free and enslaved individuals, just as much as far-reaching decisions that will affect thousands in his province. He requests that a hard-working doctor be granted Roman citizenship; he recommends a local magistrate for promotion – while Trajan repeatedly reassures the governor that 'the interests of individuals are as much my concern as affairs of state'. At a wider level, where Pliny seeks permission to build a new bathhouse, or an aqueduct to bring water to a 'thirsty city', Trajan agrees, on the condition that projects create 'no new taxes' and genuinely benefit 'the health and happiness of the people'.

The letters also reveal the fascinating ethical conundrums that challenged Roman leaders daily. What to do with a pair of runaway slaves discovered among military recruits? Should the harsh sentences of a corrupt previous governor be allowed to stand? What is the legal status of freeborn children abandoned at birth but subsequently raised as slaves by those who rescued them? Trajan's judgments are balanced and humane, but exacting in their pursuit of justice. If fugitives have been found among the troops, who was their recruiting officer, and why was their origin not discovered on the day of their enrolment? Again and again, Trajan emphasises judicial precedent and the rights of the individual in his replies.

Little did Pliny and Trajan know that one routine exchange would achieve a singular significance and continue to be scrutinised 2,000 years later. The governor had merely sought advice on how to proceed in questioning the stubborn members of a troublesome sect who were increasingly being brought before him in his province. Some of these fanatics refused to offer prayers to Roman gods or even make libations of wine to the image of the emperor. They spread the teachings of a rebel Jew, executed decades earlier after stirring up sedition in the fragile province of Judea. This man they called Christ, and themselves, Christians.

Spirit of the Age

Asked whether members of this 'wretched cult' should be interrogated under torture and executed, Trajan's concise and dispassionate response has earned him the respect of the ages. 'These people must not be hunted out,' the emperor declared. If brought before Pliny and charges proved, 'they must be punished' like any other dissidents, but those that then offered prayers to Roman gods should be pardoned, however suspect their past conduct. Most crucially, Trajan was adamant that: 'Anonymous accusations must have no place in any prosecution, for this sets a dangerous precedent, most out of keeping with the spirit of our age.'

That the opening years of the second century sparked with a unique 'spirit' – a cultural zeitgeist emphasising public provision, citizens' rights, thriving trade, and artistic excellence – is clear to see. Population of the Empire reached its absolute peak of close to one hundred million people, and the enormous material record left from the period speaks of a prosperous Roman world. The limitless creative energy of the time is evidenced in the astonishing number of intellectual heavyweights living and writing in the year 100, with Tacitus, Pliny the Younger, Plutarch, Suetonius, Juvenal, Martial, Epictetus, Apollodorus, Frontinus, and many others all simultaneously plying their trades. Embarking on his momentous 'Histories', Tacitus paid tribute to the air of open enquiry enjoyed by this lucky generation, who were free to think what they wished and say what they thought.

The possibilities of his reign seemed endless, but the reach of Trajan's ambition would ultimately exceed his grasp. Hoping to surpass his conquest of Dacia, he turned his attention east – the only direction that allowed for further Roman expansion. In 115, the ageing emperor launched a full-scale invasion of Parthia, sweeping across the vast deserts of Mesopotamia, in modern-day Iraq, in an overwhelming lightning offensive. Trajan wrote to the Senate with so many updates on his victories, they struggled to follow his campaign or even pronounce the names of newly conquered peoples. Bewildered by his successes, they simply decreed that he could celebrate triumphs over as many nations as he pleased. Capturing the legendary city of Babylon, and then the nearby Parthian capital of Ctesiphon, Trajan came as close as ever to replicating the achievements of his hero, Alexander. As they had done with Dacia a decade before, Trajan's coins now dared to declare 'Parthia Capta' – the 'capture' of Rome's greatest remaining foe. Eventually, he stood on the shore of the Persian Gulf, over 2,000 miles from Italy – the furthest east that Roman armies would ever venture. Trajan gazed out at the trade ships setting sail on the calm, azure waters. Learning that the vessels were bound for the rich realm known as India, 'Trajan began to think about the Indians and was curious about their affairs; and he lamented: "I would certainly have crossed over to India, too, if I were still young."'[27]

Jupiter had promised the Romans an empire without end – but there, on that distant Babylonian shore, the sixty-three-year-old emperor reluctantly accepted the limits of the world. With his health failing and word arriving of rebellions already springing up in his new territories, Trajan turned about and set off back to Rome. Only his ashes would return to the city. After suffering a stroke during the journey, Trajan died in August 117 at the harbour of Selinus, modern Gazipaşa, on the southern coast of Turkey. His glorious reign had lasted nearly twenty years. That Trajan may have believed he could conquer death as well as barbarian lands is evidenced in the fact that the childless emperor had stubbornly refused to adopt an heir – again following the example of Alexander. After days of intrigue that may or may not have involved the backdating of adoption papers, Trajan's nearest male relative and most obvious heir, Hadrian, was peacefully confirmed as his successor.

The 'best of emperors' required an exceptional burial place, and his most prominent Roman landmark provided the perfect location. Trajan's ashes, and later those of his wife Plotina, were interred in golden urns within the pedestal of his Column.[28] Before climbing the spiral steps to its summit, Roman visitors could offer a prayer to the deified emperor who had made it all possible. It is with some poetic irony then, that the coins struck to show the towering monument of his achievements now also showed his urban tomb – the only person granted the honour of burial inside the city's sacred pomerium since Julius Caesar.

Trajan's remarkable Forum and Column would have a long life after his reign, despite later emperors scavenging the beautiful marbles and sculpture for their own monuments. In 315, Constantine the Great pulled a number of Dacian captives and friezes from the buildings to place incongruously on his own arch which still stands next to the Colosseum, though the complex was mostly intact when Constantine's son, Constantius II, visited Rome for the only time in 359. Touring Trajan's Forum, he was rendered speechless by the construction 'unique under the heavens, beggaring description and never again to be imitated by mortal men'.[29]

During the multiple sackings of Rome in the fifth century, the ashes of Trajan and his empress were scattered into the wind, their golden urns presumably melted down. Eventually and inevitably, the Forum succumbed to the overgrowth. Earthquakes toppled sections of the complex; and statues were smashed and burnt in kilns for lime mortar. Through the Middle Ages, farm dwellings clung to its ancient walls and animals grazed among the shattered ruins. In the early sixteenth century, Pope Clement VII removed yellow marble columns from the remains for use in the new St Peter's Basilica. The dazzling columns from the second century can still be seen there today, framing the Altar of St Joseph in the South Transept. Soon all that was left was the great, unyielding Column of Trajan, now a viewpoint for the magnificent desolation all around.

In 1587 Pope Sixtus V replaced the lost bronze statue of Trajan that once surmounted the monument with one of St Peter. The spiralling Column now became a mere pedestal for the apostle's statue – symbol of the triumph of Christendom and the victory of the martyr over his persecutors. Yet this act saved it from further destruction by a pope who eagerly demolished many other ancient structures for their marble. Here too, ancient coins depicting the Column inadvertently celebrate a monument across time; a proud pinnacle from the skyline of pagan Rome, now standing as an eminent landmark in the Christian city.

That Sixtus' treatment of Trajan's Column had been relatively forgiving was somewhat appropriate for the emperor deemed a 'virtuous pagan'. Though he presided over the execution of Christians like other rulers before and after, Trajan's effective leadership, welfare initiatives, and dedication to public service had earned him the respect and admiration of early Christian thinkers. Strolling through the ruins of his Forum, the sixth-century Pope Gregory the Great is said to have been moved to tears by stories of Trajan's justice and charity. After praying earnestly for the salvation of this emperor who seemed by his actions 'more Christian than pagan', Gregory was apparently assured through divine revelation that his prayers had been answered: Trajan had been posthumously baptised, his soul freed from the fires of hell. Dante was inspired by this legend, and Trajan would subsequently make an appearance in his *Divine Comedy* as the only pagan Roman emperor to be welcomed into heaven.

His successor Hadrian had inherited an unwieldy empire. Rejecting the expansionist policies of his predecessor, the bearded lover of all things Greek quickly abandoned Trajan's territorial gains in the East and instead 'devoted his attention to maintaining peace throughout the world'.[30] His would be an empire of consolidation, of self-imposed limits – and of walls. Hadrian would be tireless in his travels around the provinces, inspecting troops and shoring up frontiers. Rome would continue to fight, to thrive, but evermore she would be on the defensive. There would be capable emperors, and many not so, but from now on the Senate would acclaim them all with that same rousing phrase: '*Felicior Augusto, melior Traiano!*' – an optimistic wish that they might prove more fortunate than Augustus, and better than Trajan.

Chapter IX

PHILOSOPHER

'Look back over the past, with its changing empires that rose and fell, and you foresee the future too.'

Marcus Aurelius

Sestertius of the philosopher-emperor Marcus Aurelius, with Salus, the goddess of health, AD 163.
Obverse: Laureate, draped bust of Marcus Aurelius.
Reverse: The healing goddess Salus feeding a snake, SALVTI AVGVSTORVM – 'To the Health of the Emperors'.

A Prayer to Salus

Rarely was the camp hospital not full during these days, but since the latest battle its wards had been overwhelmed. Injured soldiers resting on improvised beds covered the floor of every hall and corridor. Doctors clutching surgical instruments hurried between patients, while medics cleansed wounds with warm honey and pungent vinegar. Nearby, orderlies boiled linen bandages in a large cauldron, thickening the air with steam. All were used to seeing the emperor here, on one of his twilight visits to the sick and the dying. Heavily wrapped in his rough brown cloak, Marcus Aurelius moved quietly from man to man in the lamplight, careful not to interfere with work on the ward.

The emperor paused at the bedside of a soldier with a slashing wound across one of his eyes, neatly stitched with sutures of horsehair. At Marcus' gentle greeting, the legionary reeled off his name and century and assured the emperor that he had cut down a great many barbarians before taking his injury.

'Well, Plato would call yours a soul infused with gold,' answered Marcus, placing his hand on the man's shoulder. Then, summoned by a barely discernible gesture, an attendant came forward and pressed in the legionary's hand a gold aureus – one month's salary – stamped with the bearded portrait of the man before him. 'For your courage, soldier,' said Marcus before moving on.

The next man was an amputee, his leg recently sawn off below the knee. Marcus simply sat quietly with him for a time. Eventually, the legionary motioned to his absent limb and spoke with fragile voice: 'Imperator, I offered prayers to the healing gods, but as of yet . . .'

Marcus smiled at the man's good humour and leant forward: 'It gets worse – the *medicus* here will prescribe you nothing but cold baths.' Again, a reassuring squeeze of the shoulder, a nod, and a gold coin placed in the soldier's hand. 'Dig deep, my friend. Remember, Nature equips us with all we ever need.'

The emperor found the man in the next bed cold and without breath. He beckoned to the orderlies to remove him to the mortuary.

As they did so, the senior medicus explained the latest shortages: shredded robes would soon take the place of flax bandages, unmixed wine now did the job of opium, henbane, and mandrake. Marcus, maintaining his serenity, assured him he would do all in his power to repel the enemy tribes and reopen supply lines to the fortress as soon as possible. Moving to leave the ward, he glimpsed through a gap in a dividing curtain the soldiers being kept apart from the others. Those isolated souls, coughing and vomiting, their skin erupting with bleeding sores. Some nearing their end, covered head to toe in the black scabs of the pestilence. The grave expression of the medicus told him what he already knew: the pandemic was once again decimating his legions.

In the courtyard of the hospital, Marcus stood before a small shrine to Salus, the Roman goddess of health and well-being. There he solemnly invoked the goddess by name and poured a few drops of wine from a *patera* cup onto the glowing charcoal that burned on top of the altar. The libation hissed in the coals and threw up curling strands of smoke, at which Marcus offered his whispered prayer. A plea for the divine daughter of the medicine god Asclepius to look to the good health of his soldiers, and then, in a quieter murmur, a wish that she deliver all the people of his empire from the many evils being visited upon them.

The hour was late when Marcus returned to the writing desk in his private quarters. There, by the wavering flame of a simple clay lamp, he answered correspondence and read the latest strength reports of his legions, detailing precise numbers dead, wounded, deserted, and struck down by the scourge of the plague. Few cohorts could deploy half their original contingent in the field – even the volunteer units of slaves and gladiators that Marcus had recently recruited would do little to fill the gaps in his lines. Another meticulous report catalogued death tolls to the pestilence in each of the fourteen regions of the Roman capital; fatalities across the city now approached 2,000 per day. Marcus pressed his knuckles deep into his tired eyes and dragged his fingers through the thick curls of his long beard. Where along the way had Rome so angered her gods? he wondered to himself. As he often did in trying moments, the emperor looked to the small shrine mounted on the wall of his quarters. Between the columns of the miniature temple were placed statuettes of the Stoic teachers whose lessons remained for him an endless spring renewing his strength daily. Mentors like Apollonius, Atticus, Diognetus, Rusticus, and Fronto – all reminding him to pay heed only to those things within his control: his own perceptions, thoughts, and character.

With the day's tasks done, Marcus pulled a heavy bound manuscript in front of him, labelled on the front in Greek, '*Ta eis heauton*' – simply, 'notes to himself'. Wretched ramblings only fit for dedication to water or fire, he often thought, but keeping the private journal helped him restore order to a disordered mind. He flicked to the latest leaf of parchment, dipped his pen in the terracotta inkwell, and wrote.

'To be human is to be ever in flux. The body is a rushing river, the soul a dream and a vapour . . .'

A sudden chorus of Germanic war horns broke through the still of the night, tearing him away from his words. The tribes would often bellow the shrill pipes at the darkest hour, simply to invade the dreams of his men. With the faint glimmer of a smile, Marcus thought of the warriors out there in the frozen forests, gathered around their glowing fires under the circling stars, and the curious kinship shared by all men on this frontier; with the abyss of eternity stretching behind and before them, to be here together on this night in this little corner of the Earth, and that Earth itself, merely a mote of dust floating in the void. How soon each of them and their struggles – Roman and barbarian – would be forgotten to time. Quieting his mind now, and leading it back to nothing but the present moment, he dipped his pen in the ink once again and returned it to the parchment: 'Life is like warfare. A brief campaign in a strange land – and after the fame, oblivion. What then can guide us on our way? One thing and one thing alone: Philosophy.'

Princes and Promises

No other ancient ruler speaks to us across the millennia more directly, more intimately, than Marcus Aurelius. Whereas something of the character of other emperors might be gleaned through their formal letters and carefully crafted orations, in Marcus we can truly behold the man. His surviving *Meditations* – a collection of gentle and humane notes-to-self written amid bloody wars on the Germanic frontiers – reveal the complex inner life of a leader tasked with guiding the Roman Empire through its darkest decades yet. These are the private urgings, never meant for publication, of a man caught in the eye of a storm – doing all he can to resist the constant temptations of the throne and hold on to his humanity in an inhuman time. Elegantly distilling the empowering tenets of ancient Stoicism, the *Meditations* of Marcus continue to offer guidance to millions every year.

Marcus was born into a senatorial family in Rome in AD 121, just as the ruling emperor Hadrian set out on his first tour of the provinces – a journey that would take him to the northern limits of Britannia to commission 'a wall eighty miles in length to separate the barbarians from the Romans'.[1] Young Marcus would meanwhile be raised in an era of peace and prosperity surrounded by the luxurious trappings of Rome's ruling class, though a vigorous programme of home schooling left the boy little time for idle pursuits. Some of the finest minds of the age were drafted in to tutor Marcus in the Greek and Latin languages, literature, painting, rhetoric, and the subject of philosophy that would soon become an all-consuming one for the boy.

Quickly taking to heart lessons that would shape his character for life, the earnest youth 'learned not to bother with green or blue teams at the chariot races, or gladiators in the arena' and, even more crucially for his adult years, learned to endure pain and discomfort, and to never be afraid of hard work.[2] That his tutors were dealing with a uniquely intense pupil soon became clear when at just twelve years old, Marcus 'adopted the dress and hardiness of a philosopher, wearing a rough Greek cloak and sleeping on the ground'. At his mother's urging, the boy eventually agreed to sleep on a couch with some animal skins.[3]

Marcus attended every philosophy lecture that he could and devoted himself to his studies at the expense of all else, even his health. It would not take long for the childless emperor Hadrian, during the short breaks in his travels, to notice the promise in the boy; the ruler soon gave Marcus the affectionate nickname 'Verissimus' – the 'most truthful' child. Coming of age in the reign of Hadrian, Marcus absorbed the ideal that a Roman leader should be a proactive and visible presence to the people of his world. No doubt he took note as Hadrian prioritised the security of his empire, personally inspecting every border and strictly enforcing military discipline along the frontiers.

This urge to control completely the fate of his dominions would also be manifested in the ageing emperor's unprecedented succession strategy. Continuing the run of rulers without a natural heir, Hadrian designed a remarkable plan for the long-term future of his dynasty: nominating not only his immediate successor – a mild-mannered senator named Antoninus – but also the two after that, who he demanded should rule concordantly when their time came, a first in the imperial age. One of these hopeful princes was a seven-year-old boy named Lucius Verus, the recently orphaned son of Hadrian's original heir who had succumbed to tuberculosis. The other was seventeen-year-old Marcus Aurelius.

Perhaps, as the celebrated 1951 novel *Memoirs of Hadrian* imagines, the emperor saw that in Marcus he might give 'mankind the only chance it will ever have to realise Plato's dream, to see a philosopher pure of heart ruling over his fellow men'.[4] The extraordinary double adoption had indeed entrusted the studious teenager with eventual mastery of the world – and living up to his 'most truthful' nickname, Marcus made his feelings about the arrangement clear. He was appalled. Not out of any aversion to duty, but the budding philosopher had envisioned for himself a life as an intellectual, not as a ruler of men – even in the enlightened court of Hadrian he had seen the flattery, moral dilemmas, and constant compromises of character that haunted the best of sovereigns. Yet Marcus had also learned through his studies to accept all that came woven in the pattern of his destiny, embracing the fate for which he had been brought into the world. As it so often would through his life, the obstacle placed in his way now became the way.[5]

A spectacular marble relief from the city of Ephesus celebrates the dynastic adoptions with a sculpted family portrait, showing an ailing Hadrian in the last year of his life with the next two generations of imperial successors. He adopts the respected senator Antoninus, who in turn adopts the teenage Marcus and the little boy Lucius; standing, endearingly, with the men's hands resting on his small shoulders. Four Roman emperors in a single marble snapshot. Cynical observers, all too aware of the corrupting power of personal ambitions, not to mention the fickleness of the Praetorian Guard, may have held little hope of Hadrian's ambitious plan being followed in the decades after his death. Incredibly, all involved honoured it to the letter. For twenty-three tranquil years — a reign second only in length to Augustus himself — Antoninus ruled benignly over a peaceful empire, all the while holding it in trust for the two young men. Marcus would later pay tribute to his adoptive father's devotion to his role, prudent spending, self-control, cheerfulness, and humility. Patiently awaiting his turn on the throne, Marcus was gifted over two decades to ponder what type of emperor he wanted to be.

Coins advertised the harmonious dynastic plan to the people of the Roman world, and mentally prepared citizens for the future rule of the two princes. Marcus and Lucius both took the title 'Caesar', the name of the once-dictator now used to designate heirs apparent, with 'Augustus' reserved for the emperor himself. The two Caesars would soon be tasked with a revolutionary joint reign, yet coinage reveals that the elder Marcus was always envisioned as the senior partner. Double-headed issues were struck in all three metals with the kindly face of Antoninus on one side and the youthful Marcus Aurelius on the other. Even more revealingly, Marcus was soon made the emperor's son-in-law with an arranged marriage to his daughter Faustina — a union that would prove equally blessed and cursed, as we will later see. A sestertius of the time shows the emperor and his empress clasping hands, while below them, miniaturised figures of Marcus and Faustina do the same. The legend encircling the couples proudly declares 'Concord' within the imperial family: a promise to viewers that the long-term future of Rome was secured.

In March 161, after giving his guards the final watchword of 'Equanimity', Antoninus died peacefully in his sleep. Most assumed that

Four Roman emperors: an ailing Hadrian (damaged, to right) adopts
Antoninus (centre), who in turn adopts Marcus Aurelius (left) and young
Lucius Verus (bottom), as part of a long-term dynastic plan.
Ephesus Museum, Vienna.

Marcus, as the older and more publicly celebrated heir, would now push his adopted brother aside and take the throne for himself. Rome's sorry record of fraternal quarrels almost guaranteed as much. Yet in another testament to his character, Marcus actually demanded that the Senate recognise Lucius as his co-ruler. Once they reluctantly agreed, the imperial brothers set off for the Castra Praetoria to make the obligatory pledges to the Praetorian Guard as every emperor had done since Claudius. This time, it would take a gift of 5,000 denarii/200 aurei for every guardsman, to ensure their loyalty.[6]

The younger Caesar, a dashing playboy prone to excess, could not have been more of a contrast to Marcus – but a promise was a promise. And who was to say their opposing personas might not even complement each other: the impetuous Lucius winning glory in the defence of Rome's borders while the intellectual Marcus managed affairs on the home front – counterbalanced, like two sides of the coin of leadership. Rome, for the first time, had two emperors to govern her vast lands, and the future seemed aglow with optimism. The kind of splendid radiance that might tempt snakes out of hiding, and broil storm clouds on the horizon.

Feeding the Snake

The schooling of young Marcus had demanded he balance his mental exertions with physical ones like boxing and wrestling, while vigorously riding down and spearing wild boars was one of his favourite afternoon pursuits. But already Marcus found his body and constitution weakened by years of dedicated study for his role; he wrote of his battles with insomnia, sinus conditions, chest pains, and digestive problems that some believe are symptomatic of chronic stomach ulcers. Several entries in his *Meditations* offer Stoic encouragement against the fatigue that made even rising from his bed a challenge.

Faced with such ailments, Marcus was happy for his co-emperor to take the lead in confronting the first military crisis of their joint reign. Looking to test the resolve of the new rulers, Vologases IV, king of a resurgent Parthia, decided to invade the eastern buffer-state of Armenia. When a brash Roman governor marched into the client kingdom to meet the threat, he was massacred with his entire legion. The presence of a Roman emperor was needed on the front lines and, fortunately, the 'diarchy' of Rome had two; Lucius Verus soon set out for the East, with Marcus accompanying his colleague along the first leg of his journey. Almost as soon as Marcus waved him off, however, Lucius took to banqueting at every villa on his route. The playboy-emperor did not even make it to the Adriatic coast before his overindulgence led to him being taken gravely ill. When word reached Marcus of his partner's critical health, he offered public prayers to the healing gods for his salvation.

Amid these concerns for the well-being of the imperial union, a bronze sestertius was struck in Rome carrying a divine appeal for the vitality of both rulers. The coin shows us the face of Marcus, now in his early forties, with a commanding and regal portrait that gives little suggestion of his own sickly constitution. Even the austere philosopher-emperor is presented with the lavishly curled hair that had become so fashionable among men in these peaceful, and increasingly decadent, decades. Beards in the styling of Greek philosophers had been brought back into fashion by the Hellenophile Hadrian, but Marcus had grown his even longer than his predecessors; it hangs in curled tendrils similar to marble images of Socrates, the founder of Western philosophy. Earlier Stoics had even argued that shaving the beard was a sign of luxurious living, its growth as natural to a man as feathers are to birds; though his mentors had also warned Marcus that it is not the beard or the cloak, but reason that makes a philosopher.[7]

The circling legend on the reverse of the coin pronounces in the plural, 'Saluti Augustorum' – 'To the Health of the Emperors!' And accompanying the salutation is, appropriately enough, the goddess Salus. As the equivalent of the Greek deity Hygiea, Salus was recognised as the daughter of Asclepius – revered god of medicine and healing, to whom people across the ancient world might dedicate offerings when they fell sick. The snake-entwined staff of the medicine god remains a universal symbol of healthcare to this day, displayed on ambulances around the globe and on the flag of the World Health Organization. Thanks to their ability to shed and regrow their skin, as well as the antidotes that could be extracted from their venom, snakes had long been associated with health and rejuvenation; and as assistant to her father, it was the job of Salus to feed and care for the serpents. The coin shows her doing just that, offering food to a rising snake coiled around a sacrificial altar.

Extending out from the cult of her divine father and his power to cure specific ills, Salus took on a wider role in Roman religion, safeguarding the health, well-being, and security of the entire state. Just as public vows were made to the goddess at her temple in Rome, entreating the protection of the Empire and its leaders, so too Romans made private offerings to the goddess at their small household shrines, that she might watch over the health of their families.

The salvation – a word linked to the name of Salus by a common linguistic derivation – that Romans asked of the goddess also helped her imagery prevail following the rise of Christianity. Just as the enrobed figure of Salus was seen as an intercessor between humans and her healing father, so too the Virgin Mary came to be regarded as a conduit to God, to whom Christians prayed for help in times of sickness or physical suffering. One of the most revered early Christian icons, today venerated in the Roman church of Santa Maria Maggiore, is the *Salus Populi Romani*: a Byzantine painting of Mary as protectress of the 'Health of the Roman People', still evoking the name of the ancient curative goddess. Where Hygiea lives on in our modern word 'hygiene', so too we remember Salus not just in seeking salvation, but in offering each other 'salutations' or talking of healthy, 'salubrious' lifestyles.

Reverential coin tributes to Salus would take on a macabre irony with the events of coming years but for now, they seemingly had the desired effect. After a period of bed-rest, Lucius Verus was able to continue his journey east – with the obligatory stops at coastal pleasure resorts along the way. Arriving, at last, in the military garrison of Syrian Antioch, the emperor encountered what the poet Juvenal had seen as one of the 'perils of a long peace': shiftless legions demoralised by high living. Soldiers who spent more time applauding performers in the theatre than they did in their ranks, plucking their body hair while their horses became shaggy with neglect, and only riding their steed if it was saddled with a soft cushion. Verus was no model of rugged discipline himself, taking 'such pride in his blonde curls that he used to sprinkle gold dust on his head so that his hair and beard might glow even brighter'.[8] It was therefore left to his generals to kick the men into shape for the coming campaign.

With the out-of-practice legions adequately drilled, much of the subsequent assault on Parthia was likewise entrusted to a fierce commander named Avidius Cassius. Under his leadership, Roman forces swept down the Euphrates into Mesopotamia, smashing through Parthian opposition as they went. Verus, meanwhile, happily passed his time in wealthy cities far from the battlefront, playing dice through the night, and demanding urgent dispatches be sent from

Rome updating him on the results of his beloved chariot races. It had been fifty years since Trajan captured the Parthian capital Ctesiphon; now the Roman army overran the city once again and burned down the palace of the enemy king. Hoping to be spared the same carnage, the city of Seleucia on the opposite bank of the Tigris offered its surrender and threw open its gates to the Romans. Avidius allowed his men to ransack the city anyway. Rampaging legionaries massacred the citizens who had received them as friends and robbed temples of their sacred treasures. Any shame at the atrocity was outbalanced by mountains of plundered gold.[9]

This war was won, but a different battle was about to begin. Dark rumours soon began to spread that the returning soldiers carried with them another type of spoils. Some whispered gravely that the gods themselves, appalled by the sacrilege, had abandoned Rome. That a dreadful curse had been unleashed. One that no prayer to Salus could answer.

Apollo's Wrath

On reflection, signs of the coming apocalypse had been plain to see. Almost as soon as the joint emperors had taken their thrones, the Tiber burst its banks and inundated the Roman capital. The catastrophic flood left thousands homeless, drowned livestock, and spoiled the city's grain stores. Receding waters left starvation in their wake and Marcus worked tirelessly to provide aid to those worst affected. With flood and famine quickly followed by war, sacrifices for the health of the Empire surely seemed more vital than ever. Then, with Rome already wearied by disaster, the pestilence struck.

The contagion, today known as the Antonine Plague after the ruling dynasty of Marcus, surged across the Empire from east to west in AD 165. In every town, people huddled to hear the latest news of the disease, tell competing stories of its origin – and unknowingly help it spread. Most tales converged at the storming of Seleucia and its temple of Apollo, defiled by Roman soldiers. Some said that when troops ripped out the sacred statue of the god, they uncovered a hidden crypt sealed by ancient Babylonians. When they broke through in search of treasure, the germs of the pestilence burst forth.[10] Others claimed that a legionary rifling through the temple chanced on a mysterious golden casket. He prised the box open and a malignant vapour poured out to infect the city, Parthia, and before long, the world.[11] However it was released, Apollo had gifted the soldiers a deadly and invisible plunder to carry back to Rome with their riches.

While the returning legions were blamed for 'polluting everything with contagion and death', simultaneous outbreaks in Han China strongly suggest that the plague had first travelled the Silk Routes from the Far East before infecting soldiers of Rome.[12] Fascinating evidence of a Roman diplomatic mission to China during this period also adds intrigue to the pandemic's origin. Han records reveal that the emperor Huan received ambassadors from 'Antun', the ruler of Daqin – the Chinese name for the Roman Empire. The envoys brought gifts of elephant tusk, rhinoceros horn, and tortoiseshell to the Han palace and established, for the first time, direct trade links between Rome and China. If they did, in fact, return to Rome carrying plague as well as fine silks, it was an inauspicious opening to relations.

The ancient world's most famous physician Galen, court doctor to several Roman emperors, described in detail the ghastly symptoms he observed in those afflicted by the pestilence.[13] First came fever, vomiting, bloody diarrhoea, and pharyngitis that painfully inflamed the throat. In the second week, the skin of the patient erupted in red lesions which formed into a mass of black scabs covering the entire body. Many died an agonising death at this stage, but a miraculous few were able to fight off the disease, surviving scarred but immune from further outbreaks. Largely thanks to Galen's medical records, the Antonine Plague can be diagnosed across the millennia with some confidence as a smallpox pandemic.[14] Today we know that, left untreated, ordinary smallpox would have killed around 30 per cent of sufferers, while the more virulent 'flat' and haemorrhagic forms of the disease that Galen describes were nearly always fatal. The merciless pandemic would blight all the remaining years of Marcus the philosopher's reign – and beyond: it would not be until 1980, after a global vaccination campaign, that humanity was finally able to declare smallpox 'eradicated' from the world.

The ancient world, however, was one without vaccines, germ theory, or clear notions of contagion. In densely crowded and unsanitary cities the infection flourished; at the height of the pandemic, thousands were dying in Rome every day.[15] The endless corpses were packed onto wagons and wheeled out of the city for hurried burial in mass graves. Historians paint haunting images of devastated and depopulated lands: country farms left without a single soul to till the fields, and abandoned ghost towns being swallowed by the wilderness.[16] Estimates of the ultimate death toll are wide-ranging and final numbers are notoriously difficult to determine, with some speculating that it may have eventually wiped out a quarter of the people of the Empire. Altogether, it is likely that between ten million and eighteen million people perished across the Roman world.[17]

Like all pandemics through time, the scourge of the Antonine Plague drew no distinction between rich and poor. In 169, joint-emperor Lucius Verus was stricken with sickness on the road near the Venetian lagoon. After the usual bloodletting by his doctor – standard medical practice in ancient times – he lost consciousness and died three days later. Verus had been travelling in a region particularly hard hit by the disease and, while sources are unclear on his cause of death, it seems probable that the plague had carried off its first Roman emperor. Marcus had often found his younger, wilder colleague more of a hindrance than a help during the recent crises, and yet, coins of 'Divus Verus' quickly told the world that Marcus had nevertheless declared his adopted brother a god.

The weight of the collapsing world now rested solely on the philosopher's shoulders. Beset by flood, famine, and plague – with millions dying, his imperial partner among them – Marcus kicked the propaganda machine of the Roman mint into high gear. Ironically for a truth-teller nicknamed 'Verissimus', the coin messaging of Marcus Aurelius tells a relentlessly positive tale, with little hint of the consecutive disasters he faced. In what we might favourably see as Churchillian optimism rather than Orwellian doublespeak, coinage

The face of Lucius Verus, decadent imperial colleague of
Marcus Aurelius – on a denarius from the author's collection.

of his reign celebrates 'Felicitas' – the 'happiness'; 'Laetitia' – the 'delight'; and 'Hilaritas' – the 'joy' of the times. Romans using such coins may have wished for the return of these uplifting goddesses as they lived in fear of the ever-present plague. Only a notable increase in Roman and provincial coin depictions of Salus gives any clue that the health of Roman world was ever in question.[18]

In perhaps the most critical blow to the safety of the Empire, the Roman legions – initial carriers of the disease, in whose close ranks it spread rapidly – were left utterly devastated. Historians describe armies manning the frontiers 'reduced almost to extinction'.[19] Ominous echoes in the archaeological record also speak of near-annihilation in the camps. Experts have noticed that dated military diplomas given to soldiers on their retirement seem to vanish in the decade following the outbreak, implying that very few troops were reaching the end of their careers alive.[20] A more immediately striking discovery occurred in 1993 when a gigantic hoard of 2,650 gold aurei was unearthed by chance during construction work in the German city of Trier. The Roman outpost of Augusta Treverorum had been a major supply centre for legions stationed on the nearby Rhine frontier and the 18.5-kilogram cache of gold coins – equivalent to the annual salaries of 220 legionaries – was very likely intended as pay for the troops (Plate section, 12). Study of the coin types present in the hoard shows that almost all of them were deposited around AD 167, at the height of the pandemic. It is all too easy to imagine depleted garrisons, gutted by disease, concealing the fortune as the situation on the northern frontier deteriorated and Germanic warriors surged through unmanned border defences.

The Roman wolf was now an injured, limping animal – and her enemies smelled the blood. Inevitably the unified Germanic tribes would choose this moment to attack. With 'almost all his troops sunk under the disease', Marcus was forced to resurrect the desperate tactics of the Punic Wars and recruit criminals and gladiators into the ranks.[21] Leading these patchwork legions, the emperor marched north towards the most gruelling battle of his life. Into dark years of mud, blood, and iron – sure to test every tenet of his philosophy.

Weapons of Reason

The tranquil and serene Marcus Aurelius, devoted to philosophy all his days, was now called upon to fight a war 'greater than any in the memory of man'.[22] As the pandemic raged, an alliance of Germanic warriors headed by the Marcomanni tribe sensed their opportunity and smashed through the Danubian frontier near modern Vienna. Quickly skirting the Austrian Alps, the barbarian army arrived at the walls of the northern Italian city of Aquileia before Rome even had a chance to react – the first barbarian breakthrough into the lands of Italy in over 250 years. Marcus rescued the city from its siege and doggedly pursued the invaders back to their homeland, though simultaneous raids by other tribes – the Chatti to the west, the Sarmatians to the east – spread the already weakened legions even more thinly.

With seemingly all Germanic peoples now rising to test Rome's strained defences, the emperor settled in for an arduous conflict that would define the rest of his reign. For most of the next decade Marcus made his home at marching camps behind enemy lines and frontier bases at Carnuntum in Austria, Aquincum in Hungary, and Sirmium in Serbia. It was while conducting this brutal war, often surrounded on all sides by hostile forces, that Marcus wrote one of history's most inspirational philosophical works.

The personal *Meditations* of Marcus would become one of the defining texts of Stoicism, yet the emperor was the last great exponent of this ancient philosophy, first founded by Zeno around 300 BC. Named after the *stoa* colonnades in the Athenian *agora* where Zeno taught his open-air classes, Stoicism emphasises the importance of living in harmony with all aspects of Nature. Where competing Hedonistic philosophies saw the pursuit of pleasure as the chief good in life, Stoicism argued that 'virtue' should be our only goal – a moral and intellectual excellence achieved by striving to perfect only those things that are within our control. Accepting the external events and circumstances presented to them by fate, Stoics focused instead on improving their own thoughts and actions, aiming to cultivate resilience, self-control, and wisdom with which they could confidently face life's inevitable obstacles.

Asking no reverence of any holy text and concealing no mysteries behind the rituals of any priestly class, Stoicism offered people of any background practical pathways towards a better life. The egalitarian nature of its teachings was clearly evidenced in the social position of its two most influential practitioners: Seneca, the rich and powerful tutor to the emperor Nero, who called on his Stoic fortitude when the resentful ruler ordered him to commit suicide; and Epictetus, the mistreated and disabled slave, who overcame every adversity to gain his freedom and become one of Rome's greatest Stoic teachers. In a poignant dichotomy, the philosopher-slave would be one of the greatest influences on the philosopher-emperor during his dark years on the Germanic front, his rugged discourses reminding Marcus not to demand things happen as he wished, but only to wish things happen as they happened. The ultimate lesson being that while we cannot control external events, we can control our responses to them, choosing to feel angry, scorned, defeated – or indifferent. As Shakespeare's struggling Stoic Prince Hamlet would later ponder, 'there is nothing either good or bad, but thinking makes it so'.[23]

The *Meditations* reveal the emperor's constant efforts to maintain an orderly soul amid the chaos and unpredictability of warfare. Even in these private words, where many would be tempted to indulge in self-pity, Marcus remains determined to reframe every setback as a welcome test of his character – to see every impediment to action as an invitation to action. When fear and anxiety disturb his mind, Marcus urges of himself: 'Never let the future disturb you. You will meet it, if you have to, with the same weapons of reason that today arm you against the present.'[24] Words of empowerment that remain a timeless affirmation for any reader: you have navigated all life's challenges to reach the present moment and for every unavoidable battle ahead, you already have all the weapons you need.

Alert to the arrogance that often accompanies supreme power, Marcus impels himself to 'remember the emptiness of all those applauding hands', and the fickleness of his fawning admirers. *Memento mori* statements of his own mortality permeate every page; that, emperor or not, he too will soon be 'prey for worms', just 'ashes and bones' and his name merely an echo in time. After all, Alexander the Great met the same fate as his stable boy: 'both alike were dispersed into atoms and received back into the universe'.[25] As he reflects on the shortness of life, demands to seize the day follow naturally, perhaps most memorably the author willing himself to: 'Imagine each day is your last and that your life story is ended. Think of all further time given to you as a gift beyond expectation – and live it out in harmony with nature.'[26]

Despite the titanic struggle he was embroiled in, the emperor muses constantly on the insignificance of his daily battles within the massive scope of the universe. Realisations that the puny arena of his human fame inhabits just a tiny corner of the Earth, which itself is merely a speck in the endless void, seem uncannily ahead of their time. As Marcus looks up, away from the bleak battlefields 'to the circling heavens', his observations are shot through with a spiritual reverence that would make a modern astrophysicist envy his connection to the cosmos – imagining himself 'running mid-course with the stars', his mind dwells 'on that everchanging dance of mingling elements. Wonders that wash away the dust of an earth-bound life.'[27]

While Marcus simultaneously searches deep within himself for human strength and gazes off in awe at the infinity of space, we sense a hint of the spiritual crisis confronting his earthly empire. The pantheon of gods that had helped Rome to greatness seemed more absent than ever, either indifferent or powerless to halt the plague, famine, and war being inflicted on her millions. Faced with such meaningless suffering, people across the Empire increasingly looked elsewhere for spiritual nourishment that they no longer received at the smoking altars of the old gods. Stoicism had become popular with educated politicians and statesmen seeking a more humanistic worldview to help steel themselves against mounting disasters, while common people increasingly turned to new gods in search of salvation; Eastern mystery cults worshipping the bull-slayer Mithras, the unconquered sun-god Helios, or the sacred meteorites of the mother-goddess Cybele surged in popularity. In the coin portraiture of Marcus Aurelius we can see the first signs of this metaphysical shift within the Roman world: the wide eyes of the emperor seem to take on an absent gaze, as if looking away from the hardships of the age and towards another plane of existence. This artistic abstraction would develop in the coming centuries with the ascendance of Christianity, until rulers were almost indistinguishable from one another – generic faces of authority with exaggerated features and staring eyes set firmly on a higher power.

Marcus had come to the throne hoping to embody Plato's judgement that states might flourish when their philosophers are kings, or their kings are philosophers; his was meant to be an enlightened court, passing halcyon days with intellectual debates.[28] Now he found himself a mud-spattered warlord, ordering mass decapitations of Germanic prisoners on plague-ridden battlefields.[29] Likewise, the most iconic image of the philosopher-king to come down to us from ancient times shows him as a conquering general, triumphant over his barbarian enemies. The equestrian bronze statue of Marcus Aurelius in Rome is one of many such imposing statues that once adorned city squares around the Empire. With the fall of Rome, these conspicuous monuments were soon melted down for their valuable bronze, yet this lone statue of Marcus was allowed to remain standing thanks to its lucky misidentification as the Christian emperor

The replica equestrian bronze statue of Marcus Aurelius standing in
Rome's Piazza del Campidoglio, shown with an aureus depicting
the monument struck in AD 176.

Constantine through the Middle Ages. Michelangelo placed the gilded statue at the centre of his new piazza on the Capitoline in the sixteenth century, while today, a replica stands in the square and the original is displayed inside the adjacent museum. The bronze statue of Marcus represents a truly miraculous treasure of the ancient world: the only full-length equestrian statue of a Roman emperor to survive the millennia.

The statue is made even more evocative by the fact that it appears on coins of the time, celebrating hard-won victories over the Germanic tribes. A gold aureus shows the mounted figure of the emperor in a dynamic pose that almost exactly matches the Capitoline statue. Astride his prancing horse, Marcus stretches out his right hand in a gesture of clemency towards his vanquished enemies; medieval descriptions suggest a bound barbarian figure once cowered beneath the emperor's statue, benefiting from his mercy. Marcus is notably shown without armour or a laurel crown, perhaps hinting at his general reluctance to be depicted as a warlike commander. With pleasing circularity, the statue, and by extension the gold aureus depicting it, have been recreated on the reverse of the Italian 50-euro-cent coin ever since its introduction in 2002.

Marcus is certain throughout his *Meditations* that all his deeds will soon be swept away on the river of time, that his name may be spoken by a few generations until, like a dying fire, the final spark of his memory is quenched. A sort of cheerful nihilist 'whistling through the graveyard', the emperor happily faces his death without any vain hopes of immortality; how ironic then that through his coins, his unique equestrian statue, and the survival of his private journal, Marcus has achieved the eternal life he never thought possible.[30]

The emperor's 'notes to himself', thankfully preserved by an unknown individual after his death, would go on to provide comfort and wisdom to countless readers through history. Leaders of men have especially sought inspiration in the words of the reluctant warrior-king: when Captain John Smith sailed to the New World to establish his colony in Virginia, he brought with him just two books: the *Meditations* of Marcus Aurelius, and in a striking juxtaposition, the complete works of Machiavelli – Marcus therefore becoming one of the first classical authors to have his work reach North America. The four-star general and retired US secretary of defence Jim 'Warrior Monk' Mattis claims to have a carried 'a tattered copy' of the *Meditations* into combat on all his deployments. Enlightenment thinkers would also connect deeply with the humanistic ponderings of the Roman emperor. The eighteenth-century economist Adam Smith drew greatly on the Stoic ethic of cooperation and virtuous self-control in his monumental work *The Wealth of Nations*, and in the following century, philosopher John Stuart Mill would even cite the *Meditations* of Marcus as the only text to equal the moral goodness of Christ in the Gospels.[31]

Almost 2,000 years after they were written, medical experts are returning to the practical and timeless Stoic advice of Marcus and his peers to help tackle a variety of mental health conditions. The essential principles of modern Cognitive Behavioural Therapy (CBT) – one of the most widely used treatment models for those suffering from anxiety, depression, and addiction – are deeply indebted to ancient Stoicism. Like Marcus, CBT instructs us to reflect on and challenge our own negative responses to external factors, achieving peace of mind by instead focusing only on things within the realm of our control.

In a chaotic and confusing twenty-first-century world, people are seeking out these ancient lessons in fortitude and resilience more than ever before. Publishers have noted a year-on-year increase in the sales of Stoic philosophers: the *Meditations* sold over 100,000 copies in 2019, almost ten times the number purchased a decade earlier. Recent figures show that in the first part of 2020, sales surged by almost 30 per cent – a text written amid the pain and loneliness of a global pandemic, helping readers to cope during another health crisis 2,000 years later.[32]

In the pages of his philosophical journal the emperor confronted the disasters facing the Roman world, though it was equally a place where he sought the strength to endure unrelenting personal tragedies. Marcus had married Faustina soon after his adoption, and during their three decades of marriage it is thought that Faustina gave birth to no fewer than fourteen children. Coins rightfully celebrated her as the living embodiment of Fecunditas, the goddess of fertility, showing the empress surrounded by babies and toddlers. In contrast to so many childless rulers who had come before, the imperial couple surely seemed blessed by the gods. Salus, however, was evidently not one of them, and Marcus soon took to following the fateful advice of Epictetus: that every time he kissed a child goodnight, he should murmur under his breath that in the morning the child may be dead. Again and again, we hear of the couple's children dying in infancy, demonstrating that even the imperial palace was not immune to the cruel life expectancies of the ancient world. Near the culmination of his *Meditations*, Marcus quotes Homer's *Iliad* when he asks poignantly: 'What are the children of men, but as leaves that drop at the wind's breath?'

Like those fallen leaves 'were those beloved children of yours', the emperor tells himself, remembering all the infants that he and his wife have interred in tombs through the years.[33] After fathering fourteen children, the likelihood of Marcus not leaving a single male heir soon became a real possibility.

As he entered the final years of his reign, only one son remained.

Born in the Purple

Stoic philosophy had allowed Marcus to maintain his optimism in the face of plague, war, and family tragedy; however, 'one thing prevented him from being completely happy' – namely, that after rearing and educating his last remaining son in the best possible way, 'he was vastly disappointed in him'.[34] Commodus had been born one of twins in August 161, just a few months into his father's reign. He and his elder twin brother, Titus, therefore represented that rarest of occurrences in imperial Rome: sons born to a reigning emperor – commonly referred to as being 'born in the purple'. But with Titus dying in infancy like other brothers before him, and another boy, Annius Verus, following him to the afterlife in 169, young Commodus was soon the only imperial son playing in the halls of the palace.

The Greek philosopher Plato, whose teachings are often quoted by Marcus, had once compared the souls of human beings to precious metals.[35] He imagined that Mother Nature had crafted humanity, like the trimetallic coinage of the ancient world, out of gold, silver, and bronze – the nobility of our metal indicating the nobility of our character. Golden souls were governed by reason and destined to rule, while souls of silver did best as soldiers guarding society. Bronze souls were led by their appetites and were only fit to be farmers and labourers. Since parents with one type of soul could birth children of another, Plato warned that 'there is nothing that they must watch more carefully than the mixture of metals in the souls of their offspring'. It soon became clear to all that in Commodus, the gleaming and untarnished soul of the philosopher-emperor had, inexplicably, sired a soul not just of bronze, but of the basest iron.

Marcus had seen lustful, cruel habits emerging in his teenage son;

but he had also pondered in his *Meditations* 'all those royal courts, now vanished. All those memorials that read: The last of his house.'[36] Perhaps succumbing to this dynastic anxiety, perhaps out of natural fondness for a sole surviving son, Marcus broke the run of successful adopted emperors in 177 by raising the sixteen-year-old Commodus to the rank of co-ruler. With his own body weakening, Marcus commended his son to the people of the Empire with the naive hope that he might 'prove worthy'. The great teachers of his age were tasked with kicking the lazy boy into shape but it was all to no avail. The apple had fallen irretrievably far from the tree.

Later historians, struggling to fathom how one of the most virtuous emperors could father one of the most despicable, peddled rumours that Commodus was begotten through his mother's adultery with a gladiator. An understandable rationalisation – but coin portraits proclaiming the elevation of the teenage prince seem to leave little doubt as to his paternity. Denarii from my collection show father and son with the same tightly curled hair and wide, heavily lidded eyes. Commodus would soon grow a philosopher's beard to make him even more unmistakable as the son of Marcus, but for now he remains beardless and fresh-faced. All in all, he looks like a cheerful young doppelgänger of his father, which is of course the idea; their real similarities no doubt emphasised as part of state propaganda bolstering the dynastic succession. The stark contrasts between father and son would quickly be revealed, but for now, coins projected seamless continuance.

Commodus is so associated with the demented hubris of his subsequent reign – dressing as Hercules, taking to the Colosseum sands as a gladiator, even trying to rename Rome and all the months of the year after himself – it is easy to forget that he was once, as depicted here, a relatively innocent youth. Not to mention, as the only son of the beloved emperor to reach adulthood, his was surely perceived as a charmed life. But all the tutors in the world could not overcome the fact that young Commodus was, as Dio bluntly states, a bit of a 'dullard'; the youngster was 'not naturally wicked', but 'his great simplicity and cowardice made him the slave of his companions'.[37]

Why then did the great philosopher Marcus Aurelius choose

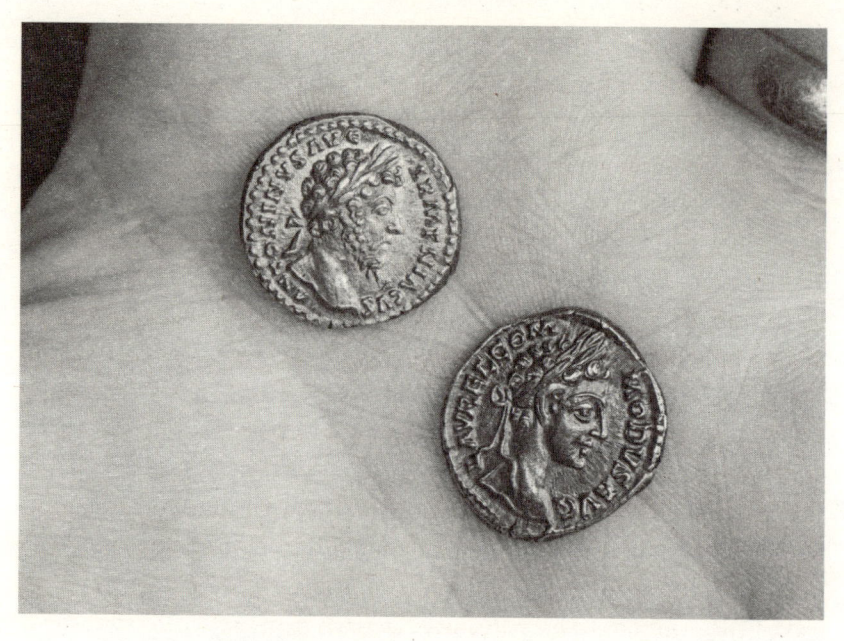

Like father, like son? Denarii of Marcus Aurelius and Commodus in the hand of the author.

Commodus as heir, when even he observed these flaws? Could he not have adopted a respected military figure to continue his tireless defence of the Empire? In reality, the mere existence of Commodus would have made such a snub a recipe for civil war, as entertainingly imagined in the movie *Gladiator*. Having narrowly fended off a revolt by the powerful general Avidius Cassius – he who had sacked Seleucia and supposedly unleashed the plague – Marcus clearly felt the need to project stability by designating an heir. Previous 'Good Emperors' had adopted carefully chosen successors in the absence of their own sons, but the lure of a blood dynasty is an intoxicating one; if Trajan or Hadrian had been blessed with sons of their own, they too would surely have placed them in the line of succession, however inferior they seemed in comparison to their fathers. Marcus was also a harried ruler and mostly absent parent – how carefully did he truly monitor the emerging character of his teenage boy? After all, while he may have been concerned about his son's abilities, he had assigned the best minds to his tuition and assumed that would suffice.

Marcus could hardly remember a time before the wars – those carefree days of boar hunts in the Italian countryside, of lively philosophy lectures and fulfilling study, when he was not battling pandemics and invasions. As one contemporary noted, 'the emperor fought for a long time, almost his entire life, you might say'.[38] By March 180, exhausted in body and spirit, he lay on his deathbed in the military camp of Vindobona, what is today Vienna. Whether the cursed disease he had somehow avoided for over a decade had finally caught up with him, we cannot say for sure; but in his last words Marcus would reference the plague that, through no fault of his own, had blighted the world during his reign. 'Weep not for me,' he urged those at his bedside. 'Pestilence and death is the common lot of us all.'[39] One of those present was Commodus, waiting to be handed sole command over the Empire at eighteen years of age. Marcus, for all his wisdom, could not foresee that his wayward son would arguably prove to be an even greater plague. It had been over 200 years since Augustus had established his Roman Empire; only now, as Commodus closed his father's lifeless eyes, did it have its first ruler 'born in the purple'.

Having lived through this transition of power, the historian Cassius Dio saw it as the precise moment that Rome began its long, inexorable decline, ending his account of the deeds of Marcus with an ominous line that again evokes the metals of Plato: 'our history now descends from a kingdom of gold to one of iron and rust'. Lacking the patience or determination of his father, Commodus quickly negotiated a treaty with the barbarian tribes before returning to the comforts of the Roman capital. There he indulged in the varied delights offered by unbridled power, leaving others to try and tackle the grave problems facing the Empire. The Salus – that good health of the Roman state longed for on a bronze sestertius of the philosopher-king – now seemed more precarious than ever; deaths to the plague would peak in 189 during the derelict reign of his son. And little salvation would be forthcoming in the century of chaos following his inevitable assassination.

But Rome would prevail. Largely thanks to the steadfast defence of its people, its ideals, and its frontiers by Marcus Aurelius, the

Roman world was able to live on despite declining health. Most impressively, Marcus had proved the exception to the rule that absolute power must corrupt absolutely. Granted god-like authority, he resisted every corrosive temptation of the throne until his dying day; so that at the news of his passing 'the people cried out in a swelling chorus, calling him "kind father", "brave general", and "wise ruler" – and every person spoke the truth'.[40]

In a later century, in the deep vaults of an unknown library, an anonymous medieval poet closed the last page on a dusty manuscript that had engrossed him. It was a copy of an ancient text written by an emperor of old – private meditations – labelled simply 'notes to himself'.[41] These were visionary words of a leader who did the best he could in trying times, without any thought of complaint. A man who loved his fate, whatever it might be. The poet, whose own age was marred with plague and suffering, was left feeling hopeful and inspired by the wisdom within. So inspired, he felt compelled to pick up his pen and write his own verse at the end of the manuscript:

> If you desire to master pain
> Unroll this book and read with care,
> And in it find abundantly
> A knowledge of the things that are,
> Those that have been, and those to come.
> And know as well that joy and grief
> Are nothing more than empty smoke.

Chapter X

SPLIT

'Money exists not by nature, but by law, and it is in our power to change it and make it useless.'

Aristotle

Silver *argenteus* of Diocletian showing the four rulers of his Tetrarchy sacrificing before a fortified city, AD 294.
Obverse: Laureate head of Diocletian, founder of the Tetrarchy or 'rule of four'.
Reverse: The four tetrarchs sacrificing over a tripod before a walled city.
VIRTVS MILITVM – 'The Strength of the Soldiers'.

The Great Debasement

The coins of Rome had proudly illustrated her rise to glory. Across thousands of miles, they passed between millions of hands – gleaming tributes to an empire of wealth and good order. But now as her fortunes waned, they would also tell the tale of a slow tumble into chaos. The fall, to begin with at least, would be a more secret story, hidden in dulled metal, and money that lay light in the palm. The same pronouncements of victory came stamped in the surface of gold, silver, and bronze; even as hostile tribes burst through frontiers. The same promises of peace and stability, pledged by an ever-changing gallery of leaders whose short reigns invariably ended in violence. Coin designs assured all that the gods still smiled on Rome, but the darkening silver of the denarius whispered an alternative narrative – one of sickness, debasement, and decline.

Money has increasingly become an abstraction in today's complex financial world of digital payments and virtual currencies, but in the classical age, money was real and tangible. Coins struck in gold and silver were worth their weight in those precious metals, operating both as efficient units of exchange and reliable stores of wealth. While modern governments print token money of no intrinsic value, accepted merely on the basis of trust in financial institutions, ancient coins were backed by the scarcity of their own lustrous metal. As a durable physical commodity, coinage formed a stable foundation for growing economies, rapidly establishing itself as an essential mechanism of trade and commerce across the Mediterranean, though its widespread acceptance as a medium of exchange relied heavily on precise standardisation of its value. Weight and purity of coinage was therefore a vital sign by which to measure a state's economic health.

Almost as soon as coins were conceived in the seventh century BC, issuing authorities looking to make their bullion go further experimented with debasement of their gold and silver. Debasement lowered the intrinsic value of coinage while maintaining its state-authorised face value. The sly practice could be implemented in two ways. The most obvious method was to reduce the weight of the coin from the agreed standard for the denomination – a tactic sure to be noticed by the observant merchants of the ancient world, quickly leading to inflated prices and economic instability. A subtler form of debasement occurred when the metal purity or 'fineness' of a coin was lowered, replacing its gold or silver with base metals like copper. This manipulation of a coin's composition was harder to identify and became a tempting way for governments to raise extra revenue in times of crisis and war.

Consequently, the purity of coinage became not just a barometer of an empire's economic well-being, but a touchstone by which the very virtue of the state and its leaders might be measured. Somewhat appropriate then that it was the decadent figure of Nero who first sought to profit by tainting the trusted metal of the denarius. As the backbone of the Roman monetary system, the denarius had maintained its reputation over the centuries as a stable and high-quality coin struck in pure silver. But after years of reckless spending compounded by the disastrous Great Fire of Rome, Nero needed a quick and easy way to generate emergency funds. Not only did the emperor lower the silver content of the denarius to around 93 per cent, he also dropped the standardised weight of the coin, further diminishing its intrinsic value. While the changes were minor at first, a disturbing precedent was set: emperors now realised that they could cover their debts through debasement.

The denarius would fluctuate around 90 per cent fineness in the following decades but confidence in the currency remained strong. Even the most successful emperors are known to have manipulated the coinage when varying supplies of silver and gold tested the bimetallic standard of the Roman monetary system; the enormous influx of gold into the Roman treasury from Trajan's Dacian conquest may have actually lowered its bullion value in relation to silver, forcing the emperor to further reduce the silver content of the denarius to maintain the parity of the two metals.[1] Such adjustments ensured the sacred ratio between the coins was protected: one gold aureus being equal to twenty-five silver denarii.

In the turbulence of the late second century, the silver of the denarius seemed to act as an uncanny mirror of the Empire's declining fortunes. Successive disasters striking in the reign of Marcus Aurelius were a perfect storm for the economy; plague tore through the population, decreasing the number of people who paid taxes and increasing financial pressure on the survivors. With Rome now on the defensive, spoils of conquest no longer flowed into the capital. Gold and silver mines, already nearing exhaustion, were emptied of their workforce and fell into disuse. At the worst possible time, Marcus was forced to wage costly wars on the Germanic frontiers, learning what Cicero had observed two centuries earlier: 'endless money forms the sinews of war'.[2] Again the denarius would have to yield a percentage of its silver purity to help fund the fight. The profligate reign of Commodus only depleted the Roman treasury further; by the year 192 when he was strangled to death in the bath by his personal trainer, the fineness of the denarius had dipped under 70 per cent silver.

Debasement had by now been normalised as a fiscal economic measure – a road that, once embarked upon, soon turned into a slippery slope. When the North African general Septimius Severus won control of the Empire the following year after a chaotic civil war in which five men fought for the throne, he came to power with a short-sighted monetary policy distilled in the lasting lesson he imparted to his two sons: 'enrich the soldiers, scorn everybody else'.[3] Not surprising then that under the rule of Severus military salaries soared, with legionary pay doubling initially from 300 to 600 denarii a year, and then jumping again to 900 denarii under the brutal reign of his son, Caracalla.[4] Having murdered his own brother to gain sole power, it seems appropriate that the corrupted character of Caracalla was matched in the corrupted metal of the denarius, now a meagre 50 per cent silver.

Recognising that the level of debasement had become untenable, Caracalla introduced a new silver denomination in 215 to help pay inflated salaries. This larger coin, today known as the *antoninianus* or 'radiate', portrayed the emperor wearing a spiked radiate crown – visual shorthand for a coin of double the value of others in the same metal. While the antoninianus was apparently tariffed as a 'double denarius', it in fact only contained the silver of 1.5 denarii, with the state pocketing the difference. Put simply, the new coin represented a knowing and wholesale monetary fraud against the Roman people. If the double denarius was intended to restore confidence in the faltering economy, it soon had the opposite effect. The ancients were no fools and, in a world where money had intrinsic metal value, made it their business to monitor the purity of their coins. Quickly realising the deceptive nature of the currency, Romans began to hoard older, higher-quality denarii while spending the new debased silver at its face value. The famous monetary principle that 'bad money drives out good' is usually attributed to the Tudor financier Thomas Gresham but the concept was well known in antiquity. As far back as the fifth century BC, the Greek playwright Aristophanes had noticed how the older coins 'untouched with alloys . . . and ringing true' hardly seemed to be used, while the 'sorry brass just struck yesterday' passed hand to hand.[5]

The Shapwick Hoard of over 9,000 denarii, buried in what is today Somerset during this precise period of economic chicanery, serves as a classic example of Gresham's Law. Not only did the hoard remove thousands of earlier denarii from circulation, it even contained 260 denarii struck by Mark Antony prior to the Battle of Actium way back in 31 BC. The wartime coins were known to have been struck in debased silver by the cash-strapped general, therefore Romans stubbornly kept them in circulation for centuries, happily spending them at their face value. Legionary denarii of Mark Antony, worn almost blank by use, are commonly found in third-century hoards having circulated around the Empire for over 250 years – the equivalent of carrying shillings of King George III (r. 1760–1820) in your wallet today.[6]

With confidence in her currency plummeting, Rome spun into a vicious cycle of hyper-inflation. As older coinage was hoarded or melted down, the monetary system became flooded by low-quality new denominations. Prices of goods and services rose accordingly, necessitating ever more coins be struck to meet demand – coins that had to pay the spiralling salaries of the soldiers in an army that was expanding massively to meet constant threats at the borders. The regular assassination of emperors by their own troops only added to the strain, with each new pretender to the throne needing to quickly conjure an extortionate cash donative to secure the 'loyalty' of the legions. Again and again, emperors felt the sharp end of their soldiers' swords after a few short years or even months in power – and the process was repeated. Sudden drops in the silver content of coinage at the beginning of reigns confirm that the dreaded tool of debasement was used to fund each donative.[7]

The precious metal steadily drained from Rome's coinage like lifeblood draining from her Empire. Around the year 240, a sombre event occurred in the Roman mint – one that may have passed people by in the turbulence of the times: a hammer-fall struck a design into the final coin recognisable as a denarius. For five centuries, the iconic silver coin had placed the Roman dream in the palms of millions across the ancient world. Now it would exist only as a hypothetical unit of account by which Romans might remind themselves how worthless their money had become. The denarius was gone. Debased into oblivion. Soon the entire Roman world seemed destined for the same.

End of Days

The turmoil that engulfed the Empire in the mid-third century is not only written in its coins; their sullied metal is often the only place the story can be told. During the fifty anarchic years following the downfall of the Severan dynasty in AD 235, upwards of twenty-five men would claim the imperial title, more than in the whole first two centuries of the Empire. These soldier-emperors were made in the barracks, elevated by their own troops, and more often than not assassinated by them the moment a better prospect came along. Each quickly minted debased silver radiates to legitimise their position and pay the legions that backed their powerplay. Romans surely struggled to keep up with the bewildering succession of stern faces passing by on their money. Indeed, the entire existence of obscure usurpers like Silbannacus, Uranius, and Domitianus would be all but lost to history if not for the coins they minted declaring themselves emperor.

While these barracks-emperors fought among themselves, existential threats to Rome mounted. Huge migrations brought fierce nomadic peoples like the Franks, Goths, and Vandals to weakened northern borders. The rival superpower of Parthia had been replaced by the ambitious Sasanian Empire, and it too was eager to expand its territory. With the denarius dead, the silver radiate coin now followed the same downward spiral of debasement until complete economic collapse seemed inevitable. As if to deliver the *coup de grâce*, the scourge of smallpox had returned to ravage the Roman world. The Christian bishop Cyprian gazed about at the unfolding cataclysm and saw nothing less than a vision of the end times, describing perpetual war, humanity wasted by disease, crops failing in the fields, and mines emptied of their metals. His prediction was simple: 'the day of judgement is drawing near'.[8]

That day must have seemed imminent in 251 when the emperor Decius and his son were killed in battle trying to defend the Danube frontier from marauding Gothic invaders. It was a grim milestone: the first ever Roman emperor to die in battle against a foreign enemy. Just a few years later in 260, the emperor Valerian met an even worse fate. Marching east to confront the Persian threat, Valerian's forces were annihilated in battle against King Shapur I. Shockingly, the emperor himself was taken as a prisoner of war. While accounts of his subsequent treatment vary, Christian historians describe Valerian being kept under the 'vilest conditions of slavery' for the remainder of his days. The slave was soon well trained, falling to his hands and knees in the dirt to act as a step for Shapur to mount his horse. The emperor of Rome had become a human footstool for an enemy king. But this was just the beginning of his humiliation. When Valerian eventually died in captivity, Shapur reportedly had the emperor skinned, stuffed, and displayed as a macabre trophy in the temple of the Persian gods. For years to come, the king proudly showed off his stuffed emperor to visiting ambassadors – a treasured memento of his greatest triumph.[9]

It was a new low for Rome – and it was reflected in the miserable silver content of her radiate coins which now sank below 10 per cent. In the decade following the disaster, the Empire came to the brink of total

A most unfortunate emperor. The face of Valerian, who was captured and enslaved by the Persian king, Shapur I – on a 'silver' radiate from the author's collection.

disintegration. Breakaway states – a Gallic Empire in the West and a Palmyrene Empire in the East – seceded from Rome to look to their own defences. One usurper after another declared themselves ruler in the provinces, all while tens of thousands of Germanic tribesmen poured across the Danube, even rampaging as far as Greece to lay waste the historic city of Athens. By 270 the 'silver' coins of Rome held less than 2 per cent precious metal. Nothing more than crude scraps of copper rushed out of the mint, without a thought of quality control. A thin silver wash on the coins only served to insult the intelligence of the Roman people, and quickly wore off to reveal the depressing base metal below. Any notion of a reliable 'gold standard' had long since vanished from the monetary system, with a single gold coin now valued at around 800 nominal denarii. As coinage ceased to hold any reliable standardised value, Rome threatened to return to a primitive barter economy.

It was therefore either a brave or foolish man who chose this moment to take the throne. When the cavalry officer Aurelian was acclaimed emperor by his troops, the crises facing the Empire seemed insurmountable. Nevertheless, he immediately embarked on an audacious mission to recover Rome's lost territories and restore some semblance of a working economy. Revealingly, his first priority was a ruthless crackdown on corruption that had infested the Roman mint, where officials had been debasing the coinage even further than instructed and stealing the silver for themselves. Aurelian ordered a full-scale military assault on the mint and after a bloody siege, executed every worker within. Once a more trustworthy workforce was in place, Aurelian relaunched the silver radiate with a heavier standardised weight and stabilised its silver content at a slightly more respectable 5 per cent. To further instil confidence in the coin he demanded the promise of its intrinsic value be struck into its surface: the enigmatic numerals 'XXI' included on his radiates are thought to represent an assurance of this 20:1 precious metal ratio.[10]

Now able to pay his forces in coin of something approaching quality, Aurelian led them against Germanic tribes who had broken into northern Italy. The invaders were defeated just 200 kilometres from the capital. It was a narrow escape for Rome and a sign of things to come. Recognising the very heart of the Empire was vulnerable to barbarian attack, the emperor ordered the construction of a twelve-mile defensive fortification to enclose the city. The massive Aurelian Walls still run their circuit around Rome today and though often ignored by visitors, remain the Eternal City's largest ancient monument.

Lightning campaigns against the separatist states of Palmyra and Gaul subsequently brought the rebel lands back into the Roman fold. The Empire was whole again. Some even sensed recovery in the air – and for his valiant efforts in pulling Rome out of the abyss, in 275 Aurelian received a thank-you indicative of the times: assassination by treacherous officers of his Praetorian Guard.

Aurelian had rightly been hailed the 'Restorer of the World', but the world he left was overstretched, unmanageable, beset by enemies within and without. Its problems were far too complex, its threats far too numerous, to be met by any one man. Perhaps, in the end, splitting the world was the only way it could be saved.

Jupiter and Hercules

It seemed like just another violent coup. Another reign founded in blood, sure to end in blood soon after. The cavalry commander from the Dalmatian coast certainly held no claim to greatness – he may have even been the son of a freed slave – but Diocles had overcome his lowly origins to reach the highest ranks of the Roman military by ability alone. When the emperor Numerian died in mysterious circumstances in 284 after just one year in power, Diocles publicly accused the praetorian prefect of his assassination and in full view of the soldiers, ran him through with his sword. With bloody blade in hand, Diocles was immediately hailed as emperor by the awed troops.[11]

It was a dramatic takeover to be sure, but standard fare for the brutal third century. Few would have predicted that the burly soldier's stint on the throne would be any longer than his short-lived predecessors, let alone that he would go on to become one of the greatest reformational statesmen of the ancient world. Having transcended his slave roots to become the sole leader of the Empire, Diocles now reinvented himself once again, Latinising his provincial Greek name to the more regal sounding Diocletianus. His personal transformation was only the beginning: almost immediately, Diocletian set into motion ambitious plans to reshape the entire Roman state.

The new emperor took stock of his vast and troubled realms: Germanic invaders breached borders in the West, Persians applied pressure in the East, rebellions ignited the lands between. Each menace demanded Diocletian's full attention – but even the best leader could not be everywhere at once. His straightforward solution showcased the rugged pragmatism of a military lifer, as well as his confidence in delegating command: if one ruler was not enough, then simply make more. Diocletian took the bold step of elevating a trusted fellow officer from the Illyrian provinces to be his imperial number two. Granted the rank of 'Caesar', Maximian was promptly dispatched to put down an insurrection in Gaul, freeing Diocletian to focus on securing the East. There he successfully defended the

Danube from Sarmatian tribes and negotiated a favourable peace with the Persians. The strategic gambit worked. Serious threats were met and overcome simultaneously, thousands of miles apart.

Acknowledging that problems shared were problems halved, Diocletian soon made the full commitment to an imperial diarchy and raised Maximian to the rank of fellow 'Augustus'. Two men were now draped in imperial purple. Rome had of course seen co-rulers before – Marcus Aurelius and Lucius Verus had inherited their shared battles with Parthians and plague; many had ruled jointly with their sons – but never before had an emperor freely chosen to split supreme power with a colleague from outside his family. Governing from dual imperial courts, the two 'Augusti' based themselves within striking distance of the most vulnerable frontiers: Maximian monitored the Alpine gateways to the Italian peninsula from his Western capital of Milan, while Diocletian made his Eastern capital at Nicomedia on the shore of the Sea of Marmara (today the Turkish city of İzmit). Notably, Rome had little part to play in Diocletian's vision for a decentralised state, the ancient city neglected in favour of these strategically located regional capitals. While she would remain the symbolic centre of the world, Rome was on her way to becoming a backwater in her own Empire.

The idea that 'Rome is wherever the emperor is' was not a new one, but Diocletian would do much to promote a reverential cult of personality around the imperial office, advertising the Augusti as semi-divine figures chosen by the gods to rule.[12] Nowhere was this clearer than in the official titles used to differentiate their parallel courts. Perhaps overcompensating for his servile background, Diocletian now became the 'Jovian' emperor, aligning his position with none other than the king of the gods, Jupiter himself. At the same time, Maximian was rebranded the 'Herculian' ruler, linking him to the mythical club-wielding action hero. An impressive moniker, but Romans would have discerned in the names the true dynamic of the partnership; just as Jupiter was the father of Hercules, so Diocletian was revealed to be the paternal figurehead of the imperial pair. Though the emperors lacked any blood ties, their new divine personas emphasised brotherhood and unity of vision between their distant thrones.

Diocletian's choice to frame their shared rule through such bold pagan iconography offered a glimpse of the staunch religious conservatism that would later become an infamous feature of his reign. Imperial propaganda would once again be steeped in reverence for the Roman pantheon of deities, whose neglect had surely been the cause of Rome's century of disaster. Diocletian struck an array of coins honouring the guardian deity of his regime 'Iovi Conservatori' – 'Jupiter the Protector', embodying the emperor's mission to preserve not just Rome's borders, but also her beliefs, values, and money. Yet 'Jovius' would prove to be both a traditionalist and a radical reformer, aware that if the Roman state were to survive at all it would need to quickly evolve to meet the unique challenges of his time. And his most monumental reforms were still to come.

After decades without a viable silver denomination, this gleaming silver coin struck around AD 294 announces to the Roman world both an overhauled monetary system and a reimagined model of government, all designed to reignite the fortunes of the Empire. On first impression the coin seems to be a resurrected high-quality denarius of the first century: struck to the same size, the same three-gram weight, and in near-pure silver of around 95 per cent fineness. In fact, it represents an entirely new silver denomination at the centre of a revamped coinage which Diocletian hoped would restore confidence and stability to the economy. Today called the *argenteus* (literally, 'of silver'), emphasising the purity of its metal, the coin was issued alongside a new bronze denomination known as the *follis*, although their standardised equivalency is lost to time. It is known, however, that despite its identical composition, the argenteus was valued at one hundred old denarii – a remarkable illustration of how far inflation had corroded the Roman economy.[13]

A domineering portrait on the argenteus shows Diocletian in his late forties, with the closely cropped hair and tightly trimmed beard typical of the militaristic barracks-emperors from the Balkans. Their generically rigid and block-headed portrayals can often be difficult to distinguish from one another – a reflection of declining artistic standards and the growing tendency to depict emperors as abstract and remote quasi-religious figures; though the uniquely determined character of Diocletian may be sensed in his piercing gaze, fixed on a visionary new future for Rome. We might expect the reverse of the new coin to celebrate the diarchy of Jovius and Herculius, but having quickly felt the benefits of shared rule, Diocletian wasted no time in taking the strategy to the next level. Rome had seen the rule of two – now it was time for the rule of four.

Divide and Conquer

On 1 March 293, two magnificent imperial ceremonies took place simultaneously, 1,100 miles apart. With the military coordination that might be expected of soldier-emperors, the two Augusti – Diocletian in Nicomedia and Maximian in Milan – each lowered a laurel crown onto the head of a new Caesar, raised to assist them in their fight to restore the Empire. Before the Jovian palace, Diocletian invested Galerius with imperial powers, while at the Herculian palace, Maximian welcomed Constantius into the ruling regime. Like their superiors, both Galerius and Constantius were no-nonsense, career soldiers from humble families in the Illyrian provinces. The days of Italian aristocrats sitting on the throne in Rome were long gone. Four military men from the Balkan lands of what are today Bulgaria, Croatia, and Serbia now controlled the Empire: a radical experiment in shared governance labelled by modern historians as the Tetrarchy or 'rule of four'.

Just as Diocletian sought to stabilise a turbulent economy with his new coinage, so his Tetrarchy was designed to end the chaotical cycle of usurpations and assassinations that had racked the century. Since the quartet were unrelated by blood, every available tactic was used to strengthen ties between them so that the Tetrarchy might be immunised against personal greed and ambition. Not only were the Caesars adopted as sons by their respective Augusti, they were also bound by marriage; Constantius married Maximian's daughter Theodora, and Galerius married Diocletian's daughter Valeria. With his Tetrarchy, the heirless but ever-inventive Diocletian had essentially conjured a ready-made dynasty, both Caesars ready to replace their

Augusti and adopt their own emperors-in-waiting when the time came.

The reverse of the silver argenteus therefore presents a family portrait of the tetrarchs to the Roman world, showing the four rulers sacrificing before a heavily fortified camp or city. Together the men offer libations over a burning tripod, emphasising the devout nature of the coalition and divine purpose to their shared mission. A sacred temple would have once provided the backdrop to such a pious scene, now we have the turreted battlements of an impregnable stronghold, epitomising the defensive tetrarchic world; theirs would be a fortress empire, of high-walled cities and militarised borderlands. The unnamed bastion may even represent the Roman Empire itself, its boundaries personally guarded by the vigilant allies. Around the scene, a legend honouring 'Virtus Militum' – 'The Strength of the Soldiers' – further underscores the martial character that now defined the Roman state. The emperors were of course soldiers themselves, and most newly minted coins only entered the economy after they had first paid a soldier's salary.

The fact that this communal sacrifice had never occurred in reality was of no consequence – it would take almost a decade for the tetrarchs to gather in one location – all that mattered was the presentation of a united front to the Roman viewer. The four rulers were too busy securing the four corners of the Empire. In the West, Constantius successfully reconquered the island of Britannia which, for ten embarrassing years, had been claimed by usurpers as a breakaway Britannic Empire. Maximian meanwhile swept across North Africa, driving rebellious Berber tribes back to the Sahara. In the East, Galerius suppressed an uprising in Egypt before he and Diocletian forced another tough treaty on the Persians. In just a few short years, victories were declared on all fronts. The Tetrarchy had proved an instant success.

Its invention had enabled Diocletian to do the impossible: in essence, to replicate himself and allow the commanding figure of the emperor to be omnipresent in every theatre of war. Imperial iconography duly presented the tetrarchs as a single entity, four embodiments of the same authority, speaking with one voice and pursuing one mission. It was no accident that only by carefully reading the name on their coin could a literate Roman identify which bearded, stern-faced tetrarch was even being portrayed. Likewise, the convened figures on the reverse of the argenteus are completely indistinguishable from one another, identical in dress, height, and pose.

This commitment to a shared but unified imperial vision is perfectly illustrated in a fascinating statue group surviving from the era. The *Portrait of the Four Tetrarchs* was carved around the year 300, in the rare purple porphyry beloved by emperors. Originally part of a monument in Constantinople, the sculpture was taken as plunder at the culmination of the Fourth Crusade in 1204 and carried back to Venice, where it was embedded in the external wall of St Mark's Basilica. There the tetrarchs still stand, rather incongruously, today (Plate section, 13). Arranged in their ruling pairs, the squat, wide-eyed figures each grip identical eagle-headed sword hilts, ready to spring to the defence of Rome, while reaching to embrace each other at the same time. The perfect picture of amity, even if their awkward poses and childlike proportions make the figures look as if they are clutching each other in fear of the passing hordes of tourists. Individual identities within the group are again impossible to discern, with all four men wearing the same armour, military caps, and severe expressions. Altogether, the sculpture presents the image of a close-knit imperial brotherhood, with no hint of a dominant *pater familias* dictating commands; though as one historian observed, in reality, the other tetrarchs 'all looked up to Diocletian as if to a father or a mighty god'.[14]

Such a group embrace may have occurred in AD 303 when all four rulers finally assembled in Rome to celebrate their decade of victories with a spectacular joint triumph – seemingly the only time that Diocletian ever visited the Eternal City. The grand parade would also mark Diocletian's vicennial anniversary; considering that many of his immediate predecessors only survived months in power, twenty years on the throne was a miraculous achievement.

Diocletian had 'quartered the Empire', hoping that by dividing the Roman world it might be held together. The gamble had worked – but now four princes led four massive armies, each demanding their own pay and logistical support. They ruled from four imperial palaces, each served by their own vast network of bureaucracy.[15] Diocletian had introduced the first true silver coin in over a century, but with greater financial outlays than ever before, its pure metal was soon tested by ongoing inflationary pressure. In the guise of Jupiter, he had remade the world to his design – and like any god, he expected it to function as intended. The soldierly existence was, after all, one of clear orders, instantly obeyed. But having dominated the field of battle, Diocletian would soon learn that it was not so simple to command the economy, to mandate belief, or indeed to legislate human nature.

The Blood is the Seed

In the forum squares of towns and cities across the Empire, heralds recited the long-winded imperial decree to sceptical crowds. Diocletian and his tetrarchs had stemmed the barbarian tides with costly but essential military campaigns, they had halted the cycle of insurrections with their political coalition; now they turned their attention to an altogether different battlefront. Their next war was to be fought in defence of the Roman economy, waged against the more abstract foes of soaring inflation, extortionate prices, and as Diocletian would perceive it, greed itself. Merchants, farmers, senators and slaves alike, all listened gravely as the new law was laid out – to be enacted under penalty of death.

Diocletian's recent coinage reform, though well intentioned, had thoroughly failed to stabilise the economy. The sudden introduction of high-quality coin denominations into a devastated monetary system had once again proved Gresham's Law, with distrustful Romans quickly hoarding the bronze follis and silver argenteus in the expectation of them soon being debased. Chronic silver shortages also meant that the pure argenteus was only ever struck in limited numbers, further encouraging the hoarding which drove the coin out of circulation. Continuing price rises therefore placed enormous pressure on the bronze follis which needed to be minted in astronomical amounts. Indeed the very name 'follis' derives from the

Latin word for the leather bag that held a fixed weight of the coins; many items were now apparently purchased, not by individual bronze *folles*, but by the sackload.

Drastic action was needed to curb the deepening financial crisis, and it came in AD 301 when Diocletian issued his Edict on Maximum Prices – unprecedented legislation that capped prices and wages throughout the Empire in an aggressive effort to counter the effects of runaway inflation. The monumental decree offers a remarkable insight into the commercial life of the late Roman world, listing as it does the relative values of over 1,200 raw materials, staple goods, luxury items, and services of all varieties.[16]

Browsing the Edict is like strolling through a vibrant ancient Roman marketplace. We learn the top price for a thirteen-litre *modius* of wheat was now set at 100 denarii, while a bottle of pungent fish sauce might cost you twelve. A barley beer was two denarii, but a helping of quality Falernian wine was twenty-four. It was sixteen denarii for a pound of smoked Lucanian pork sausage or – for that upcoming special occasion – 200 for a fattened goose (double that of the unfattened variety). Rates for essential services include two denarii for a visit to the barber, seventy-five per day for a fresco painter, and 1,000 for a lawyer to plead your case in court. The Roman super-rich may have concerned themselves with the 150,000 denarii price-tag for a pound of purple-dyed silk; interestingly, the same as an African lion for the arena. That all prices are listed in nominal denarii – a coin defunct for more than 150 years – only further emphasises the lack of economic impact made by Diocletian's newest coin types.

The reasons for such strict regulation are laid out by Diocletian in a verbose and moralising preamble to the Edict, decrying the 'burning greed' in markets of the Empire, 'which grows worse not just annually, but day by day and hour by hour'; where the new era of peace and plenty for which the emperors 'laboured mightily' has done nothing to lessen 'uncontrolled passion for profiteering' and 'unrestrained prices that mar the daily business of the cities'. Diocletian cites a revealing example of such injustice: that 'sometimes a soldier is deprived of his bonus and his pay in a single transaction', robbing not just one man of his wages, but the whole world of the taxes it pays to support the armies. As a usurping soldier-emperor himself, Diocletian knew well not to ignore the complaints of his disgruntled troops. Now he and his tetrarchs, as 'parents of the human race', had agreed 'legal intervention' was needed to remedy these failings of human nature. But rather than target the root causes of the inflationary crisis – massive military spending, bloated bureaucracy, over-taxation – Diocletian simply demanded, on pain of death, that all prices be slashed. Like a commandment issued from god-emperors on high, the Edict declared: let there be cheapness.

The misguided ruling paid little heed to the complex dynamics of supply and demand in the Roman economy, and like his failed coin reform, only aggravated the problems it aimed to solve. For instance, while the Edict goes to great pains to emphasise that its numbers represent *maximum* rather than *recommended* prices, many merchants predictably raised their already steep charges to match those listed on the decree. Others, seeing fellow shopkeepers executed for breaking mandates, were afraid to offer their goods for sale at all. Trade was therefore pushed to the black market, with the resulting scarcity of products forcing inflation higher still.[17]

Consistently policing the Edict was also destined to be an impossible task, beyond even the growing army of pen-pushing civil servants that micromanaged Diocletian's provinces. While it was apparently in force throughout the 'whole realm', the surviving copies of the inscribed Edict have almost all been unearthed in cities of the East, raising intriguing questions of how much it was truly implemented on an Empire-wide basis. Either way, after injecting needless panic and confusion into an already fragile Roman economy, the Edict was scrapped in the face of massive resistance, perhaps less than a year after its introduction.

Perceiving the economic crisis in moral terms, Diocletian had declared an unwinnable war on human avarice. On this front he was forced to concede defeat – yet he would continue to wield his imperial power as a blunt instrument, assuming his vision for a reformed Empire could simply be commanded into being. The idea that tens of millions of people from diverse lands might not blindly obey orders like one of his well-drilled legions, was seemingly hard to fathom. With his ego bruised from the failure of his financial reforms, Diocletian instead focused his attention on a more visible threat to the traditional order.

The devoutly pagan emperor had grown increasingly impatient with the growing number of mystical cults, whose adherents offended Rome's founding gods every day with their subversive rites. Roman religion had long welcomed the exotic deities of newly conquered lands into its pantheon, happily equating their attributes with existing gods – as long as libations were also made to the well-being of the emperor. In a world with no separation between church and state, reverence for the pagan gods and obedience to Roman authority were inextricably linked, especially so in Diocletian's mind: in 299 he had forced all soldiers of the Roman army to offer a pagan sacrifice or else face discharge without pension.[18] But one cult especially drew attention to itself with its secret codes and symbols, its emboldening of slaves and women, and its dissenting claim to one God. Its followers undermined sacred proceedings at pagan ceremonies by making their strange sign of the cross, and afterwards refused the meat of animals that had been sacrificed to the Roman gods. Determined to put an end to their sedition, in 303, Diocletian declared his Edict against the Christians.

The feast day of the god Terminus, deity of boundaries and endings, was chosen as the auspicious date to begin the purge. The symbolism was not subtle: Rome had reached the limits of her patience and resolved to terminate the Christian religion. At dawn, Diocletian sent a force of praetorians against the first target. The Christian church of Nicomedia was visible from his imperial palace, rising on high ground above the city as an annoying reminder to the emperor of the thriving cult. Unable to simply burn down the church owing to the risk of setting ablaze the whole city, Diocletian ordered his men to tear down the building after stripping it of its valuables. From the palace balcony, he and Galerius watched with satisfaction as the soldiers set to work with axes and demolition tools. In just a few hours the lofty church had been levelled.[19]

Diocletian's Edict did not initially demand bloodshed – more the destruction of churches, burning of holy scriptures, and barring of

Christians from public offices – but on the instigation of his firebrand Caesar, Galerius, the brutality of the persecution quickly escalated. Any who tore down the proclamations were promptly arrested and put to death. Soon Christians were being flogged, nailed to crosses, beheaded, and burnt alive in the arena. To stop their graves becoming shrines, many were tied together in large groups, weighed down with stones and dumped overboard from vessels into the sea. Subsequent additions to the Edict demanded that all suspected Christians throughout the Roman world make a public sacrifice to the pagan gods. Drawn-out death by torture awaited any who refused.[20]

The killing would continue for almost a decade. In an empire divided, geographically and spiritually, the emperor thought a return to traditional paganism could be the binding glue to unite the whole. In reality, his Great Persecution split the realm more than ever, tearing communities apart with violence and segregation. Far from eradicating Christianity, it drew sympathetic eyes and ears to the teachings of the sect while making holy martyrs out of those who died refusing to recant their faith; among them St Agnes, St Sebastian, and the patron saint of England, St George. The Christian writer Tertullian would be proved correct in his defiant statement: 'you cannot just exterminate us; the more you kill, the more we are. The blood of the martyrs is the seed of the church.'[21]

By AD 305, Diocletian was a waning autocrat in his sixties and no longer the formidable warrior of his youth. His run of faltering edicts had shown the self-styled embodiment of Jupiter to be fallible after all. And by his own design, hungry Caesars waited in the wings for their turn at the head of his Tetrarchy. Sensing this vulnerability, other rulers might have descended into paranoia. Diocletian saw one last chance for innovation. His final decree would be perhaps his most radical yet.

Dominus Noster

The old man hauled himself to his feet, strained to straighten his back, and clapped the dark soil from his hands. Adjusting the wide brim of his straw hat against the blazing sun, he surveyed the results of his labours with satisfaction. Leafy green vegetables growing, full and flourishing, in their neat rows. He had sown their seeds, watered them attentively, kept pests at bay, and watched them thrive in their orderly partitions. All exactly to his design. Unlike that chaotic world outside his palace walls, here in his vegetable garden, Diocletian had full control.

Settled back on the sparkling shores of his Dalmatian homeland, the strife and tumult of his previous life seemed a distant memory. Nothing could coax him back into that storm of rampaging barbarians, rebel cults, and harsh edicts. Those battles of empire were a young man's game. He had done all in his power to rescue Rome from disaster, to renew her for an uncertain future – but this old soldier had served his time. After more than twenty years in command, Diocletian had done what no emperor had done before: he had retired.

The joint abdication of both Augusti on 1 May 305 stunned the Roman world. That Diocletian, as senior tetrarch, had ordered his Western counterpart to surrender his throne simultaneously was in little doubt, but the motives behind the move were much debated.[22] Perhaps Diocletian simply felt he and Maximian had achieved all they could as leaders, and a transition had been agreed between the four tetrarchs at their recent assembly. The regimented hierarchies of his Tetrarchy were, after all, carefully devised to remove bloody daggers from the succession process. Nevertheless, rumour swirled that Diocletian's own Caesar, Galerius, had threatened him with civil war if he refused to step aside. Others claimed the co-rulers resigned 'out of desperation', humiliated by their failure 'to prevail over the Christians or to extinguish the herald of Christ'.[23] Whatever their reasons, in coordinated ceremonies at Nicomedia and Milan, both Jovius and Herculius made history by peacefully abdicating their thrones.

Diocletian would choose to live out his twilight years in a vast retirement palace, specially built for him on the Dalmatian coast near his home city of Salona. The fact that the residence was ready for his arrival in 305, constructed to his specifications in the preceding decade, further suggests his abdication was indeed a long-planned strategy.

Today the colossal ruins of Diocletian's Palace – home of the emperor who split the Roman world in two, and then in four – happen to enclose the historic centre of Split, Croatia. A spectacular statement of late-imperial power, the complex represents the best-preserved example of Roman palatial architecture anywhere in the world.

Combining the rigid rectangular plan of a military fortress with the grand opulence of a royal residence, the palace perfectly captures the duality of the soldier-emperor. Massive defensive walls built in blocks of shimmering white limestone rise over twenty metres in height, bolstered along their length by sixteen guard towers. Imposing gateways grant access to the compound on its three land-facing sides, while its southern facade looks out over the serene waters of the Adriatic. Straight roads strike through each axis of the palace, dividing the nine-acre interior into quadrants; even after decades of luxurious living, Diocletian evidently still drew comfort from the strict order and symmetry of an army camp.

As well as paying tribute to the emperor's military identity, the defensive architecture of the palace starkly conveys the tensions of the times. Far from the sprawling, airy imperial villas of rulers like Nero and Hadrian, here at the turn of the fourth century we have a heavily fortified stronghold, ominously designed to be resupplied by sea even if besieged by hostile armies on land. The structure once again brings to mind the reverse of Diocletian's silver argenteus, with its depiction of a similar impenetrable bastion. Increasingly, populations throughout the once-secure Mediterranean world sought protection behind such high battlements, prefiguring the castles that would be a key feature of the European landscape in later centuries.

At the monumental heart of the palace, visitors entering from any gateway arrive, inevitably, at the *peristyle* – a magnificent courtyard lined by arcades rising on pink columns of Egyptian granite (Plate section, 14). A grand portico dominates the space, through which it is believed Diocletian would emerge from his private apartments to address adoring audiences gathered in the sunken square below. Framed in the temple-like facade, beneath a cutaway 'Syrian arch' that recalls architecture of the East, Diocletian was presented as nothing less than a semi-divine being. Notably, he is thought to have introduced the

Eastern practice of *proscynesis* (prostration) to the Roman imperial court, with subjects compelled to bow, kneel, or even lie down in complete submission before emperors.[24] Here in the peristyle courtyard, even in retirement, Diocletian was venerated like a living god.

Diocletian may have relinquished imperial power to 'voluntarily return to the condition of private life' but a subtle amendment to coins honouring the veteran ruler confirms his elevation to an even higher plane of existence.[25] Added to the legends encircling his portrait were the initials 'DN', abbreviating his new title, 'Dominus Noster'. Across the Empire, coins now heralded Diocletian as 'Our Lord'. In defence of traditional paganism Diocletian had declared war on the ascendant religion of Christianity, issuing bloody edicts that sought to eradicate belief in God the Father and God the Son, yet he and the Christian God would now be acclaimed with the same ovation. As the Old Testament's Book of Psalms proclaims: '*Dominus Noster – Our Lord*, how majestic is your name in all the earth!'

It has also been observed that Diocletian's creation of a distinct-yet-inseparable Tetrarchy, with its divine fathers, sons, and single guiding spirit, is strangely similar to the Christian Trinity; his autocratic model of government and the early Christian Church evidently informed each other more than either would admit.[26] But only one of the power systems could prevail. Ultimately, like the seeds he sowed in his vegetable garden, Diocletian had inadvertently nurtured the growth of Christianity – exactly as its apologists warned. In 313, only a year after his death, a new edict was issued by his successors promising Christians an end to persecution and freedom to practise their religion throughout the Roman world.

The Romanesque bell tower soaring above the peristyle symbolises, with unforgiving irony, the total failure of Diocletian's Great Persecution. The octagonal building from which it rises began life as Diocletian's mausoleum, constructed in the heart of his palace by the retired emperor in his final years. Under its great dome, richly decorated with golden mosaics, Diocletian would lie interred in a porphyry sarcophagus; that is until the seventh century when his grave was destroyed, and the mausoleum reconsecrated as a Christian cathedral. Not only did his tomb become a seat of Christian worship, it was named in honour of St Domnius – bishop of Diocletian's hometown of Salona, who had been beheaded in the arena during his persecutions. Split's Cathedral of St Domnius stands today as one of the oldest, smallest, and most fascinating cathedrals in the world.

Other ironies abound in Diocletian's efforts to recapture the Rome of old. He strove to rekindle the failing economy, while overseeing a violent pogrom that further depleted his tax base. He took radical steps to lower prices throughout the Empire, yet dramatically increased the size and expense of the state, all but inventing the concept of a bewildering 'Byzantine' bureaucracy. He had confidently redrawn the map of the world around the Roman people, but soon struggled when attempting to remould the people themselves. In his repressive economic and religious edicts, he learned, like many political leaders across time, the futility of trying to achieve meaningful and lasting change through force.

Diocletian would even live to see the breakdown of perhaps his proudest creation. The Tetrarchy had relied, somewhat naively, on four absolute rulers playing nicely together; here Rome's track record was poor. As the Roman poet Lucan admitted, there is 'no loyalty between sharers in tyranny . . . Look at the evidence of our own nation: Rome's first walls were drenched in a brother's blood.'[27] Within a year of Diocletian's abdication the Second Tetrarchy dissolved into chaos, with spurned sons left out of the succession declaring themselves emperors anyway. Civil war returned to Rome. It seemed, after all, that the secret of the Tetrarchy's success was not the strict hierarchies of Diocletian's design – it was Diocletian himself. When Galerius appealed to his old commander to come out of retirement and restore order yet again, Diocletian's answer was final: 'If you could see the cabbages I have grown here in Salona with my own hands,' he responded, 'you surely would never judge that a temptation.'[28]

The old veteran had earned his peaceful retirement. At times he had stumbled in his radical-conservative crusade to rescue Rome, but his 'reform to preserve' strategy had undoubtedly extended the life of the Empire.[29] He tackled the financial crisis head-on, restoring pure metal coins to the monetary system and recognising the importance of quality coinage to successful economies. Reorganising the

Roman world, he formalised the notions of Eastern and Western empires which would shape Europe for millennia. His Tetrarchy had even shared power successfully, for a time. Rome was guided by a multitude of emperors and a multitude of gods – but her destiny would now echo the ancient verse of Homer, that 'ill fares the state where many masters rule; let one be lord, one king supreme'.[30]

Chapter XI

CROSS

'For it is written: "As surely as I live," says the Lord, "every knee will bow before me; every tongue will acknowledge God."'

Romans 14:11

Bronze follis of Constantine the Great struck in his new Roman capital of Constantinople, AD 327.
Obverse: Laureate head of Constantine I, known as 'the Great'.
Reverse: *Vexillum* standard surmounted by 'Chi-Rho' Christogram, piercing serpent below.

By This Sign

The vision was surely his alone. Nothing more than a foolish hallucination, spurred by thirst and exhaustion on that long road to Rome. Yet the confused shouts of his soldiers seemed to claim otherwise. As the marching column ground to a halt before the spectacle, men raised their arms to the clear sky, calling out to their emperor to witness the unfolding miracle. It took shape, by all accounts, in the rays of the midday sun. A glowing halo surrounding the solar disc, sparkling with additional rival suns where it was intersected by radiating horizontal and vertical beams – all shimmering like jewels with spectral colour. The autumn sun directly ahead of Constantine's army, guiding their way south to the capital, had become a blazing cross of light.

Shielding his eyes with an outstretched hand, the emperor filtered the blinding rays through his fingers and strained to examine the celestial omen. He was certain then of letters revealing themselves in the dazzling glare, inscribed directly on the sky beneath the symbol. Constantine asked the bewildered officers around him if they too saw the unfurling message, but only he could perceive the words in the arcing tangents of light. He would later swear by oath that accompanying the cross was the holy promise, penned in fire: '*In hoc signo vinces*' – 'By this sign you will conquer'.

The divine encouragement came at just the right moment – with the impregnable walls of Rome looming on the horizon, and the tyrant behind them holding every tactical advantage. Whichever god offered this shining banner of victory, Constantine was glad to accept it.

His battle for imperial recognition had already been an arduous one. Like every member of the Tetrarchy that dominated the Empire at the turn of the fourth century, Constantine hailed from humble family origins in the Balkan peninsula, born in what is today Niš, Serbia, to a poor 'stable maid' named Helena, the wife (or perhaps concubine) of the rising soldier Constantius. At around twenty years old, the course of Constantine's life would forever change when the mighty Diocletian inducted his father into the Tetrarchy as assistant emperor in the West. Already a promising soldier himself, Constantine surely expected to ride alongside his father on the battlefields of Gaul and Britannia – but Diocletian had other plans.

Young Constantine was instead packed off to Diocletian's imperial court in Nicomedia. On one hand the Jovian capital was the perfect place for a crown prince to complete his education. In this dynamic cultural and intellectual hub where East met West, Constantine may have attended lectures of Christian scholars active in the city. At the same time, the arrangement also revealed a darker truth behind tetrarchic loyalties. If not a hostage, Constantine was at least Diocletian's 'honoured detainee' in the imperial palace, his presence serving to limit the conquering ambitions of his father 1,500 miles away.

Constantine would have had a front-row seat in AD 303 as Diocletian and Galerius inaugurated their Great Persecution with an outburst of violence against Christians in Nicomedia. We can only guess at his thoughts as he watched the city's Christian church reduced to rubble and its sacred scriptures heaped on bonfires. That no evidence exists to suggest Constantine made any appeals to the better natures of his superiors is not surprising; whatever his opinions on the burgeoning religion at the time, without official position in the imperial hierarchy he lacked real authority to intervene and was surely mindful not to present himself as a Christian sympathiser. In his later years, however, perhaps looking to alleviate guilt at his inaction, he would strongly denounce the 'relentless cruelty and most grievous outrages' to which those 'venerable worshippers of God were daily exposed'.[1] As we will see, Constantine's journey towards open acceptance of Christianity would be a far more cautious and methodical one than is often suggested, dictated always by his need to balance the rival religious factions of his divided world. His evolving, and often contradictory, relationship with the persecuted faith will be nowhere better evidenced than in his coins, which will speak volumes in their tacit endorsements of Christianity, if not in open declarations of belief.

Two years later, Constantine was also present at the grand military parade on the outskirts of Nicomedia, where Diocletian announced with tears in his eyes to the assembled legions that having become tired and infirm, he would 'resign the Empire into hands more vigorous and able'. The confirmation that Constantius and Galerius were to be raised to the ranks of Augusti surprised no one; it was the nomination of the new Caesars that gripped the troops. Now that his father was senior emperor in the West, investing Constantine with the imperial purple was surely a mere formality. Commanding the loyalty of the legions also helped his cause; the soldiers struggled to contain their joy at his approaching appointment, with some already offering up 'prayers for his prosperity'. Bemused faces abounded then when Galerius announced the obscure names of two of his own close allies as the new tetrarchs. Confused onlookers asked their neighbours if Constantine had changed his name. The reality soon dawned – but no one dared voice any objection. The emperor's son had been snubbed.[2]

He was not the only heir apparent to be passed over that day: Maxentius, son of Diocletian's fellow retiree, Maximian, was also ignored in the reshuffle. Both young men would take the rejections personally. The Tetrarchy had, of course, been conceived as a military brotherhood that transcended fickle dynastic ambitions – based not on blood, but ability. Still, some may have wondered if the sonless Diocletian jealously excluded the heirs of his colleagues, whatever their talents. The decision would soon come back to haunt all involved.

Sensing his life would be short in the treacherous court of Galerius, Constantine fled Nicomedia under the cover of darkness and embarked on a marathon journey across Europe to be reunited with his father. They would embrace on the coast of Gaul, just in time to cross the Channel together for a military campaign against the fierce Picts of northern Britannia. Father and son made for an effective team, and the victories came quickly. Their family reunion, however, would be short-lived. In the following summer of 306, Constantius succumbed to illness in Eboracum (modern York). The tetrarchic model, designed for precisely these moments, made clear what promotions should follow. The assembled troops, loyal to the house of Constantius, had other ideas.

Some say that in his final breaths the dying emperor had bequeathed the throne, 'according to the law of nature, to his eldest son'.[3] If so, the allure of a blood dynasty had won out again. Others maintain the soldiers chose Constantine as the only one 'fit for the imperial dignity' and 'conferred the honour upon him, in hopes of being remunerated with handsome presents'.[4] They surely received their generous payday; not only did the legions salute Constantine as their new emperor, they proclaimed him a senior Augustus, in total violation of the Tetrarchy's chain of command. As he solemnly accepted the sacred laurels of office, the cheers of Constantine's troops shook the heart of ancient York – and fractured the entire Roman state.

Faced with the fait accompli of Constantine's unauthorised coronation, the Tetrarchy was immediately thrown into turmoil. When the news reached Rome, the other rejected imperial heir, Maxentius, was furious. Why should the 'son of a harlot' enjoy such good fortune, while he, 'the son of so great an emperor', remained powerless?[5] Naturally, he promptly proclaimed himself emperor too. With more rulers than there were thrones for them to sit on, the following years would see the Tetrarchy ripped apart in a ruthless power struggle where no bond was sacred. The invincible alliance – once as solid as the purple porphyry in which its members were sculpted – had crumbled, inevitably, to the human frailties of ambition, jealousy, and greed.

By 312, only the two instigators of the brawl, Constantine and Maxentius, remained alive to contest control of the Western Empire. Having crossed Britannia and Gaul, traversed the Alps, and battled his way through northern Italy town by town, Constantine bore down on Rome where his rival was holed up behind the high Aurelian Walls. And on that long road south came his solar vision.

Encamped that evening on the outskirts of the capital, Constantine debated with his inner circle the possible meanings of the miracle. All were mystified. Beset by so many enemies in recent years, each with their own favoured gods and goddesses, he had increasingly wondered if a single supreme deity might be relied on for protection and assistance. But which of the multitude of gods had offered his sigil in the rays of the sun? The answer would be revealed in the uneasy sleep of that night before battle. In the depths of his dreams, a man appeared to Constantine bearing the sign he had seen blazing in the heavens, assuring the emperor that advancing under its likeness would grant him victory against every foe. The figure, he realised now, was the 'Christ of God', and the cross was in fact a combination of the letters *chi* (X) and *rho* (P) – the first two characters of the name 'Christos' in Greek.[6]

Constantine rose at dawn and launched into a frenzy of activity. Calling together his most skilled craftsmen, the emperor stood in their midst and, like a man possessed, described to them the emblem of the 'Chi-Rho'. With no time to spare they were tasked with recreating the symbol on a large military banner in gold and precious stones. Instructions and supplies were then issued for every soldier to have painted on his shield the interlinking letters X and P – sacred cipher of Christ.[7]

The paint was barely dry when trumpet blasts called the men to formation. Under the standard of the cross, Constantine prepared to march into battle.

The Unconquered Sun

The divine endorsement may have boosted morale, but Constantine knew that overcoming Rome's massive ramparts would need more than just high spirits. Barring another miracle, a gruelling siege lay ahead. Who could doubt then, when the north gate of the city clattered open and the enemy willingly emerged, that the hand of his supreme God was guiding events?

We will never know for certain why Maxentius chose to leave the safety of the walled city and ride out to meet Constantine in the open field; whether it was overconfidence, desperation, plain military ineptitude – or a combination of them all. Maxentius probably expected a quick victory, commanding as he did up to 100,000 men, more than twice the number led by Constantine.[8] He too was certain of divine favour: this date, 28 October 312, was a charmed one, marking the sixth anniversary of his declaration as emperor. If only to confirm his blessings, Maxentius consulted the Sibylline Books – an ancient collection of oracular prophecies – and was assured in their pages that 'an enemy of Rome will perish this day'. That enemy of Rome could not be clearer in his eyes, and without delay, he marched out of the city to annihilate him.[9]

The two armies soon assembled on opposite banks of the Tiber, separated by the remains of the Milvian Bridge. After demolishing the stone crossing to hinder Constantine's advance, Maxentius now ordered his men to span the river with a hastily assembled wooden pontoon, eager to engage his rival on the far side. His legions pressed forward across the rickety bridge with every confidence in their superior numbers, but convictions began to waver as they drew closer to Constantine's battle-lines. The sight was startling: tens of thousands of shields emblazoned with painted crosses – and rising above their ranks, an enormous standard crowned with the same curious symbol, flashing, golden and bejewelled in the sunlight.

Constantine waited patiently until every enemy soldier had crowded onto his side of the river. Only then, filled with the conquering spirit of his patron God, did he order the attack. With a thundering charge, his Gallic cavalry smashed into the enemy's compressed ranks, instantly unleashing panic and confusion. He followed up with a ferocious infantry assault; and observed with amazement how his new standard swept away all before it like some invincible charm. Wherever it was directed, his men fought with untiring strength and courage, while his foes fell to their knees and surrendered immediately to its divine power.

A desperate rout ensued as Maxentius and his troops fled back to the makeshift bridge over the Tiber, their only escape from the battlefield. Surging onto the wooden walkway, many were crushed in the stampede, others thrown over the side. Then came the inevitable crack of breaking beams. Overwhelmed by retreating legions, the bridge gave way altogether. Thousands of men and horses tumbled into the water, weighed down by their heavy armour, never to resurface. Like Moses beholding the pharaoh's army engulfed by the Red Sea, Constantine watched as the mass of his enemy 'sank to the depths like a stone'.[10] Any remaining defenders were easily driven into the river to join them – among them, somewhere, the emperor Maxentius himself.

As promised in his solar vision, Constantine's victory under the sign of the cross was total. He entered Rome in triumph the following day every inch the conquering warlord; and while his golden standard may have drawn mystified looks from the crowds, its power was clearly evidenced by another object hoisted beside it. At Constantine's command the body of Maxentius had been dredged from the Tiber, decapitated, and his head mounted on the end of a spear for all to see. Yesterday he had been master of Rome – today his head was a grim trophy bobbing along above cheering soldiers.

By ancient tradition, conquering generals would ascend the Capitol and thank the thunder god in person for their victories – but no blood sacrifices would be made to Jupiter Optimus Maximus this day. Constantine instead took to the speaker's podium in the Forum to address the populace. To what extent he invoked the Christian God in his oration we do not know, though the gist of his words may have been inscribed on the base of a statue he immediately ordered to be raised, depicting himself holding his enigmatic standard of the cross. 'By virtue of this salutary sign,' its dedication proclaimed, 'I have preserved and liberated your city from the yoke of tyranny.'[11]

We might expect the Christian Chi-Rho to have been quickly stamped onto coins for promotion across the Empire, but no such celebration would take place. Pagan imagery would remain the order of the day on Constantine's coinage for years to come. It has been estimated that only 10 per cent of the Empire was Christian at the time of his victory at the Milvian Bridge – a visible minority within society, especially in urban centres, but still heavily outnumbered by followers of traditional paganism.[12] The new sole emperor in the West knew not to alienate the majority of his subjects with an open endorsement of the Christian God so early in his reign. Having witnessed first-hand the doomed overnight reforms of Diocletian, Constantine felt no need to rush his revolution.

Retrospective visions of Christ aside, how far Constantine even interpreted his solar cross as an overtly Christian symbol is open to debate. Cults of sun worship had surged in popularity in recent centuries, especially among soldiers who brought back exotic new gods and religions, as well as booty, from their conquests in the East. A hundred years earlier, the eccentric teenage emperor Elegabalus had sworn devotion to a sun god of his native Syria, building an enormous temple to the deity in Rome and even seeking to make him chief god of the Roman pantheon over Jupiter himself. A key feature of the cult of Mithraism, a major rival of early Christianity, was the worship of 'Sol Invictus' – the 'Unconquered Sun' who daily defeated the forces of darkness. The great restorer Aurelian was a devout follower of Sol Invictus (whose festival notably was celebrated on 25 December) and, if not for his assassination, had hoped to unite the fractured lands of the Empire behind worship of the single all-powerful solar god.

This growing impulse towards a monotheistic 'one faith for one empire' is reflected in stories of Constantine's youth, where in the court of his father he partook in the worship of a vaguely defined 'supreme God' – in all likelihood, the Unconquered Sun. Later accounts state that Constantine had observed how 'those who marched to battle under the protection of a multitude of gods, so often met with dishonourable ends' and therefore he 'felt it incumbent on him to honour his father's God alone'.[13] In this context then, it is no surprise that Constantine's guardian deity spoke to him in the rays of the sun; in fact, he already had form with such miraculous visions. Just two years earlier in 310, Constantine had apparently been visited by Apollo, another god of the sun, at a shrine in Gaul and promised thirty years of imperial power.[14]

His pre-battle vision of the cross might then be quickly dismissed as just more ancient propaganda, contrived after the fact by a religious convert looking to gild his own crusade for power with divine purpose; and yet, like the fiery comet of Julius Caesar in 44 BC, modern understanding of a remarkable natural phenomenon may lend the story some credibility. One exciting explanation posits that Constantine's army may have actually witnessed a solar parhelion or 'sun dog'.[15] This meteorological event occurs when the sun's light is refracted through ice crystals high in the atmosphere, resulting in the appearance of a dramatic halo around the sun and mock suns flanking both sides. In optimal conditions, a 'sun pillar' may also strike vertically through the solar disc forming an unmistakable cross in the sky, glowing with prismatic colours (Plate section, 15).

Coincidentally, the first detailed scientific observations of parhelia were also made in Rome, with a dazzling display of 'seven suns' studied by the astronomer Christoph Scheiner in 1630. Sun dogs may have even influenced the outcome of momentous battles on more than one occasion: before Yorkists and Lancastrians faced each other at the Battle of Mortimer Cross in 1461, it was reported that three suns appeared in the dawn sky. Interpreting the solar trio as the Holy Trinity and an omen of divine favour, the Yorkists swept to victory and Edward IV took the throne. The incident was later dramatised by Shakespeare who wrote of 'Three glorious suns . . . in a pale clear-shining sky', joining as one 'as if they vow'd some league inviolable'.[16] If a parhelion was indeed responsible for Constantine's conversion on the road to Rome, then it was a weather event that radically altered the course of Western civilisation.

In the wake of his victory, coinage proudly proclaimed Sol Invictus, not the Christian God, to be Constantine's heavenly ally. The sun god wearing his spiked radiate crown would now be the main pagan deity personified across all Roman money, with circling legends dedicated to 'Soli Invicto Comiti' – 'The Unconquered Sun, Companion of the Emperor'. One remarkable gold coin even shows the companions together, with busts of Constantine and Sol side by side – nothing less than equal partners on the imperial throne. Fawning tributes to the emperor further heralded him as a 'radiant sun' who 'illuminates the most distant subjects of his Empire . . . with the far piercing rays of his own brightness' – words that seem to echo biblical celebrations of Jesus as the 'Light of the World'.[17]

Christianity may have been set firmly on the road to widespread acceptance, but for now, its praise would only be conveyed to the populace by proxy, veiled behind the more palatable figure of the Unconquered Sun. Even when the ascendancy of the Christian God was undeniable, his worship would remain interwoven with that of Sol: when in AD 321 Constantine designated an Empire-wide day of rest on which all work other than farming must cease, he would of course choose the *dies Solis* – the venerable 'day of the Sun' – or as we know it: Sunday.

Another factor may have compelled Constantine to move slowly in his advancement of the Christian God: one last tetrarch survived in the East – and for now at least, they would agree to share the Empire. Unlike the Saviour God that sent his enemies to the bottom of the Tiber, Constantine was not yet the supreme king of all.

Eyes to the Heavens

Their meeting would be a momentous one. When Constantine and his Eastern counterpart Licinius conferred in Milan, just months after the former's victory at the Milvian Bridge, the direction of the Roman world was theirs to decide. Safeguarding the security and well-being of the commonwealth was crucial – a hastily arranged marriage between Licinius and Constantine's sister sealed their alliance – but top of the agenda were godly matters, namely ensuring due reverence could be paid to the divinities that each believed authored all their triumphs.

The resulting Edict of Milan, co-signed by the two emperors, would in just a few paragraphs completely transform the religious landscape of the Roman Empire.[18] In stark contrast to the despotic threats and overbearing sanctimony of Diocletian's edicts, the text reads like a libertarian manifesto promising nothing less than complete religious freedom to all subjects of Rome. Henceforth, the rulers pledge that 'all men have unrestricted right to follow the form of worship they desire'. The directives praise neither Jesus nor Jupiter in their grant of unconditional religious liberty, but simply hope that 'whatever divinity there is in the seat of heaven may be appeased' – a masterclass in compromise between the Christian-inclined Constantine and the pagan-leaning Licinius. Not to mention an inspired hedging of religious bets in a dynamic era of spiritual flux, when it was by no means certain who would win out between the old gods and the new.

Faith was now a matter of the heart. All belief systems were to be equal in the eyes of the state – yet the text's implicit recognition of Christianity as a valid faith alongside paganism was a quiet revolution. Indeed, the fingerprints of Constantine might be seen in the syntax which repeatedly places Christianity first in its instructions: every man was now 'free to devote himself to the cult of the Christians, or the religion he deems best suited for himself'.

Licinius would pay lip service to Constantine's God, and in addition to their religious toleration, each emperor agreed to tolerate the other – just so long as each stayed safely within the borders of their own provinces. It would be an uneasy truce, tested always by Constantine's conviction that he now possessed an invincible banner, and a fiery call to arms urging him to conquer by its sign. Far from Diocletian's divided worldview, Constantine increasingly 'regarded the entire world as one immense body', and the tetrarchs as a god-defying race of tyrants preventing its rightful unification.[19] So when word arrived that Licinius had reneged on their agreement and rekindled the fire of persecution against Christians in the East, Constantine had the justification he needed to march to their rescue. In reality, Licinius had probably begun expelling Christians as political dissidents, undermining his rule in their praises of his Western rival. Whatever his motives, Constantine was on his way.

The final showdown, fought on a plain near Byzantium in 324, would be a battle of both gods and men: Licinius formed up his ranks under likenesses of pagan deities, while Constantine advanced under his trusty standard of the cross. Sparkling in the sun, the insignia announcing the name of Christ had already won the psychological victory. Licinius foolishly imparted his own fear of the cross to his men, warning them of its 'terrible power', and urging them 'never to direct their attack against the standard, nor even allow their eyes to rest upon it'. Crippled with anxiety, his army stood little chance. They were devastated in a single fanatical charge by Constantine's troops.

Licinius soon surrendered, offering over his purple robes and saluting his brother-in-law as 'emperor and lord' – a gesture he was assured would buy him his life. Constantine ordered his execution anyway. Evidently imperial conquest still took precedence over Christian

The 'eyes to heaven' coin portrait of Constantine, popularised after his defeat of Licinius in 324.

forgiveness. For the first time in almost forty years the whole Empire was graced with a single ruler and Constantine's ultimate dream was realised: one God, one empire, one emperor.

A dramatic change in Constantine's coin portraits immediately following his defeat of Licinius shows the Roman world, more openly than ever before, 'how deeply his soul was impressed by the power of divine faith'. Constantine was now commonly depicted with his head turned upwards, gazing wide-eyed to the heavens. In the absence of any specific religious iconography, it is not entirely clear to a modern viewer how his celestial stare is to be interpreted. Is he beholding a vision of the cross in the sun as he did on that eve of battle, or is he still venerating 'his father's god', the Unconquered Sun? Perhaps his head is raised in a generic pose of pious worship, or does he now look solely towards the heaven of Christ the Lord? The neutrality of the portrait may have been intentional, but for Christians at least, the coins were an obvious statement of Constantine's devotion to their own faith. The bishop Eusebius, who knew the emperor personally, states that Constantine 'directed his likeness to be stamped on gold coins with his eyes uplifted in the posture of prayer to God'.[20] That historians of the time wrote about these new coins reminds us that the ancients paid close attention to, and debated the meaning behind, the designs on their money.

The gold denomination bearing this 'eyes to heaven' portrait is also significant. While Constantine would refrain from violence against pagans in the wake of his triumph, he would happily pillage the treasures from their 'temples of lies' and melt them down for new coinage.[21] Using vast quantities of confiscated gold bullion, Constantine was able to widely introduce a pure gold coin to replace the defunct aureus. The *solidus*, proudly named after its 'solid' metal, would be struck to a closely monitored weight of 4.5 grams and essentially restore the notion of a 'gold standard' to the Roman economy. Without a readily available silver denomination, however, the monetary system edged towards bimetallism and greater wealth inequality; those who could afford to conduct their transactions in gold now had abundant coin to do so, while all others were forced to complete their daily transactions with cumbersome bags of debased bronze. The reliable solidus would nevertheless prove a monetary success story, continuing in use through the Byzantine Empire until the eleventh century. The enduring gold coin would even give us our modern word 'soldier', with troops across Europe and the Middle East being associated over time with the *solidi* they were paid, an etymology also echoed in the Spanish *soldado*, the Italian *Soldato*, and the German *Soldat* – literally, 'one having pay'.

Freed of any pagan rivals, Constantine would continue to champion the Christian Church ever more boldly – short of openly declaring himself a convert. In AD 325 he summoned bishops from all over the ancient world to a sacred council in Nicaea (modern İznik, Turkey) with the goal of resolving conflict between Christian sects around the nature of Christ and his relationship with God the Father. Over 300 bishops from Europe, Africa, and Asia – Eusebius among them – gathered in a single hall to hammer out a unifying doctrine of belief that could be broadly subscribed to by Christians across the Empire. Presiding over the boisterous debate, Constantine 'dazzled the eyes of all with the radiance of his purple robe, adorned with the brilliant splendour of gold and precious stones'. The council was a success, agreeing upon the date of Easter, and the wording of a definitive creed outlining the Christian faith. Still recited today, it professes belief in 'one God, the Father' and in 'one Lord, Jesus Christ, the Son of God . . . begotten of the Father, of one substance with the Father'. The Roman emperor, for all his earthly majesty, was nowhere mentioned.

Saviours and Serpents

As foretold, the banner of the one God had secured him victory in every battle. Pagan enemies marching against him with the assurance of cryptic oracles, the encouragement of soothsayers watching the flight of birds, and the support of priests inspecting bloody entrails – all had been crushed. Preceded by that salutary sign, the armies of Constantine seemed invincible. And yet, fifteen years after the emperor supposedly beheld the Chi-Rho 'Christogram' in the shining sun, the symbol had still not been celebrated on a Roman coin.

While the last pagan portrayals of Sol Invictus had quietly disappeared from money in recent years, it would not be in favour of Christian imagery but of religiously neutral depictions of soldiers, camp gates, and Victory personified. Ultimately, the Roman emperor most famously associated with the rise of Christendom would mint almost no coins with clear Christian iconography.[22] It may be that Constantine limited himself to indirect promotion of the Church, slowly advancing its cause by degrees – or did his more secular coinage reflect a genuine stance that religious faith was a matter of personal conviction? On the other hand, the iconic visual language of Christianity was also in its formative stages, as yet offering few widely recognisable symbols for the emperor to showcase even if he so wished.

His unique battle standard, however, provided the perfect branding compromise; it had struck terror into the hearts of multiple pagan enemies but still functioned as a universal symbol of military victory. Its enigmatic crowning emblem might simply be interpreted by the majority pagan populace as the personal badge of the emperor, while admiring Christians would be thrilled to see the monogram of their Lord finally making an appearance on state coinage. Intriguingly, small versions of the Christogram have been found hidden in the designs of earlier coins of Constantine, though only included rarely on individual dies; possible evidence of Christian engravers working in Roman mints, concealing subversive tributes to their faith in their work. But no single coin had officially honoured the emperor's all-conquering sign of the cross – until now. Struck in 327, this bronze follis of Constantine gives us the first official depiction of his Chi-Rho standard, and by extension, the first open acknowledgement of Christianity ever on a Roman coin.[23]

Its portrait shows Constantine in his mid-fifties as unrivalled master of the empire of Man, and humble servant of his one God. While the square head and thick neck recall the dominating portraiture of earlier tetrarchs, a number of individualistic features show Constantine eager to distinguish himself from the brutish soldier-emperors preceding him. Gone is the regulation close-cropped army haircut, in favour of a plain swept-forward style evoking the simple fashions of Trajan, two centuries earlier. The broad jaw, projecting chin, and hook nose are also present on marble and bronze portraits of Constantine, and no doubt show something of the emperor's true appearance. Perhaps most noticeably, Constantine appears clean-shaven – the first beardless adult emperor in over a hundred years. Subsequent Christian rulers would make sure to keep their cheeks smooth in emulation of Constantine's appearance, while beards became the hallmark of any who wished to hark back to a pagan past.

The reverse of the coin provides history's first official glimpse of Constantine's triumphant trophy, surmounted by the 'symbol of salvation' that was 'both a terror to the foe and a protection against every harm'.[24] The standard would be known as the *labarum*, possibly deriving from the Latin *labare* meaning 'to sway', suggesting the motion of a waving banner. Constantine's labarum would have been a variation of the flag-like *vexillum* standards which had long been carried by legions into combat, helping to signal the location of individual units during the chaos of battle, much like modern regimental colours.

The coin's rendering of the labarum precisely matches descriptions of ancient historians like Eusebius who had observed it first-hand: a long spear intersected by a transverse bar forming the

The first official depiction of Constantine's *labarum* standard and the Chi-Rho on a Roman coin.

figure of a cross, and fixed on top, the 'Saviour's sign' of the Chi-Rho indicating the name of Christ. Hanging from the crossbar is a square cloth banner interlaced with gold and decorated with three medallions carrying portraits of Constantine and his sons.

The inscription across the face of the coin proclaims the banner to be emblematic of 'Spes Publica' or the 'Hope of the People'. As the pagan goddess of hope, Spes had appeared on coins regularly through the centuries, holding aloft a blooming flower and promising good times ahead for Rome. Here, however, she has been starkly replaced by the inanimate labarum – evidently the banner's heralding of a blessed future had rendered the ancient goddess redundant. Marching under its colours, the emperor was certain that he was no warlord battling for personal power, but merely an agent of the 'most mighty God' rescuing the Roman people from evil forces. In a thanksgiving prayer he would assure his Lord that 'by your sacred sign I have led your armies to victory, and still, on each occasion of public danger, I follow the same symbol while advancing to meet the foe'.[25]

These wicked foes may be represented on the coin in the form of a wriggling serpent being speared by the holy standard. While pagan art often incorporated snakes as protective entities magically warding off evil, monstrous serpents had also functioned as visual and literary shorthand for enemies of the Roman state; as we saw earlier, Julius Caesar had presented himself on coins as a noble elephant trampling a snake, while Roman poets had described Hannibal as 'a dark serpent, hissing with deadly blast'.[26] The scriptures of the Bible likewise presented snakes as nothing less than cursed creatures, synonymous with 'Satan, the deceiver of the whole world'.

The impaled serpent could therefore be interpreted by both pagan and Christian viewers as an embodiment of Constantine's defeated foes, most notably the rival emperor Licinius who had been overcome just a couple of years earlier.[27] In surviving letters, Constantine himself boasts of having driven 'that serpent' Licinius out of government, while Eusebius also calls the defeated enemy a 'crooked and wriggling serpent'. Both men may have also believed that Satan acted through the emperor's heathen enemies. Descriptions of a remarkable painting adorning the entrance to Constantine's palace not only precisely match the composition on our bronze coin but confirm that Licinius and the biblical Satan were to be perceived as one and the same in Christian eyes. The prominently displayed artwork showed 'the Saviour's sign, and below it that hateful and savage adversary of mankind . . . in the form of a serpent . . . pierced through with a javelin'.[28]

If we concede therefore that the creature is intended to represent both the earthly enemies of the Christian faith and 'that ancient serpent also known as the Devil', then the small bronze coin is made even more momentous to history – providing both our first image of the monogram of Christ, and our first image of Satan himself.[29]

Constantine would have most likely been pleased with such a reading, as many Romans viewing the coin may have seen in the speared serpent other antagonists whom the emperor would rather forget. Only months before the follis was struck, the imperial palace had been engulfed by a mysterious scandal that culminated in Constantine executing both his wife and eldest son. Sources are understandably vague on the sordid details of the affair, though it seems that the empress Fausta may have accused her stepson Crispus – Constantine's firstborn son from an earlier marriage – of making sexual advances towards her. Whatever the allegation, it was heinous enough that

Constantine quickly put his leading heir to death without trial. Appalled by the killing, the emperor's influential mother, Helena, then seems to have intervened and warned Constantine of his wife's possible machinations; the death of Crispus had, after all, ensured Fausta's own sons by Constantine became sole heirs to the Empire. Whether the allegations against Crispus were disproved, or if the emperor was simply trying to appease his mother, he now 'tried to remedy the evil with a greater evil': Constantine ordered that his wife be locked in an overheated bathhouse until she suffocated to death.[30]

Striking coins to celebrate triumph over evil, mere months after the murder of your closest family members, seems a curious decision; perhaps the emperor saw the serpent of Satan as having acted through them also. But Constantine was now a man seeking absolution. Having apparently been told by pagan philosophers that there could be no spiritual purification for his crimes, Constantine turned instead to the pledges of Christian bishops. They assured the emperor he could be cleansed of his sins, on the condition that he promoted their doctrines, led his subjects to the faith, and finally submitted himself to a Christian baptism.[31]

Constantine's subsequent quest for redemption would see him building Christian churches in key locations on the outskirts of Rome, most notably the first Basilica of St Peter raised atop the ruins of the Circus of Nero on the Vatican Hill – believed to be the site of Peter the Apostle's martyrdom in the first century. He would also commission fifty 'magnificent and elaborately bound' copies of the Bible for the instruction of the faith in his new churches.[32] His mother Helena would even be dispatched on an adventurous mission to find religious relics around the Empire, including fragments of the True Cross on which Jesus was crucified. But one last detail in the design of our bronze coin perhaps speaks of Constantine's most lasting contribution to Christianity – a landmark decision that would profoundly alter the shape of the ancient and modern world.

The mint mark on the coin reveals it was not struck in Rome, or at another major mint of the fourth century such as Alexandria, London, or Trier. This was one of the first coins to be struck at a brand-new mint in a brand-new imperial capital – so new it was still under construction. The abbreviated 'Cons' does not denote the name of the emperor, but a gleaming metropolis founded in his name: an earthly home for Christendom, with churches standing proudly within its walls, where Constantine could relaunch his rule, absolved of his old sins. A city not of man, but of God. In every sense, a new Rome.

Nova Roma

Following in the tradition of the greatest conquerors, when the dust settled after battle and no more enemies remained, Constantine founded a city. Having vanquished Licinius on the eastern shore of the Bosporus, he did not have far to travel in search of prime real estate. The old Greek colony of Byzantium sat on a high promontory overlooking the narrow strait, naturally defended by water on three sides with instant access to both the Mediterranean and Black seas – the perfect candidate for an imperial makeover. After only five frenzied years of construction, Constantine's glorious new capital was inaugurated in a spectacular ceremony on 11 May 330. A city raised in honour of the heavenly God, but one that would take the name of its earthly founder: Constantinople.

Where Rome was defined by its pagan monuments looming at every turn, the newly built city offered a religious blank slate, 'unpolluted by altars, pagan temples, nor sacrifices'.[33] Its founder would see that it became a fully-fledged 'city of Christ', quickly adorning it with 'many magnificent houses of prayer'; though in every other way, Constantinople was conceived as a traditional Roman metropolis. The people cheered their favourite charioteer from the stands of an enormous hippodrome, strolled through a sprawling forum, soaked themselves in a choice of bathhouses, drank from countless cascading fountains, and sheltered from the sun in shady porticoes.

Constantine would further decorate the city with the finest art imported from across the Empire. 'Graven images' from the holiest pagan sites, now treated as mere 'objects of embellishment': the colossal ancient statue of Zeus from Olympia was installed in the imperial palace alongside many other Greek masterpieces; it has even been suggested that the serene ivory face of the thunder god may have informed the depiction of Jesus in early Christian mosaics.[34] The four gilded horses now surmounting St Mark's Basilica in Venice were pulled from an unknown monument and placed atop the hippodrome, later to be carried by crusaders to Italy along with the porphyry tetrarchs. The twisting Serpent Column from the sacred Greek city of Delphi was also placed in the centre of the racetrack, where it still stands, jutting up through the modern roadway.

However, the soul of the city would be its populace, and Constantine would import many of them too. The emperor 'peopled the city with men of rank and their families, summoned from Rome and other countries' and did all in his power to make Constantinople the equal of Rome in every way. A second Senate convened there with the same honours and privileges as its Western counterpart, while that most Roman of perks, a free grain dole, guaranteed citizens their daily bread. No surprise then that the city of Constantine would become known as 'Nova Roma' – the New Rome.

A special coin would be struck to advertise the emperor's capital – like an ancient brochure selling disillusioned Romans of all backgrounds the dream of a fresh start in a new, golden city. Again ensuring the broadest appeal, the bronze follis would not side with overtly pagan or Christian imagery, but simply present the female personification of the city, helmeted, holding a sceptre, and labelled proudly, 'Constantinopolis'. The promotional campaign for the emperor's eponymous city was almost too successful: within a century of its foundation, Constantinople had overtaken Rome in population, necessitating an expansion of its massive walls. Peaking at around half a million residents, it would remain the most populous city in the world until the eighth century when it was gradually overtaken by Baghdad, and Xi'an, China.

While a neglected and beleaguered Rome quickened in its decline, Constantinople flourished. Its thriving markets flooded with the abundant gold of the rich East and luxury goods of the Silk Road – and ignited with the dynamic interchange of cultures. Perfectly located on its well-defended land bridge between Europe and Asia,

Constantinople became a true meeting point between East and West; its modern incarnation Istanbul remains the only major city in the world to span two continents. Inevitably, the Empire's centre of gravity was shifting, away from old Rome and towards Nova Roma.

As his new imperial capital bridged two hemispheres, so Constantine – now entering his sixties – continued to straddle two religious worlds. He sponsored the building of Christian churches yet as emperor he retained the position of Pontifex Maximus, chief priest of the still-pagan Roman state. He followed one supreme God yet founded cities in his own name and, in the final years of his life, still allowed towns like Hispellum (modern Spello, Umbria) to build temples in his honour. Was the emperor a devout follower of the Christian God tactfully disguising his faith, or a political opportunist judging the direction of the wind before charting a definite course? That historians still debate whether Constantine was a practising Christian or not, so many centuries on, surely emphasises how carefully he walked the line between rival religions. Only a master of realpolitik could enjoy such longevity in such a turbulent age: in 336 Constantine celebrated his *tricennalia* – the thirty-year jubilee of his reign – making him the second-longest reigning emperor behind Augustus himself.

Even his final and most famous act, a deathbed baptism the following year, can be interpreted as a shrewd manoeuvre by a lifelong political strategist. The ceremony finally saw Constantine openly accept the Christian God, though he waited until his very last days to do so. Assured by bishops that baptism cleansed the soul of all earthly sins, the emperor seemingly delayed the sacrament until his often-ruthless reign was safely at its end and there were no longer any opportunities for wrongdoing. Redeemed in his dying breaths, Constantine had timed his salvation perfectly.

The rising tide of Christianity would be unstoppable in the decades following Constantine's conversion, and almost all his successors would be followers of the faith. Anti-pagan legislation mounted during the fourth century – blood sacrifices banned, temples shut down – until in 380, the emperor Theodosius declared Christianity the official state religion of the Roman Empire. Just over fifty years since Constantine had first dared to place the strange symbol on a Roman coin, the monogram of Christ was utterly triumphant. With its military associations, the symbolically ambiguous Chi-Rho had been useful to early Christians as a covert declaration of faith; now without need for such nuance, the traditional cross of the crucifixion could be openly revered. Gradually, the simple four-pointed cross would replace the Chi-Rho as the most iconic symbol of a Christian Empire.

In its newfound dominance, the Church would soon display the same destructive intolerance towards the old religion that it once endured as a persecuted minority. The eternal fire tended by the Vestal Virgins in the Roman Forum was extinguished, their order disbanded. Marble statues were toppled and 'cleansed' of their demonic spirits with a Christian cross chiselled on the forehead. In 382 the ruling emperor removed the sacred Altar of Victory from the Roman Senate house, placed there by Augustus over four centuries earlier — a decision that would leave us one of the most poignant documents from the dying days of paganism. In a heartfelt petition, the pagan senator Symmachus urged the emperor to restore the ancient altar and preserve the city's historic monuments.[35] He asked him to imagine Rome herself standing before them pleading: 'Respect my age. Respect the ancient ceremonies that carried me through so many years . . . the worship that made the whole world obedient to my laws, the rites that drove back Hannibal from my walls and the Gauls from my Capitol.'

'We beg you emperor for amnesty,' Symmachus continued, 'amnesty for the gods of our fathers, for the gods of our homeland'; and in a moving plea to the emperor's sense of humanity, he reminded him: 'We all share the same sky, all look up at the same stars, are all encompassed by the same universe. What difference does it make which system each of us uses to find the truth? It is not by just one road that man finds answers to so great a mystery.'

For all its strength of feeling, his appeal to save the pagan monuments of Rome was denied.

Chapter XII
COLLAPSE

'My voice sticks in my throat; and, as I dictate, sobs choke my utterance.

The city that conquered the whole world is itself conquered.'

Jerome

Silver half-*siliqua* of Odoacer, the first barbarian king of post-Roman Italy, Ravenna, AD 477.
Obverse: Bust of the Germanic king Odoacer, shown with long hair and moustache.
Reverse: Monogram of Odoacer (ODOVAC) within wreath.

Refuge from the Storm

Each day brought more desperate arrivals than the last. They stumbled ashore, bewildered. Clinging to each other, half-naked and half-starved, many bearing wounds that spoke of the ravages they had suffered. Among them were men and women of noble houses who once abounded in every kind of wealth, as well as the servants who once waited on them. All now indistinguishable, offloaded onto beaches and harbours around the Mediterranean in equal poverty. Escaping the carnage of their homeland, they had prayed to find Christian charity across the sea – but human compassion was rare in these dark days. The refugees were instantly set upon by ruthless gangs who ripped off their tattered garments and rifled through their bundled belongings, looking for any gold that might have escaped the barbarians.[1]

With little left to rob, some young girls were torn from their mothers' arms and carried off to be sold as slave-brides to eastern merchants. They, at least, would fetch a fine price. After all, these were no obscure provincials from a distant frontier. These refugees had fled the ruin of Italy, mother of nations. These were the sons and daughters of Rome.[2]

Every coast that had once belonged to the imperial city was now flooded with souls escaping her sacking. Africa, Egypt, across the Holy Land; there seemed to be no part of the earth where Romans were not in exile. At his monastery in Bethlehem, the elderly monk Jerome did all he could to provide aid and shelter to the steady stream of refugees coming across the parched hills. Before long, his quiet monastic retreat had become a crowded hospice filled with the cries of anxious mothers and wails of hungry infants. All Bible studies were abandoned while Jerome and his followers worked to relieve the suffering of the displaced. They offered bread and water, treated wounds with honey and herbs – and when there was no more to give, simply sat and shared in their tears.

With his days devoted to care-giving, Jerome used the hours of darkness to chronicle events by trembling lamplight. 'The world sinks into ruin,' he lamented. 'The renowned city, the capital of the Roman Empire, is swallowed up in one tremendous fire.' Who would have believed that the citizens of 'mighty Rome, with its careless security of wealth' could be reduced to stateless wanderers, begging for food and shelter? Jerome knew he could give solace to only the smallest fraction of those escaping 'the catastrophe in the West' but even so, he was 'filled with a longing to turn the words of scripture into action – not to say holy things but to do them'.[3]

Beyond mere Christian kindness, Jerome felt a special kinship with these exiles of the Empire. Decades earlier he too had escaped the Roman capital, swapping the decadence of the metropolis for an ascetic existence of desert solitude and scholarly study. Settling eventually in a cave in Bethlehem, he laboured on a monumental Latin translation of the Bible that would become known as the Vulgate and which is still used by the Catholic Church. Following Jerome's example, complete withdrawal to pursue a life of prayer and isolation became a valid vocation among high society. A number of wealthy Roman maidens would take vows of perpetual virginity and leave Rome for Jerome's Bethlehem commune, helping him establish a monastery, convent, and hospice for pilgrims.

Their circle of elite expatriates was not an isolated example. Everywhere it seemed disillusioned men and women from the richest Roman families were renouncing their status, swearing themselves to chastity, and fleeing to monastic communities in the deserts of the Holy Land. Long before a barbarian army appeared at the walls, Romans of the ruling class were abandoning the very idea of Rome – trading the City of Man for the promise of the City of God.

The sack of Rome by invading Goths on 24 August 410 stands as a defining moment in the story of the Empire's fall and the end of the classical age – the first time in 800 years that the Eternal City was overrun by a foreign army. Recent historical evaluations have tended towards downplaying the significance of the event, arguing that the violence of the sack has been exaggerated; that Rome had long lost her political relevance and her plunder had little impact on the wider provinces. For certain, the collapse of the Western Roman Empire was a complex and gradual process that unfolded over centuries rather than days – but when news of the sacking reached Jerome in Bethlehem, his human reaction vividly captures the scale of the cataclysm in the ancient mind. The old man was left 'so stupefied' that he sat in stunned silence for a whole day and night. Such was the shock, 'I scarcely knew my own name,' he recalls, before offering a striking summation: 'when the bright light of all the world was put out, or, rather, when the Roman Empire was decapitated . . . the whole world perished in one city'.[4]

Jerome would be crushed to learn that friends among his old religious community in Rome had died violent deaths at the hands of the pillaging Goths. Appalled by stories of barbarian atrocities in the city, and the resulting humanitarian crisis that brought so many 'naked and wounded' refugees to his doors, the Christian monk reached back to the ancient verse of Virgil to convey his sorrow:

> Had I a hundred tongues and throat of bronze
> The woes of captives I could not relate
> Or ev'n recount the names of all the slain.[5]

The exodus from Roman Italy starkly illustrated how far the West had fallen, though it was just the latest in a cascading wave of mass migrations that had been set in motion decades earlier. After all, the Goths ransacking the heart of the Empire were also a displaced people, driven from their homelands by an even fiercer enemy.

The 'seed of all the ruin' was sown around the year 370, when a 'hitherto unknown race' of horse-riding nomadic warriors burst out of Central Asia, destroying all in their path 'like a whirlwind descending from high mountains'. Contemporary Roman observers paint an image of a nightmarish new antagonist, 'so monstrously ugly and misshapen, that one might take them for two-legged beasts'; a 'faithless', 'deceitful', 'savage' horde, burning with 'an infinite thirst for gold' and 'an inhuman desire for plundering others' property'. Thundering towards the barbarian kingdoms of Eastern Europe, the dreaded Huns galloped into the history books.[6]

The relentless advance of the Hunnic horsemen shunted one barbarian tribe into another, sweeping the whole confused mass towards the borders of Rome. Even the notoriously warlike Goths were 'struck with consternation at the violence of this sudden storm'. By 376 they found themselves pushed to the banks of the Danube and petitioning the Eastern emperor Valens with a desperate request: asylum for the Gothic peoples within the Roman Empire.

When permission was reluctantly granted, a gigantic body of up to 200,000 Goths poured across the dangerously swollen river on makeshift rafts. The emperor's advisers urged him to see these warriors delivered from 'the very ends of the earth' as new recruits; treated humanely and enfranchised as allies, such a force might 'form an invincible army' with which they could repel the advancing Huns. Instead, Valens treated the refugees with contempt, leaving them to starve and offering to buy their children as slaves in return for crusts of mouldy bread.

Inevitably, the beleaguered Goths soon turned to pillage, raiding towns and stripping farms of their crops. Seeing their countrymen laid so low, Gothic auxiliaries already serving in the Roman legions began to desert, returning to their native tribes with their superior weapons and military training. Soon the whole Balkan peninsula had descended into anarchy. The emperor Valens was confident that he could eradicate his unwelcome guests without the help of his Western counterpart and marched against the Goths at the head of an imposing army, attacking them near the city of Adrianople in 378. The subsequent battle was indeed a massacre and a decisive turning point in history, but not in the way Valens had intended. Ordered to fight after an arduous march in the August sun, the exhausted Roman infantry were routed and slaughtered by Gothic cavalry. Worse still, by day's end the emperor himself lay among the countless tangled bodies of the dead. Some estimates suggest that two-thirds of the Roman force, the core of the entire Eastern army, was lost in a single apocalyptic afternoon – and dying with them, any remaining notions of the Roman legion as an unassailable foe.

Rome had no choice but to allow the Goths to remain in her territory. With already stretched garrisons now at breaking point, further recruitment of barbarians as allied *foederati* troops became the only way to man imperial frontiers. Individual Goths would reach positions of influence in Roman government but their people remained outcasts aimlessly roaming the Empire. Many noticed that in the carnage of battle, Gothic units in the Roman army were the first sent into the meat grinder; expendable fodder dying by the thousand while Roman legionaries went unscathed. By the end of the fourth century the Goths had tired of 'passively serving others'.[7] Calling a great assembly, they raised up on a shield one of their finest generals and proclaimed him king – the first barbarian king to be crowned inside Roman borders. His mission was clear: to carve out a new nation for his people in a fertile corner of the Empire. United under Alaric, the Goths set out in search of a home.

A City Forsaken

The barbarian king who would bring Rome to its knees was, in reality, as 'Roman' as many in the late-imperial government opposing him. Alaric was born at the limits of Roman territory – on the island of Peuce in the Danube Delta. He spoke Latin as well as his Gothic tongue, was a practising Christian, and served with distinction as an auxiliary commander in the Roman army. Far from setting out to destroy the Empire, Alaric sought a legitimate position within its institutions and legal status for his people inside its borders – as well as fair payment for years spent fighting in its defence. History may remember him as the warlord who ransacked Rome, but Alaric would be a reluctant conqueror.

In his efforts to secure a new homeland for the Goths, Alaric had no choice but to attempt negotiations with feeble and inept emperors who epitomised Roman decline. Honorius had been raised to the Western throne in 395 at just ten years of age, while his teenage brother Arcadius was made monarch in the East. The boy-emperors would, unsurprisingly, rule as little more than lavishly dressed puppets, easily manipulated by the ambitious generals and scheming eunuchs surrounding them. Ornamental leaders would be one of the few features uniting the two halves of the Empire as their distant palaces grew ever more detached from the fate of one another. The distinct characters of East and West would be embodied in their coins, with each territory adopting completely different artistic styles in their respective money. Gold solidi from flourishing Constantinople now showed the emperor in ornately jewelled armour, confronting the viewer in a dynamic front-facing portrait. Meanwhile, portraits from the waning West remained stuck in the old style, vaguely depicting the emperor's profile in a traditional side view.[8]

Alaric found himself caught between these two dysfunctional courts and their competing agendas as he tried in vain to strike a deal with the Roman state. When discussions with Constantinople collapsed, the Gothic king marched west with his army and, in 401, broke into the lands of Italy for the first time. There he clashed with the true power behind the throne, the half-Vandal general Stilicho who ruled as regent for young Honorius. Alaric's advance was repulsed, but rumour soon swirled that his withdrawal from Italy was actually the result of a secret pact with Stilicho; pledges of a military command, a whole province for the Gothic people, and recompense for their hardships — all if Alaric would assist the depleted armies of the West in future contests with their Eastern counterparts.

Placated for now, Alaric stood down and patiently awaited his rewards. Before long, however, a succession of calamities made it clear they would never be forthcoming. In the winter of 406 a seemingly endless confederation of Germanic tribes stormed across the frozen Rhine river to escape the Huns, unleashing chaos in Gaul. Responding to the incursion, a common soldier in Britannia declared himself an emperor and sailed the island's entire military garrison across the Channel to confront the threat. Britannia was left defenceless. With borders collapsing, panic gripped the cities and anti-barbarian frenzy ignited among the populace; Stilicho — half-barbarian himself and known for his pragmatic dealings with invading tribes — would soon become its most notable victim. A bloody coup orchestrated by the eunuch Olympius would see Stilicho deprived of his head, and Alaric deprived of his only palace insider. The regent's execution escalated into a full-scale xenophobic purge as Roman soldiers set upon the Gothic auxiliaries in their ranks, slaughtering them and their families. Horrific as it was, the massacre only strengthened the cause of the barbarian king: up to 30,000 troops of Gothic heritage fled the murderous Roman persecution to join Alaric's forces.

Angry cries from his new recruits urged him to war, but still Alaric tried to forge a peace deal with Honorius. He sent ambassadors to the imperial court in Ravenna with reasonable requests: a modest allotment of land and money for the Gothic people would see him from Italy's doorstep, never to return. To the disbelief of Alaric, and many in the imperial palace, Honorius simply refused to negotiate. The emperor neither accepted a peace, nor offered battle with the remnants of his armies. Despairing of the unresponsive palace and spurred by the fury of his impatient troops, Alaric marched back into Italy.

His Gothic army barrelled through the Veneto towards Ravenna, only to bypass the heavily defended imperial capital of Honorius and make for another destination. Even now, all roads still led there. However forlorn and neglected, the Eternal City, and its centuries of accumulated treasures, remained a valuable prize. Surely, threatening the historic heart of the Empire would finally get Alaric's demands heard. A cold wave of terror swept through the streets as, for the first time in the better part of a millennium, the dark mass of a barbarian horde appeared on the Roman horizon.

Alaric ordered every entrance to the city blockaded, cutting it off from all supplies. Rome was his illustrious hostage – and he would test the will of Honorius by tightening his grip around her neck. Those imprisoned within held on to hope. Any day now, they assured themselves, an army would arrive from Ravenna to lift the siege; after all, the emperor's own sister was one of those trapped in the city. But as days turned into weeks, the realisation gradually dawned: no relief force was marching to the rescue. Rome was on her own. Grain handouts were rationed to half, then a third of the normal provision. Before long, the metropolis famed for its endless abundance was racked by starvation. Unable to bury the dead in the cemeteries outside the walls, 'the city became their sepulchre'.[9] Piles of rotting corpses mounted, choking those who clung to life with their putrid stench. Disease carried off many of those already weakened by hunger. Grim reports even circulated of cannibalism in the forsaken city.

Reaching the limits of what they could endure, and resigned to their abandonment by the emperor, Romans took charge of their own fate. A senatorial embassy trudged out to Alaric and informed him they would accept any conditions of peace. What would it take for the Gothic king to relinquish the siege? His demands were simple: every pound of gold and silver in the city, every household treasure, and every barbarian slave.

'But what will you leave for us?' pleaded one desperate senator.

'Your lives,' Alaric answered coldly.

Romans duly set to work stripping the city of its riches to pay their own ransom. Gold and silver statues of pagan gods were melted down, buildings were robbed of their precious ornaments, homes were gutted of their heirlooms. Eventually, Alaric was satisfied with a colossal payment of 5,000 pounds of gold, 30,000 of silver, and in a reminder how valued the spice was in the ancient world, 3,000 pounds of pepper.[10] Without his even entering its walls, the vast wealth of Rome had been delivered into his hands. As Jerome would mourn in Bethlehem, the city that once ruled the world now had to 'buy the right to exist', giving up all her gold and 'sacrificing all her substance' to invaders.[11]

True to his word, Alaric withdrew from the city, allowing provisions to be brought in and markets to reopen. Rome could breathe again. But in Ravenna, self-serving advisers whispered in the young emperor's ear, urging Honorius 'never to make peace with Alaric, but to wage against him a continual war'.[12] Only now did he call in reinforcements to defend Rome from further attack. Six thousand Roman troops marched obediently from Dalmatia – and were promptly ambushed by Gothic forces north of the city. Just one hundred soldiers escaped alive. Exasperated by the emperor's duplicity, Alaric renewed his siege.

In what is surely one of the most egregious examples of false advertising ever on Roman money, contemporary gold coins of Honorius show our dithering emperor, now in his mid-twenties, as a conquering military hero. Decked out in a general's armour, he raises a victorious standard and plants his foot on a vanquished barbarian cowering beneath him. We can only imagine what demoralised Romans – barely surviving in depopulated lands overrun by

Gold solidus of Honorius showing the 'victorious' young emperor with his foot on a barbarian captive.

plundering tribes – made of such far-fetched depictions. Or indeed Alaric himself, turning the coin over in his hand, ruminating on how his repeated attempts to bargain with the Roman government seemed more futile every day. Incredibly, the Gothic king would now be the one to make an emotive appeal to the emperor on behalf of Rome. Alaric implored Honorius not to allow 'so noble a city, which for more than a thousand years had ruled over so much of the world, to be seized and destroyed', or its 'magnificent edifices to be demolished by hostile flames'. He further reduced his demands for a living space and insisted that friendship and alliance could yet prevail between Goths and Romans, united against any who 'oppose the Empire'.[13]

When Honorius invited Alaric to an in-person parley on the outskirts of Ravenna, resolution to the conflict finally seemed within reach. The king eagerly awaited the emperor at the designated meeting place, and perhaps even dared to imagine the bountiful fields of a new Gothic homeland – until his daydream was broken suddenly by the unmistakable rolling thunder of galloping hooves. As if from nowhere, a warband led by the emperor's master of soldiers, Sarus, charged the Gothic delegation. Several of Alaric's men were cut down and the king barely escaped the trap with his life.

It was a betrayal too far. Enraged, humiliated, and seeing no other option left, Alaric marched on Rome for the final time.

Ashes in the Wind

We will never know who opened the gate that August night. The more dramatic narrative tells of Alaric infiltrating the city by subterfuge, disguising 300 of his warriors as lowly slaves and gifting them as peace offerings to Roman senators. At the prearranged hour, when all their masters were asleep, the men secretly converged on the Salarian Gate in Rome's north-east corner, killed the guards, and flung open the wooden doors for their fellow Goths. A Trojan horse downfall-by-deception worthy of a great city. But others told a bleaker tale: that it was the Romans themselves – broken by hunger and unable to face the prospect of another siege – who willingly opened their own gates to the enemy.[14]

Either way, the end result was the same. The first barbarian army since the Gauls of Brennus in 390 BC erupted into the city. Wholesale robbery, not slaughter, was the stated objective; Alaric ordered each of his men to 'seize as much of the wealth of the Romans as he was able' and to systematically plunder every house.[15] But the king knew Gothic fury would not be contained. As he set his warriors loose, years of pent-up frustration and grievance against the Roman state were unleashed on the populace, filling the streets with the brutality, murder, and sexual violence that inevitably accompanied sackings in the ancient world.

If they had not done so already, desperate Romans rushed to bury their valuables in gardens or hide them under flagstones as the Goths approached. One such example was the wealthy Turcii family, who concealed their most prized silver treasures beneath the floor of their townhouse on the upmarket Esquiline Hill. The hoard consisted of more than sixty gilded-silver objects crafted in the late fourth century, including plates, statues, horse trappings, and magnificently decorated cosmetic caskets. Portraits on the largest of these show a young couple, revealed in the accompanying inscription to be the hopeful newlyweds Secundus and Projecta – 'May you live in Christ!' it toasts them as they embark on their married life together. We are left to imagine what became of the treasure's owners during the sack of Rome – but every unretrieved hoard, by definition, whispers of an ancient tragedy. Neither Secundus, his wife Projecta, nor any of their descendants ever returned to recover the cherished items. The Esquiline Treasure was unearthed by chance in 1793, and today, the wedding silver that escaped Alaric's Goths can be marvelled at in the galleries of the British Museum.

We can only hope that the fate of the Turcii family was not the same as that of Marcella, an elderly widow and friend of Jerome, who ran a convent on the nearby Aventine Hill. When 'bloodstained' Goths burst in and demanded gold, Marcella received them without any fear, but merely gestured to her coarse garments to show that all her wealth had long been given away. Refusing to believe her self-imposed poverty, the Goths beat and tortured Marcella to reveal where her treasures were hidden. She is said to have given no cry of pain, but only pleaded for her attackers to show mercy on her young nuns, that they not be made to endure the violence that she 'as an old lady had no occasion to fear'. The barbarians were so impressed by Marcella's fortitude that they carried her to the Basilica of St Paul where she used her final breaths to offer joyful thanks to God before dying of her injuries.[16]

That Alaric only plundered Rome for a relatively brief three days, without complete burning of the city or mass execution of its population, has helped contribute to modern notions of the attack as a restrained affair; one recent assessment even goes as far as to label it a 'highly civilised sack'.[17] Alaric may have urged his men to 'refrain from bloodshed' but the murder of the elderly Marcella, beaten to death for her non-existent treasure, and numerous other accounts of brutality, make it clear his words were largely ignored. The British monk Pelagius, who survived the sacking, wrote that every house in the city became a 'scene of misery', with slave and master alike 'huddled together' in the same 'terror of death and slaughter'.[18] Even the famed theologian Augustine, who was keen to downplay the cruelty of the Christian invaders, had to concede that dreadful atrocities took place in the city; there was 'slaughter, fire, robbery, torture, and murder, it is true,' he admits. 'We agonise over it and often weep.'[19] Revealingly, he also penned a lengthy spiritual consolation for the many Roman women raped by the barbarians, urging them not to follow the example of the legendary noblewoman Lucretia by taking their own lives to 'avoid disgrace'.[20]

Remarkable coin evidence has even helped prove that some of Rome's most iconic buildings were consumed by fire during those three hellish days. The majestic Basilica Aemilia had stood for centuries at the heart of the city. Stretching one hundred metres along the northern side of the Roman Forum, the public hall was described by Pliny as one of the 'finest works that the world has ever beheld'.[21] Archaeologists excavating the remains of the structure in the early twentieth century encountered a destruction layer filled with ash, rubble, and thousands of ancient coins; the basilica was, after all, used for banking and commerce as well as law courts. Digging down further, excavators were amazed to find coins fused onto the ancient marble floor by the heat of the inferno that had destroyed the building. Analysis of the coin types showed that the latest among them had been struck in AD 409, confirming the basilica had burned down soon after – almost certainly during Alaric's sack of the city. The ghostly impressions of the melted coins can still be seen in the marble paving today, an evocative reminder of the fiery destruction visited upon Rome amid the chaos of the Gothic assault.[22]

While most injuries to the city would be indiscriminate – collateral damage in the relentless Gothic pursuit of plunder – one infamous act of barbarian desecration seemed intentionally designed to strike at the heart of Roman heritage and identity. For centuries, the cremated ashes of emperors and their families had been laid to rest in the shadowy inner sanctums of Rome's imperial tombs. Inside the Mausoleum of Augustus, the remains of the first emperor were accompanied by those of Agrippa, Germanicus, Claudius, and many others, all placed in golden urns that glimmered in the lamplight. Within the pedestal of Trajan's Column sat the ashes of the Optimus Princeps; and in the tomb of Hadrian, the wandering emperor rested alongside the kindly Antoninus and the wise philosopher, Marcus Aurelius. The Goths held no reverence for these pagans of old. They happily ransacked the sacred tombs, tearing the golden urns from their niches – and in the streets of the imperial city they had built, the ashes of the mighty Caesars were simply scattered into the wind.

True to form, Honorius remained indifferent to the fate of the Eternal City. The bird-fancying ruler was more likely to be found tossing seed to his feathered friends than worrying about affairs of state. One anecdote tells how when a palace eunuch broke the news to Honorius that Rome had fallen, he cried out: 'but I just fed her by hand minutes ago!' referring to his favourite hen, also named 'Roma'. When it was carefully explained to him that it was the city of Rome that had fallen, Honorius sighed with relief and replied: 'There I was thinking my beloved bird Roma had perished!'[23]

As for Alaric, he would never live to see his Goths find their promised homeland. Trundling southwards with a long train of wagons creaking under the weight of Roman spoils, the Gothic king was 'suddenly overtaken by an untimely death' near the town of Cosentia, the modern Calabrian capital of Cosenza. Recent studies have suggested that Alaric may well have succumbed to a severe form of malaria endemic to southern Italy, which would have been especially fatal to nomadic outsiders lacking any natural immunity.[24] The Goths now diverted the River Busento and ordered a band of slave-captives to dig a large grave in the exposed riverbed. In the depths of the pit they buried the king whom they 'mourned with the utmost affection', together with many of the finest treasures that had been looted from Rome. With a final prayer for the man who led them in capturing the great city, the waters of the Busento were allowed to flood back into the river channel. So that none might ever know the place of the lavish burial, all the diggers were promptly put to death. And the Goths marched ever onwards.[25]

Alaric's grave, and the Roman riches accompanying him, have never been found.

Romulus in Exile

When word of the sacking reached the East, three days of mourning were declared in Constantinople – as if marking the passing of the elder sibling-city. Rome would in fact limp on after her ravaging by the Goths, though it has been estimated that the city's population plummeted by as much as 50 per cent in the decade following the Gothic attack.[26] Sheltering some of these exiles, Jerome observed that the shame of Rome's ancient violation by the Gauls had been wiped away by the conquering of the entire Gallic nation; now, it seemed, even if Rome were to defeat every barbarian invader, she could only ever wrest back from her foes what she had already lost to them.

Roman fortunes would only dwindle further in following decades. In 455 the Germanic Vandals subjected Rome to a far more sustained two-week sacking. They were methodical in their theft, gutting the imperial palace of every treasure – even stripping the gilded tiles from the roof of Jupiter's Capitoline Temple.[27] The populace would be plundered too, with 'many thousands' of Roman captives loaded onto Vandal boats, later to be auctioned off in the slave markets of North Africa.[28] Critically, the Vandals also severed the aqueducts that had for centuries carried an endless supply of clean water to the Roman people, severely limiting Rome's future ability to sustain a large population. Such was the lasting damage caused by the sack, the very name of its perpetrators would become synonymous with the 'wilful destruction of what is beautiful or venerable', giving rise to our modern word 'vandalism'.

While the pillaging horde eventually moved on, the government of the shrinking Western Empire remained firmly under barbarian control for the final fading years of its existence. Fearsome Germanic generals with distinctly non-Latin names like Ricimer and Gundobad installed a parade of 'shadow emperors' on the throne in Ravenna – little more than disposable marionettes, ruthlessly replaced by their barbarian masters the first moment they showed any sign of independent thought. The last of these would be another bewildered boy, possibly as young as ten, grandiosely named Romulus Augustus. The belittling nickname he was given, 'Augustulus' or the 'little Augustus', better conveys the absurdity of his position: perched precariously on his seat of power with his feet dangling above the marble floor, fulfilling the purely symbolic role of Roman emperor. It would only be a few months before a barbarian coup put an end to the boy's performative reign.

When the Germanic mercenary Odoacer seized control of Italy, most surely expected him to eliminate the little Augustus and install his own imperial puppet. Yet the Western Empire had by now become so obsolete, its institutions so irrelevant, that Odoacer decided it was time to put an end to the charade. On 4 September 476, the barbarian soldier entered the imperial palace in Ravenna and, with little fanfare, told the boy-emperor his services would no longer be required. As Augustulus hopped down from his throne, Odoacer cast off all pretences and simply declared himself 'rex' in his place. The last emperor of Rome, replaced by the first king of Italy. It was no catastrophic doomsday, no sudden apocalyptic collapse – but in that subdued moment, the Roman Empire in the West ceased to exist as a formal political entity.

Soon after, the Eastern palace in Constantinople received a special delivery from Italy. Neatly packaged inside a box were the folded purple garments and regal diadem of little Romulus Augustus, along with a personal message from Odoacer: the West no longer had need of an emperor. Rome had, finally and officially, fallen.

Odoacer may have pronounced the death of Roman rule but he would still seek to continue its traditions, asserting his authority by striking a coin in his own name. Next to the artfully crafted handheld monuments that we have marvelled at from earlier centuries, this rough and ragged little coin may seem a woeful imitation. Its artistic shortcomings are more than compensated for, however, by its astounding historical significance, heralding as it does the return of kings to Italy after a thousand years.

The small silver coin, weighing just 0.8 grams, is intended as a half-unit of the *siliqua* – a silver denomination of the late Empire valued at 1/24 of a gold solidus. The siliqua helped to bridge the monetary gap between near-worthless bronze and highly valued gold currency of the time; an economic convenience that, added to the fact it was usually struck in fine-quality silver, made it perfect for the payment of soldiers and taxes. Their pure metal would see *siliquae* and solidi continue to feature prominently in post-Roman economies, as well as

Detail of the rare portrait of Odoacer, deposer of the last emperor in the West.

being a common addition to hoards as imperial authority collapsed in the West. The spectacular Hoxne Hoard – buried in Suffolk as Roman troops withdrew from Britannia and Honorius instructed Britons to look to their own defences – contained 569 gold solidi and an astounding 14,212 silver siliquae. That Odoacer wished for his coin to be recognised alongside those once struck by Rome demonstrates the Roman economic model, though much deteriorated, living on after the implosion of the state.

As well as replicating her monetary system, Odoacer would follow age-old Roman conventions in presenting his own face of power. This coin, of which just a handful of specimens are known to survive, offers the only historical glimpse of the king who did away with emperors in the West. Fifth-century viewers are presented with a traditional portrait-in-profile, evoking the imperial portraits with which they were familiar. While far from a masterpiece, the likeness clearly shows the draped and cuirassed bust of a soldier-statesman, though on closer inspection we can see this is no Roman ruler. Where the laurel wreath, and later the pearl diadem, had been an integral

The monogram of Odoacer, first king of post-Roman Italy.

part of an emperor's regalia, Odoacer makes sure to be shown bareheaded, emphasising his non-imperial status. In perhaps the most obvious sign of his Germanic origins, Odoacer is proudly portrayed with an unruly mop of long hair and even a thoroughly barbaric moustache.

The new king may not be crowned with laurel, but a wreath is included as a timeless symbol of victory on the coin's reverse, encircling Odoacer's regal monogram. First appearing on Greek coinage of the fifth century BC, monograms began as a creative, space-saving method of naming mint magistrates and cities of origin within the limited canvas of a coin, the word 'monogram' itself a combination the Greek *monos* meaning 'one', and *gramma* meaning 'letter'. Elegant monograms combining multiple letters into a single symbol were soon a must-have for Hellenistic royal houses, and as we have seen, the Chi-Rho monogram of Christ would later be utilised by Constantine as his personal emblem, heralding the kingdom of the Christian God.

Here the regal monogram merging the letters ODOVAC becomes the king's stamp of legitimacy, a function served by the symbols throughout the Middle Ages and into the modern era – notably for the British monarchy. Alfred the Great and Elizabeth I would both place monograms on silver pennies much like Odoacer, with the latter valiantly compressing all the letters of ELIZABETH R into one symbol. Today, the intertwined initials of the 'royal cypher' remain an essential part of the monarch's heraldry, famously embossed on the United Kingdom's iconic red postboxes, and making the news most recently in September 2022, with the unveiling of the cypher of the new king, Charles III.

Odoacer would rule as 'Rex Italiae' for a respectable sixteen years before he was stabbed to death by a rival during a banquet. A notably 'medieval' end for the man personally credited with ushering in the medieval age in AD 476. But what became of the little Augustus he had deposed? Surprisingly, the last Western emperor would outlive the Germanic king who unseated him. For all the moustachioed barbarism shown on this silver coin, Odoacer took pity on the cheerful young boy and felt no need to put him to the sword like so many predecessors. Not only did he spare the life of Romulus, he sent him to live a long retirement at a seafront villa in the Bay of Naples and even granted him an annual pension of 6,000 gold solidi.

The sprawling Neapolitan villa had already seen a long and eventful history. It once belonged to the Republican aristocrat Lucullus who was so renowned for his lavish lifestyle that his very name became the adjective 'lucullan', used to describe extravagant levels of luxury and indulgence. Here also, Cicero met with the assassin Brutus to discuss political strategy in the aftermath of Caesar's murder.[29] The villa, later turned into a Norman castle, is even at the heart of a fanciful local legend relating to the Roman poet Virgil. The story goes that as well as being a masterful writer, Virgil was also a powerful sorcerer; placing an enchanted egg under the building, he proclaimed that Naples could never fall as long as the egg remained unbroken – a magical fable that gives the fortress its curious modern name, Castel dell'Ovo or the Castle of the Egg.

Here the last emperor lived out his days, gazing out across the tranquil waters of the bay towards the looming peak of Vesuvius; his fortress, a bastion of peace in a collapsing world. Many noted the exquisite irony that the final Roman ruler in the West was named after both her legendary founder and her all-conquering first emperor. Romulus Augustus may have thought of his famous namesakes as he strolled in his exile, of the Empire that once was – and of Rome, once more a city of kings.

Roma Invicta

The crude silver coin of Odoacer makes tangible a moment in history that, rightly or wrongly, has become a pivotal one in the story of Rome's downfall. The swift dethroning of a powerless child – it was an event that surely went unnoticed by many in the tumult of the times. But amid a century of chaos, confusion, and rapid change, it offers us the chance, at least, for the clear turning of a page: from a Europe of emperors to one of warlord-kings; from the world of antiquity to that of the Middle Ages.

To what extent the collapse of Roman state institutions in the fifth century was a catastrophe for millions across Europe – indeed, whether the state collapsed at all – is today a subject of contention. Notions of 'decline and fall' have largely been replaced by gentler-sounding 'change and continuity'. Modern assessments tend to steer clear of apocalyptic post-Roman visions, while never failing to stress that emperors still sat in a thriving Constantinople. The spirit of Rome would certainly live on in the Greek-speaking East, where for another thousand years, citizens of the empire that we now label 'Byzantine' continued to call themselves *Romaioi* – Romans. Still, by every metric that can be measured, the collapse of the West, and the sharp upsurge in human misery that resulted from it, were real.

One of the most conspicuous casualties was that defining feature of the classical world: the city. Previously thriving urban centres across Europe saw dramatic falls in their populations in the fifth century. Many were abandoned altogether. Rome itself, which had once been home to more than a million people, dwindled to a population of just a few tens of thousands. Entire cities shrank to impoverished villages huddled within the walls of a single Roman monument, such as Arles in the south of France, where all remaining inhabitants now took refuge inside the ancient amphitheatre – building homes, churches, and even a town square in the fortified Roman arena. Other cities were simply wiped off the map by genocidal violence: the Gothic massacre of Milan saw every single adult male put to death and all women and children enslaved. Population collapse seems to have been particularly rapid in the cities of Britannia, where urban life ceased completely in the decades immediately following the Roman withdrawal. The study of animal remains found in deposits covering Roman York has shown that the metropolis quickly reverted to a grassy marshland in the fifth century, with wetland creatures like froghoppers, shrews, and water voles returning to live in the flooded, overgrown ruins.[30]

Forensic archaeology can even measure the physiological impact of the Empire's downfall. The average femur length of dated human skeletons – a reliable indicator of developmental health and nutrition – peaks in the first and second centuries, declining gradually until it drops off steeply in the fifth century.[31] Deposits of animal bones in Roman provinces, which imply meat consumption and a more protein-rich diet, similarly reach their peak in the second century but have almost vanished by the year 450. Even the animals themselves reveal the hardship of the times: the height of the average cow rose in the Roman period to 120 cm – only for them to quickly shrink back to their prehistoric height of 112 cm in the early Middle Ages.[32]

The end of Roman rule also brought with it a sharp decline in literacy at all levels in society. Where excavations of Roman towns and military forts often produce hundreds of examples of everyday writing, with graffiti carved into wall plaster and domestic objects inscribed with the name of their owners, finds from the post-Roman West are 'almost always mute'.[33] The pottery once scratched with Latin letters was now made locally, rather than imported; or in the case of Britannia, no longer made at all. Desperate Britons are known to have tipped the human remains out of old Roman cremation urns and proceeded to use the pots for cookery.[34] Likewise, the flourishing long-distance trade that once made products like wine, olive oil, and fish sauce staples across Europe abruptly came to an end.

Coinage would be part of this widespread collapse of material culture and technologies. Odoacer and other barbarian kings would continue striking coins imitating Roman denominations for a time, though in vastly diminished numbers. As abundant coinage disappeared, much of the West reverted to a primitive barter economy with goods and services traded directly without a monetary medium of exchange. This death of money would be frozen in an astonishing time capsule. Ice cores drilled from Greenland glaciers provide an annual record of atmospheric conditions dating back over 100,000 years. Since the smelting of newly mined silver for coinage releases toxic lead into the atmosphere, ice cores act as sensitive barometers by which we can measure coin production through time. Analysis shows lead pollution spiking massively in the early Empire before bottoming out to mere trace amounts in the Middle Ages – and not returning to the heights of the Roman imperial era until the eighteenth century.[35]

There would be no final ancient coin. No ringing strike of the moneyer's hammer tolling the end of classical civilisation. Although one design, struck by a Gothic king in a ruinous and depopulated sixth-century Rome, seems to offer a poignant last tribute to the ancient city and the enormous legacy of her money across the millennia. The bronze follis bears the helmeted bust of the personified Roma, alive and well even after so many ordeals. Her city had been starved, neglected, robbed of its wealth and of its people. Her Empire had crumbled. But still, the guardian goddess has donned her armour, ready to defend the remnants of a glorious past. Even though the follis was struck by barbarian hands, the legend encircling the goddess boldly declares Roma 'Invicta' – 'unconquered'.

Here at the end of the ancient Roman story, the reverse of the coin celebrates the mythical moment where it all began: the fierce and solitary she-wolf, turning to tenderly lick her adopted human twins, Romulus and Remus. It had been 800 years since the wolf and twins made their first appearance on the silver didrachm that opened our tale – and aside from the Christogram now stamped above the pagan icon, the presentation of the strange nativity remains almost identical.

The Lupa Romana would surely be proud of the relentless nation she had reared. In the centuries between the two coins, the children of the wolf had exploded out of Italy, made the Mediterranean their own personal sea – and ultimately, forged the greatest empire history had ever seen. And long after its decline and fall, Roman coins would

A farewell to Roma. The 'unconquered' goddess of the city, honoured on ancient coinage for the final time.

carry on the work of conquest. While the vast majority of ancient art and knowledge was tragically lost to time, coins survived. Unbroken and unchanged. Gleaming envoys from the past, determined to share their stories.

Collecting and studying them became the certified 'hobby of kings', and many a famous leader, hoping to learn from the mighty achievements of the Roman state, began by first building a collection of its money. Today, coins reveal to people of all backgrounds the faces, the gods, and the monuments of a vanished world – announcing their names across the millennia, and on continents the Romans never even knew existed.

In their enduring gold, silver, and bronze, Rome has finally achieved that ancient promise of Jupiter – empire without end.

Acknowledgements

This book owes its inception to the faith and foresight of Adam Gauntlett, who not only saw the potential of a work that harnessed the storytelling power of Roman coins but trusted that I might be the one to bring those stories to the page.

At home, its writing was made possible only with the constant support and encouragement of my wonderful wife, Louise, who has happily enabled my addiction to the Romans for many years. Far from resenting those small discs of ancient metal that regularly divert my attention, she has graciously lent her photographic talents to helping me capture their most minute details, not to mention, journeyed with me to countless ancient sites, and routinely displayed the patience of a saint as I slowly worked my way round every Roman artefact in many a museum gallery. I must also take the chance to praise our loyal Shetland Sheepdog, Augustus, who maintained a vigilant guard throughout the writing process. Embodying the tenacity of his ancient namesake perfectly, 'Gus' never failed to remind me when it was time to put aside the Romans and venture outside to throw a ball.

I would like to offer my sincere gratitude to Guy de la Bédoyère, not least for his many marvellous books on the Romans which line my bookshelf and so often inform my work, but also the remarkable generosity with which he shared his expert knowledge and advice as I embarked on this project. Similar thanks also go to Garrett Ryan, whose fantastic YouTube channel 'Told in Stone' is currently drawing a whole new generation to the wonders of the ancient world. The enthusiasm he showed for the idea of this book in its formative stages was a big motivation to me as I set about writing.

For centuries the collecting and study of ancient coins was a privileged pursuit reserved for kings, aristocrats, and academia's most hallowed halls. Today their beauty and lore are open to enthusiasts from all backgrounds. Newcomers enter an enchanting world where you can 'hold infinity in the palm of your hand', but it is also, as the numismatist Wayne G. Sayles described it, 'a bewildering world filled with strange names and places', where beginners 'can suffer from Robinson Crusoe syndrome. That is, they often feel alone on a vast uncharted island.' Over the years, the following individuals have all, knowingly or unknowingly, helped guide me through that wondrous isle, and affirmed my belief that ancient coins are the inheritance of us all: Aaron Berk, Dominic Chorney, Robert Cromarty, Amelia Dowler, Mike Gasvoda, Yves Gunzenreiner, Clare Rowan, Leonardo Santos e Barros, Shanna Schmidt, Simon Shipp, Peter Tompa, David Vagi, Mike Vosper, Bernhard Woytek, Liv Mariah Yarrow; all at Oxford's Ancient World Library where I have spent many a happy day, and, though she is no longer here to receive these thanks, one of my great numismatic inspirations, Elvira Clain-Stefanelli.

The legacy of the Roman world is an enduring one, and its archaeological wonders have continually shown their resilience against the ravages of time. Each successive generation, however, must step forward to become their temporary custodian, only passing them safely on to the next with the help of those who study, protect, and celebrate them in the here and now. My final thanks go to all who keep the sacred fire of Rome burning in any form; but especially the following individuals whose joyous work inspires me every day and makes ancient Rome seem more vital and relevant than ever: Darius Arya, Josep R. Casals, Bernard Frischer, Adrian Goldsworthy, Jean-Claude Golvin, Victor Davis Hanson, Robert Harris, Sophie Hay, Tom Holland, Danila Loginov, Richard Miles, Llewelyn Morgan, Matthew Nicholls, Steve Noon, Carole Raddato, Simon Sebag Montefiore, Jonathan Stamp, Barry Strauss, and all at the Association of Roman Archaeology.

Gratias vobis ago.

List of illustrations

Plate section

1: Rome's first denarius in the hand of the author. (Gareth Harney)
2: Marble portrait found in the Rhône river possibly depicting Julius Caesar. (Carole Raddato, 'Following Hadrian')
3: Roman soldier's *pugio* dagger, Denmark National Museum. (Gareth Harney)
4: Roman eagle onyx cameo, Vienna Kunsthistorisches Museum. (Gareth Harney)
5: Denarius portrait detail of Octavian/Augustus. (Gareth Harney)
6: Marble portrait of the emperor Caligula, Ny Carlsberg Glyptotek, Copenhagen. (Gareth Harney)
7: Aureus of Claudius depicting the Castra Praetoria. (Classical Numismatic Group); aureus depicting the Praetorian Guard welcoming Claudius to the throne. (American Numismatic Society, 1967.153.114)
8: Sestertius detail showing the newly inaugurated Colosseum. (Noonans Mayfair)
9: Fresco showing a hunter fighting a lioness, from the Roman amphitheatre in Mérida, Spain. (Gareth Harney)
10: Mosaic showing gladiatorial combat overseen by a referee, Roman Villa Nennig, Germany. (Gareth Harney)
11: Aureus reverse detail of Trajan's Column. (Goldberg Coins and Collectibles Inc.)
12: Aurei of the Trier Gold Hoard. (Gareth Harney)

13: The *Portrait of the Four Tetrarchs*, fixed into the wall of St Mark's Basilica, Venice. (Gareth Harney)

14: The peristyle courtyard of Diocletian's Palace, Split. (Gareth Harney)

15: Solar parhelion observed in Rhône-Alpes, France in 2015. (Wikimedia Commons)

Introduction

Denarius of Trajan in the hand of the author. (Gareth Harney)

Roman denarii displayed in coin trays. (Gareth Harney)

Prologue: Moneta

Denarius of Titus Carisius showing tools of coin minting. (Classical Numismatic Group)

Denarius of Hadrian's heir, Lucius Aelius Caesar. (Gareth Harney)

I. Wolf

Didrachm showing the she-wolf suckling Romulus and Remus. (Roma Numismatics)

Denarius detail showing soldiers of Romulus abducting Sabine women. (Gareth Harney)

Detail of the Lupa Romana on reverse of didrachm. (Money Museum, Zurich)

The Capitoline Wolf bronze statue, Rome. (Wikimedia Commons)

Silver brooch depicting the she-wolf nursing in her cave, Zadar Archaeological Museum. (Gareth Harney)

II. Nemesis

The first Roman denarius, with the goddess Roma and the Dioscuri twins. (Classical Numismatic Group)

Silver shekel of Carthage depicting elephant and rider. (Goldberg Coins and Collectibles Inc.)

Statues of the Dioscuri on the Capitoline Hill. (Wikimedia Commons)

III. Dictator

Denarius of Julius Caesar declaring him Dictator for Life. (Leu Numismatic)

Detail of Caesar denarius with portrait of the goddess Venus. (Gareth Harney)

Detail of denarius issued in 48 BC with possible portrait of Vercingetorix. (American Numismatic Society, 1937.158.247)

The 'elephant and serpent' denarius of Julius Caesar. (American Numismatic Society, 1974.26.48)

Detail of the lifetime denarius portrait of Julius Caesar. (American Numismatic Society, 1937.158.299)

IV. Ides

Brutus Ides of March denarius with cap and daggers. (Münzkabinett der Staatlichen Museen zu Berlin, 18202198)

Denarius depicting Lucius Junius Brutus, ancestor of the assassin. (Roma Numismatics)

Bronze bust commonly identified as the liberator, Lucius Junius Brutus. (Wikimedia Commons)

Detail of the denarius portrait of the assassin, Marcus Junius Brutus. (Bruun Rasmussen)

Denarius detail showing the daggers of the assassins. (American Numismatic Society, 1944.100.4554)

V. Pax

Denarius of Octavian/Augustus showing Pax, the goddess of peace. (Gareth Harney)

Denarius of Augustus depicting the comet of Caesar. (American Numismatic Society, 1944.100.39033)

Denarius with portraits of Mark Antony and Cleopatra. (Nomos AG)

Detail of denarius reverse showing the goddess Pax. (Gareth Harney)

Reverse of the Tribute Penny denarius depicting Pax/Livia. (American Numismatic Society, 1935.117.357)

VI. Kingmakers

Aureus of Claudius depicting the Castra Praetoria. (Classical Numismatic Group)

Provincial coin from the town of Bilbilis with the name of Lucius Aelius Sejanus intact. (Jared J. Clark Collection, Southern CA.)

A coin from the same issue with the name of Lucius Aelius Sejanus erased. (Classical Numismatic Group)

Sestertius of Caligula showing his three sisters as goddesses. (Numismatica Ars Classica)

VII. Arena

Posthumous sestertius of Titus commemorating the inauguration of the Colosseum. (Noonans Mayfair)

Bronze quadrans depicting an African rhinoceros. (American Numismatic Society, 1944.100.54620)

Denarius of Titus depicting an African elephant. (Classical Numismatic Group)

VIII. Zenith

Aureus of Trajan depicting Trajan's Column. (Goldberg Coins and Collectibles Inc.)

Reliefs of Trajan's Column showing Roman legionaries crossing a pontoon bridge over the Danube. (Carole Raddato, 'Following Hadrian')

Denarius detail depicting an improvised Roman victory trophy made of Dacian arms and armour. (Gareth Harney)

Colossal rock carving of the Dacian king Decebalus. (Wikimedia Commons)

Coin portrait detail of the emperor Trajan, from a silver tetradrachm in the author's collection. (Gareth Harney)

IX. Philosopher

Sestertius of Marcus Aurelius with Salus, the goddess of health. (Roma Numismatics)

Marble relief depicting four Roman emperors, Ephesus Museum, Vienna. (Gareth Harney)

Denarius portrait detail of the co-emperor, Lucius Verus. (Gareth Harney)

Aureus depicting Marcus Aurelius on horseback. (Roma Numismatics)

Equestrian bronze statue of Marcus Aurelius on the Capitoline Hill in Rome. (Wikimedia Commons)

Denarii of Marcus Aurelius and his son Commodus in the hand of the author. (Gareth Harney)

X. Split

Argenteus of Diocletian showing the Tetrarchy sacrificing before a fortified city. (Classical Numismatic Group)

Denarius of Valerian in the hand of the author. (Gareth Harney)

XI. Cross

Follis of Constantine with vexillum standard surmounted by the Chi-Rho. (Classical Numismatic Group)

Solidus portrait detail of Constantine gazing upward to the heavens. (Roma Numismatics)

Follis reverse detail of Constantine's labarum standard with Chi-Rho. (Classical Numismatic Group)

XII. Collapse

Silver half-siliqua of Odoacer, the first barbarian king of post-Roman Italy. (© The Trustees of the British Museum)

Solidus of Honorius showing the emperor with his foot on a barbarian captive. (Classical Numismatic Group)

Detail of the rare coin portrait of Odoacer. (© The Trustees of the British Museum)

Monogram of Odoacer. (OCRE, Online Coins of the Roman Empire)

Ostrogothic follis showing Roma with wolf and twins. (© Dumbarton Oaks, Coins and Seals Collection, Washington, DC)

Recommended reading

The science of ancient numismatics has, for much of its long history, been confined to the pages of weighty reference works and expensive, hard-to-find academic texts – while approachable books looking to make the case for coins to a general audience are few and far between. Indeed, one of my goals with *Moneta* has been to demonstrate, in any way that I can, how ancient coins can serve as an integral, rather than incidental focus of engaging historical narratives. I will always hope for more books celebrating the unique power of ancient coins as sources, but the following recommendations should offer any curious readers eager to learn more a well-illustrated and highly readable introduction to the topic:

100 Greatest Ancient Coins, Harlan J. Berk (Whitman, 2008)
50 Finds of Roman Coinage, Andrew Brown (Amberley, 2021)
Ancient Coin Collecting series, Wayne G. Sayles (KP Books)
Ancient History from Coins, Christopher Howgego (Routledge, 1995)
Coinage in the Roman World, Andrew Burnett (Spink, 2010)
Coins and the Bible, Richard Abdy, Amelia Dowler (British Museum, 2014)
From Caesar to Augustus: Using Coins as Sources, Clare Rowan (Cambridge, 2019)
Hoards: Hidden History, Eleanor Ghey (British Museum, 2015)
Monumental Coins: Buildings and Structures on Ancient Coinage, Marvin Tameanko (KP Books, 1999)
The Oxford Handbook of Greek and Roman Coinage, William E. Metcalf (Oxford, 2016)
The Roman Republic: Using Coins as Sources, Liv Mariah Yarrow (Cambridge, 2021)
Romano-British Coin Hoards, Richard Abdy (Shire, 2002)

Notes

Abbreviations
CIL *Corpus Inscriptionum Latinarum*
ILS *Inscriptiones Latinae Selectae*

Introduction

1 E. Clain-Stefanelli, *The Beauty and Lore of Coins* (Riverwood, 1974), p. 8.
2 King George III and his American contemporary, President John Adams, for example, were both enthusiastic collectors of ancient coins. The Adams Presidential Collection was auctioned off in 1971 and its coins, of which I am the proud owner of one, still regularly appear on the market.
3 M. Turner, *Faces of Power* (Nicholson Museum, 2006), p. 5.

Prologue: Moneta

Epigraph: E. Canetti, 'Inflation and the Crowd', *Crowds and Power*. Published in German as *Masse und Macht*, 1960.

1 Livy, *The History of Rome*, 5.42.
2 Dionysius, *Roman Antiquities*, 13.7.
3 Livy, *The History of Rome*, 6.20 and 7.28.
4 See, for instance, Turner, *Roman Coins from India* (UCL Institute of Archaeology, 1989).
5 The Antikythera mechanism, constructed in the second century BC, displayed in the Athens Archaeological Museum. See A. Jones, *A Portable Cosmos* (Oxford, 2017).

6 Extrapolated from Pliny, 33.21, claiming that 20,000 pounds of gold were extracted from the Las Médulas gold mines in north-west Spain every year.
7 J. Bennett, *Trajan: Optimus Princeps* (Routledge, 2001), p. 101.
8 K. Butcher, M. Ponting, *The Metallurgy of Roman Silver Coinage* (Cambridge, 2014), p. 19.
9 C. Howgego, *Ancient History from Coins* (Routledge, 1995), p. 35.
10 L. Yarrow, *The Roman Republic: Using Coins as Sources* (Cambridge, 2021), p. 55.
11 See for example the *Imperatorum Romanorum* made by Italian polymath and numismatist Jacopo Strada (1507–88) for the House of Habsburg in 1559, with its magnificent portraits of Roman emperors inspired by ancient coins in his collection.
12 See the Nimrud Lens, British Museum Collection, 90959, and Pliny the Elder, *Natural History*, 37.16.
13 J. Wickens, *The Production of Ancient Coins* (Lawrence University, 1996).
14 See estimates in Crawford, *Roman Republican Coinage* (Cambridge, 1974).
15 Kunsthistorisches Museum Vienna, Coin Cabinet, tessera, 32.652.
16 Gomes Eanes de Zurara (1410–74), *Chronicle of the Siege and Capture of Ceuta*, 1450.
17 CIL VI.44, a dedication to Hercules Augustus by Felix, an imperial freedman in charge of technical operations at the mint in Rome.
18 Denarius of Titus Carisius, 46 BC, Crawford 464/2.
19 Wickens, op. cit.
20 *Coin World* online article, 'Hiker in Israel discovers rare gold coin', March 2016.
21 See A. Carandini, *The Atlas of Ancient Rome* (Princeton, 2017), and the digital reconstruction work of Danila Loginov at *History in 3D*.
22 Aristotle, *Nicomachean Ethics*, 1133b.

I. Wolf

Epigraph: Virgil, *Aeneid*, Book 1.

1 Ovid, *Fasti*, 2; and Dionysius, *Roman Antiquities*, 1.79.
2 Plutarch, *Life of Romulus*, 4.1.

3 Livy, *The History of Rome*, 1.1; and Dionysius, *Roman Antiquities*, 1.79.
4 The first description of the she-wolf nursing Romulus and Remus is thought to have been from the early Roman history of Quintus Fabius Pictor, written around 215 BC.
5 Livy, *The History of Rome*, 1.4.
6 Ibid, 1.6.
7 Ibid.
8 Ibid, 1.7.
9 The 'House of Romulus' or Casa Romuli can be visited on the Palatine Hill.
10 Both the potsherd and Black Stone are displayed in the Baths of Diocletian National Museum of Rome.
11 Livy, *The History of Rome*, 1.9.
12 Ibid.
13 Other famous examples of similar marriage-by-abduction can be seen in the biblical tribe of Benjamin or Paris' abduction of Helen of Troy as described by Homer.
14 Denarius of Lucius Titurius Sabinus, 89 BC, Crawford 344/2b.
15 Livy, *The History of Rome*, 1.4.
16 Ibid, 2.1.
17 See for instance the speech 'Trusting in Money' by Mervyn King, Governor of the Bank of England, 2006.
18 Lydian staters punched with the head of a lion are generally agreed to be the first coins officially issued by a government in world history, struck from around 620 BC.
19 Sicily, Syracuse, 'Arethusa' tetradrachm with dies signed by Kimon, struck around 405 BC; described as the 'most beautiful coin' by Katherine Erhart in her dissertation on facing head Greek coins, and by numerous auctioneers.
20 See Virgil, *Aeneid*, 8.626–70, for the image of the she-wolf as described on the shield of Aeneas.
21 See C. G. Jung, *Four Archetypes: Mother, Rebirth, Spirit, Trickster* (Princeton, 1970).
22 Plutarch, *Life of Romulus*, 4.3.
23 Pope Gelasius (492–6) was still railing against the festival at the end of the fifth century AD. *Epistles*, 100.

24 Cicero, *Against Catiline*, 3.19.
25 Cicero, *On Divination*, 1.20.
26 L. Calcagnile et al., 'Solving an historical puzzle: Radiocarbon dating the Capitoline she wolf', *Nuclear Instruments and Methods in Physics-B*, Volume 455 (2019).
27 The tenth-century chronicler Benedict of Soracte writes of justice being administered in the Lateran at 'the place called the Wolf, the mother of the Romans'.
28 C. Mazzoni, *She Wolf: Story of a Roman Icon* (Cambridge, 2010), p. 23.
29 Dionysius, *Roman Antiquities*, 1.79.
30 Mazzoni, op. cit., p. 19.
31 See Chapter 12. British Museum Collection, B.12390, *nummus* of Athalaric, AD 526–34.
32 M. McGillicuddy, 'The Vatican gifts a live Capitoline wolf to Mussolini's Rome', Villa Ludovisi Online Archive, 2020.

II. Nemesis

Epigraph: Heraclitus, *On Nature*, Fragment 44.

1 Polybius, *Histories*, 3.11.
2 Livy, *The History of Rome*, 21.1 and 35.19.
3 Adapted from Silius Italicus, *Punica*, 1.106–22.
4 See Livy, 21.4, for a detailed description of Hannibal's qualities as a leader.
5 Livy, *The History of Rome*, 21.1.
6 Polybius, *Histories*, 1.63.
7 For a description of the extraction of 'Tyrian Purple' from murex sea snails, see Pliny the Elder, *Natural History*, 9.60.
8 Polybius, *Histories*, 1.20.
9 Pliny the Elder, *Natural History*, 16.74.
10 P. Connolly, *Greece and Rome at War* (Greenhill, 1998), p. 144.
11 See the RPM Nautical Foundation's Battle of the Egadi Islands Project.
12 Polybius, *Histories*, 3.28.
13 Though popularly attributed to Hannibal, the phrase is first attested in Seneca's tragic play *Hercules Furens*, written in the first century AD.

14 W. C. Mahaney et al., 'Biostratigraphic Evidence Relating to the Age-Old Question of Hannibal's Invasion of Italy', *Archaeometry* (2016).
15 Both Polybius, 3.50; and Livy, 21.32, provide sixteen-day itineraries of Hannibal's passage through the Alps.
16 V. D. Hanson, 'The Battle of Cannae', in *The Reader's Companion to Military History* (Houghton Mifflin, 2001).
17 A. Goldsworthy, *The Fall of Carthage* (Orion, 2006), p. 213.
18 J. Weber, *Pre-Industrial Bimetallism: The Index Coin Hypothesis* (University of Western Australia, 2012), p. 9.
19 Cassius Dio, *Fragments*, 14.56.
20 Between the sixteenth and twentieth centuries, British silver coins were composed of .925 fine or 'sterling' silver. Likewise, American silver coins were 90 per cent pure until the Coinage Act of 1965 which removed most precious metal from American coinage.
21 Polybius, *Histories*, 10.15.
22 Livy, *The History of Rome*, 35.14.
23 Cicero, *Life of Cato*, 27.
24 Appian, *The Punic Wars*, 19.129.
25 Polybius, *Histories*, 38.22; and Appian, *The Punic Wars*, 19.132.
26 See for instance Diodorus Siculus, 13.86, 20.14; Quintus Curtius, 4.3; and Augustine, *City of God*, 7.19.
27 For example R. Miles, *Ancient Worlds* (Penguin, 2011), p. 244, in contrast with previously held opinion of author.
28 J. Quinn et al., 'Phoenician Bones of Contention', *Antiquity*, Volume 87 (2013).
29 Matthew 20:2.
30 Mark 12:17.

III. Dictator

Epigraph: W. B. Yeats, excerpt from 'Long-Legged Fly', *Last Poems* (1939).

1 Plutarch, *Life of Caesar*, 2.1.
2 Ibid, 2.2–4.
3 Ibid, 2.5.

4 Shakespeare, *Julius Caesar*, Act 1, Scene 2.
5 Seneca the Younger, *On Clemency*, 1.12.
6 Plutarch, *Life of Caesar*, 1.4.
7 Plutarch, *Life of Sulla*, 38.4.
8 Plutarch, *Life of Caesar*, 5.9.
9 Suetonius, *Julius Caesar*, 45.3.
10 Ibid, 6.1.
11 A. Goldsworthy, *In the Name of Rome* (Phoenix, 2004), p. 204.
12 Caesar, *The Gallic War*, 8.44.
13 Plutarch, *Life of Caesar*, 23.3.
14 Caesar, *The Gallic War*, 7.76.
15 See Alesia Lidar, Département de la Côte-d'Or, Géophenix & Jonhattan Vidal, 2020.
16 Caesar, *The Gallic War*, 7.78, and see 7.26, in which Caesar states memorably: 'In the extremity of peril, fear often leaves no room for compassion.'
17 Ibid, 7.88.
18 Diodorus Siculus, *Library of History*, 5.28.
19 J. Lobell, S. Patel, 'Clonycavan and Old Croghan Men', *Archaeology*, Volume 63 (2010).
20 See Caesar, *The Gallic War*, 7.25, for a demonstration of Gallic bravery that Caesar thought 'ought not to be omitted'.
21 Plutarch, *Life of Caesar*, 32.7.
22 Caesar, *The Gallic War*, 7.88.
23 See D. L. Nousek, 'Turning Points in Roman History: The Case of Caesar's Elephant Denarius', *Phoenix*, Volume 62 (2008).
24 C. Rowan, *From Caesar to Augustus: Using Coins as Sources* (Cambridge, 2018), pp. 26–7.
25 Suetonius, *Julius Caesar*, 26.3.
26 M. P. Ben Zeev, 'When was the title of Dictator Perpetuus given to Caesar?', *L'Antiquité Classique*, Issue 65 (1996).
27 Suetonius, *Julius Caesar*, 76.1.
28 Ibid, 77.1.
29 Ibid, 45.3.
30 See criticism by M. Beard, 'Will the real Julius Caesar please stand up?', *National Geographic* (2022).

31 Plutarch, *Life of Caesar*, 57.2.
32 Shakespeare, *Julius Caesar*, Act 3, Scene 5.
33 Suetonius, *Julius Caesar*, 38.1.
34 S. Bigliazzi, *Julius Caesar 1935: Shakespeare and Censorship in Fascist Italy* (Skenè, 2019), p. 45.
35 V. Cowles, *Winston Churchill: The Era and the Man* (Grosset & Dunlap, 1956), p. 8.

IV: Ides

Epigraph: Cicero, *Letters to Atticus*, 14.14; a sentiment repeated by Cicero in numerous letters following the assassination in 44 BC, notably 14.9 and 14.21 to Atticus, as well as 12.1 to the assassin Cassius.

1 Plutarch, *Life of Brutus*, 14.3, describes how on the morning of the Ides, 'Brutus girt on a dagger, to the knowledge of his wife alone'.
2 The goddess Cloacina watched over the Cloaca Maxima or 'Great Drain', the main sewer of ancient Rome.
3 For Roman death masks or '*imagines*' see Pliny the Elder, *Natural History*, 35.2.
4 See Plutarch, *Life of Cato*, 32, describing how Caesar arranged for his supporters to dump excrement over his fellow consul, Bibulus, in the Roman Forum.
5 Plutarch, *Life of Brutus*, 1.1.
6 Plutarch, *Life of Caesar*, 62.4.
7 See Plutarch, *Life of Cato*, 70, for a dramatic description of Cato the Younger's suicide.
8 Plutarch, *Life of Brutus*, 9.
9 Plutarch, *Life of Caesar*, 60.2.
10 Suetonius, *Julius Caesar*, 81.2.
11 Ovid, *The Metamorphoses*, Book 15, 'The Deification of Julius Caesar'.
12 Plutarch, *Life of Caesar*, 17.7.
13 Plutarch, *Life of Caesar*, 63.7; and Suetonius, *Julius Caesar*, 87.
14 Plutarch, *Life of Caesar*, 63.9–12; and Suetonius, *Julius Caesar*, 81.3.
15 Suetonius, *Julius Caesar*, 80.4.

16 Appian, *The Civil Wars*, 2.124.
17 See Suetonius, *Julius Caesar*, 84; Plutarch, *Life of Caesar*, 68; and Shakespeare, *Julius Caesar*, Act 3, Scene 2.
18 Cicero, *Letters to Atticus*, 5.21 and 6.1.
19 Plutarch, *Life of Brutus*, 27.4.
20 Shakespeare, *Julius Caesar*, Act 1, Scene 2; inspired by Plutarch, *Life of Caesar*, 62.10.
21 Cassius Dio, *Roman History*, 47.25.
22 As brilliantly observed by B. Strauss, *The Death of Caesar* (Simon & Schuster, 2015), p. 221.
23 Dante, *The Divine Comedy: Inferno*, Canto 34.
24 Shakespeare, *Julius Caesar*, Act 5, Scene 5.
25 Cassius Dio, *Roman History*, 48.1; and Suetonius, *Julius Caesar*, 89.
26 Plutarch, *Life of Brutus*, 53.4; contrasting Suetonius, *Augustus*, 13.1.
27 As recounted by Lincoln's bodyguard, W. H. Lamon, *Recollections of Abraham Lincoln 1847–1865* (1895), pp. 115–16.
28 The Oklahoma Bomber, Timothy McVeigh, wore a T-shirt bearing the Latin slogan on the day of the attack, 19 April 1995.
29 Two extraordinary examples of the Brutus Ides of March coin struck in gold were auctioned in 2020 and 2022, achieving a record-breaking £3.2 million and £1.8 million respectively, confirming it as the world's most highly valued ancient coin.

V. Pax

Epigraph: Tacitus, *Annals*, 1.10.

1 A ten-day minimum for the news reaching Octavian in Apollonia is discussed in 'Baby Steps for Octavian', *The Classical Quarterly*, Volume 68, Issue 1 (2018), pp. 178–91.
2 That the letter was sent by his mother Atia, see Nicolaus of Damascus, *Life of Augustus*, 16.
3 Suetonius, *Augustus*, 25.4.
4 Nicolaus of Damascus, *Life of Augustus*, 17.
5 Cicero, *Letters to Brutus*, 1.3.

6 Cicero, *Philippics*, 13.24.
7 Virgil, *The Eclogues*, 9; and Ovid, *The Metamorphoses*, Book 15.
8 Suetonius, *Julius Caesar*, 88.
9 Shakespeare, *Julius Caesar*, Act 2, Scene 2.
10 Plutarch, *Life of Antony*, 60.1.
11 Ibid, 58.4.
12 Cassius Dio, *Roman History*, 50.25.
13 Ibid, 49.34.
14 Plutarch, *Life of Antony*, 27.
15 Cassius Dio, *Roman History*, 53.5.
16 Augustus, *Res Gestae*, 34.
17 Suetonius, *Augustus*, 79.2.
18 M. Prusac, *From Face to Face: Recarving of Roman Portraits and the Late-Antique Portrait Arts* (Brill, 2010), p. 29.
19 The head of the goddess Pax, named with the archaic spelling PAXS, was shown on a single scarce Roman *quinarius* (half denarius) struck by the moneyer L. Aemilius Buca in 44 BC.
20 Silius Italicus, *Punica*, 11.
21 Plato, *Laws*, 1.626a.
22 Augustus, *Res Gestae*, 13.
23 S. Weinstock, 'Pax and the Ara Pacis', *Journal of Roman Studies*, 50 (1960).
24 Livy, *The History of Rome*, 1.19.
25 Ibid, 30.30.
26 Tacitus, *Annals*, 1.3.
27 Martial, *Epigrams*, 5.64.
28 See Pliny the Elder, *Natural History*, 14.1, for a celebration of these 'blessings of peace'.
29 W. Churchill, *A History of the English-Speaking Peoples*, Volume 1, Chapter 3, 'The Roman Province' (Cassell & Company, 1956).
30 Tacitus, *Annals*, 1.2.
31 Ibid, 12.27.
32 Tacitus, *Agricola*, 30.
33 Gibbon, *The Decline and Fall of the Roman Empire*, Volume 1, Chapter 2 (Penguin Classics).
34 Phrases used to describe the reign of Augustus on the Priene Calendar Inscription (*IK Priene* 14), which also notably uses the term 'gospel' or

'good news'. The calendar is part of the Collection of Classical Antiquities in Berlin.

VI. Kingmakers

Epigraph: Juvenal, *Satires*, 6.

1 See Josephus, *Antiquities of the Jews*, 19.214–19; and Suetonius, *Claudius*, 1.1–4, for the discovery of Claudius.
2 Cassius Dio, *Roman History*, 55.23.
3 Tacitus, *Annals*, 1.8.
4 Ibid, 4.5, describes nine praetorian and three urban cohorts during the reign of Tiberius.
5 Suetonius, *Tiberius*, 24.1.
6 Tacitus, *Annals*, 1.7.
7 M. Bendenoun, *Coins of the Ancient World: A Portrait of the JDL Collection* (Tradart Institut, 2009), p. 48.
8 Today held in Rome's Palazzo Albani del Drago, CIL 14.2523, ILS 2662.
9 Tacitus, *Annals*, 1.17.
10 For a detailed discussion on the ratio of praetorian pay, see G. de la Bédoyère, *Praetorian* (New Haven, 2018) p. 32.
11 Tacitus, *Annals*, 1.34–5.
12 Cassius Dio, *Roman History*, 57.5.
13 Suetonius, *Tiberius*, 37.
14 Cassius Dio, *Roman History*, 57.19; and Tacitus, *Annals*, 4.2.
15 Suetonius, *Caligula*, 6.2.
16 Suetonius, *Caligula*, 1.2; and Tacitus, *Annals*, 3.16.
17 Tacitus, *Annals*, 3.16.
18 Cassius Dio, *Roman History*, 57.22; and Tacitus, *Annals*, 4.3.
19 Tacitus, *Annals*, 4.8.
20 Cassius Dio, *Roman History*, 58.4.
21 Velleius Paterculus, *Roman History*, 2.128, a rare source written prior to the downfall of Sejanus.
22 Cassius Dio, *Roman History*, 58.5.

23 Suetonius, *Tiberius*, 65.1.
24 Cassius Dio, *Roman History*, 58.11.
25 Tacitus, *Annals*, 5.9 (Fragments).
26 Suetonius, *Caligula*, 13.1.
27 Philo, *On the Embassy to Gaius*, 2–3.
28 J. D. Charry-Sánchez et al., 'Caligula: A Neuropsychiatric Explanation of his Madness', *Arquivos de Neuro-Psiquiatria* (2021).
29 Suetonius, *Caligula*, 22.1
30 Ibid, 30.1.
31 Ibid, 38.4.
32 Ibid, 55.3.
33 Josephus, *Antiquities of the Jews*, 19.153.
34 A. Camus, author's preface to *Caligula and Three Other Plays* (Vintage, 1972).
35 Suetonius, *Caligula*, 58.1–3.
36 Cassius Dio and Josephus describe the praetorians plundering and raging through the palace in a fury.
37 Josephus, *Antiquities of the Jews*, 19.200; and Suetonius, *Caligula*, 59.1.
38 Suetonius, *Claudius*, 10.3.
39 For the 15,000 sestertii donative see Josephus, *Antiquities of the Jews*, 19.247; and Suetonius, *Claudius*, 10.4.
40 Cassius Dio, *Roman History*, 60.12.
41 Tacitus, *Annals*, 11.35; and Suetonius, *Claudius*, 36.1.
42 Suetonius, *Claudius*, 21.4.
43 Pliny the Elder, *Natural History*, 9.5.
44 Suetonius, *Claudius*, 20.3.
45 Gibbon, *The Decline and Fall of the Roman Empire*, Volume 1, Chapter 5 (Penguin Classics).
46 Suetonius, *Nero*, 31.2.

VII. Arena

Epigraph: Seneca, *Moral Letters*, 7.

1 The *pompa* parade that opened amphitheatre and circus spectacles is described in Dionysius, *Roman Antiquities*, 7.72.

2 Such a gladiator procession is shown on the tomb of Gnaeus Clovatius, found in Pompeii in 1844 and displayed in Naples Archaeological Museum.
3 N. Elkins, 'The Procession and Placement of Imperial Cult Images in the Colosseum', *Papers of the British School at Rome* (2014).
4 Edible gifts described in Statius, *Silvae*, 1.6.
5 Cassius Dio, *Roman History*, 66.25.
6 Suetonius, *Vespasian*, 4.1.
7 The Loggetta of Cardinal Bibbiena in the Vatican, designed by Raphael in 1516, recreates the architecture and frescoes of the Domus Aurea.
8 As noted in A. Mahoney, *Roman Sports and Spectacles* (Focus, 2001).
9 M. Twain, *Innocents Abroad*, Chapter 26.
10 The featured sestertius is a rarer variant dedicated to Divus Titus – the emperor having died of a sudden fever in September 81 – indicating that the inaugural celebrations for the Colosseum and associated public largess continued into the reign of his brother, Domitian.
11 Martial, *On the Spectacles*, 2.
12 Figures from M. Beard, K. Hopkins, *The Colosseum* (Harvard, 2011).
13 Contrary to popular belief, the Romans usually rendered the number four with the additive numeral IIII. In texts and inscriptions, the use of subtractive numerals like IV and IX did not become the standard presentation until the seventeenth century.
14 Suetonius, *Vespasian*, 23.4.
15 As proposed by N. Elkins, 'The Flavian Colosseum Sestertii: Currency or Largess?', *The Numismatic Chronicle* (2006).
16 G. Ryan, 'How Much Would it Cost to Build the Colosseum Today?', YouTube, 'Told in Stone' (2022).
17 M. Crapper, 'How Roman Engineers Could have Flooded the Colosseum', *ICE Proceedings Civil Engineering* (2007).
18 'What Ancient Romans Ate at the Colosseum', *Popular Mechanics* (2022).
19 Details of *sparsiones* and the protective perimeter of the *balteus* described in Calpurnius Siculus, *Eclogue* 7.
20 Cassius Dio, *Roman History*, 66.25, gives this death toll and calls the Colosseum the 'hunting theatre'.
21 Martial, *On the Spectacles*, 9, 22, 23.
22 Ibid, 17.
23 As detailed on the tombstone of the farm's manager, Speclator. CIL 6.8583.

24 Plutarch, *On the Intelligence of Animals*, 12.
25 Cicero, *Letters to Friends*, 7.1.
26 Ibid, 8.1, 8.2, 8.4, 8.9, 2.11.
27 Martial, *On the Spectacles*, 5, 7, 8.
28 Tertullian, *Letter on Spectacles*, 12.
29 The oath of the gladiator quoted in Petronius, *Satyricon*, 117; and Seneca, *Moral Letters*, 37.
30 Suetonius, *Claudius*, 21.6.
31 Musée du Cinquantenaire, Brussels, inventory no. A1562.
32 Such as Juvenal, *Satires*, 3.36.
33 Cicero, *Tusculan Disputations*, 27.
34 Statistics from K. Nossov, *Gladiator: Rome's Bloody Spectacle* (Osprey, 2009), pp. 150–51.
35 CIL 10.7297, Palermo.
36 CIL 10.6012, from Minturno.
37 Seneca, *Moral Letters*, 70.20.
38 Pliny the Elder, *Natural History*, 28.2.
39 Ibid, 15.5 and 28.13.
40 G. Caneva et al., 'Analysis of the Colosseum's floristic changes during the last four centuries', *Plant Biosystems* (2002).
41 Bede, *Collectanea*.
42 Cicero, *Tusculan Disputations*, 27.
43 Seneca, *Moral Letters*, 7.

VIII. Zenith

Epigraph: Tacitus, *Histories*, 1.1.

1 Cassio Dio states Trajan always marched on foot with the body of his army, *Roman History*, 68.23.
2 B. Jones, *The Emperor Domitian* (Taylor & Francis, 1992), p. 74.
3 Pliny the Younger, *Panegyric in Praise of Trajan*.
4 P. Connolly, *Greece and Rome at War* (Greenhill, 1998), p. 233 puts the weight of reconstructed segmented armour cuirasses at just 9 kg.
5 Vegetius, *Military Matters, Book 1, Not to Cut, But to Thrust with the Sword*.

6 R. A. Gabriel, *The Great Armies of Antiquity* (Greenwood, 2002), p. 232.
7 Josephus, *The Jewish War*, 3.7.
8 Procopius, *Buildings*, 4.6.
9 P. H. Blyth, 'Apollodorus of Damascus and the Poliorcetica', *Greek, Roman and Byzantine Studies*, Volume 33 (1992).
10 L. Seymour et al., 'Hot mixing: Mechanistic Insights into the Durability of Ancient Roman Concrete', *Science Advances*, Volume 9 (2023).
11 Cassius Dio, *Roman History*, 57.6, describes Decebalus as 'a worthy antagonist of the Romans for a long time'.
12 See M. Speidel, 'The Captor of Decebalus: a New Inscription from Philippi', *Journal of Roman Studies*, Volume 60 (1970) for analysis of the gravestone.
13 Today the tombstone is displayed in the Archaeological Museum of Drama, Eastern Macedonia and Thrace, Greece.
14 Cassius Dio, *Roman History*, 68.14.
15 J. Bennett, *Trajan: Optimus Princeps* (Routledge, 2001), p. 101.
16 M. Schmitz, *The Dacian Threat* (Caeros Publishing, 2005), p. 8.
17 K. Butcher, M. Ponting, 'The Reforms of Trajan and the End of the Pre-Neronian Denarius', *Annali dell'Istituto Italiano di Numismatica*, 61 (2015), p. 40.
18 Ammianus Marcellinus, *Roman History*, 27.3, for Trajan's 'wall ivy' nickname.
19 Column statistics from L. Lancaster, 'Building Trajan's Column', *American Journal of Archaeology*, 103 (1999).
20 Cassius Dio, *Roman History*, 68.5, also paraphrases the Column inscription, restating that 'the entire section had been hilly, and he had cut it down for a distance equal to the height of the column'.
21 J. E. Packer, *The Forum of Trajan in Rome* (University of California, 2001), p. 75.
22 Frontinus in his *Aqueducts of Rome* claims a supply equivalent to around 300 million gallons per day, while most modern estimates arrive at around 200 million; see K. Rempp, 'Water Supply and Urban Development in Ancient Rome and Modern Cities', at EngineeringRome.org
23 See J. R. Brandt, *Warehouse of the World* (2005) for detailed estimates of import tonnage for these commodities.
24 Aelius Aristides, *Roman Oration*, 13.

25 Fronto, *Elements of History*, 17.
26 J. Hanson, S. Ortman, 'Urbanism and the Division of Labour in the Roman Empire', *Journal of the Royal Society Interface* (2017) place the total number of provinces in AD 117 at fifty-one.
27 Cassius Dio, *Roman History*, 68.29.
28 Aurelius Victor and Dio both describe Trajan's ashes being sealed in the base of his Column; Eutropius, 8.5, describes his 'golden urn'.
29 Ammianus Marcellinus, *Roman History*, 16.10.
30 *Historia Augusta, Life of Hadrian*, 5.

IX. Philosopher

Epigraph: Marcus Aurelius, *Meditations*, 7.49.

1 *Historia Augusta, Life of Hadrian*, 11.2.
2 Marcus Aurelius, *Meditations*, 1.5.
3 *Historia Augusta, Life of Marcus Aurelius*, 2.6.
4 M. Yourcenar, *Memoirs of Hadrian* (Secker & Warburg, 1955), p. 279.
5 Marcus Aurelius, *Meditations*, 5.20.
6 *Historia Augusta, Life of Marcus Aurelius*, 7.9.
7 See Musonius Rufus, *Lecture 21, 'On Cutting the Hair'*; and Epictetus, *Discourses*, 4.
8 *Historia Augusta, Life of Verus*, 10.7.
9 The sacking of Seleucia as described in *Historia Augusta, Life of Verus*, 8.1.
10 Ammianus Marcellinus, *Roman History*, 23.6.
11 *Historia Augusta, Life of Verus*, 8.1.
12 The 'contagion' of the soldiers described by Ammianus Marcellinus, *Roman History*, 23.6.
13 Galen, *Method of Medicine*, 5.12.
14 F. McLynn, *Marcus Aurelius* (Vintage, 2010), p. 464.
15 Cassius Dio, *Roman History*, 73.14.
16 Orosius, *History Against the Pagans*, 7.15.
17 As concluded by McLynn, op. cit., pp. 466–7.
18 For example in Corinth, see *Corinth in Context* (Brill, 2010), pp. 183–4.
19 Jerome, *Chronicle, 236th Olympiad*.

20 R. P. Duncan-Jones, 'The Antonine Plague Revisited', *Arctos*, 52 (2018).
21 Eutropius, *Roman History*, 8.
22 Ibid.
23 Shakespeare, *Hamlet*, Act 2, Scene 2.
24 Marcus Aurelius, *Meditations*, 7.8.
25 Ibid, 6.24.
26 Ibid, 7.56.
27 Ibid, 7.47.
28 *Historia Augusta*, 27.7, says this judgement of Plato was always on Marcus' lips.
29 Such a mass execution is shown in the reliefs of the Aurelian Column in Rome.
30 As described by Dr Michael Sugrue in his lecture 'Meditations: The Stoic Ideal', available on YouTube.
31 J. S. Mill, *The Utility of Religion* (1874).
32 Vice, *'The Revival of Stoicism'*, June 2021.
33 Marcus Aurelius, *Meditations*, 10.34, quoting Homer, *Iliad*, 6.147.
34 Cassius Dio, *Roman History*, 72.36.
35 Plato, *Republic, Book 3*, 'The Myth of the Metals'.
36 Marcus Aurelius, *Meditations*, 8.31.
37 Cassius Dio, *Roman History*, 73.1.
38 Ibid, 71.3.
39 *Historia Augusta, Life of Marcus Aurelius*, 28.4.
40 Herodian, *History of the Empire*, 1.4.
41 A copy of the *Meditations* preserved in the enormous Byzantine encyclopedia known as the *Suda*. Translation of the added verse by Gregory Hays.

X. Split

Epigraph: Aristotle, *Nicomachean Ethics*, 1133a.

1 J. Bennett, *Trajan: Optimus Princeps* (Routledge, 2001), p. 129.
2 Cicero, *Philippics*, 5.5.
3 Cassius Dio, *Roman History*, 77.15.
4 G. de la Bédoyère, *Gladius* (Little Brown, 2020), p. 95.

5 Aristophanes, *The Frogs*, c.405 BC.
6 The Shapwick Hoard is displayed in the Museum of Somerset, Taunton.
7 C. Howgego, *Ancient History from Coins* (Routledge, 1995), p. 119.
8 Cyprian, *Address to Demetrianus, Treatise 5*.
9 Lactantius, *Deaths of the Persecutors*, 5.
10 Howgego, op. cit., p. 127.
11 *Historia Augusta, Lives of Carus, Carinus and Numerian*, 13.
12 Herodian, *History of the Empire*, 1.6, quotes the phrase 'Rome is wherever the emperor is' being addressed to Commodus in the late second century.
13 Howgego, op. cit., p. 127.
14 Aurelius Victor, *Lives of the Roman Emperors*, 39.29.
15 In the East, Diocletian ruled from Nicomedia, and Galerius from Thessaloniki. In the West, Maximian ruled from Milan, and Constantius from Trier.
16 Text and prices from the *New English Translation of the Edict on Maximum Prices*, Academia.edu (2016).
17 Lactantius, *Deaths of the Persecutors*, 7.
18 Eusebius, *Church History*, 8.4.
19 Lactantius, *Deaths of the Persecutors*, 12.
20 Eusebius, *Church History*, 8.2.
21 Tertullian, *The Apology*, 50.
22 Eusebius in his *Life of Constantine*, 1.18, says that for 'some unknown reason, Diocletian and Maximian resigned their power in the first year after their persecution of the churches'.
23 John Zonaras, *Epitome of Histories*, 12.33.
24 S. Williams, *Diocletian and the Roman Recovery* (Routledge, 2000), p. 111.
25 Diocletian's retirement described by Eutropius, *Roman History*, 9.28.
26 A. D. Lee, *Pagans and Christians in Late Antiquity* (Routledge, 2016), p. 63.
27 Lucan, *Pharsalia*, Book 1.
28 Aurelius Victor, *Lives of the Roman Emperors*, 39.6.
29 'The voice of great events is proclaiming to us, Reform, that you may preserve.' The famous appeal made by Thomas Babington Macaulay in his speech to the House of Commons on 2 March 1831.
30 Homer, *Iliad*, 2.204.

XI. Cross

1. Eusebius, *Life of Constantine*, 2.52.
2. Diocletian's abdication described in Lactantius, *Deaths of the Persecutors*, 19.
3. Eusebius, *Life of Constantine*, 1.21.
4. Zosimus, *New History*, 2.9.
5. Ibid.
6. Constantine's dream described in Eusebius, *Life of Constantine*, 1.29.
7. Lactantius, *Deaths of the Persecutors*, 44, and Eusebius, *Life of Constantine*, 1.30.
8. Milvian Bridge battle numbers as estimated by S. Dolezal, *Reign of Constantine* (Springer, 2022), p. 287.
9. Lactantius, *Deaths of the Persecutors*, 44.
10. Eusebius, *Life of Constantine*, 1.38, eager to compare Constantine to Moses by quoting Exodus 15:5.
11. Eusebius, *Life of Constantine*, 1.40.
12. K. Hopkins, 'Christian Number and its Implications', *Journal of Early Christian Studies*, 6 (1998).
13. Eusebius, *Life of Constantine*, 1.27.
14. *Latin Panegyric*, 6, delivered to Constantine in AD 310.
15. As argued by P. Weiss, 'The Vision of Constantine', *Journal of Roman Archaeology*, 16 (2003).
16. Shakespeare, *Henry VI, Part III*, Act 2, Scene 1.
17. Eusebius, *Oration in Praise of Constantine*, 3.4.
18. The famous 'Edict' of Milan was more a set of directives dispatched to provincial governors following the imperial conference. The instructions of the emperors are preserved in Lactantius, *Deaths of the Persecutors*, 48; and Eusebius, *Church History*, 10.5.
19. Eusebius, *Life of Constantine*, 1.26 and 1.5.
20. Ibid, 4.15.
21. The emperor's description of pagan temples from the 'Prayer of Constantine' quoted in Eusebius, *Life of Constantine*, 2.56.
22. M. Dunning, 'First Christian Symbols on Roman Imperial Coins', *The Celator*, 17 (2003).
23. See A. Burnett, *Coinage in the Roman World* (Spink, 1987), pp. 146–7, for further discussion of Christogram mint marks.

24 Eusebius, *Oration in Praise of Constantine*, 9.8.
25 Eusebius, *Life of Constantine*, 2.55.
26 Silius Italica, *Punica*, 3.
27 Licinius as Satan discussed in D. Woods, 'Constantine I and a New Christian Golden Age', *Greek, Roman, and Byzantine Studies* (2018).
28 Eusebius, *Life of Constantine*, 3.3.
29 Description of the Devil from Revelation 12:9.
30 Zosimus, *New History*, 2.29.
31 Sozomen, *Ecclesiastical History*, 1.5.
32 Eusebius, *Life of Constantine*, 4.37.
33 This and later descriptions of Constantinople from Sozomen, *Ecclesiastical History*, 2.3.
34 S. Moorhead and D. Stuttard, *AD 410: The Year That Shook Rome* (British Museum, 2010), p. 46.
35 Symmachus, *Petition to Valentinian II for the Restoration of the Altar of Victory in the Roman Senate*.

XII. Collapse

Epigraph: Jerome, *Letters*, 127.

1 Jerome, *Prefaces to the Commentary on Ezekiel*, Book 7.
2 The enslavement of Roman refugees described in Jerome, *Letters*, 130.
3 Jerome, *Letters*, 128, and *Prefaces to the Commentary on Ezekiel*, Book 3.
4 Jerome, *Letters*, 126, and *Prefaces to the Commentary on Ezekiel*, Book 1.
5 Jerome, *Letters*, 123, quoting Virgil, *Aeneid*, Book 6.
6 Ammianus Marcellinus, *Roman History*, 31.
7 Jordanes, *The Origin and Deeds of the Goths*, 29.
8 As noted by A. Burnett, *Coinage in the Roman World* (Spink, 1987), p. 146.
9 Zosimus, *New History*, 5.39.
10 Ibid, 5.41.
11 Jerome, *Letters*, 123.
12 Zosimus, *New History*, 5.49.
13 Ibid, 5.50.
14 Procopius, *The Vandal Wars*, 1.2.

15 Sozomen, *Ecclesiastical History*, 9.9.
16 Jerome, *Letters*, 127.
17 P. Heather, *The Fall of the Roman Empire* (Pan, 2006), p. 228.
18 Pelagius, *Letter to Demetrias*, 20.
19 Augustine, *De Excidio Urbis Romae*, 2.3.
20 Augustine, *City of God*, 1.16–17.
21 Pliny the Elder, *Natural History*, 36.24.
22 University of Warwick, 'Coin Finds from the Basilica Aemilia' Project, Department of Classics and Ancient History website.
23 Procopius, *The Vandal Wars*, 1.2.
24 F. Galassi et al., 'The Sudden Death of Alaric: A Tale of Malaria and Lacking Immunity', *European Journal of Internal Medicine*, 31 (2016).
25 Jordanes, *The Origin and Deeds of the Goths*, 30.
26 From as much as 1,000,000 in 410, down to 500,000 by 419. M. R. Salzman, *The Falls of Rome* (Cambridge, 2021), p. 122.
27 Procopius, *The Vandal Wars*, 3.5 and 4.9.
28 Prosper, *Epitoma Chronicon*, 1375.
29 Cicero, *Philippics*, 10.8.
30 R. Fleming, *Britain After Rome* (Allen Lane, 2010), p. 28.
31 Human and animal bone data from W. Jongman, *Gibbon was Right: The Decline and Fall of the Roman Economy* (Brill, 2007), pp. 192–4.
32 B. Ward-Perkins, *The Fall of Rome and the End of Civilization* (Oxford, 2005), p. 145.
33 Ibid, p. 166.
34 M. Morris, *The Anglo-Saxons* (Penguin, 2022), p. 39.
35 Jongman, op. cit., p. 189.

Index

Abduction of the Sabines, 27–8
Achaemenid Empire (550–330 BC), 158
Acropolis, Athens, 120
Adrianople, 293
Adriatic Sea, 98, 107, 207, 222, 262
Aegates Islands, 46
Aelius Caesar, 15
Aeneas, 24–5, 42, 68
Aeneid, The (Virgil), 21
aes signatum, 31, 32
Agnes, Saint, 260
Agrigento, 30, 31, 45
Agrippa, Marcus, 107, 115, 123, 125, 139, 301
Agrippina the Elder, 139–40, 142, 148
Agrippina the Younger, 148, *149*, 160
Alaric, King of the Visigoths, 198, 294–303
Alba Longa, 23, 25
Albania, 5, 107, 130, 180
Alesia, Gaul, 71–3
Alexander the Great, 33, 55, 92, 99, 113, 158, 187, 211, 231
Alexandria, Egypt, 111, 113, 115, 284
Alfred, King of Wessex, 306
Alimenta scheme, 208
alphabet, 44
Alps, 48–9, 229, 251
Amazonian Guard, 158
amphitheatres, 166, 175, 184
Amulius, King of Alba Longa, 25
Anatolia, 30, 62, 64, 164, 175, 201, 211, 251
  Cilicia, 62, 67, 175
  Nicomedia, 251, 253, 259, 261, 268–9

animals, 157, 173–7, 183–4
Antioch, Syria, 113, 141, 224
Antonine Plague (165–180 AD), 216, 225–8, 239, 244
antoninianus, 244–5, 246, *248*, 249
Antoninus Pius, 219, 220–21, *221*, 301
Antony, Mark, 64, 82, 139, 245
  Caesar, assassination of (44 BC), 91, 93, 96, 97
  Caesar's dictatorship (49–44 BC), 81
  Civil War (32–30 BC), 112–15, 136
  Civil War (43–42 BC), 99, 104, 110
  Civil War (49–45 BC), 75
  Cleopatra, relationship with, 111–15
anvils, 9, 13
Apicata, 144
Apollo, 225–6, 274
Apollodorus of Damascus, 195, 201, 202–3, 207, 210
Apollonia, 107
Apollonius, 217
Aponius, 149–50
Aqua Traiana, 207
aqueducts, 13, 130, 169, 173, 207
aquila, 187
Aquileia, 229
Aquincum, Pannonia, 229
Ara Pacis Augustae, Rome, 122–3
Arabia, 59, 129, 164
Arcadius, Roman Emperor, 294–5
Arethusa, 31
argenteus, 241, 252–3, 254–5, 256, 262
Aristophanes, 245
Aristotle, 241

Arles, 80, 308
Armenia, 129
AS Roma, 39
Ascanius, King of Alba Longa, 25
Asclepius, 216, 223
Asper, Marcus Pompeius, 138
asses, 51, 144–5
Athena, 30, 120, 230
Athens, 30, 120, 248
Atlas Mountains, 175
atomic spectrometry, 19
Atticus, 217
Augusta Treverorum, 228
Augustine, Saint, 183, 300
Augustus, Roman Emperor, 98, 99, 104, *106*, 107–27
    Civil War (32–30 BC), 112–15
    death (14 AD), 127
    empire, foundation of (27 BC), 116–18, 135
    Mausoleum, 123–4, 301
    portraits of, 118–19
    succession, 124–7
aurei, 14
    Claudius' Praetorian Guard (41 AD), *133*, 153–6
    Marcus Aurelius' equestrian statue (173–4 AD), *233*
    Trajan's Column (113 AD), *186*, 205
Aurelian, Roman Emperor, 248–9
Aurelian Walls, Rome, 249, 270
Austria, 117–18, 229, 239
Aventine Hill, Rome, 26, 300

Baal Hammon, 41–2, 57
'baby in a basket' myths, 25
Babylon, city of, 211
Babylonian Empire (1894–539 BC), 226
Bacchus, 25
Baghdad, 286
Balearic Islands, 53, 192

ballista, 194
Barbary lions, 175
barbers, 257
barley beer, 257
Basilica Aemilia, Rome, 301
Basilica Ulpia, Rome, 202, 203, 206
Batavia, 192
Baths of Titus, Rome, *162*, 170
Battle of Abritus (251 AD), 247
Battle of Actium (31 BC), 115, 118, 127, 136, 245
Battle of Adrianople (378 AD), 293
Battle of Alesia (52 BC), 71–3, 76
Battle of the Allia (390 BC), 10–12
Battle of Cannae (216 BC), 50, 53
Battle of Milvian Bridge (312 AD), 267–8, 270–75, 276
Battle of Mortimer's Cross (1461), 275
Battle of Philippi (42 BC), 104, 110–11
Battle of the Teutoburg Forest (9 AD), 129
Battle of Zama (202 BC), 54–5, 56
Bay of Naples, 31, 195, 307
Bayeux tapestry, 204
beards, 100–101, 206, 223
bears, 176
Bede, Saint, 183
beer, 257
bell-bronze stamps, 14
Berbers, 254
Bethlehem, 290–92, 297
Bible, 53, 60, 131, 266, 283, 284, 291
Bilbilis, Hispania, 144
Bithynia, 99
Bithynia and Pontus, 208–9
Black Sea, 208
Black Stone, 27
bog bodies, 73
Booth, John Wilkes, 104–5
Boudica, Queen of the Iceni, 130
'bread and circuses' 208

Brennus, 10, 299
bribery, 66, 68
bride kidnapping, 27–8
Britain, 19, 20, 59, 128, 309
    Boudican revolt (60–61 AD), 130
    Caesar's expeditions (55–54 BC), 70–71, 83
    Carausian Revolt (286–96 AD), 254
    Claudius' invasion (43 AD), 129, 156, 165
    Constantine's Pictland campaign (305–6 AD), 269
    Hadrian's Wall, 218
    Honorius' withdrawal (410 AD), 305, 309
    Hoxne Hoard, 305
    Shapwick Hoard, 245
British Museum, London, 113, 300
brockage, 18
bronze, 7, 12, 14, 18
    currency bars, 31, 32
    Punic Wars and, 51
brothels, 34
Brothers Grimm, 34
Brutus, Lucius Junius, 29, 89, 90–91, *90*, 100
Brutus, Marcus Junius, *85*, 86–105, 307
Bulgaria, 253
bullfighting, 184
Burj Khalifa, Dubai, 195
Busento River, 302
Byron, George Gordon, 6th Baron, 182, 185
Byrsa, Carthage, 42, 57
Byzantine Empire (330–1453), 279, 308
Byzantium, 130, 277, 285

Caesar, Julius, 5–6, 17, 27, 35, 61, 62–84, *81*
    assassination (44 BC), 86–105, 107–10, 135, 274, 307
    Britannia expeditions (55–54 BC), 70–71, 83
    Civil War (49–45 BC), 75–6, 78, 83, 91, 93
    Cleopatra, meeting with (46 BC), 114
    dictatorship (49–44 BC), 79–84, 86–105, 117
    gladiatorial displays, 178
Caesonia, 151–2
calcio storico, 185
Caledonians, 130
Calgacus, 130
Caligula, Roman Emperor, 6, 134–5, 140, 142, 143, 147–52, 159
Calpurnia, 94–5
Camargue, France, 184
cameos, 117–18
Camulodunum, Britannia, 130, 156
Camus, Albert, 151
Canaletto, 182
Canetti, Elias, 9
Cannae, 50, 53
'cap and dagger' denarius, *85*, 100–103, *101*, *102*, 105
Cape Bon, 46
Cape Ecnomus, 45
Capitoline Brutus, *90*
Capitoline Hill, Rome, 10, 12, 14, 24, 32, *52*, *90*, 273
    mint, 24, 32, 90, 92, 100, 119, 154, 164, 200, 227, 246, 249
    Temple of Jupiter, 78, 303
Capitoline Wolf, 35–9, *36*
Capri, 142, 147
Capua, 53, 178
Caracalla, Roman Emperor, 244
Carausian Revolt (286–96 AD), 254
Carisius, Titus, 9, 17
Carnuntum, Pannonia, 229
carnyx, 76

Carolingian dynasty (613–1120), 59
Carpathian mountains, 187, 193
Carpophorus, 174
Carrara marble, 172, 201
Cartagena, 54
Carthage (c. 814 –146 BC), 41–60, 64, 130
Casca, Publius Servilius, 93, 95
Cassius, 93, 94, 95, 96, 99, 102, 103, 104, 105
Cassius, Avidius, 224, 238
Cassius Dio, 101, 143–4, 205–6, 237
Castel dell'Ovo, Naples, 307
Castor and Pollux, *40*, 52–3, *52*
Castra Praetoria, Rome, 140, 141, 143, 152, 154–5, 157, 159, 221
Catalonia, 60
Cato, 55–6
cerebral palsy, 154
Chaerea, Cassius, 150–52
chariots, 78, 150, 167, 169
Charlemagne, Holy Roman Emperor, 59
Charles III, King of the United Kingdom, 307
Chatti, 229
Chi-Rho, *266*, 271, 273, 280–83, *282*, 288, 306
Childe Harold (Byron), 182
China, 12, 109, 128, 226, 286
Christianity, 35, 53, 58, 60, 131–2, 209–10, 212–13
  basilicas, 202, 224
  Constantine and, 267–8, 270–71, 273–88
  Council of Nicaea (325 AD), 279
  crucifixion of Jesus (c. 30 AD), 60, 132
  Crusades, 255
  Diocletian and, 259–60, 263, 268

Edict of Milan (313 AD), 276
  gladiatorial martyrs, 176, 183, 184
  Trajan and, 209–10, 212–13
  Virgin Mary, 224
Churchill, Winston, 83, 128, 227
Cicero, 36, 64, 94, 99, 108, 114, 175, 180, 183, 244, 307
Cilicia, Anatolia, 62, 67, 175
Cimber, Lucius Tillius, 93
Cincinnati, Ohio, 39
Circus Maximus, Rome, 26, 167, 206
civic crown, 118
Claudius, Roman Emperor, *133*, 134–5, 152–9, 165, 301
  Britain, invasion of (43 AD), 156, 165
  gladiatorial displays, 178
  orca hunt, 157
Clement VII, Pope, 212
Cleopatra, Queen of Egypt, 6, 64, 78, 82, 111–15, 117
Cognitive Behavioural Therapy (CBT), 234–5
Col de la Traversette pass, 49
Colchester, Essex, 130, 156
Cologne, 191
Colosseum, Rome, 6, 161, *162*, 163–4, 167–85, 237
  animals, 173–7, 183–4
  architecture, 169
  audiences, 171–3
  Byron's visit (1817), 182, 185
  construction, 161, 168
  earthquakes, 184
  facilities, 172–3
  gladiators, 177–82, 183, 185
  inauguration (80 AD), *162*, 163–4, 168
  plant life in, 183
  sparsiones, 172
  velarium, 172

Colossus of Nero, Rome, 166, 183
comets, 108–9, 274
Commodus, Roman Emperor, 236–9, *238*, 244
Concordia, *149*
Constantine, Roman Emperor, 37, 159, 212, 233, 266, 267–88, *278*
   accession (306 AD), 269–70
   Chi-Rho, 266, 271, 273, 280–83, *282*, 288, 306
   conversion (312 AD), 267–8, 270–71, 273–5, 280
   Council of Nicaea (325 AD), 279
   Edict of Milan (313 AD), 276
   'eyes to heaven' portrait, 278–9
   Fausta, execution of (326 AD), 384
   follis, 266, 281–3, *282*, 288
   labarum, 266, 281–3, *282*
Constantinople, 255, 266, 284–8, 302–3, 304, 308
Constantius I, Roman Emperor, 253, 254, 268, 269–70
Constantius II, Roman Emperor, 212
consuls, 29, 43, 64, 67, 89, 91, 143
   Incitatus anecdote, 150
   power sharing, 26, 29, 66, 68, 137, 144–5
copper, 198, 243
Corinth (900–146 BC), 58
Cornelia, 66
cornucopia, 123
corona civica, 118
Corsica, 41, 42, 46
corvus, 45–6
Cosentia, 302
Council of Nicaea (325 AD), 279
Covid-19 pandemic (2020–23), 235
Creation of Adam (Michelangelo), 35
Crispus, 283–4
Croatia, 37, 253, 262

Crowds and Power (Canetti), 9
crucifixions, 60, 63, 132, 260
Crusades, 255
Ctesiphon, Mesopotamia, 211, 225
cults of personality, 100
Cunobelin, 59
Cupid, 68
curule, *162*
curule aedile, 67
Cybele, 232
Cyprian, Bishop of Carthage, 247
Cyprus, 99

Dacia, 14, 129, 183, 186, 187–205, 243
daggers, 102, 104
Dalmatia, 250, 261–4, 297
Damascus, Syria, 164
damnatio ad bestias, 176
damnatio ad metalla, 13
damnatio memoriae, 144–6
Dante, 103, 213
Danube River, 138, 139, 187–8, *189*, 190, 191, 229, 247, 248, 251
   Trajan's Bridge, 194–6, 199
dates, 164
David (Michelangelo), 172
debasement, 242–6, 256
Decebalus, King of Dacia, 188, 191, 193, 194, 196–200, *199*
Decimus, Junius Brutus, 93, 94, 96
Decius, Roman Emperor, 247
Delphi, Greece, 286
denarii, 14, 19–20, 51, 53, 58–60
   Aelius Caesar (137 AD), *15*
   Antony and Cleopatra (34 BC), 113–14, *114*
   Augustus' 'Pax' (c. 29 BC), *106*, 119–22, *121*, 128
   Augustus' 'Sidus Iulium' (19 BC), *110*
   Brutus' 'Ides of March' (42 BC), *85*, 100–105

denarii, – cont.
   Brutus' 'Lucius Junius Brutus' (54 BC), *90*, 99
   Caesar's 'Dictator for Life' (44 BC), *61*, 79, 81
   Caesar's 'elephant' (49–48 BC), 76–7, *77*, 283
   Caesar's 'Venus' (45 BC), *69*
   Caesar's 'Vercingetorix' (48 BC), 73–4, *74*
   Cohortium Praetoriarum, 136
   debasement of, 243–6
   final (c. 240), 246
   Roma (211 BC), *40*, 51–2
   Sabine women (89 BC), 28
   Shapwick Hoard, 245
   Titus Carisius (46 BC), *9*, 17
   Titus' 'African elephant' (79–81 AD), *174*
   Trajan's 'tree stump', *198*
   Tribute Penny (14–37 AD), 60, 131–2, *132*
Diarchy
   First (286–93 AD), 251–3
   Second (313–24 AD), 276–7
dictatorships, 66–7, 79–84, 117
Didius Julianus, Roman Emperor, 159
didrachm, 21, 32–4, 35, 37
dies, *9*, 13, 14–16, 17
dinars, 59
Diocletian, Roman Emperor, 241, 250–65
   abdication (305 AD), 260–61, 268–9
   Edict against the Christians (303 AD), 259–60, 268
   Edict on Maximum Prices (301 AD), 257–8
   religious beliefs, 252, 259–60, 263, 268
   Tetrarchy established (293 AD), 241, 253–4, 268

Diodorus, 180
Diognetus, 217
Dioscuri, *40*, 52–3, *52*
Divine Comedy (Dante), 103, 213
Divus Augustus, 127
Divus Julius, 98, 108–9
Divus Verus, 227
Domitian, Roman Emperor, 190, 191
Domitianus, 246
Domnius, Saint, 264
Domus Aurea, Rome, 160–61, 166, 168, 170
double headed coins, 113, 220
double strikes, 18
drachms, tetradrachms, 31, 44, 113, 120
drachms, 32–4, 35, 37, 51
draco, 202
Druids, 130
Drusilla the Elder, 148, *149*
Drusilla the Younger, 151
Drusus Julius Caesar, 139, 142
Dubai, 195
Durrës, Albania, 180

eagles, 118, *186*, 187, 202
earthquakes, 184
Eboracum, Britannia, 156, 269–70, 309
Ebro River, 48
Eden Park, Cincinnati, 39
Edict against the Christians (303 AD), 259–60
Edict of Milan (313 AD), 276
Edict on Maximum Prices (301 AD), 257–8
Edward IV, King of England, 275
Egypt, 6, 64, 78, 82, 111–15, 117
   Alexandrian War (48–47 BC), 78
   grain exports, 207
   granite from, 201, 262
   hippopotami, 175
   Medjay guards, 158

Pompey's assassination (48 BC), 78
revolt (293–4 AD), 254
War of Actium (32–30 BC), 112–15, 136, 245
Elegabalus, Roman Emperor, 274
elephants, 47–9, *49*, 54, 76–7, 174–5, 176, 283
   denarius depiction, 76–7, *77*, 283
Elizabeth I, Queen of England, 306
embossing, 14
England, *see under* Britain
engraving, 13, 14–16
Ephesus, 55, 111, 180, 219–20
Epictetus, 210, 230
epilepsy, 111, 148–9, 182
Epistle to the Romans, 265
Eppillus, 59
Esquiline Hill, Rome, 299–300
Etruscan civilization (c. 900 – 27 BCE), 31, 36, 37
Euphrates River, 224
Eusebius, 278, 279, 281
extortion, 99

face value, 52
Falernian wine, 257
'falling sickness', 111, 148
falxes, 193, 198, 202
Farnese, Alessandro, 184
Fascist Italy (1922–43), 38, 83, 170
Fausta, Roman Empress, 283–4
Faustina, 220, 235
Faustulus, 23–4, 25
Fecunditas, 235
Felicitas, 228
Fenrir, 34
Field of Mars, Rome, 122
figs, 56, 164, 173
'first among equals', 117
fish sauce, 207
Fiumicino airport, Rome, 208

Flaminius, 49
Flamma, 181
*flan*s, 13, 14
Flavian Amphitheatre, *see* Colosseum
Flavian dynasty (69–96 AD), 164
Florence, 185
follis, 252, 256–7, *266*, 281–3, *282*, 288, 310
Ford's Theatre, Washington, DC, 104
forgery, 16
Fortuna, 45, 76, 99, 125, *149*
Forum, Rome, 27, 68, 86, 97, 201
   Antony, denunciation of (35 BC), 111
   Basilica Aemilia, 301
   Caesar statue, 109
   Caesar's assassination (44 BC), 93, 94
   Caesar's funeral (44 BC), 98, 107
   Claudius' accession (41 AD), 153
   gladiatorial displays, 167, 178
   Sejanus' arrest (31 AD), 143
   Sulla's coup (82 BC), 66
   Temple of Janus, 122
Forum of Trajan, Rome, 201, 212
Fourth Crusade (1202–4), 255
France, 73, 130
Franco-Prussian War (1870–71), 73
Franks, 247
fresco painters, 257
Freud, Sigmund, 34
Frontinus, Sextus Julius, 210
fruit, 164
funeral rites, 178

Gaddafi, Muammar, 158
Gaius Caesar, 125
Galen, 179, 226
Galerius, Roman Emperor, 253–4, 259, 261, 264, 268, 269
Gallic Empire (260–74 AD), 248, 249, 250

Gallic War (Caesar), 83
Gallic Wars (58–50 BC), 69–75, 76, 77, 78, 79
Gardon River, 130
Gaul, 117, 128, 129, 130, 192
    Gallic Empire (260–74 AD), 248, 249, 250
    Gallic War (390 BC), 10–12, 299, 303
    Gallic War (58–50 BC), 69–75, 76, 77, 78, 79
gazelle, 176
Gazipaşa, Turkey, 211
Gemini constellation, 53
Genesis, 35
George III, King of the United Kingdom, 245
George, Saint, 260
Germanic tribes, 70, 121, 129, 191
    Battle of the Teutoburg Forest (9 AD), 129
    Gothic War (248–253 AD), 247
    Gothic War (376–82 AD), 293
    Gothic War (410 AD), 290–92, 295–303
    Gothic War (535–54 AD), 308
    Marcomannic Wars (166–180 AD), 215–17, 229–30, 232, 233, 244
    Third Century Crisis (235–84 AD), 248, 249
Germanicus, 134, 139–43, 152, 301
Gérôme, Jean-Léon, 180
Gibbon, Edward, 131, 159
Gibraltar, 41, 47
Gladiator (2000 film), 238
gladiators, 5, 15, 150, 157, 167, 177–82, 183, 185, 237
gladius, 134, 192, 193
gods/goddesses, *see* pantheon
gold, 7, 12, 14, 153, 225
    Dacian Wars (101–6 AD), 188, 189, 194, 198, 200, 243

    debasement and, 242–4, 248
    Siege of Rome (408–10 AD), 290, 297
    solidi and, 279
Golden House, Rome, 160–61, 166, 168, 170
Goths, 198, 247, 291–303
    Byzantine War (535–54 AD), 308
    Roman War (248–53 AD), 247
    Roman War (376–82 AD), 293
    Roman War (408–10 AD), 290–92, 295–303
Gratus, 134
Great Fire of Rome (64 AD), 160, 243
Greece, 3, 13, 30, 44, 51, 64
    Corinth (900–146 BC), 58
    Magna Graecia (c. 800 – c. 205 BCE), 30–31, 44
    military service in, 167
    Nero's tour (66–67 AD), 165
    pantheon, 51
    Pyrrhic War (280–275 BC), 32, 55
    theatre in, 166
Greek language, 218
Greenland, 310
Gregory I, Pope, 213
Gresham, Thomas, 245, 256
griffins, 52
Gundobad, 303

Hadrian, Roman Emperor, 6, 37, 183, 211, 213, 218–19, *221*, 238, 301
hair gel, 73
Hamilcar Barca, 41–2, 46, 47
Hamlet (Shakespeare), 230
hammers, 9, 16, 17, 18
Han Empire (202 BC–AD 220), 109, 226
Hannibal, 41–2, 47–51, 53, 54–5, 56, 76, 283
Hasdrubal, 47, 54

Hedonism, 230
Helios, 232
Helvetii tribe, 70
Henry VI (Shakespeare), 275
Heraclitus, 40
Hercules, 21, 32, 33, 237, 251
Hesiod, 120
Hilaritas, 228
hippopotami, 175
Hispania, 67, 117, 129, 144, 191
Hispellum, 287
History of Rome (Livy), 24, 122, 125
Hitler, Adolf, 158
Holy Roman Empire (800–1806), 59
Homer, 24, 204, 235, 265
Honorius, Roman Emperor, 294–5, 296, 297, *298*, 302, 305
horn of plenty, 123
household deities, 88
Hoxne Hoard, 305
Huan, Han Emperor, 226
Hungary, 229
Huns, 292–3, 295
hunting, 157, 173–7, 183–4
hydraulic systems, 168
Hygiea, 223, 224
hyper-inflation, 51, 245

Iadera, 37
Iberia, 41, 47–8, 53–4, 58, 60, 64, 67, 117, 129, 144
Icarus, 177
ice cores, 310
Iceland, 12
Iceni tribe, 130
Ides of March, 88, 92, 95, 102, 105, 135
denarius, *85*, 100–103, *101*, *102*, 105
Iliad, The (Homer), 24, 235
Illyria, 250, 253
Immortals, 158
Incitatus, 150

India, 12, 33, 176, 211
Indian Head coins, 73–4
Inferno (Dante), 103
inflation, 51, 245, 256–8
Iraq, 210
Ireland, 130
Iron Age (c. 1100–700 BC), 27, 29
Iron Gates, Dacia, 192–3, 200
Israel, 19
Isthmus of Corinth, 83
Italy Kingdom of Italy (1861–1946), 38, 83, 170
Italy Republic of Italy (1946–), 38
İzmit, Turkey, 251
İznik, Turkey, 279

Janus, 122
Japan, 34
javelins, 192
Jerome, 289, 290–92, 297, 300, 303
Jerusalem, 132, 165–6, 168, 170, 200
Jesus Christ, 58, 60, 131–2, 275
Jewish War (66–74 AD), 164, 165–6, 168, 170, 194, 200
Jonson, Ben, 146
Josephus, 150, 194
Judas Iscariot, 103
Judea, 129, 131–2, 164, 165–6, 168, 170, 194, 200
Julia (daughter of Augustus), 123, 124–6, 139
Julia (daughter of Caesar), 75
Julia (daughter of Germanicus), 148, *149*
Julian Calendar, 83
Julian Star, 108–10, *110*
Julio-Claudian dynasty (27 BC–AD 68), 126, 135, 139, 148, 165
Julius Caesar (Shakespeare), 64, 82, 97, 100, 103–4, 110
Jung, Carl, 34

Junii clan, 89, 91
Juno, 9, 11–12, 17, 163
Jupiter, 12, 19, 32, 78, 94, 118, 150, 163, 202, 251–2, 256, 273
Juvenal, 133, 208, 210, 224

killer whales, 157
Kimon, 31
King James Bible, 60
King's Men, 146
Kingdom of Italy (1861–1946), 38, 83, 170
Kingdom of Lydia (1200–546 BC), 30
Kunsthistorisches Museum, Vienna, 117–18

labarum, 266, 281–2, *282*
Laetitia, 228
Lake Trasimene, 49
lanista, 178
Lateran Palace, Rome, 36
Latin, 5, 27, 59, 60, 83, 200, 218
lead, 200, 310
Lebanon, 44
Leeds Museum, West Yorkshire, 38
legions, 18, 65
    Antonine Plague (165–180 AD), 216, 226, 228–9
    helmets, 193
    numerical designations, 129
    pagan sacrifices, 259
    pay, 59, 77, 117, 136, 138, 215, 228–9, 244
    Praetorian Guard, relations with, 138
    shields, 138, 192
    terms of enlistment, 136
    weapons, 102, 192, 193, 194
leopards, 175–6
Lepidus, Marcus Aemilius, 93
Leukaspis, 181

Libertas, 90, 102
Libya, 5, 158
Licinius, Roman Emperor, 276–8, 283, 285
Lincoln, Abraham, 104–5
lions, 175, 176, 257
literacy, 35
Livia, Roman Empress, 124, 125, 126, *132*
Livy, 24, 122, 125
Loki, 34
Londinium, Britannia, 130, 156, 284
'Long-Legged Fly' (Yeats), 61
Lucan, 264
Lucanian pork sausages, 257
Lucius Caesar, 125
Lucretia, 301
Lucullus, 307
Ludus Magnus, Rome, 178
ludus, 178
Lullus Antonius, 126
lupa, 34
Lupercal cave, Palatine Hill, 34, 37
Lupercalia, 34–5, 81
Lupus, 151
Lydia, Kingdom of (1200–546 BC), 30

Macedonia, 60
    Empire (c. 650–148 BC), 33, 55, 62, 92, 99, 113, 158
    Roman period (148–476 AD), 98, 99
Machiavelli, Niccolò, 234
Macro, 143, 147
Maecenas, 107
Mago, 47, 54
malaria, 302
malliatores, 18
Manlius, Marcus, 11
Marcella, 300
Marcellus, Marcus Claudius, 124–5

Marcomannic Wars (166–180 AD), 215–17, 229–30, 232, 233, 244
Marcus Aurelius, Roman Emperor, *214*, 215–40, *221*, *238*, 244, 251, 301
   Antonine Plague (165–180 AD), 216, 225–8, 244
   equestrian statue, 232–4, *233*
   Marcomannic Wars (166–180 AD), 215–17, 229–30, 232, 233, 244
   Meditations, 218, 222, 230–31, 234–6, 237
   Parthian War (161–66 AD), 222–26
mare nostrum, 58
Marius, Gaius, 65, 66
Mars, 3, 23, 25, 30, 32, 45, 163, 120, 122
Martial, 86, 127, 174, 210
Mattis, James, 234
Mausoleum of Augustus, Rome, 123–4, 301
Maxentius, Roman Emperor, 269, 270, 271–3
Maximian, Roman Emperor, 250, 253, 254, 261, 269
Maximus, Tiberius Claudius, 197
Meditations (Marcus Aurelius), 218, 222, 230–31, 234–6, 237
Medjay guards, 158
memento mori, 231
Memoirs of Hadrian (Yourcenar), 219
Mesopotamia, 210, 224
Meta Sudans, Rome, *162*, 170
metal detectorists, 4
Michelangelo, 35, 38, 166, 172, 233
Milan, 251, 253, 261, 276, 308
Miletus, 63
Mill, John Stuart, 234
mines, 13–14, 16, 48, 188, 244, 247, 310
minting, 9, 13–20
   die engraving, 14–16
   ice cores and, 310
   tools, 9, 17–19

mints
   Antioch, 113
   Capitoline, 24, 32, 90, 92, 100, 119, 154, 164, 200, 227, 246, 249
   Constantinople, 284
   Syracuse, 31
   Temple of Juno Moneta, 12, 19
   travelling mints, 17–18, 85, 100
Misenum, 172
Mithras, 232, 274
moneta, 12
money lending, 99
monograms, 306
Moses, 25, 272
Mount Vesuvius, 167, 307
munera, 178
murex sea snails, 44
Mussolini, Benito, 38, 83, 170

Naples, 32, 307
Napoleon I, Emperor of the French, 83, 84
Napoleon III, Emperor of the French, 73, 83
Native American peoples, 34, 73–4
Nazi Germany (1933–45), 146, 158
Nemausus, Gaul, 130
Nemean Lion, 32
Nero, Roman Emperor, 6, 15, 159–61, 165, 166, 230, 243
Nerva, Roman Emperor, 191
Nicaea, Anatolia, 279
Nicolas V, Pope, 184
Nicomedia, Anatolia, 251, 253, 259, 261, 268–9
Nîmes, France, 130
Niš, Serbia, 267
'noble savages', 73
Norse mythology, 34

North Africa, 5, 42, 47, 48, 54, 56, 58, 60, 64
  animals from, 175, 207
  Carthage (c. 814 –146 BC), 41–60, 64, 130
  imports from, 207
  marble from, 201
  Maximian's Berber conflict (c. 296–8), 254
  Vandal Kingdom (435–534), 303
Numa, King of Rome, 122
Numerian, Roman Emperor, 250
Numidians, 53
Numitor, King of Alba Longa, 23, 25
nymphs, 31

oak wreath, 118
obverse side, 13
  commemorative coins, 170
  double striking, 18
  living people on, 76, 79–80, 82, 100
  value on, 52
Octavia the Younger, 139
Octavian, *see* Augustus
Odin, 34
Odoacer, King of Italy, 289, 304–, *305*
Odyssey, The (Homer), 24
Offa, King of Mercia, 59–60
olive branches, 120, *121*, *132*, *162*, 170
olive oil, 44, 128, 129, 207
Olympia, Greece, 285
Olympius, 295
On Analogy (Caesar), 82
Optimus Princeps, 190
orcas, 157
Orșova, Romania, 199
Osiris, 25
Ostia, Rome, 157, 174, 207
ostriches, 176
Ostrogothic Kingdom (469–553), 37, 308
Othello (Shakespeare), 146

Ovid, 109
owls, 30, 93, 120
Oxford University, 57–8

Paestum, 31
Palatine Hill, Rome, 26, 27, 34, 37, 118
palm trees, 44
Palmyrene Empire (260–73), 248, 249
Pannonia, 229–30, 239
pantheon, 3, 10, 20, 88, 92, 100, 232, 252, 259
  Asclepius, 216, 223
  Concordia, *149*
  Divus Augustus, 127
  Divus Julius, 98, 108–9
  Divus Verus, 227
  Fecunditas, 235
  Felicitas, 228
  Fortuna, 76, 99, 125, *149*
  Hercules, 21, 32, 33, 237, 251
  Hilaritas, 228
  Janus, 122
  Juno, 9, 11–12, 17, 163
  Jupiter, 12, 19, 32, 78, 94, 118, 150, 163, 202, 251–2, 256, 273
  Laetitia, 228
  Libertas, 90, 102
  Mars, 3, 23, 25, 30, 32, 45, 120, 122, 163
  Pax, *106*, 119–23, *121*, *132*
  Roma, *40*, 51–2, 58, 88, 310, *311*
  Salus, 214, 216, 223–4, 225, 228, 235, 239
  Securitas, *149*
  Sol, 166, 274
  Terminus, 259
  Venus, 68, *69*, 109, 163
  Vesta, 171
  Victory, *61*, 122, 204
panthers, 175
Parthian Empire (247 BC–AD 224), 92–3, 111, 210–11, 222–6

Index

patrician families, 89
Paul III, Pope, 184
Paul, Saint, 53
Pax, *106*, 119–23, *121*, *132*
Pax Britannica, 128
Pax Romana, 128–32
Pelagius, 300
pennies, 59–60
Pergamum, 179
peristyle, 262
Perpignan, France, 48
Persia
   Achaemenid Empire (550–330 BC), 158
   Parthian Empire (247 BC–AD 224), 92–3, 111, 210–11, 222–6, 238
   Sasanian Empire (224–651 AD), 247, 254
   Seleucid Empire (312–63 BC), 62
Pertinax, Roman Emperor, 159
Peter, Saint, 53, 284
Pharisees, 60
Pharsalus, 78
Philip II, King of Macedon, 158
Philippi, 104, 110–11, 197
Philostratus, 113
Phoenician civilisation (c. 2500–64 BCE), 44
Piacenza, Italy, 49
Piazza del Campidoglio, Rome, *52*
Picts, 269
Pietà, 196
pileus cap, 102
Pillars of Hercules, 41, 47
pilum javelin, 192
piracy, 62–4, 67
Piranesi, Giovanni Battista, 182
Plato, 121, 215, 219, 232, 236, 239
Pliny the Elder, 109, 157, 301
Pliny the Younger, 208–9, 210
Plotina, 211

Plutarch, 94, 114, 175, 210
polio, 154
Pollice Verso (Gérôme), 180
Polybius, 54
pomerium, 136, 212
Pompeii, 167
Pompey, 64, 75–6, 78, 91, 93, 96, 98, 178
Pont du Gard, France, 130
Pontifex Maximus, 67–8, 77, 287
populism, 97
Porcia, 87–8
Portrait of the Four Tetrarchs, 255
Portugal, 60
Portus, Rome, 207
pottery, 27, 128, 309
pozzolana cement, 195
Praetorian Guard, 134–61
   Augustus and, 117, 135
   Aurelian and, 249
   aureus of Claudius, *133*, 153–6
   Caligula and, 135, 147, 149
   Claudius and, 134–5
   Hadrian and, 220
   Marcus Aurelius and, 221
   Sejanus' regency (25–31 AD), 142–6
   Tiberius and, 127, 137–46
princeps, 117
Prometheus, 177
proscription, 66
proscynesis, 263
prostitution, 34
provincial coining, 18
Ptolemaic dynasty (305–30 BC), 113, 115
Ptolemy XIII, King of Egypt, 78
pugio daggers, 102, 104
punch dies, 9, 17
Punic Wars (264–146 BC), 41–60, 122, 229
Puteoli, 138

Pyrenees, 48
Pyrrhic War (280–275 BC), 32, 55
Pyrrhus, King of Epirus, 32, 55

*quadran*s, 174
*quaestor*s, 67
Quirinal Hill, Rome, 203
Quran, 59

radiates, 244–5, 246, *248*, 249
Ragnarök, 34
Raphael, 166
Ravenna, 289, 296, 297, 298, 303, 304
referees, 179–80
Regia, Rome, 27
Remus, 21–6, *33*, 35–9, 310
Renaissance (c. 1450 – c. 1650), 14, 158, 166, 196
reverse side, 13
　double striking, 18
Rhea Silvia, 23, 25
Rhine River, 129, 138, 191, 228, 295
rhinoceroses, 174, *174*, 176
Rhodes, 62
Rhône valley, 48, 80
Ricimer, 303
roads, 19, 83, 128, 129, 132, 156, 207
　Via Egnatia, 130
　Via Traiana, 207
Röhm, Ernst, 146
Roma, *40*, 51–2, 58, 88, 310, *311*
Roman Empire (27 BC–AD 476), 116–19, 127
　Antonine Plague (165–80 AD), 216, 225–8, 239, 244
　Britain, conquest of (43–87 AD), 130, 156, 165
　Caledonian campaign (80–84 AD), 130
　Caligula assassination (41 AD), 134–5, 151–2

　Civil Wars (306–24 AD), 267–8, 270–78
　Dacian Wars (101–6 AD), 14, 183, 186, 187–205, 243
　Diarchy, First (286–93 AD), 251–3
　Diarchy, Second (313–24 AD), 276–7
　dissolution (476 AD), 304
　Edict against the Christians (303 AD), 259–60, 268
　Edict of Milan (313 AD), 276
　Edict on Maximum Prices (301 AD), 257–8
　foundation (27 BC), 116–19
　Germania campaigns (12 BC–AD 16), 129
　Gothic War (248–253 AD), 247
　Gothic War (376–82 AD), 293
　Gothic War (408–10 AD), 290–92, 295–303
　import economy, 207
　Jesus, execution of (c. 30 AD), 60, 132
　Jewish War (66–74 AD), 164, 165–6, 168, 170, 194, 200
　Marcomannic Wars (166–180 AD), 215–17, 229–30, 232, 233, 244
　Mutinies (14 AD), 138
　Parthian War (115–17 AD), 210–11
　Parthian War (161–66 AD), 222–26, 238
　Pax Romana, 128–32
　Praetorian Guard, 117, 127, 133, 134–47, 149, 151–2
　Sasanian War (c. 253–60 AD), 247
　Sasanian War (c. 296–99 AD), 254
　Sejanus' regency (25–31 AD), 142–6
　Tetrarchies, *see* Tetrarchy
　Third Century Crisis (235–284 AD), 246–9
　Vandal invasion (455 AD), 303

Roman Kingdom (753–509 BC), 26–9, 31, 68, 122
Roman noses, 118
Roman Republic (509–27 BC), 29, 31, 35
   Britannia expeditions (55–54 BC), 70–71, 83
   Caesar's dictatorship (49–44 BC), 79–84, 86–105, 274
   Civil War (32–30 BC), 112–15, 136, 245
   Civil War (43–42 BC), 99–104, 110–11
   Civil War (49–45 BC), 75–6, 78, 83, 91, 93
   Civil War (83–82 BC), 65–7
   first coin (c. 269–266 BC), 21, 24, 32–4, *33*, 35, 37
   Gallic War (390 BC), 10–12, 299, 303
   Gallic War (58–50 BC), 69–75, 76, 77, 78, 79
   Punic Wars (264–146 BC), 41–60, 122, 229
   Pyrrhic War (280–275 BC), 32, 55
   Sabine abduction legend in, 28
   Sulla's dictatorship (82–80 BC), 65–7, 79–80
   War of Spartacus (73–71 BC), 178
Roman roads, 19, 83, 128, 129, 132, 156, 207
   Via Egnatia, 130
   Via Traiana, 207
Romania, 14, 129, 183, 186, 187–205
Romanitas, 3
Rome, city of, 5
   aqueducts, 173, 207
   Ara Pacis Augustae, 122–3
   Aurelian Walls, 249, 270
   Aventine Hill, 26, 300
   Basilica Aemilia, 301
   Basilica Ulpia, 202, 203, 206

   Baths of Titus, *162*, 170
   Capitoline Hill, *see* Capitoline Hill
   Castra Praetoria, 140, 141, 143, 152, 154–5, 157, 159, 221
   Circus Maximus, 26, 167, 206
   Colosseum, 6, 161, *162*, 163–4, 167–85, 237
   Colossus of Nero, 166, 183
   Esquiline Hill, 299–300
   Field of Mars, 122
   Forum, *see* Forum
   Forum of Trajan, 201, 212
   foundation (c. 753 BC), 21–6
   Gallic sack (390 BC), 10–12, 299, 303
   Golden House, 160–61, 166, 168, 170
   Gothic siege (408–10 AD), 290–92, 295–303
   Great Fire (64 AD), 160, 243
   Lateran Palace, 36
   Ludus Magnus, 178
   Marcus Aurelius statue, 232–4, *233*
   Mausoleum of Augustus, 123–4, 301
   Meta Sudans, *162*, 170
   Ostia, 157, 174, 207
   Palatine Hill, 26, 27, 34, 37, 118
   pomerium, 136, 212
   Portus, 207
   Quirinal Hill, 203
   Regia, 27
   Senate house, 82, 83
   St Paul's Basilica, 300
   St Peter's Basilica, 184, 212, 284
   Subura, 64, 68
   Temple of Janus, 122
   Temple of Juno Moneta, 12
   Temple of Jupiter, 78, 303
   Temple of Saturn, 14, 76
   Temple of the Deified Julius Caesar, 109
   Theatre of Pompey, 93, 94, 95

Rome, – *cont.*
    Trajan's Column, 186–90, 191–7, 199, 202–5, 212, 301
    Vandal invasion (455 AD), 303
Romulus, 21–8, *33*, 35–9, 116, 310
Romulus Augustus, Roman Emperor, 303–4, 307
Rubicon River, 76, 83, 91, 93
Rusticus, 217

Sabines, 27–8
Sabinus, Lucius Titurius, 28
Saguntum, 48
Salona, Dalmatia, 261, 264
salt, 200
Salus, *214*, 216, 223–4, 225, 228, 235, 239
Samnites, 31
Sanguineto, 49
Santa Maria Maggiore, Rome, 224
Sardinia, 37, 41, 42, 46
Sargon of Akkad, 25
Sarmatians, 229, 251
Sarmizegetusa, Dacia, 193, 196
Sarus, 298
Sasanian Empire (224–651), 247, 254
Satan, 283
sausages, 257
Scheiner, Christoph, 275
Scipio Aemilianus, 56–7
Scipio Africanus, 54–5, 56
scorpions, 138
Scotland, 130
scutum shields, 192
Sea of Marmara, 251
Sebastian, Saint, 260
Securitas, *149*
Segesta, 31
Sejanus, Lucius Aelius, 140, 141–6, 148, 150
Seleucia, Mesopotamia, 225, 238
Seleucid Empire (312–63 BC), 62

Selinus, Anatolia, 211
Senate, 39, 64, 83
    Augustus' accession (27 BC), 116–17, 122
    Caesar assassination (44 BC), 93, 94, 95
    Caesar's dictatorship (49–44 BC), 79–80, 82, 83
    Caligula's reign (37–41 AD), 150, 152
    Civil War (32–30 BC), 112
    Civil War (43–42 BC), 99
    Civil War (49–45 BC), 76
    Claudius' accession (41 AD), 152–3
    dual command structure, 26, 29, 66, 68, 137
    Gallic Wars (58–50 BC), 75
    Punic Wars (264–146 BC), 50, 53, 56
    Sejanus' regency (25–31 AD), 143, 144
    Sulla's dictatorship (82–80 BC), 66
    Tiberius' accession (14 AD), 137
    Tiberius' adoptions (23 AD), 142
    Tiberius' tribuneship (6–14 AD), 127
Seneca, 159, 162, 181, 183, 230
Septimius Severus, Roman Emperor, 244
Serbia, 229–30, 253, 267
sestertii, 138, 144, 147
    Antoninus' 'Concord' (142 AD), 220
    Caligula's 'Sisters' (37 AD), 148–9, *149*
    Marcus Aurelius' 'Salus' (163 AD), *214*, 222–4, 239
    Titus' 'Flavian Amphitheatre' (81 AD), *162*, 164, 168–71, 185
    Trajan's 'Danube Bridge' (107–9 AD), 196
Severan dynasty (193–235), 246
Seville, Spain, 191
Shakespeare, William, 6
    Antony and Cleopatra, 115

Hamlet, 230
Henry VI, 275
Julius Caesar, 64, 82, 97, 100, 103–4, 110
Othello, 146
Shapur I, Sasanian King, 247
Shapwick Hoard, 245
shekels, 48, 49
Shinto, 34
shipbuilding, 45–6
Sibylline Books, 272
Sicily, 30–31, 41, 42, 44, 45–6, 175
Sidus Iulium, 108–10, *110*
signed bronze, 31, 32
Silbannacus, 246
siliquae, 289, 304–5
silk, 128, 257
Silk Roads, 226, 286
silver, 7, 12, 14, 18, 32
    Dacian Wars and, 189, 198, 200
    debasement and, 242–6, 248
    ice cores and, 310
    Punic Wars and, 51
    Siege of Rome (408–10 AD), 297, 299
    solidi and, 279
Sirmium, Pannonia, 229–30
Sixtus IV, Pope, 35
Sixtus V, Pope, 212–13
slavery, 56, 86–7, 89, 94, 95, 102, 129, 164, 168, 207
    gladiators, 5, 15, 150, 157, 167, 177–82, 183, 185
    Gothic invasion (408–10 AD), 299, 302
    Vandal invasion (455 AD), 303
smallpox, 226–7
    Antonine Plague (165–180 AD), 216, 225–8, 239, 244
    Cyprian Plague (c. 249–62 AD), 247

Smith, Adam, 234
Smith, John, 234
snakes, 283
Socrates, 223
Sol, 166, 274, 275
solar parhelion, 274–5
'soldier', term, 279
solidi, 279, 295, *298*, 304
souls, 236, 239
Spain, 13, 47–8, 53–4, 58, 60, 67, 117, 129, 144, 191
Spartacus, 178
Spello, Umbria, 287
Split, Croatia, 262
Spurinna, 92, 95
St Albans, Hertfordshire, 130
St Elmo's Fire, 53
St Mark's Basilica, Venice, 255, 286
St Paul's Basilica, Rome, 300
St Peter's Basilica, Vatican City, 184, 212, 284
Stilicho, 295
Stoicism, 181, 217, 218, 222, 223, 230–32, 234–6
Strait of Gibraltar, 41, 47
strigimentum, 182
sub-Saharan Africa, 130
Subura, Rome, 64, 68
Sudan, 121
Suetonius, 94, 118, 137, 157, 210
Sulla, Lucius Cornelius, 65–7, 79–80
sun dogs, 274–5
sun worship, 166, 273–4
Sunday, 276
Surus, 48
Swiss Guard, 158
Switzerland, 70
Syracuse, 30–31
Syria, 20, 113, 141, 164, 181, 192, 195, 224, 274

Tacitus, 127, 130, 138, 186, 210
Tang Empire (618–907), 286
Tarpeia, 28
Tarquin the Proud, King of Rome, 29
Taylor, Elizabeth, 112
Temple of Janus, Rome, 122
Temple of Juno Moneta, Rome, 12, 19
Temple of Jupiter, Rome, 78, 303
Temple of Saturn, Rome, 14, 76
Temple of the Deified Julius Caesar, Rome, 109
Terminus, 259
Tertullian, 183, 260
*tetradrachm*s, 31, 44, 113, 120
Tetrarchy
   First (293–305 AD), 241, 253–60, 264, 268
   Second (305–6 AD), 261, 264, 269
   Third (306–7 AD), 267, 270
   Fourth (308–10 AD), 270
Thanksgiving, 120
Theatre of Pompey, Rome, 93, 94, 95
Theodosius, Roman Emperor, 287
Thessaloniki, 181
Third Century Crisis (235–84 AD), 246–9
Thracians, 192
thumbs down gesture, 180
Tiber River, 22, 25, 123, 168, 272
Tiberius, Roman Emperor, 60, 125–7, 131, 137–48
tigers, 176
Tigris River, 225
Titus, Roman Emperor, *162*, 163–4, 165–6, 168–71, 174, 183
togas, 67, 78, 79, 86–7, 88, 89, 150, 155
tongs, 9, 17
tools, 9, 17–19
   dies, 9, 13, 14–16, 17
   hammers, 9, 16, 17, 18
   tongs, 9, 17

Tophet, Tunis, 57–8
Traianus, Marcus Ulpius, 191
Trajan, Roman Emperor, 1–2, *2*, 13–14, 183, *186*, 187–213, *206*, 238, 301
   administration, 208–9
   Christianity and, 209–10, 212–13
   Dacian Wars (101–6 AD), 14, 183, 186, 187–205, 243
   death (117 AD), 211–12
   infrastructure development, 206–8
   'Optimus Princeps' title, 190, 205, 301
   Parthian War (115–17 AD), 210–11
   welfare policies, 208
Trajan typeface, 203
Trajan's Column, Rome, *186*, 187–90, *189*, 191–7, 199, 202–5, 212, 301
   construction of, 202–3
Trajan's Forum, 212
Transylvania, 193
tria nomina, 77
Tribute Penny, 60, 131–2, *132*
Trier, Germany, 228, 284
Tunisia, 44, 46, 54, 57–8, 60
Turcii family, 299
Turin, Italy, 49
Turner, Joseph Mallord William, 182
Tyrian Purple, 44

Umayyad Caliphate (661–750), 286
United Kingdom, 52
   see also Britain
United States, 51, 52, 73–4, 104–5, 120, 158
Uranius, 246
urban praetor, 91
ustrini, 49–50

Valens, Roman Emperor, 293
Valeria, 253
Valerian, Roman Emperor, 247, *248*

Vandals, 247, 295, 303
Varus, Publius Quinctilius, 129
Vatican City, 158, 166, 184, 212
velarium, 172
venationes, 173
'*Veni, Vidi, Vici*', 78
Venice, 227, 255, 286
Ventotene, 126
Venus, 3, 68, *69*, 109, 163
Vercingetorix, 71–5, 79
Verica, 59
Verulamium, Britannia, 130
Verus, Annius, 236
Verus, Lucius, 219, 220, 221–5, *221*, 227, *228*, 251
Vespasian, Roman Emperor, 164, 165–7, 169–70, 190
Vestal Virgins, 25, 28, 112, 171
Vesuvius, 167, 307
vexillum, 266, 281
Via Egnatia, 130
Via Traiana, 207
Victory, *61*, 122, 204
Vienna, Austria, 117–18, 229, 239
Villa Romana del Casale, Sicily, 175
Vindobona, Pannonia, 239
Virgil, 21, 86, 109, 120, 292

Virgin Mary, 224
Virginia Colony (1606–1776), 234
Visigoths, *see* Goths
Vologases IV, Parthian Emperor, 222
Vulgate, 291

War of Actium (32–30 BC), 112–15, 136, 245
War of Spartacus (73–71 BC), 178
Wars of the Roses (1455–87), 275
water nymphs, 31
Wealth of Nations, The (Smith), 234
wild boars, 177
wine, 59, 115, 126, 128, 257
wolves, 34
'Wonky wolf', 38
World Health Organization, 223

Xi'an, China, 286

Yeats, William Butler, 61
York, Yorkshire, 156, 269–70, 309

Zadar, Croatia, 37
Zama, 54–5, 56
Zeno, 230
Zeus, 285–6

About the Author

Gareth Harney is a historian and coin collector striving to bring the wonders of the ancient world to a wider audience. For two decades he has explored the ruins of the Roman Empire, from the rugged landscapes of Hadrian's Wall to the desert sands of the Sahara, all the while celebrating every aspect of ancient Rome with his large online following.

Tweeting @OptimoPrincipi he combines rigorous historical research with thrilling storytelling to make classical history vital and relatable. Having built his own ancient coin collection since childhood, he now uses his website, blog, and high-definition coin photography to promote the joys of the hobby to a whole new generation.